Their Benevolent Design

Études d'histoire du Québec / Studies on the History of Quebec

Magda Fahrni et/and Nicolas Kenny
Directeurs de la collection / Series Editors

23 The Empire Within
Postcolonial Thought and Political Activism in Sixties Montreal
Sean Mills

24 Quebec Hydropolitics
The Peribonka Concessions of the Second World War
David Massell

25 Patrician Families and the Making of Quebec
The Taschereaus and McCords
Brian Young

26 Des sociétés distinctes
Gouverner les banlieues bourgeoises de Montréal, 1880-1939
Harold Bérubé

27 Nourrir la machine humaine
Nutrition et alimentation au Québec, 1860–1945
Caroline Durand

28 Why Did We Choose to Industrialize?
Montreal, 1819–1849
Robert C.H. Sweeny

29 Techniciens de l'organisation sociale
La réorganisation de l'assistance catholique privée à Montréal (1930–1974)
Amélie Bourbeau

30 Beyond Brutal Passions
Prostitution in Early Nineteenth-Century Montreal
Mary Anne Poutanen

31 A Place in the Sun
Haiti, Haitians, and the Remaking of Quebec
Sean Mills

32 The Pauper's Freedom
Crime and Poverty in Nineteenth-Century Quebec
Jean-Marie Fecteau

33 Au risque de la conversion
L'expérience québécoise de la mission au XXe siècle (1945–1980)
Catherine Foisy

34 From Old Quebec to La Belle Province
Tourism Promotion, Travel Writing, and National Identities, 1920–1967
Nicole Neatby

35 Genre, patrimoine et droit civil
Les femmes mariées de la bourgeoisie québécoise en procès, 1900-1930
Thierry Nootens

36 L'Église et la politique québécoise, de Taschereau à Duplessis
Alexandre Dumas

37 Grossières indécences
Pratiques et identités homosexuelles à Montréal, 1880-1929
Dominic Dagenais

38 Taking to the Streets
Crowds, Politics, and the Urban Experience in Mid-Nineteenth-Century Montreal
Dan Horner

39 Colonialism's Currency
Money, State, and First Nations in Canada, 1820–1950
Brian Gettler

40 Deindustrializing Montreal
Entangled Histories of Race, Residence, and Class
Steven High

41 La guerre d'indépendance des Canadas
Démocratie, républicanismes et libéralismes en Amérique du Nord
Julien Mauduit

42 Countercurrents
Women's Movements in Postwar Montreal
Amanda Ricci

43 Cette science nécessaire
Dissections humaines et profession médicale au Québec
Martin Robert

44 Their Benevolent Design
Conservative Women and Protestant Child Charities in Montreal
Janice Harvey

Their Benevolent Design

Conservative Women and Protestant Child Charities in Montreal

JANICE HARVEY

McGill-Queen's University Press
Montreal & Kingston • London • Chicago

ISBN 978-0-2280-2027-1 (cloth)
ISBN 978-0-2280-2056-1 (paper)
ISBN 978-0-2280-2028-8 (ePDF)
ISBN 978-0-2280-2029-5 (ePUB)

Legal deposit first quarter 2024
Bibliothèque nationale du Québec

Printed in Canada on acid-free paper that is 100% ancient forest free (100% post-consumer recycled), processed chlorine free

This book has been published with the help of a grant from the Canadian Federation for the Humanities and Social Sciences, through the Awards to Scholarly Publications Program, using funds provided by the Social Sciences and Humanities Research Council of Canada.

Funded by the Government of Canada | Financé par le gouvernement du Canada | Canada | Canada Council for the Arts | Conseil des arts du Canada

We acknowledge the support of the Canada Council for the Arts.
Nous remercions le Conseil des arts du Canada de son soutien.

McGill-Queen's University Press in Montreal is on land which long served as a site of meeting and exchange amongst Indigenous Peoples, including the Haudenosaunee and Anishinabeg nations. In Kingston it is situated on the territory of the Haudenosaunee and Anishinaabek. We acknowledge and thank the diverse Indigenous Peoples whose footsteps have marked these territories on which peoples of the world now gather.

Library and Archives Canada Cataloguing in Publication

Title: Their benevolent design : conservative women and Protestant child charities in Montreal / Janice Harvey.
Names: Harvey, Janice (Researcher), author.
Series: Studies on the history of Quebec ; 44.
Description: Series statement: Études d'histoire du Québec / Studies on the History of Quebec ; 44 | Includes bibliographical references and index.
Identifiers: Canadiana (print) 20230538843 | Canadiana (ebook) 20230538916 | ISBN 9780228020561 (paper) | ISBN 9780228020271 (cloth) | ISBN 9780228020295 (EPUB) | ISBN 9780228020288 (ePDF)
Subjects: LCSH: Women in charitable work—Québec (Province)—Montréal—History. | LCSH: Protestants—Québec (Province)—Montréal—History. | LCSH: Charities—Québec (Province)—Montréal—History. | LCSH: Poor children—Services for—Québec (Province)—Montréal—History.
Classification: LCC HV541 .H37 2024 | DDC 361.7082/0971428—dc23

To my daughter Angela,

and in memory of my parents, Muriel and Allen Harvey

Contents

Tables and Figures

TABLES

FIGURES

Acknowledgments

This book is the result of research conducted over a long period of time, branching out, expanding, and evolving over the years. I would like to thank Brian Young for invaluable insights and critique from the beginning, and for his ongoing advice and support. Comments from Bettina Bradbury have also been extremely helpful. Countless stimulating discussions with the late Jean-Marie Fecteau and other members of the Centre d'histoire des regulations sociales (UQAM), opened up new avenues of intellectual pursuit and helped me to mature as an historian. I am extremely grateful for this and for their continuing friendship. Particular thanks goes to Martin Petitclerc and Kim Petit. I am also indebted to the two external readers of the present book whose thoughtful comments and suggestions have resulted in a number of improvements. Any errors that remain are my entire responsibility.

The research has benefited from the support of grants from the Social Science and Humanities Research Council (of Canada), the Fonds québecois de la recherche sur la société et la culture (Québec), and the McConnell Foundation (McGill University). I gratefully acknowledge this support, without which the research would not have been possible. The book itself has been published with the help of a grant from the Federation for the Humanities and Social Sciences, through the Awards to Scholarly Publications Program, using funds provided by the Social Sciences and Humanities Research Council of Canada. I thank them for their financial support and their confidence.

This funding support enabled me to work with a number of research assistants who helped in the construction of databases and provided me with other research support. I owe all of them a real debt: Annie Lyonnais, Vincent

Garneau, Jeffrey Clark, Brenda Harvey, and especially Caroline Robert, as well as my daughter, Angela Harvey, for her assistance with graphic design and photography.

I also extend my thanks to Batshaw Youth and Family Services, now under the Centre intégré universitaire de santé et de services sociaux de l'Ouest-de-l'Île-de-Montréal (CIUSSS), for granting me access to the Summerhill Homes Collection (LAC MG 28, 1388) that holds the papers of the two main institutions under study; and to Frank Campanile, Archives, for his constant interest, support, and good humour while I worked. The list of other archives and institutions that gave me access to their papers can be found in the bibliography. I am grateful for all of their help.

A number of colleagues and friends including Brian Young, Magda Fahrni, Eileen Manion, Martin Petitclerc, Jean Trépanier, Joy Moore, and Jo Lapierre read earlier drafts of the manuscript or parts of it, and I thank them for their invaluable comments and suggestions. Thanks also goes to the McGill-Queen's publishing team, especially Magda Fahrni, series editor, and Jonathan Crago, editor-in-chief, for their insights and encouragement with the manuscript preparation; Lara Minja for the superb cover design and Elena Goranescu, production manager; Kathleen Fraser, managing editor, for having a ready answer to all of my questions; and the marketing team. I want to extend a grateful thanks to Grace Rosalie Seybold, copy editor, for making the book more readable and Catherine Marjoribanks for producing the index.

Finally, special thanks go to my friends, my siblings (Karen, Paula and Kevin), and my parents, whose help, support, and encouragement saw me through this process. A particular thanks to Émile Laforest and my daughter, Angela, who forgo many family outings to give me time to work. Unfortunately, my parents, Muriel and Allen Harvey, did not live to see the work come to fruition. I would like to dedicate this book to them and to my daughter.

Over the years, earlier versions of parts of the research included in the book have been published. In particular, the discussion of the Ladies' Benevolent Society Industrial School in chapter 4 draws on some of the material in parts of two articles: "'Endangered' Children and the Montreal Ladies' Benevolent Society Industrial School, 1883–1921," in *Youth and Justice in Western States, 1815–1950: From Punishment to Welfare*, edited by Jean Trépanier and Xavier Rousseaux (London: Palgrave Macmillan, 2018), 131–60; and "The Montreal Ladies' Benevolent Society Industrial School: An Interface of Public and Private," in *Modernité, Citoyenneté, Deviances et Inégalité. Pour une analyse comparative des difficultés du passage à la modernité citoyen*, edited by Fernando Mora Lopez (Cordoba, Spain: Presses de l'Université de Cordoba, 2010), 309–27. Parts of the discussion on agency use examples from "Agency and Power in Child Charity: A Study of Two Montreal Charities, 1832–1900," in *La régulation sociale entre l'acteur et l'institution. Pour une problématique historique de l'interaction*, edited by Jean-Marie Fecteau and Janice Harvey (Sainte-Foy: Presses Universitaires du Québec, 2005), 328–42.

Abbreviations

ADA	Anglican Diocese Archives
AVM	Archives de la Ville de Montréal
BANQ/ANQ	Bibliothèque et archives nationales du Québec
CCCC	Canadian Conference of Charities and Correction
CIHM	Canadian Institute for Historical Microreproductions
CAS	Children's Aid Society
CHRS	Centre d'histoire des régulations sociales (UQAM)
COS	Charity Organization Society
DCB	Dictionary of Canadian Biography
DLAUC	Debates of the Legislative Assembly of United Canada
FBS	Female Benevolent Society
LAC	Library and Archives Canada
LBS	Montreal Ladies' Benevolent Society
MCSA	Montreal Council of Social Agencies
LCW	Montreal Local Council of Women
MM	McCord Museum
MUA	McGill University Archives
NCCC	National Conference of Charities and Corrections
NCWC	National Council of Women of Canada
POA/H	Protestant Orphan Asylum/Home
SJEAC	St John the Evangelist Anglican Church
SPWC	Society for the Protection of Women and Children
WHM	Welcome Hall Mission
WWM	Welfare Work in Montreal – Reports of the Federation, MCSA

Figure 0.1 James Duncan (attributed to), *Jane Davidson Ross*, c. 1830–40. Jane Davidson Ross was a long-term Directress of the POA.

Figure 0.2 William Notman, *Mrs. Robert S. Tylee, Montreal*, 1866. Mary-Jane Ross Tylee served as Treasurer or First Directress of the POA until she moved from the city.

Figure 0.3 *Mrs. John Samuel McCord*, about 1855. Anne Ross McCord held the office of Secretary of the POA for almost forty years.

Figure 0.4 William Notman, *Miss Annie McCord, Montreal*, 1866. Anne McCord served as Secretary of the POA after her mother and remained in office for twenty-five years.

Figure 0.5 Notman & Sandham, *Miss F. Evans, Montreal*, 1882. Fanny Evans was Secretary of the LBS for many years.

Figure 0.6 Notman & Sandham, *Miss J. Evans, Montreal*, 1881. Jane Evans was secretary of the LBS for many years.

Figure 0.7 Notman & Sandham, *Mrs. John H.R. Molson, Montreal*, 1881. Louisa Frothingham (Molson) was a very active member of the POA for sixty-four years and spearheaded many policy reforms after the 1870s. She also made important contributions to the funds of both the LBS and the POA.

Figure 0.8 James Duncan (attributed to), *Eliza Ross (1810–1874)*, c. 1830–40. Eliza Ross was a very active long-term member of both the POA and the LBS.

Figure 0.9 William Notman, *Mrs. H. Lyman, Montreal*, 1862. Mary Corse Lyman was a very active long-term member of both the POA and the LBS.

Figure 0.10 *Mrs. Thomas Wheeler*. Annie Wheeler was responsible for many administrative reforms in the LBS.

Their Benevolent Design

Introduction

In 1815, a group of Montreal women formed an association to "relieve indigent women and small children, the sick, the aged, and the infirm poor of the city."[1] The Female Benevolent Society eventually became two female-directed private charities: the Protestant Orphan Asylum of Montreal (POA) and the Montreal Ladies' Benevolent Society (LBS). Both flourished into the mid-twentieth century.[2] The women who ran them received thousands of orphans, young children, elderly women, convalescents, and destitute widows over the course of these years. In their typically humble and understated way, they spoke of their charity work as "quiet usefulness"; we will see that what these women undertook and accomplished was much more than that. In fact, their "benevolent design" was a form of dedicated service and a testimony to a genuine concern for the well-being of those under their care; it represented an ambitious project of female benevolence, one that was committed, proactive, collective, and organized.

This study aims to highlight the major contribution these Montreal bourgeois women made to the network of Protestant social services in the nineteenth and early twentieth centuries, to understand the challenges they faced in doing this, and to examine the steps they took to face these challenges and overcome the obstacles put in their way both by polite society and by the grim reality of dealing with poverty. These were women who made a difference. This is their story and that of the institutions they founded.

It was not unusual across the Western world for bourgeois women or "ladies of the leisure class," as Bonnie Smith has called them, to assume responsibility for philanthropic endeavours.[3] Montreal was an excellent example of this, and Protestant women directed almost all the private associations that took in women and children of the city's Protestant community. This book follows the work of some of these benevolent women for approximately a hundred years – from the founding of the two most important child charities, in 1822 for the Protestant Orphan Asylum (POA) and 1832 for the Montreal Ladies' Benevolent Society (LBS), until 1921 when the *Public Charities Act* began the shift to more extensive state financing and new models of addressing child poverty became more popular among the city's Protestant community. This lengthy framework makes it possible to evaluate the essential role these two charities and the women who ran them played in the city at a key period, as the elite responded to the social inequality associated with the processes of urbanization, immigration, and industrialization connected to Montreal's transformation from a pre-industrial colonial town to a booming industrial and commercial city.

When British authorities assumed responsibility for New France in 1763, they did not introduce the Elizabethan Poor Law with its system of local tax-supported workhouses and public hospitals. Neither did Upper or Lower Canada once they had the power to do so under the 1791 *Constitutional Act*.[4] Catholic nuns continued to run institutions such as the Hôtel-Dieu and the Hôpital Général that provided some aid to the poor, the sick, the elderly, and foundlings. Early legislation empowered judges and justices of the peace to name guardians for orphans and abandoned children or to apprentice them, and begging permits could be secured on a parish basis.[5] Otherwise, the existing system was left in place. Essentially pre-industrial in nature and designed for a small, stable, and Catholic population, the model was not well adapted to respond to an industrializing society in which a sizeable number of those in need (including many British immigrants) were not Catholic, at least not without some major changes. These changes were made by the newly arrived Protestant elite and the reorganized and strengthened Catholic Church.

Montreal's dual ethnic and religious makeup provides a unique opportunity to study the development of Protestant poor relief. As one of the major centres in the new British colony, the city was dominated by an English-speaking, Protestant economic elite; however, except for a thirty-year period at mid-century, it had a French-speaking majority. Moreover, the combination of French and Irish Catholics resulted in a Catholic majority. Hostility between the two communities was increasingly visible by the 1830s and '40s with the crushing of the rebellions of 1837–38 and the creation of ethnic national societies.

The absence of a tax-supported public poor-relief system makes nineteenth-century Montreal an interesting example of a mixed social economy where poor relief was largely allocated to the private sector, the state providing only nominal financial support. This model was complicated by the fact that social services evolved along confessional lines, with the Catholic Church controlling aid destined to Catholics and, from mid-century on, actively establishing an extensive network of charities and services to maintain that control. This obliged Protestants to develop their own network of social services, not as a supplement to state aid, as was normally the case in Protestant jurisdictions, but as the only aid available, all the while conscious that available Catholic relief services might attract Protestants (and their souls).

Faced with the influx of immigrants and the misery that was attendant on large numbers of displaced families trying to survive in a new city in the middle of a cold winter, the wives and daughters of Montreal's Protestant elite sprang into action. On 23 February 1815, an announcement in the *Montreal Gazette* opened the public funding campaign that preceded the founding of the Female Benevolent Society ten months later. It informed inhabitants that a subscription, "liberally patronized by His Excellency, Sir George Prevost, and many of the respectable inhabitants of Montreal," was ongoing "for the purpose of providing for all of the destitute poor of the city."[6] The patronage of both the governor and leading citizens established the project's credibility; nonetheless, its financing was to come from voluntary subscriptions (not the state), and the actual work would be assumed by "Ladies." The founding of this first Protestant benevolent society points to several themes that run through this book: the extent to which private charities were an integral part of Protestant Montreal's response to poverty and depended on that community for support; the central role women played in this; and their basic approach as conservative women influenced by their class duty to the poor, their maternal instinct to help children, and their humanitarian and Christian resolve to address need in their midst.

The women who founded and managed the child charities were members of the city's Protestant bourgeoisie. They included women whose family names mark the streets or public buildings of Montreal to this day – McCord,

Torrance, Molson, Redpath, Galt, Workman: families whose contributions as fur traders, merchants, bankers, manufacturers, land owners, and transportation developers were important to the economic development of the city, and professionals (doctors, lawyers, ministers) as well as politicians, judges, and mayors who contributed to the well-being of their own community and that of the city as a whole. Some had come from England, Scotland, or Ireland, but many were Americans; all of them had arrived to take advantage of the emerging trade and economic possibilities represented by Montreal's integration into colonial trade routes and both the growth in its own population and the potential markets represented by the interior.

As a colonial elite, but a cultural and linguistic minority within Quebec for most of the century, these citizens' Protestant religion and their sense of Britishness, including a focus on Empire, served as cohesive factors.[7] Being the economic power in the city, they were in a position to enforce their influence over public space and public morals through their control of institutions, at least for their own population. Much of Montreal's propertied class, and the wives of this colonial bourgeois elite in general, shared many of the cultural values that Brian Young has referred to as "patrician," including the importance of religion, Christian morality and the family, the respect for traditional social and patriarchal authority, a "sense of social responsibility" to others in the city, and the desire for social harmony.[8] Their families were interlinked by marriage as well as friendship and business ties, and, by mid-century, many were neighbours living in the Golden Square Mile north of St Catherine Street; some had large estates on the side of the mountain. They worked to build a thriving urban community, establishing institutions and associations, an extensive network of educational and cultural facilities, hospitals, and scientific and cultural events.

It was a natural extension of the power, social prominence, and status of these families for the wives and daughters of this bourgeois elite to manage the city's child charities. Through this type of activity, women played a crucial role in the social organization of class and class identification.[9] Many families maintained their connection with the Societies over several generations. Daughters worked on the management boards alongside their mothers, mothers-in-law, and aunts, or took their place when the time came. Sisters and sisters-in-law carried out committee work together. The majority of members were married, although a few high-profile single women including

Louisa Goddard Frothingham (Molson) and Eliza Ross worked tirelessly for these charities and a number of others were among the original founders. Some of these single members married and continued their benevolent endeavours as married women. Many women worked on these charity boards for extensive periods of time, often until their deaths; some of their husbands died during their tenure and they continued on as widows.[10]

The ladies[11] did not work in isolation cut off from their community, nor did they carry out their benevolent designs without the support of that community. Their charities received substantial encouragement from the community at large and from individual clergymen, businessmen, and professionals. These men tended to be their husbands and sons, but several men such as Peter McGill were active in their philanthropic support of the child charities even though their wives were not members. This support from the male establishment provided the ladies and their Committees with social credibility as well as important contacts that facilitated their work in the public sphere. It is imperative, though, not to overestimate the importance of male support for these two female charities. First, women both founded and managed the charities; neither worked under a male Advisory Board and they appealed to men only for specific tasks such as investment and building-related questions. Second, the charities did not depend on male supporters for their financial viability – most of the POA's funding came from female subscription members, and this represented a major source of LBS funding as well until the latter part of the nineteenth century. Finally, we will see that, although they took advantage of men's advice, they did not need the approbation of community leaders for their policies and occasionally simply refused this advice.

Both of the charities under study began as voluntary associations and eventually were incorporated for legal and property-holding purposes, the LBS in 1841 and the POA in 1843; official by-laws were established at that time.[12] This incorporated status recognized the ladies' power to act as a legal entity and removed them from any restrictions associated with the concept of *femme covert*. The Act of Incorporation outlined the responsibilities and scope of the societies; the managers followed these to the letter, seeing them as prescriptive. The Committees ran their charities as formal associations, adopting an administrative business model with regular meetings, votes on matters of importance, and carefully kept records. Being private associations responsible to their supporters, both Societies held annual public meetings to present an account of the year's work and the financial statement, as well as to elect the management Committee and office-holders for the following year. This type of structure ensured that the project would survive after the founding members were no longer able to carry it on.[13]

Opened and chaired by ministers, these meetings included speeches by male supporters. Normally after motions of thanks and the benediction, the children sang and visitors could inspect the institution. The meetings were carefully designed as community events and covered by the newspapers. Both the meetings themselves and the published reports, which included lists of subscriptions and donations, were the physical proof that philanthropy was a community undertaking and that the city's elite, through its female members, were responding to the problems in their midst. Originally situated in the lower part of the city, the charity "homes" followed their supporters uptown around mid-century. This had the added advantage of securing larger parcels of land for their permanent buildings in a healthier environment surrounded by gardens.

Montreal women were the first to respond to need in their community, but they did not carry out their work in isolation. They were integrated into the community they served – both the families who applied to them for aid and the supporters who provided the funds to make their work possible. But they were also an integral part of the wider context of poor relief in the city. It is crucial to understand this overall structure, as it clarifies the options available for families in the city and the pre-eminent role female-directed child charities played in family support as a result. Increasingly influenced by liberalism, the larger structure reflected changing notions of poverty, poor relief, and social order.

In the absence of any public relief structure, the choices the elite made as to the types of services they would provide and their admission criteria determined what aid was available and who had access to it. Most of the aid available in nineteenth-century Protestant Montreal, both that for children and what little was available for adults inside the House of Industry, was institutional in form, thus allowing for isolation and treatment (education and training in the case of children); the distribution of food and clothing through depots or to people's homes, what was known as "outdoor relief," was available only in the latter part of the century, apart from that provided by churches and ethnic societies. In fact, the continued preference for institutional aid, even for children, is one of the characteristics of the Quebec model, both Protestant and Catholic, that distinguishes it from other places in North America, which by the late nineteenth century were adopting models of foster care known as "placing out." The shift to foster care only began in English Montreal in the 1920s.

The particular mode of regulation – that is, the normative, institutional, and legislative framework that structured social relations – was linked to the elite's response to the increasingly destabilizing factors in urban society caused by massive (im)migration and the poverty associated with the fragility of wage work in industrializing economies. It was in this context that a social services structure evolved. The theoretical framework that best explains this overall structure and the integration of relations of power and community that it represented is that of social regulation. The most eloquent explanation of this framework, in Quebec, is provided by the late Jean-Marie Fecteau in his studies on the charitable and penal network in Montreal.[14] In his seminal work, *La Liberté du Pauvre* (*The Pauper's Freedom*), Fecteau links the development of the social regulation system in nineteenth-century Quebec (by the 1840s) to the rise of liberalism. Given the concept of freedom and individual responsibility underlying this liberal mode of regulation, both crime and poverty were seen as the responsibility of the individual, necessitating targeted measures. Crime, as "a conscious act of will," became the responsibility of the public sector with its legislative capacity for confinement (punishment or rehabilitation). Poverty, as a "deficiency of good intentions" and a failure to make "the proper use of freedom" by not preparing for economic setbacks such as unemployment, was considered more of a personal weakness, and moral aspersions of laziness and immorality were commonplace. As such, charity in relation to "normal" poverty, which was assumed to be temporary and simply a natural part of social inequality, was left to the private sector and aimed at self-help.[15] However, extreme chronic poverty, stigmatized as dependency and referred to as "pauperism," was cast, across much of the Western world, as a moral problem that called for state intervention and the use of confinement.[16] Given that this public response did not occur in Quebec, the private sector found itself responsible for the entire range of poverty.

Although he recognizes the directive role of the elite and their power, Fecteau's interpretive framework is sensitive to the part working-class agency played in influencing (and using) the relief system that constituted a component of the overall regulation structure. In the context of social assistance, power and regulation are not abstract concepts of domination and control; they are dialectic, reactive, and changing. In effect they exist as relations, not fixed categories. In the elite's interaction with target populations, resistance and accommodation may occur, and original objectives are not always met and may be adjusted over time. Many poor families integrated charity into their survival strategies – as temporary child care, as labour-force training/entry for themselves or their children, or as custodial care of the ill and the old – although the aid available was not always what was needed and families often had to manoeuvre to be able to use it in the way they wanted.[17] From this perspective, charitable institution-building and social policies designed to reproduce approved social forms by integrating segments of the population, especially immigrants and the young, into what was believed to be an appropriate normative system became a complex interactive process between the organizers and the users of their services.[18] Nonetheless, it is important to remember that client agency in this context was shaped and limited by social structure, and that institutional organizers had considerably more power in this type of interaction, given that the aid structure reflected their values and beliefs.[19]

Influenced by this liberal approach to poverty, the leaders of the Protestant community were hesitant to establish a relief structure that might encourage dependency or laziness. This led to a situation where a permanent House of Industry was not established until 1863 and charities, other than those founded and directed by women, were only formed in the last quarter of the century and were targeted to meet the needs of particular groups. The examination in chapter 1 of the gradual piecing together of this network will reveal how this constrained benevolence on the part of the elite left the city's poor with limited access to assistance, and how the child charities were so central to family services as a result.

As part of this larger structure and the city's Protestant elite, the women who directed the child charities were influenced by this context, but they also distinguished themselves from it. This book addresses this by looking first at the women who ran the charities and did the charity management work; then, at the admission and departure policies they developed, how these differed from policies advocated by others, and why; and finally, at the impact contemporary gendered notions had on the Committees and their work.

With their direct approach to providing aid, these women came to their benevolent projects from within a more conservative world-view based around religious commitment and a sense of class duty towards the poor; as such, they moderated some of liberalism's restrictive and moralist notions in relation to poverty and poor relief, at least in terms of women and children, although their charities were nonetheless part of the social regulation structure. When I refer to these women and their benevolence as "conservative" in the book's title, I am adopting the definition developed by historians Nancy Hewitt and Anne Boylan and subsequently used by Lori Ginzberg. In their studies of women's activism, these historians distinguish between associations of (conservative) "benevolent" women and those with a reform approach, whom they identify as either "perfectionist" (reformist) or "ultraist" (feminist).[20] In this context, "benevolent" or "conservative" refers to a world-view based on a hierarchical social order, the central importance of tradition, social status, and religion, and the duty of the privileged to help the poor (that is, a needs-based response to poverty). Furthermore, conservative women's associations, such as the two discussed in this book, tended to focus their efforts on the benevolent project at hand rather than on social reform work in the community at large or on striving for more individual rights of citizenship for themselves. Both charity Committees modified a number of policies over the course of the century on the basis of their experience managing the child charities and in light of changing notions of children's needs; nonetheless, they continued to approach their work from a basic "charitable" perspective, one that differed in important ways from that of women involved in social reform work who supported "scientific philanthropy," which the ladies viewed as overly restrictive.

Our examination of admissions and discharges enables us to investigate the interface of upper-class power and working-class agency in the context of child charity. We find examples of parents designing their aid applications in the most favourable light possible, with a number of mothers even entering the institution as workers to secure a place for their children; we also see parents resisting unfavourable discharge decisions by stealing their children from the institution or by initiating court cases. Although the ladies who ran the child charities agreed to help needy families by admitting children, caring for them, and educating them, not surprisingly, they tended to understand child care from the perspective and values of their own class. This perspective

– centred as it was on child protection, religious salvation, and the inculcation of middle-class values – served as the foundation of their benevolent design and could, on occasion, diverge from the aims of parents to use the charities as temporary shelter.

Children are integral to the story of the Montreal institutions at the centre of this book. A brief look at the historiography of childhood and children helps to highlight some of the relevant issues and concepts and put the experiences of the children we meet into a broader context. Much of the early historical work on children focused on how adults saw children and the actions they took as a consequence. It is important to remember that "childhood" – that is, the category that considers children grouped together according to their stage of life – is a social and cultural construct whose meaning changes over time. Hence expectations about children and attitudes towards them must be situated within a given historical period.[21] Over the late eighteenth and nineteenth centuries, earlier concepts of the "wicked" child in need of strict discipline slowly gave way to the "precious," innocent child.[22] This shift was more pronounced for middle-class children than for the children of the poor, but the widespread urge to protect children was pervasive by the end of the century. These changing notions of childhood were not lost on the Montreal charity managers; their policies by late century demonstrate a marked increase in the recognition of childhood innocence and children's need for protection.

In the wider society, a consensus arose that destitute children should be removed from general poorhouses and placed in age-specific institutions such as orphanages where they could receive specialized care.[23] However, this construct of "innocence" held within it clear tensions: children were recognized as malleable but also corruptible, in need of protection but also regulation and training. This ambiguity was particularly pronounced for poor children, whom many saw as victims and threats at one and the same time. Bruce Bellingham has argued that alongside the concept of the innocent middle-class child, a working-class-child concept, framed by the "street," started to gain currency about mid-century. This politicized working-class-child concept and the "myth of misery" linked to it cast poor parents as unfit and their children as in need of "rescue."[24] Reformers tended to agree that due to their malleability and basic innocence, even these children were salvageable given the right environment and moral-religious guidance, and that indeed it was the responsibility of the elite (and the state) to provide this.[25] Nonetheless, the distinctions between various categories of children were vague and overlapped, making some version of this dual regulation/training role standard for all nineteenth-century child institutions (even schools and orphanages). As American historian Steven Mintz observes, basically all "child-saving" was driven by a "mixture of hope and fear."[26]

By mid-century, both philanthropists and governments began to identify certain groups of children as candidates for specialized intervention, either to protect those who needed help or to rehabilitate those who were considered a threat to social order. This concern centred mainly on the potential danger posed by the urban "working-class child" and, in particular, homeless youth labelled "street arabs" or "urchins" and described as "running" in the streets (although most were probably working).[27] Several historians have analyzed this discourse in Canada in relation to Toronto.[28] Similar fears about the link between "little wanderers" and criminality are evident in Montreal's English press across the century.[29] In response to these fears about the threat of rising levels of delinquency, governments across Western Europe and North America intervened to "protect" children by removing them from normal prisons (where they were incarcerated alongside adult criminals who might influence them) and placing them in age-segregated reformatory institutions designed to rehabilitate them using a regime of strict training, work, and moral influence.[30] The creation of these institutions is an excellent example of the state's power to use law to define deviance and then act on that definition.

It was in this context that United Canada created reformatory schools in 1857.[31] Once Quebec assumed power for this type of social legislation, it passed the *Reform School Act* in 1869 to establish institutions for young delinquents.[32] In the same session it extended state intervention to include non-criminal children, creating industrial schools for the "protection" and training of children judged to be "endangered," that is, vulnerable to abuse or delinquency.[33] Although, in Quebec, responsibility for these institutions was allocated to private associations having secured state accreditation, they were clearly part of the larger governance structure. These "schools" were designed to be stand-alone training institutions, but the reluctance of

Montreal's English-speaking elite to invest in social welfare structures led to a situation where no separate reformatory institutions were created for Protestant children. In this context, the Ladies' Benevolent Society received certification as an industrial school in 1883 and simultaneously served as both a child charity and an industrial school until 1923.

By late century the reform scope in terms of children had widened and so-called "child-savers" lobbied for more state involvement to implement legislation to protect children from exploitation on the labour market and to force school attendance. Reformers also argued for legislation that would open the way for state intervention directly into poor families targeted as "bad" parents. Newly formed Societies for the Protection of Children were empowered to "rescue" children from what were feared to be abusive or negligent families.[34] The Society for the Protection of Women and Children (SPWC) was established in Montreal in 1881.[35]

In this way, the institutionalization of children was a central feature in the attempt to integrate children into societal norms. While schools taught Canadian values and proper behaviour to children in a position to attend them, other components of the social regulation structure served different roles in this reform project. Reform and industrial school administrators established congregate institutions designed for rehabilitation and/or training. Delinquent and vulnerable children were admitted through the judicial or the municipal court systems respectively for a fixed term. Private child welfare institutions such as orphanages received children directly from families who applied to place their children, often for short periods of time during a family crisis. Although these institutions were designed to shelter and protect dependent children, and certainly the Montreal institutions respected parents' rights to remove children, they also aimed to (re-)educate them into "useful citizens," and therefore were a part of the larger regulation structure.

Recent revelations around residential schools for Indigenous children have raised the public's interest in the institutionalization of children in the past. Although the two Montreal child charities under study shared the basic aim of training children in Christianity, morals, and acceptable social norms, they differed in crucial ways from the legal reformatory institutions mentioned above – ways connected to admissions, discharges, training, and resident labour – and in even more important ways from the federal system of residential schools managed by religious communities. In the latter "schools," children were placed in institutions far from their families and their communities where they were meant to learn "Canadian" ways, ostensibly to help them integrate into society. However, the aim of these congregate institutions was not simply re-education or training, as it was in institutions that received non-Indigenous children; it was cultural and "racial" assimilation through the destruction of their Indigenous cultures. Furthermore, the abysmal conditions and mistreatment that characterized these institutions betrayed the determination with which administrators undertook this task and their total disregard for the children's well-being.[36]

As well as the literature already referred to on changing attitudes to children and action taken in response to these, the current study has benefited from a number of excellent histories of childhood and edited collections of articles.[37] More recently, historians have focused on children as actors in their own lives, making "age" a category of analysis in its own right.[38] Since children rarely left written records with which historians can evaluate their experience or agency, it is necessary to read documents written by others, often those with power over them, "against the grain" in order to tease out meaning in relation to children. Ideally this allows the researcher to find children's perspectives on their own lives.[39] Mona Gleason warns that, in doing this, historians must be careful to avoid what she calls the "agency trap" – that is, not to create binary categories and to keep in mind the complexity of childhood and its existence within a given normative structure.[40] Mona Gleason and Kristine Alexander have proposed using "emphatic inference," which Alexander explains as "the ability to imagine what events and experiences might have meant and been like from the perspective of a young person," as one approach to uncover children's voices and get at their experience.[41] The present book uses this method to evaluate how children might have experienced institutional life.

A number of other researchers, including Karen Vallgårda, explore what insights can be found by putting the history of childhood/children in a global context. In her work on Tamil children and Danish missions, for example, Vallgårda examines the complexities of agency. Her analysis of these missions as part of "a greater bourgeois project of civilizing the lower class" is of particular relevance to the current study.[42] Living in a settler colony, most Montreal children were not confronted with the same level of "civilizing" that Tamil children encountered, but what Vallgårda refers to as the "transmission of social knowledge," or socialization in a more general sense, was clearly a priority for the child charity managers, who tended to believe that this had not been done properly by the children's families. Furthermore, the Montreal directors were convinced of the possibility of religious salvation. Hence, the children found themselves faced with a situation in which they were being taught "new habits, new attitudes, new values."[43]

Stephanie Olsen, Karen Vallgårda, and Kristine Alexander also propose linking the history of emotions and the history of childhood to understand children's experience. Their concept of "emotional formation," that is, "a set of emotional structures ordered in a particular *pattern*" and "the process through which [these] codes of emotions are learned and imparted,"[44] recognizes the cultural specificity of emotional structures. Accepting that training children in the proper emotions and "ways of being" is a central component of all socialization,[45] they argue that in certain circumstances children might be confronted with an "emotional frontier" – "a boundary between different emotional formations."[46] Especially true in a colonial context, this could also be experienced when a child moved between different class, ethnic, or social milieux. This concept of emotional frontier is key to understanding the experience of children in child charities. Even though the Montreal charity children were not rescued from their families, differences in class norms and even material factors could result in them experiencing the shift from family home to institutional home as an emotional frontier.

Class and gender intersect in the Montreal managers' charitable work and their response to poverty, but gender was the determinant factor. Bringing their maternal and caring perspective to their work with children, the ladies structured their societies and their benevolent design around religious salvation, education, and providing a home for children who found themselves in need of one. Overall, they approached their work more in terms of need than morality and developed child-centred policies.

The ideologies and norms that influenced the social construction of gender and its meaning in the period are relevant to this study of female-directed charities, and, to some extent, represent an even more complex factor than class. At one and the same time, a female charity director in the nineteenth century was part of the power structure by virtue of her class while her gender made her part of the less-than-powerful, herself subject to the legal, social, and moral prescriptions of a highly gendered society that dictated a secondary and restrictive place for women. Gender as constructed and conceived in the nineteenth century was largely about boundaries. These Montreal women demonstrated agency as they pushed certain boundaries and respected others, all the while fulfilling both their social/Christian duty of charity by taking direct action to address need around them and their class duty by moulding poor children into good Christians and well-trained citizens.

The dominant gender ideology at the time was premised on the belief in gender-specific qualities and in "separate spheres" of action for men and women.[47] This discourse held that men and women had different inherent "natures" which lent themselves to distinct spheres of activity – for men, the world of business and politics; for women, the family and the home. This ideology is relevant to our study, in Mary Ryan's words, "by virtue of its power in the creation of meaning."[48] That meaning was created through prescriptive discourse in the press and popular literature,[49] where woman's sphere, centred on her role as mother, wife, and household mistress, and women's supposed special qualities including modesty, piety, charity, and morality were idealized.[50] Even more importantly, as Cecilia Morgan has established in the case of Canada, by 1840, with the rise of liberal capitalism, the ideology was far-reaching as it also "wielded considerable power in shaping the legal, political, social and economic structures that affected their subjects' lives," and, in fact, women's rights were reduced in a number of ways in Quebec.[51]

It is important to recognize that, despite its influence, this ideology was a constructed discourse.[52] In their important, and still relevant, study of class and gender, Leonore Davidoff and Catherine Hall argued that women's lived "experience" cannot actually be reduced to this type of a binary and in fact the boundaries between the spheres were "ragged" and "blurred," with women crossing them regularly.[53] As Denyse Baillargeon explains, the public and private spheres were not separate and divided, but formed two worlds with fluid frontiers constantly moving, linked to each other, and acting on one another.[54]

When considering the distinction between the public and the private as it applied to the myriad of semi-public activities nineteenth-century women were involved in, Mary Ryan proposed that we should make a distinction between the formal public sphere, "the authoritative, legally sanctioned public arena," and charity work that was mainly "conducted under private auspices," if somewhat in the public sphere.[55] Recognizing the existence of this intermediate space between the "spheres," Denise Riley and Cecilia Morgan speak of voluntary societies, including charities, and activities such as visiting the poor as being included in a "social sphere."[56] This category of the social sphere, or, as Magda Fahrni describes it, "a feminized 'social,'" is a good characterization of the Montreal benevolent societies under study and the way they pushed back against any strict definition of boundaries while still respecting certain aspects thereof.[57]

Even more important than abstract notions of boundaries, even nuanced ones, this gendered ideology has meaning for our present study to the extent it was internalized by women. In *The Gentleman's Daughter*, Amanda Vickery argues that she has not used the conceptual vocabulary of separate spheres because it did not resonate with the eighteenth-century British women she studied.[58] Looking at the elite women who ran the private charities in Montreal, however, we find that the concept definitely did resonate there, with its prescriptions about propriety in public and its notion of special qualities intact. In fact, it affected what these women believed about their position as women in society and what those around them expected of them as reflected in the press, public lectures, and statements made at their annual meetings.[59] Nonetheless, in managing their charities in the intermediate "social" space, the Montreal ladies forged an important place for themselves in the city and its socio-charitable structures.

The charity managers acceded to this power by virtue of their class status and exercised it with the support of the male establishment. Following prevailing gender prescriptions was important to maintain this support as well as their social credibility as elite women or "ladies." Therefore, although working in the social sphere – performing numerous political and economic activities and providing relief services for thousands – the women on these charity committees carefully respected social conventions in terms of propriety and the restrictions placed on women's interventions in public space, such as not speaking in public forums or travelling alone, even to rescue children who found themselves in abusive placements. Furthermore, out of respect for notions of distinct and gendered qualities/capacities, in the last half of the nineteenth century they allocated "male" activities such as investments to men's committees formed specifically to assume these responsibilities, although women's subcommittees worked in conjunction with them.

Yet notions of gendered specific "qualities" could also be empowering. The ladies accepted, and even requested, advice from male supporters on finance and building matters, but they were confident of their own abilities in areas defined as within the women's sphere, such as child-care/training and household management (and by extension their charity homes), and hence in the validity of their decisions in relation to these domains. On the basis of this strength they took an active role in the city's charity network, managing their charities in the face of adversity and budget constraints, making admission and placement policies, and defending them even when members of the male elite disagreed. We see evidence of both the limiting and the empowering aspects of this ideology in relation to management style and policy development.

All of these factors – their class power, their conservative benevolent approach, and their gendered beliefs – converge to influence the ladies, their benevolent design, and policy development. The women's culture that evolved from this and was at work in charity management was a female culture based on what Veronica Strong-Boag calls "a highly gendered ethic of care" and a person-centred orientation.[60] From this perspective of "care" as well as their conservative approach with its belief in the duty of charity, the women who managed these charities based their philanthropic endeavours on responding to the needs of families and resisted the drive to limit and rationalize aid that became more prominent by the turn of the century. It was also a female culture infused with religious dedication and humanitarianism, both of which were key to their work with children. Nonetheless, it was a class culture – it united the upper-middle-class "ladies" who managed the charities but distinguished between them and the "women" they helped or who worked in the charities. We find very few examples of social solidarity overcoming or mediating class other than that the LBS admitted destitute widows as well as elderly women and that it occasionally sheltered a battered or abandoned wife. Even the ladies' relationship with the matrons who managed the daily running of the institutions was hierarchical.

Managing a charity as these women did involved a significant commitment of time and energy – attending meetings; visiting the asylum; making policies; interacting with parents, apprenticeship families, and government representatives; fund-raising; and committee work. The sources used for this study provide the opportunity not only to investigate charity work and what it involved in detail, particularly aspects such as fund-raising and visiting, but also to analyze participation rates. The findings, presented in chapter 3, force a re-evaluation of generalizations about the large numbers of upper- and middle-class women involved in charity work and the skills they developed as a result. Nonetheless, one does find a small core of hard-working women and another group of women who actively supported their work. This lack of commitment on the part of so many members was problematic for the charities, especially for the LBS with its larger budget needs.

The project the Montreal ladies had undertaken was providing care for destitute children. The work of Timothy Hacsi on American orphanages has been helpful in analyzing some of the overarching policy aspects of work with children.[61] Hacsi uses the basic aim of charity directors and their interaction with families to distinguish among child charities that were isolating, protective, or integrative. The two Montreal charities under study have aspects of both isolating and protective asylums, but for the most part are protective, as neither deliberately tried to break families apart and their more isolating policies were aimed at protecting the children. The emphasis both charities placed on protecting children increased over time as new members joined the Committees and as changing social attitudes to children as innocent made the ladies less concerned about public criticism of their caring approach. Another key factor in changes to both internal and placement policies was the expertise the managers acquired on the basis of their experience using different placement policies. By the end of the century, the policies they developed as a result of this put them directly into conflict with so-called "new" child-care methods being advocated by the growing group of "experts" in the field.

As more and more emphasis was placed on children as innocent and malleable, proper Christian nurture was touted as crucial to educating and training children. Families, especially mothers, were seen as central to this nurture, alongside properly supervised schooling.[62] Child charities that took in destitute children and acted as substitute families received widespread support, and from the mid-nineteenth century more age-specific institutions opened. However, alongside this profusion of child charities, a number of child charity workers began to advocate placing children in foster families, preferably in rural areas, and vocally attacked institutionalization. This movement, known as "placing out," grew in popularity through the 1880s. Its support was based on the ideal of the family and the superiority of families over institutions, but also on the desire to rescue children from families many among the middle class felt were inadequate. In effect, the more the elite saw children as needing protection and as being susceptible to negative environmental influences, the more they became suspicious of the ability of poor urban families to provide "adequate" child nurture.

The LBS and the POA were aware of this discourse but both Committees rejected the movement's underlying objective to remove children from their natural families. Furthermore, they did not see "placing out" as a new method, but rather as similar to methods such as adoption and apprenticeship that they had used for years and had often found lacking, if not downright dangerous for the children so placed. Their experience revealed a regular disregard of contractual stipulations in relation to education, church attendance, and training; and mistreatment including medical neglect, overwork, and physical, mental, and even sexual abuse. This convinced the ladies that placement families could not always be trusted, even under supervision. As their own emphasis on child protection increased they defended institutions as a perfectly equipped environment in which to educate, train, and protect destitute children – in effect, to perform the functions of a "fictive" family for those who had lost their families or needed a temporary one. By the mid-1880s, they were convinced, in fact, that only their institutions, where the managers themselves and their staff monitored the children's care, could provide a safe haven and superior training for the children, and had introduced prolonged residence in the institution at least for girls, who did their training inside the charity and left to go directly into service. In this way, their experience with placement methods led them to opt for an even more developed institutional model, in direct contradiction to trends that were increasingly popular among professional child workers and some of the Montreal elite.

The other major movement the ladies found themselves in conflict with by the end of the century was the push to make relief more "scientific" and organized. By mid-century many argued that readily available relief aggravated the problem of poverty by creating relief dependency. They believed that relief should be designed to force the poor to self-reliance and thus eliminate dependency. This movement found echoes and proponents in Montreal as elsewhere. A short-lived Associated Charities was created in 1883, followed by a Charity Organization Society in 1900.

The women who ran the two Montreal child charities did not agree with this restrictive approach to relief that limited the aid available to many of the poor. They also vehemently rejected "scientific" charity's aims to rationalize, organize, or centralize the charitable services available across a city, aims that could have the effect of reducing the number and type of charitable services available. They accepted general notions of the "deserving poor" and of poverty as individual fault, but their religious motivation, humanitarianism, and traditional world-view led them to focus more on need than on morality or concepts of individual freedom and forced self-reliance – to design their aid to *relieve* rather than *reform*; in effect, to *personalize* rather than *systematize.* In this way, they moderated some of the more extreme and moralizing voices from both the male establishment and groups of more reformist women in the city.

Neither class nor gender provide a complete explanation of the workings of the charities. In several important areas, these women made policy choices related to poverty relief and placement methods that differed in fundamental ways from those made by other women and men of their class. Their conservative benevolent approach distinguished the charity managers from more reform-oriented groups of women in the city such as the YWCA or the Local Council of Women. Their practical experience and expertise in child charity work and the policies they developed in consequence were also key to these differences. It was through this experience that the ladies defined their "voice," and the particularities of this voice distinguished them from other groups of women working in the social sphere who advocated what many considered to be more "modern" approaches.

A number of recent studies have focused on the reformist or activist women's associations that aimed to forge a place for women in the public arena. These include those by Sarah Deutsch, Maureen Flanagan, Andrea Geddes Poole, Eleanor Gordon and Gwyneth Nair, Stephen King, Daphne Spain, and, in terms of Montreal and Canada, Yolande Cohen, Elizabeth Kirkland, and Carmen Neilson.[63] The current study will shift the emphasis to put the spotlight on more traditional women who did not aspire to political involvement. Rather, they worked within a framework of conservative benevolence, providing crucial services to families but deliberately limiting their public intervention to that project. Our ability to do an in-depth analysis of policy development over time allows us to build on the model of women's associations that Nancy Hewitt created to flesh out our understanding of benevolent societies, the choices they made, and the factors that influenced those choices.

In looking at the shift to placing out in late-nineteenth-century Ontario, Neil Sutherland speaks somewhat disparagingly of institutional charities making "a determined effort to survive." He concludes that, once the zeal of the original founders faded away, many child institutions "displayed both a grim determination to persist and, at best, a cautious drabness in their management."[64] This study shows that, in the case of these two Montreal charities, the defence by the Committees of their charities and their methods was not at all a reactionary resistance to change nor simply an attempt at self-preservation. Their policies evolved over the century and into the twentieth century as the ladies identified and responded to problems in placement methods and identified new needs among the city's poor families with considerable respect for parental rights.

The study of these charities contributes to an understanding of a number of questions related to child charity, women's benevolence, working-class agency, placement methods, and social regulation. Finally, it provides a much-needed study of the Protestant charitable network in the nineteenth and early twentieth centuries and of Protestant female-managed charity in Montreal. The sources do not lend themselves to a developed study of particular women; even dissension within the Committees is difficult to assess and has only been developed in a few instances. Thus, this is really a collective history of the women who made up these charity committees, the work they accomplished, and the institutions they managed as they worked together on their joint project in close networks of kinship, friendship, community, and sisterhood.

The study is largely based on the remaining archival material for the two charities, supplemented by municipal and church archives, government documents, contemporary literature and reports, a survey of the nineteenth-century press, and relevant secondary sources. A full set of annual reports is complemented by admission registers, minutes of meetings, and daily journals. Taken together, this remarkably complete archives enables us to examine the characteristics of resident populations as well as policy discussions and thus to analyze actual services and policy shifts.[65] The admission registers are single-line data entries that include both admission and discharge circumstances, but they are not case files in the modern sense of the term. Although, as Mariana Valverde notes, this type of register does not allow us to "know" individuals the way case reports would, the information, supplemented by commentary in the minutes and the matron's journals, allows us to determine the institutional demography and the circumstances that led families to seek help from charities.[66] It is important to establish that, although the examination of policies follows both charities until 1921 and in some cases to 1936, the statistical analysis, except that for the LBS Industrial School, is based on the nineteenth century. Twentieth-century data is treated as a separate entity and used mainly for comparative purposes.

A note on vocabulary is needed. The fact that Committee members deliberately and clearly differentiated between themselves as "ladies" or even "Ladies" and their female clients and hired staff as "women" speaks eloquently to their class-defined self-image. This labelling or symbolic representation both united the Committee members as a group and separated them from women of an inferior social class. The rhetorical trope of the "lady" evoked specific notions of both domesticity and respectability; that is, it had both gender and class connotations.[67] The term highlights the directors' status and the social expectations they lived with; in this way it was part and parcel of their identity and their position in the nineteenth-century city. The reader will note the change in name from the Female Benevolent Society in 1815 to the Ladies' Benevolent Society when it was resurrected in 1832, a change that better reflected the social respectability of its members.[68] Although an organization such as the Women's Christian Temperance Union, for example, hoped to appeal to all women, the Ladies' Benevolent Society was addressing only those women who could lay claim to the social status and social capital of "the lady." In recognition of the symbolic importance language had for these elite women and their approach to charity work, I refer to the Committee members as ladies throughout the book. It could be argued that, as a construct, the term should be placed in quotation marks; I have not done this to avoid cluttering the text. In a similar attempt to respect the historical importance of language, I have systematically capitalized Committee to distinguish it as a corporate body, and have adopted the capitalization norms used in the period for elected officers.

This book is divided into seven chapters. The first chapter establishes the context of benevolence in the city, that is, the Quebec social welfare model and the Protestant private relief network, particularly services available for children. Chapter 2 begins the more detailed examination of the two charities under study, looking at the identity of the charitable elite who ran them, their funding, and the factors that influenced these benevolent women's groups, including their conservative benevolent approach. Chapter 3 examines the management of female-directed charities, the work involved in running a charity, participation in it, and relations with the staff.

Chapters 4, 5, and 6 look at the interface of the managers and the families applying for help by analyzing the children admitted to and discharged from these two institutions: the circumstances under which families placed children in a charity; what life in an institution was like; how long children stayed; and where they went when they left. These chapters answer a number of questions in relation to the charities' role in bolstering families, the difficulties encountered in finding adequate placement families for children who could not return to their birth family, and how the ladies dealt with problematic, even abusive, placements when they occurred, as well as how the ladies attempted to make their institutions into homes and how successful they were in this. These answers provide a context for the discussion of policy changes in the final chapter.

Chapter 7 addresses policy development in more detail, specifically the impact of the "separate spheres" ideology, the rejection of both placing out and scientific charity by these Committees, and the policies they chose instead. The chapter also considers the interaction between these two benevolent Committees and the more reform-minded YWCA and the Local Council of Women, both of which actively supported the newer approaches. Finally, the Epilogue looks briefly at some of these policy conflicts in the twentieth century and the ladies' fight to defend their place in the charitable network in light of the growth of foster care and system-wide organizational structures.

Like the Chicago women at the centre of Maureen Flanagan's study, we could speak of these Montreal women as "seeing with their hearts."[69] As benevolent associations, they forged an important place in the city's social regulation system, but at points they needed to defend this place and their policies. As elite women, they needed to straddle two different worlds – that of the meeting room and the benevolent association, where, in the context of a female culture based on care and a person-centred approach, they worked alongside fellow women to address need and care for children, and that of the larger society, where, as members of the elite, they were exposed to ideologies that judged their "clients" harshly and possibly even questioned the existence of their charities and their policy orientations. It was impossible for them not to be influenced by this larger liberal perspective in some ways and certainly their charities were an integral part of the social regulation structure whereby they socialized poor children in "appropriate" attitudes and skills while they cared for them, but countervailing ideologies of religious motivation, humanitarianism, and traditional class obligations, as well as their maternal and caring approach to work with children and the expertise they developed from years of doing this, also contributed to the complexities of their "benevolent design."

1

A Poor Relief Network for Montreal's Protestant Poor

As Montreal industrialized over the nineteenth century, an increased proportion of the population became wage-dependent. A tenfold increase in population and the instability of the evolving wage market meant that larger and larger numbers of people lived under the constant threat of unemployment, under-employment, destitution, hunger, and even homelessness.[1] Much of this systemic unemployment occurred during the winter slowdown with the closure of the port and was concurrent with increased fuel and clothing costs, making it even more devastating, as seen in figure 1.1. The large number of immigrants crowding into the city each summer, often with little more than the clothes on their backs, was another problem, and many of those who remained in Montreal did so not by choice but because they were without the resources to continue further west.

For most low-wage workers and recent immigrants, poverty was a way of life accompanied by the appalling sanitary and health conditions prevalent in an unregulated, rapidly growing city. The fragile balance of income strategies that individuals and families devised was easily upset by any sustained period of unemployment or illness or by the death of a wage-earning spouse, all of which occurred on a regular basis, leaving families faced with destitution.[2] Particularly at risk were families with young children as yet unable to contribute to family income, the families of widows, and other female-headed households who could not count on a male wage, as well as elderly couples or single individuals without the support of a family wage system.[3] As our charity files show, in times of need people usually turned to kin, friends, or even neighbours. Those without these help networks, or for whom these options were already

Figure 1.1 Auguste Trichon, *A Winter Scene*. An illustration that appeared in *L'Opinion publique* in 1875 with an article describing the misery of many poor families, especially during the winter. The society ladies are "visitors" probably bringing aid.

stretched to capacity, turned, as a last resort, to charity. Although those in need were often able to use relief structures for their own purposes, the aid available usually reflected the prejudices and interests of the elite much more than the needs of the destitute. This was particularly true of places such as Montreal, where no state relief system was developed until the twentieth century.

"A MIXED SOCIAL ECONOMY"

The basic model of social welfare that developed in central Canada over the late eighteenth and early nineteenth centuries was one of mixed public/private responsibilities, with the role of each sector taking different forms depending on the specific area of intervention – what Mariana Valverde has called a "mixed social economy."[4] Consistent with liberal beliefs about individual freedom and responsibility, poor relief was generally allocated to the private sector with only minimal public financial support, although the exact mix of public and private varied from one region of the country to another. Two of the biggest influences on the specific model that developed in Quebec, and certainly in Montreal, were the region's religious divide and the growing power of the Catholic Church, with its deliberate campaign from the 1840s to consolidate its social role and assume responsibility for social service delivery in the absence of active state intervention in this area. Thus the Quebec social services model came to mirror yet another divided responsibility – that between the state and the Catholic Church – in which the Church assumed an increasing role in civil society.[5] This placed the Protestant community in the position of providing for its own population separately, and resulted in two parallel social assistance networks. This model, both private and confessional, differed from that developed in Ontario, for example, where historians have found that the state and its municipalities, including Toronto, were more interventionist and that generally the churches, other than the Catholic Church, did not have a significant role.[6]

Besides refusing responsibility for a poor relief structure, the early Lower Canada government was also hesitant to allocate public funds to support private relief efforts. Thus requests from the nuns to continue the support they had been receiving under the New France regime were unsuccessful until 1801. So too were requests from others in 1789 and 1792, for support to create new institutions that would be nondenominational and able to cope with a larger scale of need.[7] Similarly, early applications from groups seeking incorporation, such as the first application of the Montreal House of Industry in 1808, met with rejection.[8] Undaunted by the state's rejection of these petitions, the urban elite began private relief initiatives to deal with the poverty and illness resulting from rising immigration. Through this process they added a new component to Quebec's poor-relief model: private charitable societies that were not run by the Catholic Church but nonetheless tended to be organized along confessional lines. In Montreal, Protestant women formed the Female Benevolent Society in 1815 (dissolved in 1822), the Protestant Orphan Asylum in 1822, and the Montreal Ladies' Benevolent Society in 1832, while Catholic women formed the Roman Catholic Orphan Asylum in 1832 and a group of Protestant businessmen founded the Montreal General Hospital in 1821. Although the permanent network was organized on denominational lines, there were several examples of non-sectarian cooperation early in the century. The original Montreal House of Industry (1817/19–46), for example, took a parish approach, being formed by committees of leading Catholics and Protestants.[9] However, its existence was both seasonal and sporadic, and when permanent institutions were formed in the 1860s they were confessional.[10] Other associations, such as child charities, although sectarian, occasionally cooperated in fund-raising events.[11] All of these societies were private, lay, and specialized – in effect an early version of voluntary associations. Alongside these lay undertakings, the Catholic Church and a number of religious communities continued relief services to the Catholic population and slowly increased their scope.

From the beginning there was an expectation, at least on the part of English-speaking Protestants, that the public sector should provide some support for these private efforts in the form of infrastructure. The state remained hesitant to do so. Thus, a year after its foundation, the Protestant Orphan Asylum applied to the Governor-in-Chief to grant them a piece of land on which to erect a permanent building. His denial of their petition clarified the state's position in relation to poor relief. He argued he "did not feel himself authorized to bestow the land for such a comparatively private purpose."[12] Not surprisingly, this refusal to extend public power and funds to what the Governor considered a "private" undertaking was consistent with previous refusals to grant incorporation status and subsidies to charities. It reflected the increased separation between public and private that Jean-Marie Fecteau has identified as a component of the liberal mode of social regulation, a separation that allocated responsibility for the relief of "normal" poverty to civil society and which granted associations that assumed this responsibility a substantial amount of autonomy.[13] During the period 1800–60 the legislature debated the role of the state in relation to poor relief several times, but consistently rejected any direct intervention for ideological and financial reasons, although it began granting some financial support from the 1830s.[14]

By mid-century, the government was taking a more direct role in areas such as prisons, reform schools, industrial schools, and insane asylums, convinced that intervention in these areas was justified for social regulation and/or youth protection purposes and that the cost was beyond the capacity of the private sector.[15] Nonetheless, even here, Quebec was keen to limit the state's financial liability and responsibility.[16] Once it gained power over the realm of social policy under the *British North America Act*, Quebec replaced the former non-sectarian state-run reformatory institutions created in United Canada with state-certified but privately managed, confessional ones which were paid on the basis of small per-diem fees.[17] This type of public-private model whereby private institutions assumed infrastructure costs as well as full administrative responsibility was feasible given the willingness of the Catholic Church to move into the vacuum created by a weak state presence and establish a social services network. In fact, it was ideal as long as some government oversight could be maintained. Mechanisms such as inspection and using the courts to control admissions effectively created these conditions, enabling the state to "rule from a distance" at a minimal cost. In terms of direct poor relief, however, the Lower Canada/Quebec government was much more circumscribed than this, unusually so. Even the various Houses of Industry in Montreal were privately managed and financed despite being the type of institution where public financing would have been the norm, and was, for example, in Toronto.[18]

STATE SUPPORT FOR PRIVATE RELIEF INITIATIVES

While not taking a direct role in poor-relief distributions, the state assumed a supportive role for private initiatives through small but regular subsidies as early as the 1830s. Published government budgets from 1840 reveal that the number of Montreal charities receiving some state support increased from three in 1840 to twenty-five in 1899. After funding increases in 1843 and 1863, though, cuts began in 1884. In this way, despite an increase in the number of charities, overall government costs were controlled through decreasing individual grants. By the end of the century, government grants for most Montreal Protestant charities, for example, had been cut to almost half their 1863–83 level. However, these remained a reliable, if small, source of income for private undertakings. Although subsidies were not forthcoming from the city, Montreal gave charities a tax exemption after 1856.[19]

In areas where the state or its institutions (such as the police and the courts) were directly involved in institutional placements, more financial support was forthcoming and this grew over the period. From 1887, for example, the city paid substantial sums for the board of children in the city's reformatories and industrial schools. By 1892, this had reached an annual total of $30,000;

by 1910, $47,852.[20] Part of this was the result of legislation that shifted the financial responsibility for subsidizing these institutions from Quebec to municipalities.[21] It also reflected Montreal's decision to use these institutions, particularly industrial schools, in the city's front-line response to poverty among its citizens.

Besides funding, the state facilitated private welfare initiatives by using its legislative powers to grant incorporated status to voluntary associations. This was beneficial to both parties. Controlling access to incorporation enabled the state to ensure that associations were non-profit and to standardize the form charters took and the rules included in them across the country. Meanwhile, incorporation was essential to voluntary associations since it gave them a legal existence as collective entities and the ability to act as corporate entities. Clauses establishing limited liability freed members from any personal responsibility for debts and contracts incurred by the corporate entity.[22] Incorporation was particularly important for female-directed associations to manage their work efficiently, since it granted them the legal status to carry on business affairs and sign contracts despite the legal obstacles inherent in the common-law doctrine of *femme covert*.[23] In effect, incorporation allowed voluntary associations freedom of action and ensured their ability to function in perpetuity.

Governments' early hesitation to recognize voluntary associations had subsided by the 1830s as these associations became more common.[24] Nonetheless, extensive debate on the question occasionally took place in the legislature of United Canada. In 1849–50, a more standardized process was established, but an attempt in 1852–53 by Attorney General George Drummond to further simplify the process and eliminate the need to discuss each application separately provoked vociferous protest motivated by the fear of creating an uncontrollable profusion of sectarian institutions with recognized property rights and so on.[25] When the bill was finalized in 1856, it included a clause limiting property acquisition to that actually needed by a corporation to carry out its specific realm of activity.[26]

Although the incorporation process was thus simplified, the aims of standardization remained. In 1857, the government extended its control over private charities receiving public funds by placing them, along with prisons and hospitals, under the jurisdiction of the *Prison Inspection Act* and the newly formed Board of Inspectors.[27] Inspectors were "to visit, examine and report" on "every Hospital or other Benevolent Institution supported wholly by grant of public money" as well as those supported "partially" when requested.[28] At Confederation, this responsibility passed to the provinces. The new Quebec board listed its duties as the inspection of twenty-five public institutions, as well as "more than thirty charitable or benevolent institutions" when instructed.[29] Unlike Ontario, where Carmen Neilson has argued that powers such as inspection led to an increase in state control, the Quebec government was not interested in actually exercising this control and rarely gave instructions to inspect charitable institutions. The Reports of the Inspectors of Prisons, Asylums, etc. from 1869 to 1899 include only a few comments on private charities other than those for the disabled and industrial/reform schools, which received substantial funding and were regulated by government contracts.[30]

Occasionally over the nineteenth century the state, especially at the municipal level, provided some emergency aid to boost the capacity of charitable networks during economic crises and natural disasters.[31] Mounting need linked to high levels of unemployment after the 1880s as well as continued funding problems for the charitable network led to increased city initiatives in the twentieth century. The city paid for the admission of more and more children into industrial schools and placed both the application process and the funding allocation under the jurisdiction of the Bureau of Municipal Assistance, formed in 1907. A city refuge for the unemployed and homeless, the Meurling Refuge, was opened in 1912.[32]

In 1916, in an effort to generate funds, Montreal received permission from Quebec to levy an amusement tax with part of the proceeds going to hospitals and other charitable institutions. This *sou du pauvre* was the first step towards a more systematic state support.[33] The *Public Charities Act* of 1921 was an even more significant step and established the model for state financing that would persist well into the twentieth century. Under this law, set amounts of minimal support were established for various categories of relief – charitable, hospital, and so on – and awarded to associations/institutions (according to their number of residents) as long as they provided congregate/residential care.[34] The financing was organized on the basis of a shared responsibility – one-third Quebec, one-third municipality, one-third private organization. Nonetheless, given the permanently precarious budgets of most private institutions, this was an important turn of events. Three points are relevant in relation to this legislation. First, the responsibility of the private organization to provide some of its own support was a central principle, and, at least for Protestant institutions with large wage bills, the amounts per inmate were always substantially less than real costs. Second, aid was awarded to organizations, not given directly to individuals. Third, this financing was only available for congregate institutions, a situation that reflected the predominant place of institutional aid in the Quebec model.[35]

Thus, the global Quebec welfare model was characterized by the strong presence of private and/or Church associations managing relief efforts, by some version of state support for this (increased in 1921), and by a bifurcation along confessional lines. The government became more directly involved through regulatory control and/or extensive funding in the case of reformatories, industrial schools, prisons, and insane asylums; this was also true of institutions for hearing-impaired and disabled children. This basically private model satisfied the elite (and the Catholic Church) in charge of the voluntary associations, since it left them with control of their benevolent projects but able to depend on at least some state funding. It left those who needed help, however, in a less than ideal situation – forced to turn to their Church or to a private charity for what relief they could find. This makes a study of private charity crucial to understanding nineteenth-century Montreal.

THE PRIVATE RELIEF NETWORK

Montreal's social assistance network had several characteristics that were shared by those in most Western countries.[36] First, women were responsible for much of the relief work. Women from the city's elite, both Protestant and Catholic, managed private charities and supported church relief work; alongside this volunteer lay effort, female religious orders dominated the hands-on work of the Catholic network. Second, institutions formed the core of the structure, supplemented by outdoor services. Third, charity was seen as a gift, not a right, and hence was recognized as both voluntary and discretionary. This "gift relationship" assumed gratitude and humility on the part of recipients; donors had the responsibility to distribute charity wisely.[37] The small role for the state and the confessional split, resulting in two parallel structures (three by the end of the century with the addition of the Jewish network), were particularities of Montreal's system.

Montreal's Catholic community adapted easily to a private bifurcated welfare model since it opened the opportunity for the Church to assume an increased role in the public realm. As a number of historians have explained, during the nineteenth century an extensive Catholic charitable network was established, organized by the Sulpicians, the Bishop, religious communities, and lay groups including the Ladies of Charity and the St Vincent de Paul Society.[38] The actual management of the institutional network was largely the work of the religious orders, especially the Grey Nuns and the Sisters of Providence, although specialized religious orders, brought in from Europe, worked with targeted groups. By the end of the century this well-organized network contained approximately thirty-eight residential institutions including a number of hospitals, an insane asylum, institutions for orphans, children and the elderly, two industrial schools, two reform schools, a refuge for the homeless, institutions for the seeing- and hearing-impaired, and homes for unwed mothers, as well as several large outdoor-relief depots and dispensaries.[39] The possibility that this large Catholic network could be used to proselytize was recognized as a threat and, on occasion, even stimulated Protestants to increase the services available for their own community.

In the Protestant tradition as developed in England and the United States, the state played a major role in poor relief through its poor law provisions, but the uniqueness of Quebec's situation obliged Montreal's Protestant community to develop new models. The resulting network was the combined effort of churches, ethnic national societies, and private charities or voluntary associations, and was influenced by a mixture of Christian duty, evangelicalism, and liberal ideology. This private model gave the city's Protestant leaders the ability to control the forms of aid available, as well as access to that aid, through eligibility requirements. This effectively enabled them to both regulate behaviour and impose their beliefs about domesticity, family, childhood, and morality on their community. Their ideology is central to the way Protestant relief developed in the city.

According to Protestant dogma, charity was an individual duty with numerous obligations and rewards. But by the late eighteenth century the rise of liberalism rendered the concept of charity-as-duty somewhat ambiguous and few members of the Protestant elite advocated that charitable giving should be unrestricted. Liberalism, with its emphasis on freedom and individual responsibility, held all individuals, even the poor, to be autonomous members of society. Poverty then became a personal responsibility blamed on the failure to adjust or to make adequate provision for economic changes. These ideological shifts paralleled the massive economic and social processes associated with industrialization and urbanization, which, as feminist political philosopher Joan Tronto argues, created a new form of social distance and (lack of) connectedness between the social classes.[40] In Montreal, as a colonial port city, this situation was aggravated by the number of recent immigrants struggling to survive without family support networks while trying to find employment in a changing economy. As a result, at many points in the nineteenth century, segments of the population were not yet fully integrated into the fragile wage economy.[41]

Although the elite believed that destitution demanded some redress to avoid the threat of social disorder, they were equally concerned by their conviction that easily available aid could create relief dependency or "pauperism," which they saw as a moral and social problem, associated with a constellation of other social "evils" including crime, indolence, intemperance, illiteracy, and disease.[42] This association of destitution and dependency with crime and even the association of poverty with personal weakness tended to marginalize at least some of the poor as "Other." In this case, as Linda Gordon has argued, "Other" had connotations of "not simply different but lacking."[43] This reinforced distinctions philanthropists had begun making in the eighteenth century between the "deserving" poor and those they called the "undeserving," and encouraged them to carefully define what comprised real "charity" as opposed to "indiscriminate giving."[44]

With this moral and class-based perspective, the organizers of relief efforts visited applicants to ensure that relief would neither be wasted nor create dependency. This process asserted their control over aid distribution, but, in a place such as Montreal where no public workhouse existed for the undeserving, it involved a balancing of ideological beliefs with basic humanitarian instincts and was not always straightforward. As the wardens of the Anglican Christ Church Cathedral explained in 1871: "Those who claimed to be the poor of the Church have given your Wardens a great deal of trouble and anxiety, lest by a rigid weeding out of the impostors and unworthy … they should cast off some one who might possibly be worthy of charity."[45] In 1873, the St Andrew's Society pointed to the same ambiguity: "To separate

Figure 1.2 *Frozen to Death.* A *Canadian Illustrated News* front-page illustration depicting the discovery of dead children in their lodgings, January 1872.

the deserving from the undeserving, to know when it was charity to give and when not to give, to guard the funds of the Society so that there should be neither careless lavishness, nor worthy poor sent away empty-handed." Care was taken to determine "worthiness," but the Committee admitted to occasionally aiding others out of "feelings of humanity" and "fear they might perish from cold and hunger."[46] Figure 1.2 reveals that this was not an unrealistic fear on their part.

Accordingly, Montreal's Protestant community was torn between the need to create its own relief network to alleviate poverty and the prevalent ideology against making relief too easily available or too abundant. This resulted in a somewhat constrained benevolence, a benevolence that did not reflect the real wealth of the community as much as it reflected their moral and ideological views. More importantly, it led to a network of services that did not recognize the real level and scope of need, and severely limited private donations to the institutions that were created, including the child charities, which consequently suffered from tight budgets and even deficits. The women of the elite, including those who managed the child charities, were doubly caught by this situation as they attempted to mesh this liberal perspective with considerations of religious and humanitarian motivations to rescue souls and protect children and their own conservative beliefs of their class duty to the poor. As we saw in the Introduction, their solution to this dilemma was to act on their own beliefs and organize services mainly for children, whom most considered deserving and who could be trained in middle-class values. Through this action the ladies bolstered poor families and helped many women and children.

PROTESTANT CHURCHES

Protestants could not expect their churches to take a leadership role in poor relief similar to that of the Catholic Church. Without the substantial landed endowments of the Sulpicians or access to the inexpensive and dedicated labour of Catholic religious orders, and lacking a centralized structure since the Protestant population was divided into different denominations, efforts in this area fell to individual churches or denominations.[47] Most churches organized poor funds that helped provide small pensions and aid in kind to the elderly and poor members of their congregation, to pay to board children and the elderly in city charities, to cover burial costs, and to hire needy members for odd jobs.[48] All applicants were visited to ensure "worthiness" and to maintain contact with the church. Those churches that could afford it named a clergyman to work specifically with the poor and/or had District Visiting committees.[49] Women's groups such as Dorcases and Ladies' Aid Societies played a major role in this work, making clothing and visiting the poor to distribute clothing, boots, grocery tickets, fuel, and Christmas dinners. Young women helped through the Young Women's Association and the Dominion Order of King's Daughters. Missionaries working in connection with the Montreal Woman's Missionary Society also did some relief work.[50]

Slowly, over the nineteenth and into the twentieth centuries, churches became more active in the fight against poverty. In 1876, the Anglican Church formed the Committee on Works of Mercy to enable the Diocese to supplement and extend the work of individual churches.[51] This committee assumed responsibility for a number of services: the Immigration Chaplain (1883), the city missionary (1884), the district visitors, the Church Home / Ladies' Home (1855), and the Robert Jones Convalescent Hospital (1895). Despite these new undertakings, Bishop Bond used his Synod addresses in 1891, 1892, and 1893 to call for more effort to establish "general diocesan charity" and to find a way "of ministering to the waifs and strays of a great city, to the unknown men and women … who creep into our cities in winter seeking the shelter of our streets and refuges."[52] A timely bequest from Henry Ogden Andrews in 1894 made it possible to open Andrews Home in a three-storey building on Belmont Park in connection with the immigration chaplain.[53] The Home ran a placement bureau for domestics and provided lodging and meals for immigrants searching for work. As of 1900 it opened a special dormitory and placement service for boys aged seven to twenty.[54]

Another new development near the end of the nineteenth century was the arrival first of Anglican nuns in connection with St John the Evangelist church, and then of Deaconesses. The Anglican Sisters of Saint Margaret came to Montreal from Boston and opened the Saint Margaret's Anglican Home for the Incurable and Infirm (women) in 1883.[55] Other Anglican orders opened two missions for the homeless associated with St John's.[56] Alongside this practical work, the twentieth-century church under Bishop Farthing increasingly focused on expanding its social and educational role.

Unlike the Anglican churches, Presbyterian and Congregational churches focused much of their efforts on mission work in working-class districts. Every church contributed to the support of missionary Sunday schools and/or city mission work.[57] A number of them established missions in the second half of the century when churches began to move uptown to follow their middle-class and elite clientele, or helped form new churches in working-class districts.[58] These missions (Nazareth Street, Chaboillez Square/Inspector Street Chapel, Victoria, and Centre Street) provided some temporal aid and job referrals alongside evangelical religious services.[59] Many ran Sunday schools, mothers' meetings, temperance groups, sewing classes, and libraries. Several paid nurses and bible women to visit families.[60] Although they enforced moral and gender prescriptions, the missions also provided poor families and immigrants with facilities that were in sharp contrast to the hard conditions of their lives – places where they could meet, listen to church music, and learn practical skills.[61] As the Crescent Street Church missionary in Griffintown pointed out in 1886: "The relation of the Church to the poorer classes is demanding more and more attention, and not only in Montreal, but in every city on the continent."[62]

Montreal had a number of other evangelical missions. The Old Brewery Mission, which opened as a soup kitchen in 1890 on Dalhousie Street, drew support from the Dominion Square Methodist Church; however, a commitment from the city's Methodist churches as a group enabled them to move to larger quarters on St Antoine Street quite quickly. The Welcome Hall Mission, opened in the 1890s further west on St Antoine Street south of the CPR station, was the project of a group of young men from Calvary Congregational Church. These missions were an important addition to the network since they provided services for homeless men: bed, meals, and bath. In the twentieth century they extended their work to include services for families: mothers' meetings, summer camps, classes, savings banks, job referrals. Both missionaries and Deaconesses worked as the link with neighbourhood families.[63] When the Salvation Army arrived in the city in 1884 they immediately started rescue work with men and also opened the Young Women's Lodge boarding house. By 1905 they had added the Working Women's Home, an Industrial Home for men, a home for the elderly, relief bureaus, and food and clothing depots.[64]

The Protestant churches, therefore, provided small amounts of aid for some of the congregational poor, mainly in the winter months. By the end of the century, missions, the Salvation Army, and Andrews Home had undertaken important work with the homeless and recent immigrants, accompanied by a heavy dose of evangelism. However, unlike their Catholic neighbours, Protestant families could not depend on their church for help with child care, and even outdoor aid was limited. For these services, the Protestant poor turned to either the ethnic national societies or private charities.

PROTESTANT NATIONAL SOCIETIES

Much of the Protestant population was British-born, and ethnicity served as a focus of identity as much as religion did, especially in such an ethnically diverse city as Montreal. The national societies were central to this identity.[65] Although they satisfied needs of a political and social nature, these societies were also aid societies whereby ethnic communities cared for their own. They constituted one of the major components of the Protestant relief network, providing aid for the elderly poor and outdoor relief in the winter season. But their main contribution was the services they provided through their immigrant reception homes for the large number of sometimes destitute and friendless immigrants entering the city every summer. Overall, their charity work was on a much larger scale than that of the Protestant churches but more limited in its range.

The St George's Society (English)[66] and the St Andrew's Society (Scottish)[67] were formed in 1834 and 1835 respectively at about the same time as the Saint Jean Baptiste Society, the German Society, and the St Patrick's Society. The latter included both Catholics and Protestants until the Irish Protestant Benevolent Society was created in 1856.[68] Over the winter months, the Charitable Committees met once a week to receive applicants and to distribute food, clothing, and fuel. Help with burial costs, job referrals, and passage money to return to Britain or to move west was also possible. A few elderly pensioners received assistance all year long, often for many years. St Andrew's helped an average of 111 families, or between 300 to 500 persons, each year over the winter months.[69] The numbers for St George's were even larger as it served a much larger population. In 1903 it was estimated that, since 1834, a total of 10,000 families or 56,000 people had benefited from outdoor relief over the winter months.[70] Total numbers are not available for the Irish Protestant Benevolent Society but we know that over the 1870s and 1880s approximately fifty families a week received assistance.[71] The Committee rented a woodlot in Pointe-St-Charles to distribute wood over the winter and put aside funds in anticipation of the spring floods since so many Irish lived in high-risk flood areas.

In the spring and summer months, representatives met newly arrived immigrants at the docks to offer help to any who needed it. In 1857, the St Andrew's Society made this help more tangible with the opening of St Andrew's

Home.[72] Serving as a temporary shelter for immigrants, it housed up to 200 persons a year, most of them for several days. By 1900, close to 5,000 persons had been residents. Since there were always large numbers of applicants whom the Committee judged to be "tramps" who "could not properly claim a shelter," the Home also ran an outdoor soup kitchen to provide these "questionable" applicants with meals.[73] By the late 1860s, St George's had built a similar home on St Antoine Street where, from 1872 to 1900, a total of 22,816 persons were admitted.[74] It was this home that the Irish Protestant Benevolent Society used for outdoor relief until they opened a reception home on Belmont Park in the early 1880s.[75]

Thus, national societies established front-line services for immigrants in the summer, and, in the winter, supplemented the aid provided by Protestant churches to city residents with larger-scale outdoor relief. Although they helped many people, this aid was designed to be temporary and did not directly address the problems of most of the elderly, the homeless, or families unable to support their children. For these needs, Protestants turned to the private charities founded by groups of philanthropic citizens.

PROTESTANT PRIVATE CHARITIES

Protestant Montreal was part of a larger process of institution-building and organized private charities that was reproduced in cities across Canada, the United States, and England as urban elites responded both to need and to the perceived threat to social order, but the Montreal process had several particularities. To begin with, due to a lack of state support, a permanent House of Industry (workhouse) did not exist until 1863. A House of Industry was founded in 1819 but it was both seasonal and sporadic and closed for good in 1846. Although city council considered forming a municipal institution, these efforts also faltered.[76] Thus, Montreal did not follow the usual pattern where the workhouse was one of the first institutions established, if not the first, and specialized charities, such as those for women and children, followed. Instead, by the time the permanent Protestant House of Industry was opened in 1863, three female-directed charities for women and children already existed (dating from 1822, 1832, and 1847) as well as a sewing room for widows (1855). In the absence of a general institution, the common jail assumed its function to some extent, sheltering the homeless under the guise of vagrancy charges and thereby coming close to criminalizing poverty.[77] Finally, the earliest Protestant charity, the Female Benevolent Society (1815–22), was established by women, not men, and at an earlier date than even the original short-lived House of Industry.

Indeed the women of Montreal responded to the plight of the destitute early in the century and played a central role in organized charity. While men applied for charters and funds and debated the wisdom of state poor-relief systems versus private ones, women took a more proactive approach – they simply rented facilities and began to provide aid. In this, they could look to examples of American women, who had been organizing charities since the early 1800s.[78] In return, the Protestant Orphan Asylum, formed much earlier than the norm for such organizations in Canada,[79] became the model for many other Canadian Protestant child charities founded in the decades that followed.[80]

Most of the women's charitable work, though, was limited to women and children. Except for the early Female Benevolent Society and the short-lived Protestant Industrial House of Refuge (1854–56), there is no evidence of Montreal Protestant women running a general charity that distributed outdoor relief as women did in several other North American cities,[81] although many women were involved in the distribution of outdoor relief to families in their homes in connection with churches or national societies.[82] Thus a gender division developed in Montreal's Protestant private charity network, roughly along the lines of the gender-defined separate spheres, whereby women established and managed services for the care of other women and children. In her work on women's benevolence in San Francisco, where a similar gender division evolved, American historian Mary Ann Irwin refers to this as "lifeboat benevolence" – a particularly feminine version of charity in which women and children always came first.[83] Furthermore, with the exception of the Boys' Home, mainly for boys over thirteen, the Mackay Institute for Deaf Children, and the Society for the Protection of Women and Children (SPWC), which were run by men, women carried out all of the social assistance work with women and children in the city. It was men, however, who supervised larger-scale undertakings such as outdoor relief and who managed the Montreal

Protestant House of Industry and Refuge. This situation seems to have been influenced by the scope of the work involved and by an inferred restriction on women giving aid to men as well as the belief that caring for women and children was naturally within "the women's sphere."

Another unusual influence on Montreal's Protestant network was the existence of the large Catholic network. This served as a model of women managing charities, but it also created a troubling religious concern among the city's Protestants. Referring to the importance of child charities at the annual POA meeting in 1863, John Greenshields indicated: "It would do well to take a leaf out of the book of the Roman Catholics, and while viewing their charitable institutions, and looking at the good they were accomplishing, ourselves also determine to go and do likewise."[84] Charities could be a way of keeping the faithful in the flock or bringing wayward Protestants back to the faith. In his address to the LBS meeting in 1858, Rev. Charles Bancroft praised the institution's new building and spoke of the need for many such institutions in these terms: "should we not be zealous in providing for our own people, for, in providing for their bodily wants, had we not the opportunity of training them for heaven?"[85] This was not simply a question of mimicking good works. In the absence of corresponding Protestant services, there was a chance that Protestant families might be forced to apply to the nuns for services unavailable in their own community and be "lost" to the faith in the process. Not surprisingly, with only a few exceptions, Protestant charities refused aid to Catholics. This reflected an unwritten understanding whereby Protestants hoped to avoid the Catholic Church using its charitable services to proselytize. It was far different from the pattern in cities such as Boston and Toronto, for example, where Protestants were in the majority and openly used child charities to proselytize.[86]

Montreal's Protestant private network grew slowly over the century. The earliest charities, all run by women, provided institutional care for children and elderly women, both identified as "proper" objects of charity, or work for destitute women. The creation of the Montreal Protestant House of Industry and Refuge in 1863 added facilities for the elderly of both genders, night shelters for the homeless, and permanent outdoor relief services, including a soup kitchen. As the community and its leaders adjusted to new economic and social realities, new needs were identified and more specialized associations such as the Boys' Home, the Protestant Infants'

Table 1.1
Charitable institutions with a residential component in Montreal, 1841–1901

Year	Total institutions	Catholic institutions	Protestant institutions
1841	10	7	3
1861	37	26	11
1881	54	35	19
1901	73	38	35
1921	97	49	48

Source: Fecteau and Harvey, "Montreal's Network of Social Regulation," 679.

Home, the Mackay Institute, the Day Nursery, and the Foundling and Baby Hospital were created. These organizations slowly filled the gaps in services available for families.

Residential institutions represented the major component of the charitable network. From three such institutions for the Protestant population in 1841 (two child charities and a hospital), the network grew to include a total of forty-eight institutions by 1921. Counting Catholic institutions as well, there were ninety-seven charitable institutions with a residential component in 1921. This evolution is clear in table 1.1.

The number of "external" associations and services such as depots and repositories also increased over time. This included dispensaries (which distributed medicine, meals, and basic care), job services (registers and sewing rooms), training services such as those run by the YW/YMCA, summer camps and fresh air funds, and so on. The outdoor relief services (the distribution of clothing, wood, and food) provided by the Protestant House of Industry and the United Board of Outdoor Relief it coordinated in conjunction with the national societies, as well as woodlots, and soup kitchens were part of this group. Finally, the network was completed by services based on direct aid to recipients in their homes. Very few private charities were involved here, but this was the main form of aid provided by churches and their visiting committees.

The poor had to manoeuvre through this mosaic of potential assistance. The help of ministers and eventually the SPWC was indispensible in finding and securing the specific form of help they needed. Families often resorted to a variety of different charitable resources, sometimes at the same time. Some of the charitable services, particularly the early ones run by women, emphasized need and protection and were designed to alleviate poverty; others including the Protestant House of Industry enforced notions of "worthiness" much more strictly; still others such as the School of Industry (Hervey Institute), the Boys' Home, and the groups associated with the YW/YMCA emphasized training and self-improvement. All of them, though, approached relief from the perspective of middle-class cultural and moral values.

The remainder of this chapter provides a brief overview of the Protestant private charities set up over the nineteenth century, organized by type of service (institutional or not) and target population. The main emphasis is placed on alternatives that existed for families needing help with child care. This puts the more detailed analysis of the two child charities that follows in the rest of the book in a clearer perspective. The appendix shows the evolution of the network, listing the services (other than hospitals) by date of foundation.[87]

RESIDENTIAL CHARITIES FOR CHILDREN

The child charities, designed for orphans, abandoned children, or destitute children whose parents could not provide for them, formed the earliest group of Protestant charities, all of them residential institutions. A few, such as the Female Benevolent Society and the Ladies' Benevolent Society, provided some services for women, but the care of children remained their main focus. Described by the Secretary of the Protestant Orphan Asylum as "the most helpless, the most interesting, of God's creatures," children were normally seen as deserving and the charities placed a great deal of emphasis on evangelical notions of soul-saving as well as the need for guidance, education, and protection.[88] Thus, although charities were not controlled by the church, religion permeated much of their work.

As we saw in the introduction, the Female Benevolent Society (1815–22) was formed in December 1815 to help the indigent, the sick, and the aged; men are listed among recipients and the majority of recipients were recent immigrants.[89] The Society organized supply depots (food, wood, clothes,

Figure 1.3 St Maurice Street. Location of the original home of the Montreal Ladies' Benevolent Society, c. 1817. This is the House of Recovery and school opened by the Female Benevolent Society on St Maurice Street.

and medicine) in the summers of 1816 and 1817. In 1817, they made the undertaking more tangible, renting a house on St Maurice Street in the Récollet suburb, seen in figure 1.3. By 1819 they had two houses that served as a day school, a home for orphans, widows, and their children, a House of Recovery for sick women, and a food dispensary for the city's poor; they also ran a soup kitchen in 1818–19.[90] Their endeavour filled a real need in the city; by 1820, 739 people, including 87 orphans and 90 school children, were aided annually. The ladies were helped in some of this work by the Montreal Medical Institute and the Society for the Relief of Emigrants, an interdenominational association that organized assisted passage westward.

Gradually, some of these services were taken over by others. In 1817 a House of Industry was organized on a temporary basis to provide aid for the destitute poor and recent immigrants. Between 1819 and 1822, the patients in the House of Recovery were transferred to the early Montreal General Hospital. A National School was opened and the British and Canadian Schools Society created others. In light of these developments the Female Benevolent Society was dissolved in 1822. The soup kitchen and dispensary services were closed. The resident children were given into the care of the Protestant churches, but almost immediately many of the women associated with the Society joined forces to form the Protestant Orphan Asylum to assume the children's care.

The two main child charities families turned to for help in the city were the Protestant Orphan Asylum (POA) and the Ladies' Benevolent Society (LBS). They serve as the basis of our discussion for the rest of the book; at this point we will review their main features and then look briefly at the other institutions or associations that made up the Protestant network. Over the nineteenth century, the Protestant Orphan Asylum (1822–1946) admitted 939 children between the ages of two and twelve; from 1900 to 1921 a further 223 entered.[91] The number in the institution at any one time, though, was relatively small. Using the number present at the time of the annual meeting as an indication, we find an average of thirty-three, with the largest number being fifty-nine, in 1891. The total number of children aided over the course of a year averaged forty-two, although sixty-eight were helped in 1899. After the formation of the LBS in 1832, the POA took on its vocation as a real orphanage and admitted very few children who were not full orphans (that is, bereft of both parents) until the twentieth century.

The orphanage rented premises first on St Lewis Street, and then on St Antoine. In 1849 it constructed a permanent home on St Catherine Street, between Drummond and Stanley, seen in figure 1.4. Several businessmen donated the building lot, which was part of the McTavish estate, and the Committee purchased an adjoining lot.[92] They added a third lot in 1856 as a playground and garden. In 1893, this building was sold and the Committee constructed a larger building on Summerhill at Côte-des-Neiges.

In 1832, Montreal experienced a cholera epidemic that left many orphans, as well as widows and widowers, in its wake. Knowing that the POA was unable to respond to the increased number of destitute Protestant children and that it was not designed to help needy women, a group of Montreal ladies, many of them from the original Female Benevolent Society committee and others from the POA, reorganized the Female Benevolent Society, now named the Ladies' Benevolent Society (1832–1946).[93] The new society was designed to extend aid to "widows with small children and to all others who either from infirmity, age or want of employment are unable to procure the means of subsistence."[94] Over the nineteenth century the LBS performed these ser-

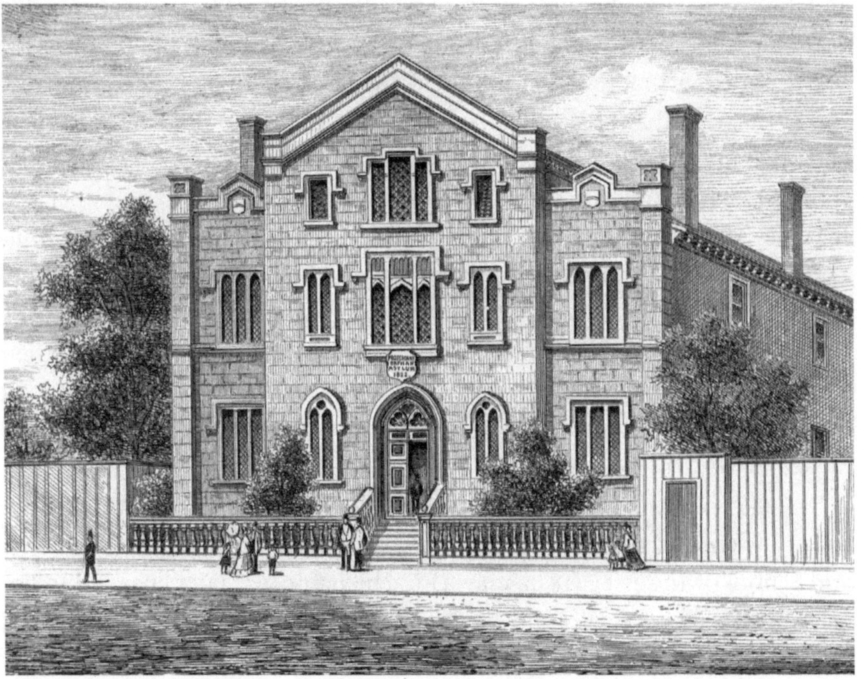

Figure 1.4 *Montreal. The Protestant Orphan Asylum, St. Catherine Street,* 1875. The orphanage's home dated from 1849 and was situated on three lots near the corner of Stanley. It was sold in 1893 and a new home built on Summerhill at Côte-des-Neiges.

vices, acting as a sort of poorhouse for women and children. The institution's main work, though, was with destitute children between the ages of two and twelve, and by 1900, 2,572 children had been admitted.[95] From 1900 to 1921, a further 1,135 entered. The admissions policy stipulated children from destitute one-parent families, but a number of children with both parents were admitted, as were children whose parents paid board for their stay. In 1883, the LBS was certified as an industrial school. Four hundred and sixty-two children were admitted to the industrial school from 1884 to 1921 but they intermingled with the other children, no distinction being made other than in the register.

The LBS was much bigger than the POA. Using the number present at the annual meeting on 1 October as an indication, we find an average of forty-three from 1832 to 1852, and sixty-one in the early 1850s. The number increased dramatically when the institutional home was constructed in 1856 and the average number present from 1856 to 1900 was 98, the most crowded year being 1894 with 124 children. Since many of the children remained for only a short period, the total number of children helped in any given year was even larger than this, at 154 on average from 1856 to 1900. Between 1832 and 1856, the LBS rented accommodations and moved regularly. Sufficient space was constantly a problem, and after 1847 the Committee complained that they were able to help only half of all applicants.[96] In 1856, the LBS built a large three-storey home on Berthelet between Bleury and City Councillors Streets (247 Ontario), but within a few years, space was again a problem. Additions in 1871, 1881, and 1898 helped relieve overcrowding. Still, in years when the house was full, the attic, the infirmary, and even the Committee's meeting rooms were used as dormitories. Figure 5.2 shows how large the building was by 1920.

The 1847 typhus fever immigration saw the founding of yet another child charity when Eliza Hervey, herself an Irish immigrant, formed the Home and School of Industry (1848–c.1924).[97] The name was later changed to the Hervey Institute in her honour.[98] After renting premises at various locations, the institution moved to a more permanent residence on Mountain Street in 1875, and, then, in 1908, to an even larger building at the corner of Windsor Avenue and Claremont in Westmount. It was originally a day school, but girls began to board as well in 1854. With a solid focus on reform and training, the Hervey Institute provided girls aged eight to fourteen with "a plain education" and training as domestics.[99] In 1889, the Committee began special classes for training servants.

Although the school was designed for girls, their brothers were admitted to keep families together. According to the rules, boys were to leave at seven years old, but this rule was not enforced. The Committee made several unsuccessful appeals to the LBS and the Boys' Home to accept boys as transfers. When they requested such a transfer in 1879 there were twenty boys between the ages of five and ten in the asylum.[100] Once the Society moved to Windsor Avenue, they established a separate department for boys to the age of fourteen.[101] The number of children admitted was limited by the building's size; applications often exceeded capacity.[102] Before 1864 there were fewer than thirty. The Mountain Street building saw sixty-one present in 1889 and the move to Windsor Avenue allowed more again; seventy-five were there in 1909. Parents paid what board they could afford, but some children were always

Figure 1.5 Wm. Notman & Son, *Hervey Institute Children*, 1887. The children are posing on the steps of the Mountain Street institution.

accepted free of charge.[103] Figure 1.5 shows the children on the front stairs of the Mountain Street building in 1887. The Hervey Institute was another possible choice for families looking to place girls, especially if they could pay board, and many of the boys in the LBS had sisters there. Its managers emphasized training more than shelter and protection, but worked from the same religious perspective as the women who ran the POA and the LBS.

Eliza Hervey and the women who worked with her were more reform-minded than the benevolent women who ran the POA and the LBS. In addition to their work with children, the Committee ran a job register and provided some relief and visiting services to needy families.[104] A work repository was added in 1847 and sewing rooms in 1855. This latter became the Protestant Industrial Rooms in 1861, which we will look at later in the chapter.

The Hervey Institute Committee was also the first to address the problem of care for infants, and Miss Hervey opened a convalescent home for women and children in Murray Bay. Many of the same women helped form the YWCA.

More specialized child charities were added in the second half of the century in a deliberate attempt to fill the gaps in the Protestant network. The first of these was the Protestant Infants' Home (1869/70–1936). The Infants' Home is of particular interest as it provided a much-needed service for new mothers and acted as a feeder institution for the two charities under study. Poverty forced many women, especially unwed mothers, to abandon their infants or young children and take on employment as wet nurses or servants. With no Protestant institution to receive infants, women left their babies with the Grey Nuns, where they were baptized as Catholics and had only a small chance of survival (mortality there was 90 per cent).[105] By mid-century, Protestant philanthropists were increasingly concerned about this and hoped not only to stop the exodus of babies to the nuns but also to find a way to reduce mortality rates.

The Hervey Institute made the first attempt to address this problem, setting up three nurseries for infants and their mothers in 1855, but funding problems forced them to close these after only two years.[106] In 1869, their Committee began to investigate the feasibility of opening a separate nursery institution.[107] This led to a public meeting to discuss the issue, and by January 1870, the Protestant Infants' Home of Montreal was incorporated.[108] The new charity was designed to accept infants with their mothers as well as children under four from destitute families. It was managed by many of the same reform-minded women who ran the Hervey Institute.[109] From 1875 to 1905, a total of 2,329 children and 747 nursing mothers were admitted.[110] The institution was located first on St Antoine, then on Notre-Dame, and finally on Sussex. In 1878 the committee purchased the home of the late Dr Philip Carpenter, a renowned public health campaigner, on Guy Street. They remained there until 1910 when they moved to Queen Mary Road.

The novel approach of admitting mothers with their infants was based on the desire to reduce infant mortality and the practical recognition that mothers were the most efficient providers of "good care and plenty of nourishing food."[111] It had the added advantage of providing both a place where unwed mothers and deserted wives or widows could find shelter and employment while caring for their infants, thus reinforcing maternal ties and giving the women time to rebuild their lives. During the first year the institution cared for thirty-two mothers and ninety-three children; in the 1880s this averaged closer to eighty children but by the end of the century had increased to more than 100. The Committee admitted unwed mothers and illegitimate children without prejudice, but very few foundlings, because they insisted on meeting mothers to encourage them to either enter the institution with their child or pay towards their support. The presence of nursing mothers kept mortality rates much lower than those of the Grey Nuns' Foundling Hospital, at approximately 22 per cent in the 1880s, although the restrictive admission policies and forced vaccination were also a factor in this.[112] Children could remain in the Infants' Home until they were four or five. At that point, if they had not returned to their relatives or been adopted, they were placed in another child charity (the LBS, the POA, or the Hervey Institute) depending on their familial status.

Although the child charities often admitted teenage girls to train them for service and/or allowed girls to remain in their institutions into their teens, they were hesitant to keep boys much older than ten or twelve. Hence, older boys from families experiencing difficulties and homeless boys alone in the city had nowhere to turn for help. Furthermore, boys who worked in the street trades (as bootblacks, newsboys, and the like) or as apprentices without a boarding arrangement had difficulty finding lodgings inexpensive enough to match their paltry incomes. In February 1871, a group of men from Zion Congregational Church, including Charles Alexander and John Dougall, editor of the *Montreal Witness*, addressed this problem when they opened the Boys' Home of Montreal (1871–1930).[113] Their aim was to provide an inexpensive boarding alternative (like a newsboys' home) linked to a Christian training program for citizens.[114]

The institution was built on Mountain Street below the tracks. Additions were made in 1883, 1886, and 1893. Alongside dormitories and bedrooms, the buildings had workrooms, classrooms, a savings bank, reading rooms, and a library. A new wing in 1905 added a swimming pool and exercise rooms. Although educational classes and lectures were held in the evenings and manual training courses were added by 1901, boys worked in the city during the day and returned to the Home only in the evening hours. Hence the institution was very different from the industrial schools found in the city and not custodial in the normal sense of the word.[115] The citizen-training program implemented by the Board of Directors placed an emphasis on liberal values such as self-reliance, education, religion, and independence.[116] Boys were helped to secure positions as skilled apprentices or in other work; the board they paid out of their earnings kept the institution almost self-sufficient. From 1871 to 1900, more than two thousand boys used the institution. By 1921, an additional 900 had been residents.[117] The male superintendent earned an excellent reputation among other charities for shepherding boys. This led the Boys' Home to play an important role in relation to both the POA and the LBS by the end of the nineteenth century. Boys returning from apprenticeships, those needing unusual boarding arrangements during a city apprenticeship, or those needing more discipline than the matron and female Committee felt able to provide were sent there.

Early in the twentieth century the Boys' Home Board of Directors became concerned about the treatment boys received in the government-run Sherbrooke Reform School for Protestant Boys (inside the Sherbrooke prison), where Montreal boys were sent since no Protestant reform school had been established in the city.[118] They questioned the school's physical and sanitary conditions as well as the insufficiency of its training program.[119] Following a major funding campaign, they opened the Boys' Farm and Training School in Shawbridge and received accreditation as a Reform School in 1908 to replace the Sherbrooke institution.[120] In 1930, the Boys' Home itself moved to a new building on Weredale Park in Westmount, and unofficially took the name of Weredale House.[121]

Another group of children for whom Protestant families had difficulty finding adequate help in standard city charities was children with disabilities or handicaps. This problem was addressed in 1869 when a residential school for children with disabilities, the Protestant Institution for Deaf-Mutes and the Blind, was created, managed by a mixed male-female Committee led by Charles Alexander. Adequate funding was difficult to find until Joseph Mackay took an interest in the project in 1878 and made a large donation. The society's name was changed to the Mackay Institution for Protestant Deaf-Mutes in his honour and he became President.[122] In 1883, a legacy from his brother Edward provided a more solid financial footing and enabled the Committee to admit and train blind children as well as the hearing-impaired.[123] As an institution working with children with disabilities, it eventually received a substantial government grant.[124]

The Institute housed both boys and girls between the ages of seven and fifteen, although until the 1880s and 1890s the number of boys was always larger, reflecting gender-based assumptions about the need for schooling. Before 1877 the number of children in a year was fewer than twenty-two but averaged thirty-three from 1878 to 1883. With the admission of blind children, the total increased into the forties and was as high as sixty-eight in 1895–96. There were always some children who paid board, but usually about half were admitted free. Boys were trained in carpentry, printing, typesetting, chair caning, and cabinet-making, and girls in dressmaking and cooking.

Another important service for families was added by the YWCA when they opened the Montreal Day Nursery in 1888, on Belmont Park.[125] With this institution, poor Protestant women finally had access to a daycare service where they could leave their children while they worked and then take them home again at night. Beginning with only ten children, the number in the Nursery increased steadily and by the late 1890s an average of 170 children a year attended. Many families sent more than one child. Children attended from 7 a.m. to 7 p.m. and were "fed, kept clean, medically treated, and, when necessary, clothed."[126] They spent their mornings in school and their afternoons learning practical skills such as sewing, mending, and housewifery as well as gymnastics and singing.[127] These long hours were designed to allow mothers to work a full day and meant that they did not have to worry about feeding the children supper. Many of the mothers worked as charwomen, taking advantage of the employment centre the Nursery ran to help find the mothers work and to find workers for its supporters.

Since the Infants' Home accepted so few foundlings, many Protestant babies still ended up with the Grey Nuns. The Associated Charities (founded in 1883 to coordinate Protestant relief)[128] created a subcommittee to address this problem in 1886, at which point it represented about sixty infants a year.[129] Deciding foster care was too expensive and not wanting to increase the number of institutions, they requested that the Infants' Home accept foundlings.[130] The Committee refused since it was against their mandate and they lacked additional space and funding. Finally the (Anglican) Sisters of Saint Margaret opened St Margaret's Nursery in 1887, designed specifically for foundlings but based on the principle of encouraging mothers to enter the institution or pay board. Despite the support of the Associated Charities, which claimed that within eighteen months no Protestant infant left the Montreal Maternity destined for the Grey Nuns, this institution remained controversial and was hounded by budget problems. The role of the sisters, the lack of a female Board, and the fact that its work was thought to duplicate that of the Infants' Home to some extent all led to criticism.[131] In 1891 a group of women took over the work and opened the Montreal Foundling and Baby Hospital. Designed for "deserted and sick children under the age of two," foundlings made up about half of its admissions.[132] A special ward for sick babies was opened in 1897. Located on Argyle Street, the hospital was managed by a female committee aided by a Medical Board. When it was incorporated in 1914 it was on St Urbain Street.[133]

A yearly average of 167 infants were admitted between 1891 and 1905, with approximately thirty-six present at any point. Another twenty babies were admitted to the sick baby ward. The hospital originally admitted mothers, but this practice ended in 1897 when the sick baby ward opened.[134] From that point on, infants were fed with modified cow's milk prepared in the institution. The hospital established a milk depot in 1901 in connection with the Local Council of Women, and the next year sold 4,000 bottles of modified milk at cost.[135] Thus, the Foundling and Baby Hospital pioneered the distribution of milk several years before the Gouttes de lait movement gained force in Montreal in 1910 or Well Baby Clinics opened in Toronto in 1912.[136]

In this way, services for families needing help with child care were built up slowly over the century. By 1900, a core of residential institutions admitted orphans, children with parents, infants and their mothers, foundlings, children with disabilities, and young boy workers, and day care was available for children of working mothers. Many of these institutions had links with the POA and the LBS as children were transferred from one institution to the other, and all of them represented possible alternatives for families needing some form of child care, either temporary or more permanently. The provision of aid to young mothers and widows themselves, however, was complicated since many of the elite saw the working class as a whole, and women in particular, as morally suspect. Protestant leaders were hesitant to help two-parent working-class families since they feared it would encourage dependency and make it too easy for men to shirk their economic responsibilities for familial support. However, even widows or deserted wives could become victims of this deeply held belief in self-reliance and were often criticized for not adequately providing for their children by middle-class standards.[137]

WOMEN

It was an economic reality, unfortunately, that the families of widows, deserted wives, and single mothers were especially poor as a result of the gendered labour market that undervalued the work of women and children. Much of the aid available to women was designed to help them fulfil their dual role as mother and provider. Residential child charities took in children to reduce their costs (and domestic responsibilities) and enable them to work, while other "external" services provided them with work such as sewing or work referrals. It was only with the introduction of mothers' allowances in the twentieth century that women were accepted foremost as mothers, but even here the moral ambiguity about helping women remained.[138]

A number of younger women – abandoned mothers, widows unable to support their families, adolescent girls without work, recent immigrants, and women in poor health needing a rest – entered the Montreal Ladies' Benevolent Society for a short time, sometimes with their children. More than 100 are recorded in the institution's register over the nineteenth century. They tended to remain for short periods of time until they could get their lives back on track. The LBS also admitted 350 female convalescents from 1856 until about 1900, providing a place for them to regain their strength after they left hospital and before they returned to work, often in service. These women were housed in a separate wing of the building; they tended to remain less than a month, with the rule specifying two weeks as a norm. The LBS largely depended on donations to provide the convalescents (and the elderly) with the foods and beverages that were considered restorative.

Women in need of some form of assistance could also enter the Anglican Church Home, although the latter tended to attract mainly elderly women. More importantly, both the YMCA and the YWCA established training courses and supervised boarding facilities for young men and women. The YWCA in particular opened several lodging facilities in the early twentieth century for young women, one of which included convalescent care.

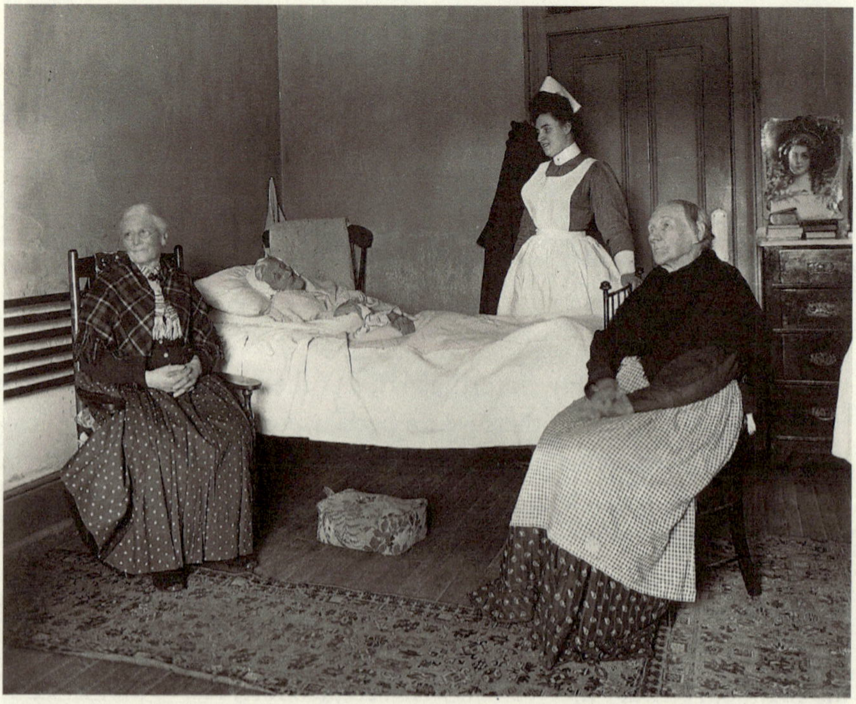

Figure 1.6 Wm. Notman & Son, *Ladies' Benevolent Institution, Montreal,* QC, 1909. Many of the elderly women in the LBS needed constant care; others helped with sewing and knitting.

THE ELDERLY

The elderly were usually recognized as deserving and were admissible into several charities. Close to 200 elderly women or invalids were recorded in the Montreal Ladies' Benevolent Society from 1832 to 1900 and others entered until 1917. Many did not remain for very long, but there were a number who stayed for long periods of time, several for upwards of fifty years, often until their deaths. Most of these elderly women needed constant care as a result of illness or infirmity, but those who were healthy enough contributed to the cost of their care by sewing and knitting clothing for the institution. Figure 1.6 shows several of these elderly women keeping their bedridden friend company in her room.

The Anglican Church Home (1855–2021), founded in 1855 and mostly occupied by elderly women, was another option for women of that congregation. Originally managed by the Cathedral Dorcas under Bishop Fulford's wife, Mary Drummond, it was taken over by the Diocese in 1870. From 1874, elderly genteel women entered as boarders alongside the poor. This dual arrangement ended in 1889 when admission was limited to those who could pay board. Housed in the building on Guy Street where it existed until it was closed in 2020, the home became known as the Ladies' Home and then the Fulford Residence.[139]

THE MONTREAL PROTESTANT HOUSE OF INDUSTRY AND REFUGE (1863–1953)

The main charity for the elderly was the Montreal Protestant House of Industry and Refuge, opened in 1863 by a committee of elite men.[140] The Protestant House of Industry had two buildings on Bleury at the corner of Dorchester (René-Lévesque) with dormitories for the elderly poor as well as shelters for the homeless, which we will discuss below. In the 1860s, there was an average of eighty "permanent" residents, most of them elderly or infirm. The number grew steadily to an average of 129 over the 1890s. Despite being seen as deserving, the elderly were subjected to the standard workhouse rules that emphasized confinement and included forced labour, uniforms, separation by gender, and strict regulations on behaviour. Although improvements were made to the building, conditions were designed for the moral improvement of the residents and reflected the elite's suspicion of the poor. For this reason, an elderly single woman would have applied to the Ladies' Benevolent Society before the Protestant House of Industry.

The Board hoped to move the elderly residents to the country, but this did not happen until 1885 when the Country House (later known as the Old People's Home) was opened on land in the east end of the city bequeathed to them by Thomas Molson.[141] Despite the President referring to this work as "this noble work of beneficience," the residents were expected to work if possible and little had changed in terms of workhouse rules.[142] Slowly the Board began to place more emphasis on the importance of domesticity, religion, and the environmental advantages of the rural setting and hired helpers to work the farm. By the twentieth century the increased medical needs of the elderly residents were recognized and a constellation of medical services was opened on the grounds alongside the original building: a convalescent home (1894), a home for incurables (1916), and several additional infirmaries/hospitals, each bigger than that which preceded it (1929, 1955, and 1959). As new medical facilities were built, the old ones were converted into additional wards, especially for men.[143] There remained some flow of residents between the country installations and the city building.

THE HOMELESS

Alongside its work of sheltering the elderly poor, the privately managed Protestant House of Industry established the first permanent facilities for Protestant homeless men and women. Designed to be open from October to May, the Night Refuge, as the shelter was called, was in fact kept open year-long, although it was used more extensively in the winter season. Strict rules were enforced: lights out at 8 p.m. and no smoking or alcohol in the building. Inmates were to leave by 8 a.m.[144] The shelters certainly filled a need and were often crowded. The total annual aggregate nights' lodging increased from approximately 6,715 in the 1860s to more than 14,000 by the late 1870s, 25,000 in the 1880s, and 32,000 in the 1890s, with as many as 40,563 in 1889. These numbers decreased sharply in the early 1900s. There were always more men than women. Within a few years of opening, the Protestant House of Industry began to impose a work test, requiring two to three hours of work as payment for a bed and two meals.[145] Women sewed, and originally men did stone-breaking. Finding this work too difficult for many, the Board switched to the production of kindling wood that was then sold to the public. In 1875 they started an outdoor labour service, advertising men to do various types of labour. A portion of the wages was paid to the institution; the men kept the rest.

Despite the work test, the suspicion that some might choose to take charity rather than work was strong. As a result, very little effort was put into keeping the shelters in an inhabitable condition. In effect, both the poor conditions and the forced labour were designed to discourage casual use and thus hopefully avoid dependency – in effect, a version of the principle of "less eligibility."[146] The organization continued to house the homeless and even developed specialized services for young men during the 1930s but closed the city building entirely in 1953 when the city expropriated the land to expand Dorchester Boulevard.[147] The Missions seen earlier in the chapter also worked with the homeless.

ANCILLARY INSTITUTIONS

Alongside these residential charities, a number of medical charities such as dispensaries and hospitals provided medicine and medical care for the poor. Hospitals were traditional charitable institutions, but over the nineteenth century, under the influence of both a medicalized approach to poverty and the needs of the massively increased population, they grew in number, size, and specialization (maternity, children, TB, fever, contagious diseases, or insanity, for example). General hospitals such as the Montreal General Hospital (1821) established large outpatient departments and clinics that acted as dispensaries of medicine and advice. Many more people used these services than were hospitalized.[148]

Moral regulation played a large part in all charitable undertakings, but found its most visible manifestation in institutions created directly to "rescue" groups thought to have transgressed moral codes such as unwed mothers, prostitutes, and former prisoners. These services tended to be residential. Here women could find shelter and work, along with what was considered moral "guidance." The Protestant Home for Friendless Women founded in 1874 took in maternity cases and, after 1888, young female minor offenders sent by the Recorder. Most of the maternity cases placed their babies in the Infants' Home and a good many of these women entered the latter institution for a time. The ambiguity around institutions for more serious cases of transgression was clear by the fact that the main institution changed management often – the Montreal Protestant Magdalene Asylum (1848–66) and the Female Home (1868–85) were run by mixed-gender Boards. In 1885 the home changed its name to the Sheltering Home (1885–1950) and was reorganized by Emma Barber and a female board, although men are included on the Act of Incorporation in 1898. Not limited to "maternity" cases, it admitted a wide range of women including ex-prisoners, convalescents, and the "feebleminded."

As a colonial port city, Montreal also had a Sailors' Institute formed by shipping magnate Hugh Allan and a group of leading citizens in 1862. Situated near the docks, the institute offered sailors recreational facilities such as reading and letter-writing rooms, a smoking/games room, concerts, coffee, and evangelical services. It was designed to provide an alternative to the area's bars but had clear moral regulation and evangelical overtones, although the sailors tended to use the secular services more than the evangelical ones.[149]

"EXTERNAL" SERVICES

The main source of outdoor relief to Protestant families, including soup, bread, clothing, fuel, and so on, was the Protestant House of Industry. The institution ran a soup kitchen for its residents and the Protestant poor; more importantly it coordinated the United Board of Outdoor Relief. Every Thursday relief was distributed at the institution's building on Bleury and many families also received soup daily and a hot meal once a week from the soup kitchen.[150] As a norm men did some work in connection with the institution to "pay" for their family's aid. Most of the Protestant poor lived in the southwest working-class districts of Griffintown, St Henri, and Pointe-St-Charles, or down by the docks. All of these areas were far from the Bleury Street building and applying for aid involved a long trek, especially on cold winter days. This was probably one of the reasons why the national societies never actually suspended their own distribution of relief once the United Board, of which they were members, was created.

One of the most important non-residential services for poor women was the provision of work. In an effort to help the mothers who appealed to them for assistance with childcare, as well as other women in similar situations, the Hervey Institute created a job register and a work repository, and opened sewing rooms during the winter months from 1855 for "the relief of the industrial poor by their own labour."[151] In 1861 these workrooms became a separate organization known as the Industrial Rooms.[152] The Rooms moved into the Protestant House of Industry when it opened in 1863 to save on rent, but the Committee maintained its autonomy with distinct funding and reports.[153] The Industrial Rooms was incorporated in 1899 and moved to a newly purchased house on Metcalfe Street.[154] Running the Rooms involved a lot of hands-on work for Committee members, some of whom worked several days a week purchasing and preparing the material to be given out to the sewing women and then examining the finished products.[155] The Committee met on Fridays to distribute work and receive new applicants, all of whom were visited to determine need.

A yearly average of 121 women over the century, most of them Protestant, found employment at the Rooms.[156] In the 1890s numbers increased and usually more than 150 women received sewing consignments. Women could work in the rooms and benefit from the instruction provided by the lady superintendent, but most took the work home to do while they supervised their children. A lack of skill meant that much of the work was "coarse" sewing and the organization often had trouble selling it. By 1895, 4,700 surplus garments were on hand; by 1899, the number had increased to 7,000.[157]

The Rooms were basically self-supporting. The exact wages paid are unknown, but in their 1872 annual report the Committee explained that their objective was "to give a higher price for work than can possibly be given by any other business Establishment."[158] This appears to be a form of "fair wage policy" similar to that used by several American charities.[159] Certainly the Committee maintained both their level of service and their wages during recessions in the 1890s when the number of women helped increased. Some work was done on order or sold at bazaars. Clothing was also sold to the poor below cost and to charities or churches at reduced cost; much of this latter was in turn donated to city charities such as the LBS. The Rooms also provided several support services for the women it employed.

A number of health-related undertakings completed the Protestant network. The most important of these was the Montreal Diet Dispensary, opened in 1879 by the YWCA to provide nourishing food to the sick poor in their homes or boarding houses.[160] Open six days a week, the Dispensary made and delivered food at no cost to individuals with an order signed by a physician, clergyman, city missionary, or Committee member, and at or below cost to others. This specially prepared food could include beef tea, chicken broth, calf's foot and wine jelly, gruel, light puddings, cooked meats, milk, eggs, fruits, and vegetables. City doctors testified to the important role this institution played in people's ability to rebuild their strength.[161] From 2,560 meals in 1884, the Dispensary grew to 17,336 meals in 1899, of which 16,338 were delivered for free.[162] By 1911 this total had grown yet again.[163] As of 1885, the dispensary had also hired a visiting nurse; by 1899 three were on staff, adding to the "health" outreach this association was able to provide.

Finally, the lack of green spaces and the overall unhealthy conditions in working-class districts raised many concerns. The city opened a park on Saint Helen's Island in 1874 and another on Logan's farm (Lafontaine Park) in the 1880s, both designed for the working class. Mount Royal Park was also opened in 1876, but was used mostly by the Anglophone elite who lived at its base.[164] Several charitable associations addressed the problem by taking women and children from centre-city families to the country. One of the earliest such organizations was the Murray Bay Convalescent Home, formed in 1874 by Eliza Hervey. Despite its location, the institution was run by a Montreal Committee and supported by the Protestant elite. Every summer groups of women and children, some sent by charities such as the POA and the LBS, went by steamer down the St Lawrence River to Murray Bay (La Malbaie) for two-week stays. The Fresh-Air Fund Committee, formed in 1887, also sent women and children for two-week stays in Chambly on the Richelieu River. From 1887 to 1894, 8,356 women and children stayed at their home and a further 18,762 went on excursions.[165] These external services and medical charities rounded out the services available to the Protestant poor.

In the absence of any substantial role for the state, the regulation of poverty, even homelessness and destitution, was left to the private sector. The Catholic Church took on this role for Catholics. In the case of Protestant Montreal it was assumed by churches, national societies, and private incorporated associations. The prevailing assumption that poverty was an individual fault and responsibility led to a constrained benevolence on the part of the elite, who did not recognize the real level of need among the community. The same distrust of the "destitute" explains the largely institutional nature of the Protestant network, since institutions allowed for both confinement and the introduction of a reform agenda. In the case of child charities, they provided shelter, education, and religious training – in a sense, a form of socialization into appropriate norms. Nonetheless, as a colonial entry port city, Montreal's elite, the women in particular, responded to the need created by massive immigration and economic dislocation as early as 1815. Slowly over the century a network of private residential charities, reform-oriented associations, outdoor relief, and other types of external services was formed, as well as aid being distributed to people in their homes, although access to some of these services was restricted by notions of the deserving poor. Many of the voluntary associations and the residential institutions, especially those for women and children, were created and managed by the wives and daughters of the city's elite. With these benevolent projects they provided critical support for families in crisis and those needing long-term solutions for child-care difficulties.

In the next chapter we begin our examination of the two main female-directed child charities, looking at the characteristics of the women who formed them, the support they received from the Protestant community, and the culture and values they brought to their undertaking.

2

"Endeavours to Do Good"
The Protestant Orphan Asylum and the Ladies' Benevolent Society

> The yearly reports of an Institution such as the Ladies' Benevolent Institution must, of necessity, be monotonous; the same record of want of means, of occasional sickness and death, and continual evidence of so much obliged to be left undone, that ought to have been done, in spite of all the endeavours of those managers and friends who take an active interest in the affairs of the Society. Still something has been accomplished, children rescued from want, and worse than want, taught to read and write, given the chance, at least, to become useful men and women, and no destitute case has been turned away from their door.
>
> ~ LBS, *Annual Report*, 1885

This was the way the Ladies' Benevolent Society Secretary described the work of female benevolence and the role her charity played in the city. The secretary of the Protestant Orphan Asylum could have said something very similar, and in fact many annual reports included this type of comment. These two child charities were the oldest and most important ones for Protestant families in need of help; they serve as our example of female-directed child charity work in Montreal for the rest of the book. This chapter introduces some of the general aspects, including finances, in order to set the framework for the more specific discussions of management work and structures, services (admissions, departures), and policy development that follow in subsequent chapters. The chapter looks at the elite women who sat on the management boards and the community that supported them, paying specific attention to their conservative benevolent approach and the women's culture they brought to their works of charity.

THE CHARITABLE ELITE

Charity work was an accepted and even expected activity for upper- and middle-class women in the nineteenth century, and many of Montreal's Protestant English-speaking elite were involved in their community's charities. A total of 589 women served on either the POA or the LBS Committee during the nineteenth century: 220 in the POA and 369 in the LBS. About sixty were members of both. Many Montreal women were connected with other charitable institutions: the School of Industry / Hervey Institute had 253 members from 1867 to 1900; the Protestant Infants' Home had 155 (1871–1900); the (Anglican) Church Home another 116 (1855–1900); and the Industrial Rooms had 86 (1864–67, 1884–1900).[1] Sixty-six of these women were also on either the POA or the LBS Committee, and a number served on more than one of the other Committees. Some worked alongside other women in church Dorcas or Missionary societies, on the Ladies' Committees of the national societies, or in the YWCA and its affiliated organizations such as the Day Nursery and the Diet Dispensary.

A closer look at the 589 women on the POA or the LBS Committees reveals an intricate web of family interconnections; several groups of linked families account for many of the members and, importantly, for many of the Directresses. There was almost always a representative of the Ross/McCord/Tylees, the Corse/Savage/Lymans, the Moffatts, the Greenshields, and the Armour/Ramsays in the POA; and of the Greenshields, the Mackenzies, the Ogdens, and the Evans in the LBS. The various Torrance and Molson families were well-represented on both Committees.[2]

Mothers and daughters, sisters and sisters-in-law worked in the same bonds of kin, friendship, and sisterhood that historians have found in other cities, either working together or following each other in the family tradition.[3] A minimum of thirty-six family units of mothers and daughters existed; new ones emerged in the twentieth century. As well, a minimum of ten sets of mothers and daughters-in-law appear and an almost equal number of aunts and nieces.

In addition to these, many of the LBS members had daughters working on the Young Ladies' School Committee that supervised the institution's school. At least fifteen groups of sisters worked in the charities, as did an equal number of sisters-in-law, who were often linked through family business connections as well as marriage.

An excellent example of these family linkages is found in the Corse-Lyman-Savage Committee members. For a visual representation of this see figure 2.1. Susannah Lyman (Roswell) Corse and Anne Jones (Henry) Corse,[4] for example, were both on the POA Committee from its beginnings in the 1820s to the late 1840s. The family's connection was maintained into the next generation by Susannah's two daughters. Mary Corse (Henry) Lyman (see figure 0.9) worked alongside her mother before Susannah's health forced her to leave; her sister, Susan Corse (Dr Arthur) Fisher, took Susannah's place at that point. Both Mary and Susan were active members for many years. During the 1880s, Mary's daughter-in-law Louisa (F.S.) Lyman joined her, and in the 1850s and '60s so did her sister-in-law, Hannah Lyman (John Easton) Mills.[5] When Hannah moved to England, her daughter, Mary's niece, Hannah Jane (N.S.) Whitney, took her place.[6] Thus representatives of these interconnected families served on the POA Committee throughout the century. During much of this time Mary Lyman was also a member of the LBS Committee. Her cousin Abigail Jones Lyman (Joseph) Savage also worked in the LBS alongside her sister-in-law Jane (Alfred) Savage. Abigail's daughter-in-law, Mary Workman (Joseph) Savage Jr, joined them in the 1860s. Mary's mother Annabella Eadie (Thomas) Workman was a long-time POA Committee member (1850–89).[7] This example highlights other types of family linkages, including cousins, aunts/nieces, sisters-in-law, and daughters-in-law, all of whom worked together or consecutively for the same cause. Committees often pointed proudly to these various associations in their minutes as evidence of their charity's continued relevance to prominent families and its important place in the community.

The Molson family is an interesting example of a family whose members worked on both Committees. (See figure 2.2.) A few of them maintained their association after they left active duty by joining the LBS Honorary Committee, thus allowing the Society to retain the family's name among their supporters.[8] Both Thomas Molson's first and second wives, Martha and Sophia, worked on the LBS Committee, as did Elizabeth Molson, daughter of William Molson, before she married David Lewis Macpherson. Sophia worked alongside her

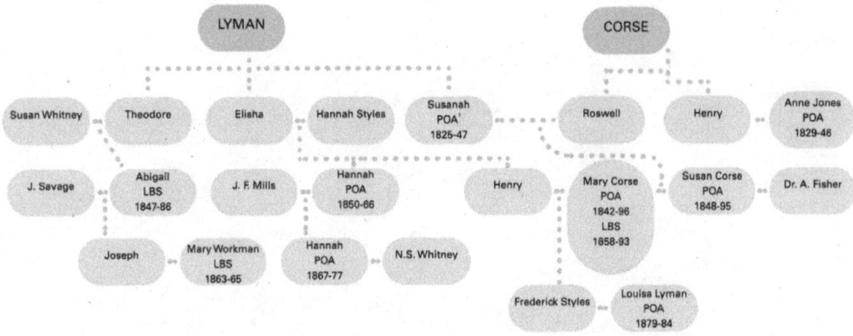

Figure 2.1 The Lyman/Corse families Committee members: years in the Committee.

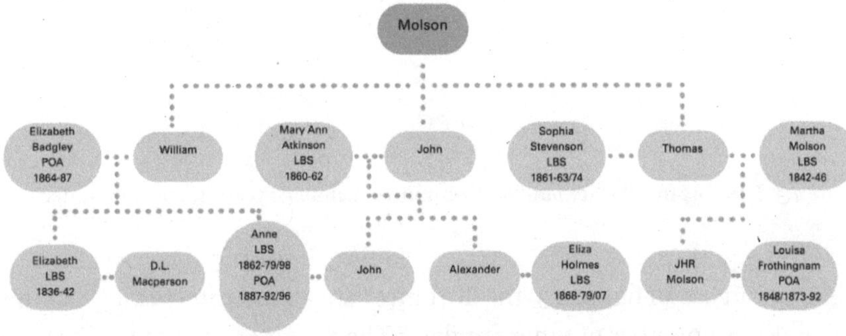

Figure 2.2 The Molson family Committee members: years in the Committee.

sister-in-law Mary Anne Atkinson (John) Molson Jr. At her death, Mary Anne was succeeded by her daughter-in-law and Elizabeth's sister, Anne Molson (John) Molson III. Anne's sister-in-law Eliza Holmes (Alexander) Molson, was also a member. Eliza herself came from a family closely connected to the LBS. Both her mother, Elizabeth Arnoldi (Benjamin) Holmes, and her sister, Maria Holmes (Charles) Dewey Day, had worked on the Committee before her. Her grandfather Dr Arnoldi had been the doctor for the institution, as well as for the POA, for many years. Members of various Molson families also worked with the POA. Elizabeth Badgley (William) Molson was on the Committee for more than twenty years followed by her daughter Anne (John) Molson III. Long-time POA member Louisa G. Frothingham became part of this family effort in 1873 when she married J.H.R. Molson. Elizabeth's Badgley's mother (Anne Molson's grandmother) had worked in the LBS.

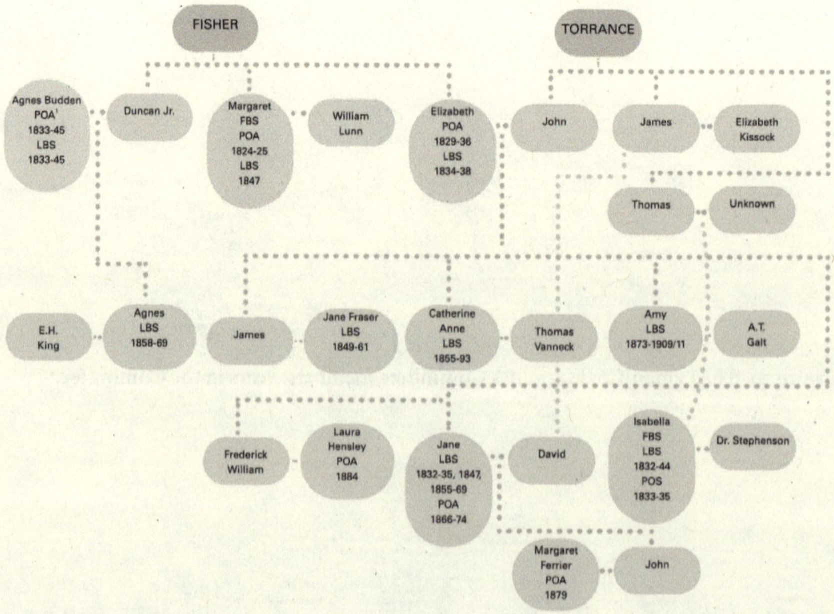

Figure 2.3 The Torrance/Fisher families Committee members: years in the Committee.

As we can see in figure 2.3, the Torrances are another interesting example with links to a number of other families.[9] The daughter of Thomas Torrance, Isabella (Dr John) Stevenson, was a member of the original Female Benevolent Society and then worked on both Committees. Elizabeth Fisher (John) Torrance, the daughter of Duncan Fisher, also worked on both Committees. Her sister Margaret Fisher (William) Lunn and her sister-in-law, Agnes Munn Budden (Duncan) Fisher Jr, served with her. Agnes Budden's daughter, Agnes (E.H.) King, joined the LBS Committee later. Several of Elizabeth's fifteen children followed her example. This included her daughters Jane (David) Torrance, Catherine (Thompson) Vanneck, and Lady Amy (A.T.) Galt; her daughter-in-law Jane, the wife of her son James; and Margaret Ferrier, the wife of her grandson John. Margaret's family too had a long connection with the LBS through her mother Mary Todd (James) Ferrier. Finally, Laura (Hensley) Torrance, the wife of the son of Elizabeth's brother-in-law, James, was a part of this family effort.

A number of other families had connections that spanned several generations and crossed several family trees. Jane Davidson Ross, for example, served on the POA from 1823 until her death in 1866. Three of her daughters – Mary-Jane Ross Tylee, Anne Ross McCord, and Eliza Ross – joined her, as did her grand-daughter Anne McCord. (See figures 0.1–4 and 0.8.) But rather than simply acting as Committee members, the women of this family virtually monopolized the positions of POA Directress for four decades from 1835 to 1875 and then again from 1879 to 1883, during which time two or three of the four POA Directress positions were held by Ross-McCord family members. While her mother and sister Mary-Jane served as First Directress or Treasurer, Anne McCord became Secretary shortly after she joined and held the position until she died in 1870. When she was ill her sister Eliza filled in for her, but at her death the Committee decided to ask her daughter Anne (who was only twenty-two years old) to accept the position, "notwithstanding her youth, as a way to perpetuate the record and name of her mother."[10] Here we see an excellent example of the deliberate tendency to request daughters to take their mothers' places to maintain family connections with the charity. This was a norm in the charities; so was inviting women of bourgeois families new to the city to join the Committee if there was an opening, or to become subscription members and thus support the charities with their money, if not their time.

A similar pattern of extensive involvement at the leadership level was evident in the LBS with the example of the family of Thomas and E. Evans. Fanny and Jane Evans, unmarried sisters, consecutively held the position of Secretary from 1856 to 1892. (See figures 0.5 and 0.6.) Mrs E. Evans served as First Directress and J. Frances Evans as Treasurer. There are only four years from 1856 to 1903 in which a member of the Evans family was not an LBS Directress.

The sixty ladies who were members of both of these Committees illustrate some of these familial trends; they also foreshadow other trends we will examine in the next chapter on management work. Almost half of them (twenty-eight of sixty) worked on both Committees for about the same amount of time either consecutively or concurrently. Six of them were also associated with the original Female Benevolent Society. However, for thirteen of these twenty-eight women, their association with either group represented less than five years. This tendency towards short membership is one pattern we will find in our later investigation. The other fifteen women worked on both Committees for many years, a few such as Eliza Ross (42-POA, 31-LBS) and Mary Corse Lyman (55-POA, 35-LBS) for long periods of time as very dedicated and hard-working managers.

The remaining ladies (thirty-two of sixty) put their main effort into one organization. There are a number of possible explanations for this. One is a question of affinity. Isabella Boston, for example, found her home in the LBS where she served for thirty-eight years until her death, compared to only three on the POA; while Agnes Armour (Hew) Ramsay felt more affinity with the POA where she served forty-seven years (until her death) but was a member of the LBS Committee for only one year, albeit the difficult year of 1847 when the Committee certainly benefited from her experience. Others joined both Committees but naturally put most of their efforts into the Society where they could work alongside family members. This was the case with Jane Davidson Ross and Anne Ross McCord, for example, both members of the LBS for a few years (five and eight) but who remained active members of the POA for twenty-eight and thirty-eight years respectively. In a similar manner, the tendency we noted to continue family connections was clearly illustrated by Anne (John) Molson III, who took her mother-in-law's place in the LBS and then her own mother's place in the POA, where she worked with her sister-in-law Louisa G. Frothingham (J.H.R.) Molson on a number of committees. A final reason is connected to access to leadership positions. Catherine (Samuel) Ogden and Harriet Geddes, for example, joined the POA Committee for one or two years, but were members of the LBS for long periods of time (thirty-one and thirty-seven years). For much of this time they served as Directresses, something that would have been difficult to do in the POA given the Ross-McCord monopoly over these positions. This factor almost certainly influenced their choice.

We noted in the Introduction that the ladies who founded and managed these charities were members of the larger bourgeoisie, coming as they did from families who were part of the collective elite of the propertied, the commercial, and the professional linked together by cultural and personal ties – a group that Amanda Vickery refers to as the "genteel."[11] The class position of Committee members was examined using the occupation of either a woman's husband or her father as indicated in the *Montreal Directory* and the biographical sources consulted. Each woman was checked in her first or second year on the Committee. Positive identification was problematic for women with common surnames, for those from the early years before the city directory existed, and for those who lived outside the city limits. Nonetheless, occupation was established for 152 of the POA members and 224 of those in the LBS, an ample sample on which to base an analysis, especially since a detailed occupation scale is not necessary for our purposes. The results are found in table 2.1.

Table 2.1

Montreal Ladies' Benevolent Society and Protestant Orphan Asylum Committee members, by husbands'/fathers' occupation, 1830–1900

Occupation	LBS No.	LBS % of known members	POA No.	POA % of known members
Merchant	64	28.6	48	31.6
Manufacturer	19	8.5	6	3.9
Businessman	21	9.4	22	14.5
General manager	18	8	8	5.3
Broker	15	6.7	11	7.2
Agent	8	3.6	3	2
Publisher	2	0.9	6	3.9
Building contractor	3	1.3	2	1.3
Total bourgeois	150	67	106	69.7
Doctor	19	8.4	8	5.3
Judge	6	2.7	8	5.3
Clergy	21	9.4	9	5.9
Lawyer	12	5.4	10	6.6
Other professional	5	2.2	2	1.3
Total professional	63	28.1	37	24.4
Military	5	2.2	3	2
Government	6	2.7	6	3.9
Grand total	224	100	152	100
Total members	369	100	220	100
Known members	224	60.7	152	69
Members not in data	145	39.3	68	31

Source: *The Lovell's Directory, Main Series*, 1842–1900.

Occupations are organized using general categories: merchants (import-export, retail, and general), manufacturers, general managers, professionals, agents (land and insurance), brokers, and government employees (Sheriff, Post Master General, Customs Controller). A category of "businessman" was created to identify those families whose investments crossed over into many areas, such as the Molsons, the Torrances, and the Van Hornes. Many other families also had multiple business interests and several had rental income from urban real estate or seigneuries, but none were found to have income from landed wealth alone.

The largely middle- and upper-middle-class origin of Committee members holds no surprises.[12] Neither does the fact that, in a commercial city such as Montreal, the most common occupation was that of merchant. Grouped together, the bourgeois occupations (merchants, manufacturers, brokers, contractors, publishers, and the powerful general managers of banks and large family companies) made up more than 66 per cent of members.

Professionals were the next largest group, accounting for approximately a quarter of the members. Most were from the upper strata of their profession – doctors who serviced an upper-class clientele and were lecturers at the McGill Medical School, and lawyers who later became judges or successful politicians. The wives of the city's leading Protestant clergymen were also prominent and lent their moral authority to the Committees. Less than 10 per cent of members did not fit into one of these two categories. As the wives of the military elite stationed in Montreal when it was a British garrison post or of high-level government officials such as sheriffs, however, they were undoubtedly associated with the upper middle class. The occupational structure showed little change by decade other than an increase in the number of company managers and agents, and of several professions after the 1870s, an increase that mirrors the growing importance of these occupations in the Montreal economy. This masks changes in the profile of the city's elite, however, and by late century the wives of some of the new industrial elite such as the Drummonds, the Van Hornes, and the Stephens were either not associated with these charities or were only marginally involved. We will see in chapter 7 that this was no accident.

The Montreal charitable elite had more in common than membership in the bourgeoisie. As E.P. Thompson and others have explained, class is a "lived experience," a conscious identification with a group through the recognition of common experiences and in distinction from (or in opposition to) other groups – that is, a socially constructed formation.[13] In a similar vein, when commenting on how the American bourgeoisie built an "articulation of shared interests," Sven Beckert and Julia Rosenbaum point to the consensus among a number of European historians that the "social glue provided by the construction of a shared culture" was what worked to bind "competing, heterogeneous social groups."[14] In Protestant Montreal, that shared culture included the sense of "Britishness," which both Catherine Hall and Linda Colley identify as being characterized by Protestantism, respectability, the importance of Empire, and trade. In fact, Hall specifically identifies the "English" identity as being "constituted in relation to 'others,'" that is, "what it is not as much as what it is"; so does Colley, who refers to the unifying power of the "reaction of an 'Other'" as being integral to the forging of this British identity.[15] As a colonial elite but a cultural and linguistic minority within Quebec for most of the century, these awarenesses of both similarity and difference would have served as important cohesive factors for Montreal's Protestant elite and for the building of a shared culture.

Personal, social, and cultural connections reinforced occupational, business, and financial connections. Intermarriage was common; so were friendships. By mid-century, many Committee members were neighbours on the estates built on the south side of the mountain known as the Golden Square Mile; in death, they shared high-profile areas in the Protestant cemetery.[16] Ethnicity, religion, and language were additional unifying factors. The national societies, where men served as Office Bearers and women served on the Ladies' Committees, were central to this ethnic cohesion.[17] So were Protestant churches, whose clergy acted as moral leaders in the community. During the period of its ascendancy the Protestant elite established an extensive network of educational and cultural facilities as well as social events, sporting clubs, and associations of a political, literary, or scientific nature; all of these helped this Protestant bourgeoisie to mould the city's social space in its image and reinforced kin, friendship, and business networks.[18]

Membership in these various associations or service on a charity Board of Directors or Committee of Management acted as a way to build class cohesion as well as to reflect a family's social status and standing in the community, and its sense of social responsibility. Both Leonore Davidoff and Bonnie Smith find that membership on a charity Board was almost an adjunct to "Society"; Amanda Vickery refers to this as "fashionable benevolence."[19] This is one reason why so many of the women from prominent families served as members of these Committees at some point and why some of the male elite, usually the husbands of these women, served as special advisors.

Married women and widows predominated on the Committees.[20] In the LBS, there were 298 married women and 71 single ones; in the POA, 172 were married and 48 single. Several of the single women in each Committee married and remained members.[21] Several other single members, including Elizabeth Molson and the Misses Richardson, left one or two years before their marriages, after several years of service.

Of the married women, thirty-two were widows at some point while working on the LBS Committee and twenty-six among the POA Committee members that we know of. Some of these women (twelve in the LBS and six in the POA) joined the Committee as widows. The others lost their husbands during their tenure; two of them remarried while they were members. Widows tended to remain on the Committees an average of nine or ten years. If we consider their total years of membership, though, we find that this increases to eighteen years for the LBS widows and twenty-two for those of the POA. Clearly this group of ladies included many of the long-term managers we will meet in the next chapter: twenty-three of them had more than twenty years of service, and a number, more than thirty. Furthermore, seven women left active membership one or two years before they became widows, probably propelled by the demands of their husbands' ill health. This was the case, for example, with Mary Corse Lyman, who left the POA after fifty-five years at the age of seventy-three, one year before her husband, Henry, died (she had left the LBS three years earlier). A minimum of thirty ladies remained on the Committees until their own deaths or left one or two years before. A number of others left Committee work when they moved from the city.

To the extent these charities were run by the wives of the city elite, it is interesting to have a sense of the connection between marriage and charity work. At what point in her life cycle did a married "lady" tend to take on charitable work by joining one of these Committees? The biographical sources consulted provided pertinent data on this for 75 married women in the POA and 112 in the LBS. Although not complete, this sample reveals some patterns. The tendency was to join the Committees between 0 and 9 years after marriage. Grouped together, this accounted for 85 women or 45 per cent of those for whom we have data. Another large group joined between 14 and 24 years following their marriage (70 women or 37 per cent), probably once their families were established. It is important to note that twelve women, ten in the LBS and two in the POA, joined the Committee the year they married and established their status as a married woman, and a further sixteen in the following year. This reveals the importance of marriage in the lives of elite women. In her perusal of the diaries of elite Montreal women near the end of the century, Elizabeth Kirkland concludes that women tended to describe marriage as the commencement of their lives as "women."[22] Indeed, their new status removed them from under their fathers' authority and placed them in the position of "adult" in relation to children in their families. Marriage conferred a form of respectability and changed the nature of societal expectations. Here we see proof of this in terms of social commitment. The priority for most women was to establish their marriage and family first, and then turn their attention to other things such as charity work, but not to wait too long before doing this.

Understandably, few ladies with large families were able to devote a lot of time to charitable work when the demands on them as mothers were greatest.[23] Even with the help of household staff, attending meetings and doing committee work took a great deal of time many women would be unable or unwilling to give. Unfortunately information on family size was even more difficult to secure than that on marriage and is only available for 116 Committee members, which makes it difficult to establish any real pattern in relation to children and charity work.[24] We find that about one-third of these members (forty) had very small families with fewer than two living children, which could explain their ability to devote time to philanthropy. Another thirty-two (28 per cent) joined twenty years or more following their marriages, once their families must have been well-established; in fact, several worked alongside a grown daughter at some point during their tenure. If women were dedicated to working on one of these Committees, however, they would find a way to continue charity management while raising a family, and there are many examples of extraordinary commitment among the Montreal Committee members. A few of these suffice to illustrate this fact; all of them were very active managers, several assuming leadership positions. Anne Ross McCord, for example, joined the POA at her marriage and raised six children while she was the Secretary.[25] Jane Mackay also joined at her marriage and raised nine children while she was a manager.[26] Mary Corse Lyman joined the POA one year after her marriage and remained for many years, during which time she had eight children (she would join the LBS sixteen years later). Harriet Thomas joined the LBS within eleven years of her marriage, when her family of nine children must have been very demanding.

Combining charity management, certainly in a committed way, with child care could be difficult, however, and probably was a real balancing act. Annie Wheeler, for example, joined the LBS nine years after her marriage but left due to sickness after only six years of very active involvement at the leadership level; this might have been connected to one of her six children. She returned years later and played a key role in many leadership changes in the Society. (See figure 0.10.) Sarah Lovell joined the LBS when she married in 1849 but left within eleven years. Since she was to have twelve children, it is possible she found it too difficult to juggle active charity work and her growing family. Elizabeth Torrance is another example of a very active manager/Directress with a large family. She joined the POA in 1829. Although this was eighteen years after her marriage, she remained only eight years, possibly because the demands of fifteen children (or maybe grandchildren) proved too difficult. Her daughter Jane (David) Torrance's association with the charities exposes the difficulty of juggling child care and charity work with a growing family. Jane was a member of both Committees but her participation was disjointed as she actively participated, left, and then returned while she raised her family of ten children.[27]

A number of single women (119 of 589) worked on these Committees. Unlike the pattern found by Susan Porter Benson in her work on Providence, this number was not disproportionately large, nor did these ladies as a group demonstrate a higher level of commitment than their married counterparts,[28] possibly because most had extensive family and social obligations.[29] Nonetheless, a number of single women were among the most dedicated and active Committee members, several of them spearheading policy reforms. Probably even more than their married co-workers, single women brought a need for social recognition and personal fulfillment to their charity work. It is also clear that, to some extent, the charity children served as a substitute family for some of them, and several regularly volunteered to do visiting duty and extra teaching in the asylums.

Three examples suffice to illustrate this. Louisa Goddard Frothingham was a POA member for sixty-four years, from the age of eighteen, continuing after her marriage to J.H.R. Molson. Having postponed her marriage for thirty years out of a sense of duty to her widowed father, she married at forty-six and remained childless. Throughout this time she organized annual Christmas Eve celebrations for the children and the POA staff in her home. Her sense of purpose and self-confidence led her to actively initiate and work on many projects connected to the institution's diet and the building's condition, all designed to improve the children's health. She was also in a position to use her substantial wealth to help both the POA and the LBS.[30] (See figure 0.7.)

Eliza Ross worked on both the LBS and the POA Committees for more than thirty years. She visited the asylums regularly and taught the children singing and religion, as well as teaching a young hearing-impaired girl in the orphanage. When her sister, Anne Ross McCord, was away, she assumed the duties of Secretary for her; Eliza was also LBS Secretary from 1847 to 1850. (See figure 0.8.)

Finally, Emma Badgley was a Directress of the LBS Young Ladies' School Committee for many years before she joined the main LBS Committee, where she worked for another twenty-four years, until her death. Over these years she visited the children regularly and taught them singing, and often ran the institution during the summer months when the First and Second Directresses were away on holiday with their families by the sea. Despite this long involvement, Emma did not serve as an LBS Directress.[31]

It is interesting that despite the level of commitment illustrated by the example of these three women, very few single women served as office-holders, including these three. Both societies had single Secretaries (six for the LBS, one for the POA) and single Treasurers (three in the LBS and one in the POA), but, with one or two exceptions, single women did not serve as either First or Second Directress in either society. Although a discussion of this was never recorded in the minutes, it is probable (if we consider the experience elsewhere) that as much as possible the Committees restricted key leadership roles to married women.[32] These charities served as substitute homes for the children they took in, and notions of domesticity and family were central to their work and to their public image. From this perspective, leadership positions such as that of Lady Directress called for the moral authority and respectability more "naturally" associated with married women or widows than with single women irrespective of class or age. In the case of Louisa Frothingham, her Unitarian faith was probably also a factor in this.

CHARITABLE SUPPORT

Community support was crucial to these societies, and it was forthcoming from a core group of female and male members of the city elite. As private organizations, both the POA and the LBS depended on revenue from private sources for much of their funding. This included annual subscriptions from members, donations, and collections from individuals, companies, and churches. Special events such as bazaars or concerts brought in funds from the wider public, and the LBS received some board payments from parents who were able to pay towards the cost of their children's care. Legacies and endowments went into investment funds that generated interest paid to the General Fund. Finally, both received small government grants, and the LBS received state board payments for their industrial school post-1883. Specific aspects of the work connected to raising these funds will be analyzed in chapter 3; at this point we will examine the major components of revenue as a form of community support.

Figures 2.4 and 2.5 illustrate the revenue sources (and their proportional importance) for the two Societies from the 1840s to 1899. The data is organized into five-year periods to facilitate analysis. Looking at the opening balance, we can see that both, but particularly the POA, tended to be prudent about spending all of their income in the years before the 1870s in case revenues did not match needs the subsequent year, so balances were common. In the LBS, opening balances were always much smaller, and by the 1880s they had actually run deficits in several years. The clearest overall tendency visible in figure 2.4 for the POA is the rise of investment income in both actual dollar value and proportional importance, where, by 1884, it had surpassed private funding as a source of revenue. Investment income also increased for the LBS over the period, but private funding remained the most important revenue source alongside government revenue, other than in years when bazaars were held.

Community involvement could take many forms, but the most common, other than Committee membership itself, was financial support in the form of private subscriptions and voluntary donations. Committee members volunteered their time, which was a crucial investment, but arguably even more importantly, they paid annual subscription dues to ensure the financial viability of the project. Many other women who did not work directly on the Committees contributed to the work's success through this annual financial support as subscription members and through occasional donations. The volunteer donation of services by city doctors, dentists, lawyers, pharmacists, notaries, and printers, and donations of goods including fruits and vegetables from neighbouring farmers, were additional forms of community support and were important to budgets, given the expenses they helped avoid.

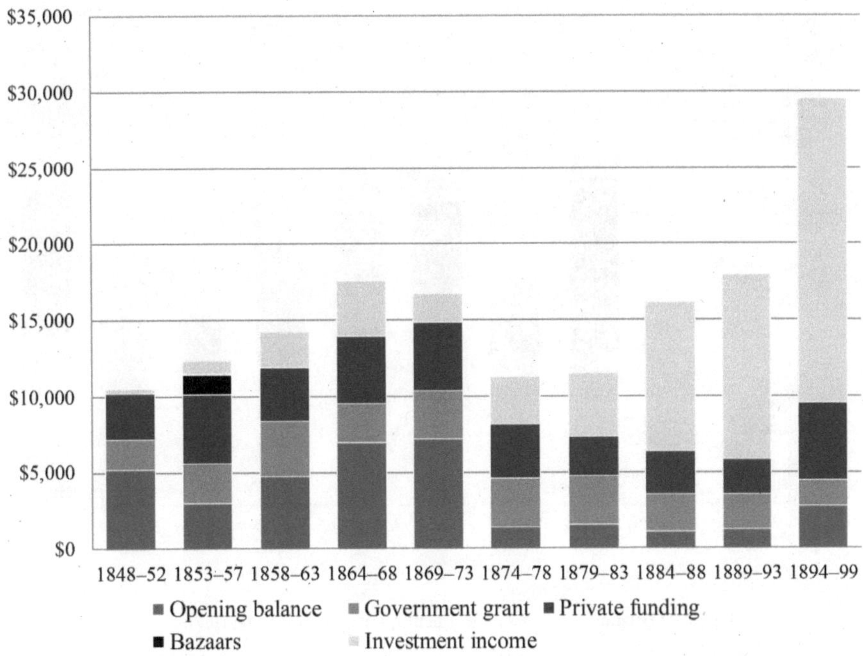

Figure 2.4 The Protestant Orphan Asylum, General Fund account, five-year totals, 1848–99 (in dollars). Conversion rate from British pounds was $4 = £1. "Private funding" includes all private donations, annual subscriptions, and legacies if entered into the General Fund account. Source: Montreal Protestant Orphan Asylum, *Annual Reports*, 1848–99.

Looking more closely at charity subscribers for the two charities reveals some interesting differences.[33] The total number of contributors to the POA's General Fund (through subscriptions or donations) was small and decreased over the century, with an average of 109 across the century, but only seventy-one by the period 1880–95. Most were subscribers, paying an annual subscription of at least five dollars. More than three-quarters of contributors (78 per cent) were women, and they donated a large proportion of this form of private income. In 1855 the Secretary proposed that they solicit more "gentlemen to become permanent annual subscribers,"[34] but the suggestion was never followed up.

The LBS records reveal a very different pattern. First, as a bigger institution with more than three times the number of residents and subsequently much larger financial needs, its volume of annual operating funds collected through

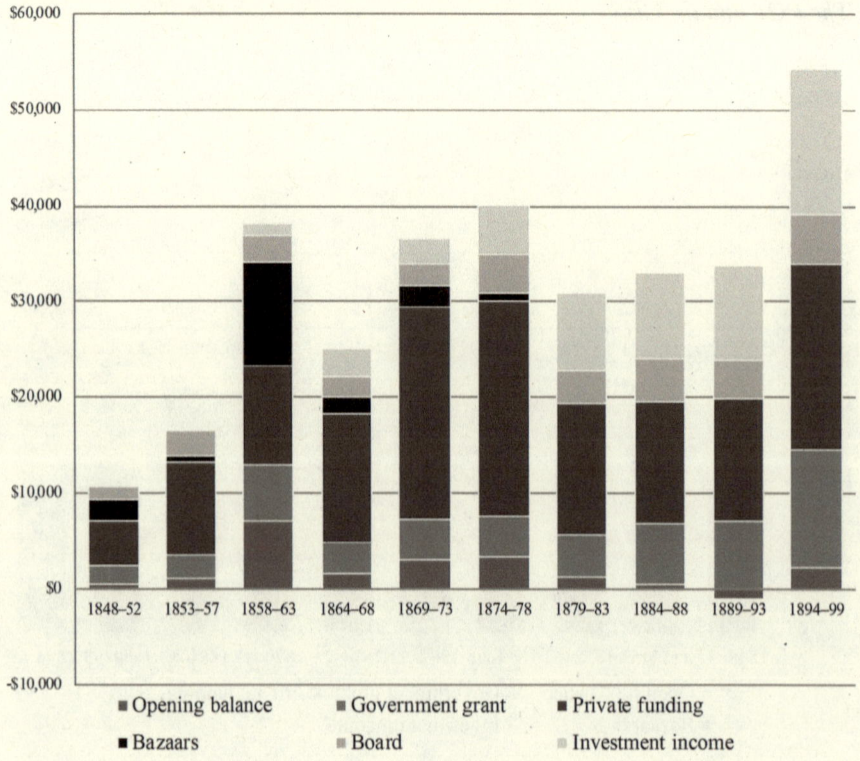

Figure 2.5 The Montreal Ladies' Benevolent Society, General Fund account, five-year totals, 1848–99 (in dollars). Conversion rate from British pounds was $4 = £1. "Government grant" includes the grant for the Protestant Industrial House of Refuge from 1858 and government board for the Industrial School children from 1883. "Private funding" includes all private donations, annual subscriptions, and legacies if entered into the General Fund account. "Board" includes private board paid for children or elderly inmates. Source: Montreal Ladies' Benevolent Society, *Annual Reports*, 1848–99.

subscriptions and donations was substantially larger than in the POA, with an average of $1,702 over the century compared to $623 for the POA; the LBS contributions had passed the $1,000 mark by the early 1850s. Much of this came from donations rather than subscriptions. Furthermore, the subscriptions and donations lists were much larger than those of the POA, with an average of 467 persons. The large street canvasses begun in the 1890s increased the number of donors substantially, and by 1899 this had reached close to 1,400 persons. The average donation, however, was always below the standard five-dollar subscription level, especially after 1890, since most of the street collections were for small sums of less than one dollar. Nonetheless, as figure 2.5 shows, for much of the century and certainly after 1865, the combination of subscriptions and donations was the largest single source of income for the LBS.

The gender pattern of contributions also reveals an important difference. The percentage of women contributors to the LBS's yearly private income, at 61 per cent, is smaller than that of the POA (78 per cent), and women accounted for only 49 per cent of total contributions. This is due to the large number of male and business contributors (counted as male) who were reached by special collections in the financial district. It is also due to the fact that company donations tended to be much larger than the standard subscription fee women normally donated. Before 1865–66 when these collections began, women made 73 per cent of contributions; afterwards, their proportion dropped to 39 per cent. As a result, the two charities had somewhat different income profiles. It is clear that, with its much larger budget needs, the financial support of the male elite was important for the LBS, while the POA, as a smaller charity, could manage on the subscriptions of its female members and the income generated by its growing investment fund.

In an attempt to avoid fluctuating income levels and constant appeals for support, both charities created investment funds for special donations and legacies – the POA in 1851, the LBS in 1858. During the same period they both purchased land and constructed buildings to reduce their costs. This landed capital served as a further asset.[35] Interest on the special endowment funds went towards annual operating costs, but the capital was kept distinct to ensure the funds' stability. The ladies hoped these funds would eventually become large enough to make the charities self-financing. Although they never reached that point, the interest the funds generated became a major source of revenue by the 1880s. This was especially true for the POA, whose budget needs were smaller than those of the LBS. The POA Endowment Fund grew quite rapidly with the regular addition of dividends and interest payments on investments and the influx of a portion of the profit associated with the sale of their St Catherine Street property. Payments from this Fund to the General Fund contributed approximately 50 per cent of revenues in the 1880s and 69 per cent over the 1890s. By 1899, the Fund had surpassed $100,000 in market value.[36] The LBS Permanent Fund was somewhat smaller and grew more slowly as they drew on it regularly to offset debt, repairs, and the like, but investment income accounted for 25 per cent of income in the 1880s and close to 30 per cent through the 1890s. By 1899, the Fund had a value of about $50,000.[37]

These funds testify to the fact that a number of supporters and Committee members left legacies to the charities or made donations directed to the endowment funds rather than to current expenses. This was the best way to ensure continued future support to the charities. Although historians Frank Prochaska and Suzanne Lebsock have found that women predominated among legators in the female-directed charities they examined in England and Petersburg, Virginia respectively, this is not the pattern in Montreal.[38] Indeed, as we can see in table 2.2, the gender pattern that emerges is quite different, given that a significant number of men contributed to these funds, and their contributions tended to be large. This different pattern is likely due to the fact that men wanting to support work with children in Montreal were forced to leave legacies to the female charities, since no male-directed child charity existed in the city. In England and Petersburg, men had the option of leaving their money to a much wider range of charities.

In the POA, only 33 per cent of contributors to the Endowment Fund were women and their legacies represented only 21 per cent of total funds. Thus, although female subscribers paid much of the orphanage's operating costs, it received substantial support from men to its Endowment Fund. In this way men actually indirectly contributed an increasing proportion of the POA's financing by late century through the interest revenue secured on investments.

In the LBS, women made up 45 per cent of contributors to the Permanent Fund and accounted for more than half of total funds. This seemingly different pattern is largely explained by two unusually generous sums given to the LBS in the 1890s by Louisa Frothingham Molson (a $10,000 donation) and by Agnes Gale Stuart, a former Young Ladies' School Committee member (a $12,775 legacy). With these two amounts removed, the remaining sums donated by women represent 32 per cent, a proportion closer to that found in the POA. With the exception of the $25,000 legacy allotted to the LBS by Edward H. King in 1896, both were much larger than donations left by men. The King endowment is not included in the pre-1900 statistics since the LBS did not receive it until 1906, as Agnes Budden King (who had been on the LBS Committee as had her mother, Agnes Budden Fisher, before her) retained usufruct

Table 2.2
Contributions to the permanent/endowment funds of the Protestant Orphan Asylum and the Ladies' Benevolent Society, 1850–1900

	Total Number	Women	Men	Women as % of	Total funds ($)	% of known funds from women
POA						
Donations	15	5	10	33	2,413.91	22
Legacies	71	26	45	37	23,069.17	21
Unknown	8	–	–	–	1,830	–
Total known	94	31	55	33	27,313.08	21
LBS						
Donations	12	3	9	25	13,106	83
Legacies	83	40	43	48	52,181.55	49
Unknown	1	–	–	–	100	–
Total known	96	43	52	45	65,387.55	56

Source: POA, "Account of the Endowment Fund," in *Annual Reports*, 1856–1900; LBS, "Account of the Permanent Fund," in *Annual Reports*, 1860–1900.

on the sum until her death. At that point Agnes left the Society a further $25,000.[39] These large gifts reflect the central role charity played in the lives of many women and their willingness to devote their wealth to its support. It is also interesting that Louisa F. Molson made her substantial donation while she was still alive and could see its impact, and that she made it to the LBS, a society on whose Committee she had never worked but one that was struggling financially and needed the money much more than did the POA with which she was so closely associated. In recognition of this financial need, she would leave a further $10,000 to the LBS but only $4,000 to the POA when she died in 1910.[40]

As was the case with most of the city's private charities, both the POA and the LBS received small government grants from 1832. This support was important to them, although, as evidenced in the two graphs, the amount of these government grants fluctuated over the century. Until the cutbacks to the POA grant began in 1884, this source contributed about 20 per cent of POA income; afterwards its proportional relevance dropped substantially. In the LBS, the government grant represented about 20 per cent of revenue in the 1830s and 1840s. The grant increased in 1856 when the Society assumed the work of the defunct Industrial House of Refuge but then stabilized at about $800 annually. Despite this relative increase, its proportional importance dropped to 15 per cent by the 1860s and 12 per cent in the 1870s as overall income increased. Requests for an increased grant remained unsuccessful. Income from government sources would increase as of 1884, however, when both the province and the city began to pay board for the LBS Industrial School children. By the 1890s it accounted for 22 per cent of total revenue. The LBS generated an additional 10 per cent of its income from board payments by parents, income that was especially important in the latter part of the century.[41]

Although investment income was substantial by late century, and, combined with the government grant, provided a dependable base income, it was never large enough to eliminate the need for private funds. Organizing fund-raising events and finding ways to encourage people to become subscription members or to donate money was demanding work, and these Committees often had problems raising more funds than the bare minimum. This was particularly the case in years when provisions were costly, when they needed to raise funds for construction, renovations, or land purchases as well as for operating costs, and when the city was in an economic recession. As a result, budgets were frequently very tight. This situation was aggravated for the LBS by the fact that their fiscal year began in October just before the winter supplies were purchased. Too many late subscriptions could cause havoc; in several years in the 1880s and '90s, funds were insufficient to cover costs and expenses were carried on the books. The Committee often only managed to cover debts by borrowing from the Permanent Fund, and repaying that fund if and when finances permitted.

In relation to their finances, the ladies were always conscious of their dependence on private contributions and of the responsibility this implied for frugality. Although speakers at the annual meetings often complimented them on their economical management, on several occasions the Committees decided against expenses such as a piano or specialized teachers for reasons of economy or a concern that the public might not see something as a "necessary expense."[42]

Even with the moral and financial support of the community, they were constantly worried about the appearance of waste or extravagance and the impact this might have on their ability to secure enough funds to run their institutions. Perhaps budget constraints and minimal conditions were simply in the nature of private charities and accepted as such.[43] It was often with some fatalism that the LBS Committee, in particular, carried on in spite of precarious finances, pointing to the social and religious role of the work to justify renewed and continued efforts and inevitably to their role as elite women doing "women's work" caring for those in need of both their help and their moral guidance.

BENEVOLENT WOMEN'S SOCIETIES

The POA and the LBS are both excellent examples of benevolent women's societies as identified by Nancy Hewitt in her work on women's activism. Although we will see that their specific policies changed somewhat over the century as they responded to new needs and/or concerns, as they gained experience on which to base new orientations, and as new members joined, their basic benevolent perspective remained. One important characteristic of this perspective was its conservatism. With few exceptions, these women came from bourgeois families and most were members of Anglican or Presbyterian churches. From this class perspective they understood the world as being ordered on traditional principles. One of these principles was the duty of the privileged to help the poor; another was the status difference accorded to different social classes as they accepted their respective "stations" in life and interacted with each other.

The ladies of the POA, in particular, spoke of this hierarchical order on several occasions. This was less common in the LBS, which received children directly from their families, often for very short periods. As late as 1874, in their address to the visiting Governor General, for example, the POA Committee assured supporters that they "ever endeavour to train the children entrusted to their care in a manner which will qualify them to fulfill the duties of the station in life which they will be called upon to occupy upon leaving this institution."[44] For the POA Committee there was no ambiguity about what station that would be. Although they educated and trained the children to become useful citizens, they did not harbour any aspirations of real social mobility for them. In 1858, the Committee engaged a teacher to supplement the work of the superintendent responsible for the children's education, since "the Ladies felt convinced, that, without exceeding the limits to which children in their station of life were entitled, much useful knowledge might be added."[45] The next year they invited supporters to visit the orphanage and witness the "happy little faces that may be seen, industriously employed in the acquisition of that humble knowledge suited to their station in life."[46]

Their beliefs do not seem to have changed much over the century. In 1893, when they fired their last male superintendent (and his wife), in his letter protesting his dismissal he claimed it was because he was teaching the children to aspire to social mobility: "At the same time we were informed, that the children here are charity children, and a strong intimation was given us, that they should not be taught to aspire beyond their condition." He admitted he had "not strictly observed this injunction."[47] These ideas were still evident in the early twentieth century. Although the Committee sent some gifted children to high school, they continued to find most of them positions as servants (albeit as upper servants with higher wages) and office boys when they left the institution.

Like other benevolent women's groups, these two Montreal societies enjoyed the support of the male elite. The prominent role of church leaders at their annual meetings lent moral approbation; other men in attendance lent public support and credibility. In fact to some extent these charities were social projects that drew on the support of a large spectrum of the city elite. Protestant ministers were in attendance at the founding meeting of the Female Benevolent Society in 1815 and then called the original public meeting that formed the POA. The community's support for the undertaking never faltered over the century. This was also true for the LBS, which grew naturally out of the city's response to the cholera epidemic and to which men contributed financial support when appealed to, as we have seen. Prominent male supporters attended the charities' meetings, newspapers covered them, and the institutions were among those that tourists visited when seeing the "sights."[48]

Cracks were beginning to form in this support by the 1880s and '90s as old supporters died and new agencies proliferated and competed for funds. These cracks widened to a gulf in the twentieth century as new approaches to relief and especially to child charity gained popularity, and certainly with the rise of professional social work. In fact, by the 1920s and '30s the Societies found themselves in direct confrontation with an important component of the city's Protestant charitable elite over methods.[49]

Throughout the period, both Committees received the support and advice of regular male advisors and/or men's committees (after the 1850s) that helped with building matters and investment questions. That the ladies were very aware of the contribution some of these "gentlemen" made, is evidenced by the statement the POA presented to their Treasurer, Mary-Jane Tylee, on the death of her husband, who had helped her manage the institution's finances: "what a serious loss our Institution has sustained, in the death of your beloved husband, his efforts were most unceasing to further the interests of the Orphans, and to his good management, we are mainly indebted for the present successful state of our finances."[50] As Nancy Hewitt has argued, this cross-gender class collaboration was important to the success of women's public activism, providing the three crucial resources of legitimacy, money and material, and political contacts.[51] An interesting example of this latter is found in 1852 when the LBS received a £50 donation from the Provincial Secretary. In the private Committee minutes, the LBS Secretary identifies the sum as "money they [the government] had on hand" and explains that the First Directress "heard of this," applied, and received the funds.[52] Even more interesting, though, is the comment in the annual report that year thanking the First Directress's husband, David Davidson, for procuring the said money.[53] Clearly conversations around the dinner table with those in the know could advance the cause. Networks were key to these associations in terms of both links on the Committee and their ability to use their supporters' influence to lobby in the political realm.

Elite women's moral authority rested on their class status, but it was also grounded in women's religious and spiritual qualities. Historians such as Ruth Compton Brouwer, Marguerite Van Die, Nancy Christie, Michael Gauvreau, Leonore Davidoff, Catherine Hall, and Frank Prochaska remind us that it is important to recognize the significance of religion and personal spirituality for women and of religious ideology as a cultural force for middle-class Protestants in general. In its connection to civilizing missions and rescue work, religion was a particularly strong driving force in women's philanthropy.[54] In fact, in the comparative studies on philanthropy that Kathleen D. McCarthy coordinated, the first hypothesis the group worked with was that "[r]eligion was the most important factor in shaping women's philanthropy and civil society."[55] Like their contemporaries, religion was central to the culture the Montreal women shared, to their understanding of the world, and to the way they acted in it. Their deep religious faith and conviction were integral to their identity both as individuals and as "Committee" women. They saw benevolence as a class duty (a form of noblesse oblige) connected to the public good, or what Frank Prochaska refers to as practical Christianity; but even more importantly, they saw it as a Christian duty and a religious commitment, a duty and obligation that quite naturally fell to them as women.[56] In effect, women claimed the authority associated with their religious nature as moral entities, even if at that point in time they lacked recognition as legal entities. Their assertions in relation to the importance of charity and women's role in dispensing it reflected the beliefs of many of their contemporaries.[57]

In the sermon he gave at the official opening of the Female Benevolent Society in 1816, and which was later published to raise funds for the charity, Rev. Robert Easton used the lesson of the good Samaritan to illustrate the duty of charity and remind his audience of the role of both poverty and charity in the divine design: "Yea verily, Heaven created these inequalities, that compassion and liberality on the one hand, and gratitude on the other might be carried through all varieties of human woe."[58] Touching on the importance of "discriminating" aid and "the assiduity of female tenderness," he encouraged the ladies not to let any difficulties discourage them from "pursuing a plan of benevolence, which is as becoming in your sex, as it is highly profitable."[59]

Years later, Rev. William Snodgrass opened the 1864 POA annual meeting with another typical commentary on the duty of charity in relation to the work of female Committees: "It was a great Christian duty performed on behalf of a portion of our fellow creatures who were very helpless, to maintain this institution, and manage it so efficiently ... a privilege as well as a duty – a solemn Christian obligation incumbent upon them."[60] A survey of the major religious and secular press in both Montreal and Toronto over the nineteenth century reveals that writers echoed these words, consistently presenting benevolence as a Christian duty, a proof of faith, and a privilege that gave life its "best dignity and its most essential importance."[61] Authors emphasized the personal advantages to be gained by donors and promised "that to him who patiently continues in well-doing, there is reserved glory, honor, immortality, eternal life."[62]

The annual reports, historical sketches, and minutes of these two charities reveal this same combination of religious piety and conservative benevolence. Recognizing charity as a "high and solemn duty,"[63] the ladies emphasized the responsibility of the wealthy to help the "poor and needy whose wants would otherwise have cried unto heaven against those amongst us whom God has given the means to help."[64] In a typical mixture of religion and self-effacement, they referred to their charitable work as "their humble mission," "endeavors to do good," "quiet usefulness," and "cheerful and self-denying work." They regularly repeated lessons of proportional giving, pointing to the personal and spiritual value of charity, and invited donors "to the honor of being God's almoners, and to be twice blessed in being bountiful to the poor."[65] To encourage generosity, the Committees frequently alluded to the benefits bestowed upon the benevolent. They particularly reminded donors how supporting charities allowed them to "carry out their benevolent designs" while being "spared much personal effort" since the voluntary association would act as intermediary for them with the poor.[66]

It is important to note that this emphasis on religion was not simply a part of the charities' public discourse. Annual reports are filled with these types of references and usually both open and close with some comment about the religious nature of the work, but the Committees' minutes consistently demonstrate this same religious commitment. Meetings were opened with prayer and members carefully considered questions such as ministers visiting the institution and presiding at annual meetings and the children attending church and Sunday school.

The evangelical belief that individual salvation was possible through carefully guided education, faith, and virtue was central to the work of these two child charities. Indeed, religious salvation was one of the major roles they saw themselves fulfilling in terms of destitute children, and they pointed to this on many occasions. In 1867, for example, the LBS Committee spoke of how "[e]ntrusted with the care of childhood it is ours to surround these little ones with holy influences watching as we sow the seeds of the precious Gospel."[67] By the end of the century they still highlighted this aspect in their funding appeal, referring to "every opportunity being used to draw them [the children] into that better knowledge that pertains to everlasting life."[68] The POA spoke of their "higher responsibilities" in relation to the children, explaining that, "while training them for usefulness in this world, we endeavour to inculcate in their hearts the higher aims, principles and motives which will lead their steps to the Good Shepherd,"[69] and appealed for endowments "whereby donors may see their seedlings produce fruit, to the honor of God, and the comfort and happiness of their fellow creatures."[70] This was not social reform work; it was moral and religious rescue. This distinction would differentiate these two Committees from other female associations as the century progressed.[71]

Convinced of the religious importance of their charitable undertaking and their work with children, both Committees had faith that the public would recognize its Christian duty to help the poor and provide the funding necessary to run the charities.[72] In this the ladies trusted not only to the public but also to Divine Providence to meet their needs. Annual reports opened with thankful prayers to Providence and hopes for future support. The 1878 POA Annual Report, for example, begins with an interesting comment on the mixture of work and Providence responsible for their success: "Therefore, let us plan wisely, work patiently, and wait prayerfully, confident that He that has begun this work, and thus far blessed us, will be with us to the end."[73] In comments such as these the ladies referred to the planning and work implicit in their charity undertaking but, in their typical style, did not take full credit for the success of their benevolent project, couching it instead in the context of practical Christianity.

Charity was a duty thought to be particularly well-suited to women because of their natural benevolence, their moral character, and their maternal instincts. As Frank Prochaska has pointed out, "it remained an article of faith right through the century that in the performance of good works women's nature and mission joined in near perfect harmony."[74] On several occasions, speakers at annual meetings made allusions to the appropriateness of charitable work being carried out by women. Thus Rev. Donald Fraser ended his comments at the 1855 LBS meeting: "I must not omit to say that we place great confidence in the internal management of the Institution, because it is in the hands of *Ladies*. All the gentlemen present concur in acknowledging and admiring the peculiar aptitude of the other and more amiable sex for conducting institutions of mercy."[75]

Recognizing and accepting this, many ladies used their charity work to initiate their daughters and other family members into their role as ladies of the elite. Daughters worked with mothers on the committees or in the LBS Young Ladies' School Committee. An interesting example of wider family influence is Elizabeth (John) Greenshields, whom we see in figure 2.6 with her daughters. When the POA needed a new Treasurer in 1874, Elizabeth's daughters were too young, but her niece Margaret accepted to join the POA and take on the position given that her uncle, Elizabeth's husband John, was the society's main financial advisor and could support her in this role. Younger children attended the Christmas dinner at the institutions with their mothers, and some shared their birthday celebrations with the charity children. Children were encouraged to donate funds individually or through school collections, and a few offered prizes at the year-end school presentations. Subsumed within this lesson in religious benevolence was another lesson: the role of charity in social regulation and in class relations in general.

In child institutions such as these, the religious and humanitarian aspects of child-saving were mixed with the social-regulation role of training useful citizens and good Christians. The prevalent association of poverty with moral weakness made the urban elite increasingly concerned about the children of the poor and their potential for delinquency.[76] Alongside the creation of specific reform institutions, many recognized that child charities could play a role in the fight against this possible threat to social order by rescuing children from the streets or from marginal families and by teaching them appropriate values or "civilizing" them to help build the bourgeois cultural norm.

For about a twenty-year period at mid-century when this type of discourse was at its height, supporters of the charities and occasionally the ladies themselves vocalized these concerns at the annual meetings. Speakers referred to charity as a "safety-valve" for society, assuming that, if left to themselves, destitute children would inevitably become criminals who would "prey upon society" and cause innocent citizens "to go to bed in terror."[77] They spoke of the savings charitable works represented and thanked the ladies for their social contribution. In 1858, one speaker applauded the LBS in the following terms: "Public institutions of benevolence forced themselves upon communities from the very wants and exigencies of the masses, and it was not a question of will, but of necessity."[78] In 1871, *Gazette* editor Thomas White Jr offered thanks to the LBS for "the great good that was done by rescuing these children, who otherwise would become the social pariahs of society, and training them up to be useful members of society."[79]

Although admissions were largely driven by parental unemployment, insufficient income, or illness, the ladies publically bought into this construct

Figure 2.6 William Notman, *Mrs. John Greenshields and Daughters, Montreal*, QC, 1871. Women such as Elizabeth Greenshields often initiated their daughters and other extended family members into charity work. Her niece, Miss Margaret Greenshields became Treasurer of the POA and held the position for twenty-two years.

of "poverty linked to crime" for a short period at mid-century. As early as 1849, the LBS reminded supporters that their work helping destitute women "has afforded a home to many houseless wanderers, who would otherwise have become abandoned to misery and destitution, and their concomitants vice and crime."[80] Echoing contemporary beliefs that bad environments also led children to vice and crime, they spoke of their work as "preserving the young from the paths of vice, and fitting them for becoming useful members of society";[81] or, in another instance, reminded supporters that otherwise these children would "in all human probability, grow up in ignorance and vice, and reap the fruits of their neglected youth in the gaol or penitentiary."[82] On occasion, the POA recognized that parentless children without supervision could pose a social risk for the city. A comment made in 1854 is a good example: "Let us consider that without such an Institution, to rescue the poor and abandoned Orphans from the contagion of vice to which they must be otherwise inevitably exposed, they would most assuredly be consigned to the ranks of that host of juvenile offenders, which throng our prisons."[83]

Particularly in the case of the LBS, where this discourse is more prevalent, we find evidence of a profound suspicion of working-class parents. Comments tended to cast parents in a negative light, emphasizing their immoral character and the debilitating, even dangerous, environments to which they exposed their children. Thus charity children were characterized as the "illused [*sic*] and neglected children of worthless parents" who were exposed to "that training which fills our prisons, disturbs our streets, and leads on ever towards a dreadful death."[84] Parents were described as "drunken, worthless, and degraded" and children as having to be untaught everything they knew.[85] Committee members were particularly appalled by "drunken mothers," as we can see from the LBS Secretary's description of the children in 1861: "truly unfortunate in their remaining parent, and are consequently worse than orphans, with drunken fathers, and alas! sometimes with drunken mothers also, whose only anxiety is to keep them with them for the purposes of mendacity or intemperance, and ... from which dreadful preparation for greater crimes they are rescued by this Society."[86] The LBS annual reports in the 1860s even began to include lists of descriptions of cases taken from the admissions register, although they used this technique infrequently "from consideration for the unfortunate."[87] In a few years they simply referred to "the same calamitous effects, from the same miserable causes, with only a few honorable exceptions."[88]

The emphasis on this role of social regulation, however, was limited to the mid-century period as the city adjusted to massive immigration and economic change. By 1872, the LBS annual reports began to make less of a distinction between the children of what could be considered "immoral" parents and respectable temporary aid cases, even merging the two in descriptions such as "and all with the usual melancholy story of destitution, or desertions by one or more parents, or the equally sorrowful tale of the remaining parent, a widow or forsaken wife, being unable to support them."[89] By the mid-1870s the anti-parent and child-rescue discourse had all but disappeared.[90]

It is important to note that this mid-century public discourse did not reflect any real change in the ladies' work, and actual patterns of admissions and discharges to the LBS did not change; the majority of children were still admitted by their parents and then returned to them after a short stay. Moreover, it is almost exclusively a feature of the charity's public representation. The discourse found in internal sources such as the admission registers and Committee minutes was much more focused on responding to need and on protecting and educating children than on child rescue. These aspects reflected the real work and orientation of the two Committees much more accurately than did a spattering of public posturing during a period of extreme public uneasiness.

WOMEN'S CULTURE AND ITS IMPACT ON CHARITY WORK

In December 1868, Eliza Ross presented the POA Committee with a portrait of her mother, Jane Davidson Ross, who, as her daughter explained, "surrounded by the friends she so truly loved, had, in that Committee Room, passed many happy hours, laboring in the cause of the Orphan."[91] That her fellow committee members had appreciated working alongside Jane, some of them since 1823, was clear by the motion they passed on her death in 1866: "Always judicious in whatever she said or did, kind and affable to all, Mrs Ross combined the character of a Christian Lady with that of a wise and conscientious Directress."[92] The epitaph on her tombstone pointed to the same Christian nature, referring to her as "An humble Christian woman."[93] It seemed appropriate, then, to hang her portrait in the Committee room as Eliza proposed. By the end of the century Jane shared the space with other long-term members, including three of her daughters (Eliza herself, Anne McCord, and Mary-Jane Tylee) and her colleague Agnes Armour Ramsay.[94] We know that the LBS Committee room held the portraits of Jane and Fanny Evans.[95]

Class and class concerns played an important role in the way these ladies approached their charity work. But gender was equally, if not more, important. As mothers and daughters, benevolent women brought their "ethic of caring" and their maternal approach to their charity work.[96] They also brought a culture shared among women of the elite that was grounded in domestic values and close personal contacts with family and friends, a sociability of sorts. American historians such as Kathleen McCarthy, Suzanne Lebsock, and others have identified women's emphasis on people and relationships as well as on a personal approach as "personalism."[97] For the purposes of this book I will refer to this as "person-centred." Whatever term one chooses, this approach was an extremely important aspect of female philanthropy.

One form of this person-centred approach is evidenced by the example of the portraits hanging in the Committee rooms and the personal interconnections between Committee members. Another aspect is the ladies' attitude to their child charges. In her discussion of this in relation to women's charity work, Kathleen McCarthy argues that "the Board members identified with their charges and sought to establish ongoing relationships and programs tailored to individual needs."[98] This same emphasis is evident in the Montreal charities and influenced their policies and their management. Both were basically designed to respond to the needs of families, and as a general rule the ladies viewed the children under their care as individual young people in need of protection and training, not as a social category such as "the poor" or "dangerous children."

Although many of the ladies did not visit the asylum other than for meetings, the Committee members' interest in the children as individuals is evident in the structure of their monthly meetings, which were essentially organized around reports on the children and the institutional home. One does not find discussions of abstract ideological approaches to poverty or charity; even the business aspects of the work such as funding and building considerations were discussed only when they were a problem. However, every meeting included reports by the Committee members who had supervised the charity homes in the previous month; a reading of the matron's or superintendent's journal outlining daily events, special needs, and problems (this included any comments made in the visitors' journal by visiting dignitaries or friends); and the reading of all letters from or about child apprentices or residents. In recording these reports and discussions, the minutes are filled with comments on the children and on the daily occurrences in the institution. Through these reports, one can follow the cases of children having difficulties or those returning to visit and what some were doing after their apprenticeships. Thus the primacy the ladies accorded to these very personal aspects of their work is evidenced by both the structure of the meeting, centred as it was on these reports, and the fact that all of this detailed information on the children was considered important enough to be recorded in the official minutes. Kenneth Cmiel refers to this as a "hands-on type of management" where the committee members were "directly involved in all details of the asylum," a very specific cultural space, "managerial yet personal."[99]

The ladies who ran these charities were volunteers, not charity professionals trained in social work. Their conservatism did not lead them to try to reform the poor, to force self-reliance, nor to solve the problem of dependency (which they publicly recognized as a problem). Rather, they saw their work as helping families in difficulty or providing a "family" for children who were without one, looking after the children placed in their care, and doing their best to educate the children even if budget constraints meant that often the quality of this care was somewhat minimalist. This practical and rather personal approach of addressing the issues at hand rather than theoretical concepts predominated.

Another aspect of this person-centred approach was the central place the institutional home itself played in their work. All meetings were held in the institution, both the LBS and the POA buildings having been specifically designed with a meeting room on the first floor. This meant that Committee members could visit the home and the children before or after monthly meetings. Holding the annual meeting in the institution gave supporters the same opportunity, placing the institutional home and its residents front and centre as the reports were being read and discussed. Comments by journalists or speakers that refer to the children confirm that they were present at the meeting and that they frequently closed the proceedings by singing hymns.

Particularly in the POA, where children remained for longer periods of time and most of them were actually parentless, an even greater emphasis was placed on each individual child. Children were introduced to the Committee at the monthly meeting following their admission, and the ladies also met with each child before she or he was apprenticed to give them personalized advice. The minutes occasionally recount the earnestness with which children received this advice and their sorrow at leaving the orphanage. After 1868 the ladies had each child photographed just before they left for an apprenticeship.[100] Often when ladies were going out of town, the Committee asked them to check on an apprentice or to scout out potential new apprenticeship situations. By the later part of the century the POA had introduced a visiting system to keep contact with most of the apprenticed children and had the children write letters to them. Finally, the ladies regularly made special personal donations at their meetings to purchase Christmas presents for the children and other "luxuries" (such as a piano, a singing teacher, and occasionally toys) they wanted to provide them but did not feel warranted the allocation of official funds for these purposes. They used the same form of personal private charity to pay for gifts to thank staff after a trying experience (such as an outbreak of disease) or after many years of dedicated service.

This person-centred approach is also evident in the organization of the committees themselves on the basis of kinship and friendship networks – a group cohesion that helped give the ladies the confidence in their ventures into the social sphere they otherwise might have lacked. The funeral soliloquies composed at the monthly meetings, and occasionally published later in the year in the annual report, testify to this very personal aspect of their work and the bonds they built with the other elite women who worked alongside them.[101] These are filled with the heartfelt sense of the personal loss of a close friend, but more specifically they recognize the loss of a fellow worker – the valued ideas, the good judgment, the experience, special skills and knowledge, and the mutual support. Again and again, we find tributes to women's commitment and to the moral and religious qualities that suited them to charitable endeavours.

This personal approach as an element of charity management is particularly associated with women's committees, especially conservative benevolent ones, and with women's culture. Analyzing the nineteenth-century minutes of two Montreal charities directed by male Boards (the Boys' Home and the

Protestant House of Industry) and comparing them with what we have seen for our two female-directed charities provides striking gender differences.[102] The Boys' Home of Montreal (for adolescent boys) was established in 1871 by a male Board with ten members and five Directors.[103] We know this particular charitable project was very important to these evangelical men by the fact they remained involved in the work for many years, most of them until their deaths. Charles Alexander, for example, was President from 1871 until he died in 1905. John Redpath Dougall, who assumed the Presidency at that point, had been on the Board since 1871 (where he served alongside his father) and would remain associated with the charity into the 1930s. Alexander had personally donated the funds to build the original building and other Directors helped pay part of the mortgage on the land although none of them were among the city's wealthy citizens. Finally, a number of Board members gave the boys educational lectures in the evenings.[104] Despite this clear personal involvement in the project and their private links to each other through collective membership in an evangelical community, if we analyze the charity as an organization we do not find the same person-centred approach that is evident in the female-directed charities.

Unlike the minutes of the female charities, a reading of the minutes of the Boys' Home monthly meetings reveals no evidence of a personal approach. On the contrary, they read like the reports of a business and include very few references to the boys themselves. The emphasis was consistently on the state of the finances and the property – that is, on the institution or the corporation itself. It was rare to find a report on the boys, rarer still for an individual boy to be singled out for extensive comment, both of which were common in the minutes of the ladies' Committees. The Boys' Home superintendent started to make regular monthly reports on the boys in the 1890s, but even these included only general comments on their overall health and conditions, rather than reports on specific boys and their progress.

Another difference is the regularity with which discussion on the nature of work with boys took place. The early minutes recounted the research several Board members undertook before they embarked on the project by travelling to New York City to investigate work with boys and the ensuing discussions as to the type of service to create and the target residents. For several months following the opening, the Board recorded many discussions on the specific orientation they should take and adjustments to it. Throughout the period discussions took place on the best way to train the boys as citizens and "gentlemen." Then, in the early twentieth century, the minutes related the discussions in connection with the opening of the (Shawbridge) Boys' Farm and Training School to replace the boys' reformatory in the Sherbrooke Prison and aspects of this type of training work. Even here, though, we see gender differences, as the men's discussions centred on theory, which was rare in the ladies' minutes. Moreover, the possibility for more extensive "public" action was clear from the fact that Alexander and J.R. Dougall were able to travel freely, first to New York and then later to Sherbrooke, and to discuss and negotiate regularly with the Inspector of Prisons.[105]

The role of the Boys' Home superintendent raises another difference between the conservative female-directed charities and the male ones – that of the delegation of power. The Boys' Home's Board members were reform-minded, not conservative, and this difference was relevant here. Their hired superintendent was made a member of the Board and in this capacity attended all meetings. Like a modern CEO, he kept the Board abreast of occurrences in the Home and, alongside Alexander, was the public face of the institution. This was never a characteristic of the benevolent female charities, in which power relations between the Committee and their hired staff were completely hierarchical. Staff, even the matron or superintendent, were never invited to attend meetings and certainly had no public role other than that outlined in their work duties.

A reading of the nineteenth-century Minute Books for the Montreal Protestant House of Industry and Refuge confirms the absence of a person-centred approach in male-directed charities in the city.[106] Buildings and budgets also have a predominant place in these minutes. As a charity dealing with adults, it is perhaps not surprising that the Board did not discuss individual cases. However, this was not uncommon in the LBS, where minutes regularly included commentary on the elderly women resident in the institution. The Protestant House of Industry minutes also included regular discussions on the nature of their work generally, particularly in relation to that with the elderly and the homeless.

It is entirely possible that these two male Boards discussed many matters related to the residents in their institutions at length in their meetings but did not consider these subjects important enough or appropriate content to include in official minutes. This in itself would be telling. Notwithstanding this possibility, the male members of these two Boards seem to have focused on the global project, its business, and its ideological aspects more than on the work in relation to the residents as individuals. Ultimately what is most important is the fact that their official minutes reflect this preoccupation and this hierarchy of importance. In both these aspects the comparison with the more personal approach of the female-directed charities is striking.

Created and managed by the wives and daughters of the city's Protestant elite, these two child charities received the community's moral and financial support. Gender was an important influence on these conservative women in terms of the values and the culture they brought to their works of benevolence and the way in which they managed their incorporations and their charity "homes." They developed a protected female world inside institutions organized around a charity infused with religion, caring, and a personal approach – an emphasis on the children and their needs, on friendship ties among the Committee members, and on their common religious dedication. But gender was not the only factor at play. Two other elements are key to their undertaking: first, their conservative benevolent approach, and second, the expertise they developed as a result of years of experience running child charities. These factors, as well as their protective attitude towards the children in their care, led both Committees to moderate some aspects of the liberal approach to charity and to develop policies that differed from those of other charity workers in the city by the end of the century. In the more detailed analysis that follows, although the two charities under study had many similarities, the reader will also see that there were important differences. These are a result of specific institutional realities linked to the type of services, the number of children in the institutions, the influence of parents, and the level of budget independence.

The next chapter looks at the management aspects of these two female charities and their Committees as they worked to provide services and ensure that their benevolent designs were implemented successfully.

3

Charity Management and Work

Managing a charitable society was recognized as an acceptable activity for elite women for whom humanitarian and religious motivations merged with the sense of social obligation and duty that accompanied their wealth and social status. In many ways this was a sociable activity, as women worked alongside friends, relatives, and neighbours and within a female world of sociability and female culture, but it was also an activity that required a great deal of work, challenging administrative tasks, and serious responsibilities. The aim of this chapter is to examine this management work as illustrated by the POA and the LBS.

Historians who have looked at women's activism and benevolence have found that the management of charitable institutions provided women with important work in the social sphere. Nancy Hewitt, Anne Boylan, and Lori Ginzberg clarified any assumptions that this activism in and of itself led women to feminism, finding that certainly women they refer to as "benevolent" did not inevitably become feminists – a position confirmed by this book.[1] It is clear that running private charities involved challenging work that required a wide range of administrative and leadership skills, but to date, little research has been done on the actual tasks such committees performed. The wealth of sources available enable us to fill this gap in our knowledge of women's activism through an examination of these two Montreal committees for a seventy-year period, from approximately 1830 to 1900. The sources also provide an opportunity to address the underlying assumption that the women who served as members of charity Boards actively participated in the charity's work and acquired new skills as a result. Clarifying this is important as it helps us to better understand the workings of the charities and the problems encountered in running them.

Committee members and Directresses were elected at the annual public meetings; these lists were published in the annual reports and often in the City Directory or in city newspapers. Given this publicity, as well as the central role charities played in the Protestant community, being elected to a charity Board was an excellent way for a "lady" to assert her family's social standing and to publicly demonstrate her own respect for social conventions and duty. Certainly the newspaper reporter in 1863 took the class and status aspects of charitable work for granted when he commented on the POA annual meeting as being "largely and fashionably attended by ladies,"[2] as did the LBS Secretary who reminded supporters in 1896 that on the LBS's "list of Subscribers and Managers can be found many names of our wisest and best."[3] It is quite possible, therefore, that some ladies were motivated more by a desire to gain this public recognition than by a real interest in immersing themselves in the thousand and one details involved in charity work. Were the lists of members really lists of women (or families) who publicly supported the charities and their work – a kind of public relations document – or were they lists of women who were actually actively working in the management of the charities? This analysis uses several indices to evaluate this: the Committee structures, the number of years women remained members, their attendance at monthly meetings, and their participation in work-related activities such as visiting the institution, fund-raising, and subcommittee work.

At first glance, on the basis of the published lists, the two charities fit the pattern of large active committees. However, an examination of the actual involvement of individual members forces us to qualify generalizations about widespread participation. The chapter is divided into three parts. The first part looks at the organizational structure, the second deals with the work involved in charity management and the extent to which members participated in this, and the third looks at the interaction of the ladies and the hired staff.

ORGANIZATIONAL STRUCTURE

Voluntary associations such as these charities, especially those that were also incorporated societies, had well-developed organizational structures. Their purpose or mission was clearly stated in their Statutes, By-Laws, and Act of Incorporation. These also outlined the number and rhythm of meetings, the number of elected officers, the size of the Committee of Management, the election process, and the accountability and duties of all officers, as well as the internal rules by which the institutions would be run. Both of the organizations had made sets of rules when they were formed and then updated and passed new by-laws in connection with their incorporations. The POA's official Constitution and By-Laws were written in 1844 and revised in 1852. The official Rules and By-Laws for the LBS were drawn up in 1841 and revised in both 1874 and 1896. These documents became, in effect, a form of self-regulation and were one of the ways the private societies established and proved their credibility to the public whose donations they managed. Thus, although membership on a charity board had an important social aspect, it involved clear responsibilities of an administrative, political, and economic nature.

Both of these societies elected Committees of Management of at least twenty members and four or five Directresses. Membership on the Committee and nomination as a Directress were determined at the last meeting of the year, with elections ratified at the annual public meeting usually held the next month. Although the POA Constitution set the size of the Committee at twenty-nine, it was smaller than that until 1851. The LBS Committee was larger for much of the century. Ranging from twenty-two to thirty from 1832 to 1846, it increased at that point and remained near sixty until 1869. In that year the list was divided between those members who agreed to be actively involved – the Committee – and those who were unable to devote the necessary time but wanted to maintain their association with the LBS – the Honorary Managers.[4] The new Committee averaged thirty-five throughout the 1870s but dropped to the low twenties after 1885.

Both Committees held regular monthly meetings in the institution's meeting room. In the event of contagious illness, the meeting was held at the home of the First Directress. A quorum – set at eight for the POA and five for the LBS – was necessary to conduct official business; otherwise only reports were read. The meetings were structured. The minutes of the previous meeting were read and approved, after which reports were made by the Secretary, the Treasurer, and the Monthly Visitors who had supervised the institution over the previous month. The Secretary also read the written reports of the (hired) matron and the teacher as well as any correspondence regarding the children. Members reviewed any issues raised in these reports. This structure enabled members to keep up-to-date with occurrences inside the home and with ongoing decisions. Elaborate and careful record-keeping systems existed. The minutes included records of attendance as well as discussions and decisions. Careful records were kept in the registers of all the children entering and leaving the institutions, including descriptions of the circumstances for most cases. Contracts were entered into for the adoption or apprenticeship of children.

Both Committees had a small core of experienced members who remained for many years and provided the charities with both stability and continuity that were of immeasurable value to their work. Forty-one of the 220 women who served on the POA Committee and thirty of the 369 women on the LBS Committee were members for more than twenty years.[5] Many of these long-term managers (nineteen in the POA and thirteen in the LBS) had memberships of more than thirty years. This included members we met in the last chapter such as Agnes Armour Ramsay, Mary Corse Lyman, Louisa Frothingham (Molson), Eliza Ross, and Anne Ross McCord. Another group (thirty-six POA members and seventy in the LBS) were members between ten and twenty years. The majority, however (65 per cent of members in the POA and 73 per cent of those in the LBS), remained for less than ten years, most of them less than five years, and a third for either one or two years.

With so many members remaining for short periods of time, there was a constant turnover. In more than half the years from 1835 to 1900, at least ten members were replaced in the LBS; in several years half the membership changed. The POA was a little more stable, with two or three members changing each year. This pattern of turnover was not unusual for the city's private charities. In both the Protestant Infants' Home and the Hervey Institute, for example, 90 per cent of members remained less than ten years. This was also true of 93 per cent of members of the Diet Dispensary, 80 per cent of the Montreal Maternity's Board, and 74 per cent of the (Anglican) Church Home.[6] It appears that many women were associated with charities at some point in their lives, but only for a few years.

It is difficult to determine why some women remained on these committees longer than others and why so many remained for such a short period of time. Changing life experiences seems to be the only explanation. We know that a minimum of thirty-four women maintained their membership until their deaths and that many others left active duty as a result of poor health, a move from the city, the demands of a growing family, commitments in other charities or church groups, or, as in the case of the LBS Honorary Managers, because they were no longer able to participate actively. Patterns of meeting attendance were affected by similar factors. Some of the short-term members might have joined the Committees intending to be active members but then left because of changing personal or family priorities, because they found the work too demanding or the power too centralized in the hands of a few members, or because they disagreed with policy directions; others might have joined mainly as a result of social pressure or simply to demonstrate support for the charity.

The structures as outlined in the by-laws tended to invest a lot of power into the hands of "Directresses" elected to their positions on an annual basis. The responsibilities of each position reveal a wide range of administrative duties. The First Directress presided at meetings, determined the agenda, and called special meetings; she was also responsible for all "external" affairs, including contacts with city officials such as the sanitary inspector, and with the institution's doctor, lawyer, and notary.[7] In her absence, the Second Directress assumed her duties. Besides her duties as official representative of the Committee, the First Directress tended to assume a supervisory role in relation to the institution, many of them visiting almost daily.[8]

The Secretary was responsible for correspondence and records. She kept minutes of meetings, lists of members, and the admissions register, wrote the annual report, and sent out the notices of meetings.[9] The POA's Secretary was also in charge of apprenticeships and all dealings with masters and parents, except for fees, which were administered by the Treasurer. In the LBS, a special position of Secretary for the Children was created in 1843 to carry out these duties.[10]

The Treasurer managed and paid accounts, kept lists of subscriptions and donations, as well as legacies and special subscriptions,[11] and wrote the annual treasurer's report. She also managed numerous accounts including the General Fund, building/land funds, in-trust accounts for apprentices or children, the Reward Fund (POA), and the Endowment or Permanent Funds, which included the stock portfolio, savings, and mortgages. Her job was quite complicated, especially in years when several concurrent accounts existed and once the Endowment Funds became substantial; the job also crossed gender boundaries. For this reason, from about mid-century on, the Treasurer was aided by a men's committee or an advisor, as we will see in chapter 7. In the POA, from 1851, two other Committee members also helped audit the monthly accounts, and by the 1890s, a ladies' Finance Committee helped with financial questions alongside the Gentlemen's Committee.

From 1835 to 1900, a total of sixty-nine ladies, or 19 per cent of LBS members, held one of these leadership positions, and a few served in two different positions (normally the Second Directress assuming the First Directress position). This included sixteen First Directresses, twenty-one Second Directresses, fifteen Secretaries, eleven Treasurers, and fourteen Secretaries for the Children. A number of them had lengthy terms of office – three more than twenty years and six for periods ranging from eleven to seventeen years – but most terms were shorter than this, and in two-thirds of the years from 1835 to 1899 at least one LBS Directress position was vacated and filled by a new candidate. Such a regular turnover often caused problems, since many members were unwilling to accept elected office, given the amount of work and responsibility the positions entailed.

Turnover was less of a problem in the POA, where Directresses tended to serve for many years. As a result, only twenty-seven ladies or 11 per cent of members held office in the century. By 1895, for example, the POA had had only four Secretaries (with terms of eleven, one, thirty-six, and twenty-four years) and three Treasurers (with terms of twenty-eight, twenty-five, and twenty-one years). The new Secretary and Treasurer, elected in 1895 and 1896 respectively, remained in office into the twentieth century. The offices of First and Second Directress changed a bit more frequently, with eleven First Directresses and twelve Second Directresses over the century, serving an average term of office of seven years.

Despite this marginal stability, even in the POA, age and poor health often forced Directresses to submit their resignations. This was particularly a problem in the 1860s, '70s, and '80s when many of the members from the early years began to grow old and several died. In 1871, for example, the POA was forced to fill the positions of both First and Second Directress in the same year when Sophia Moffat, who had served as a Directress for twenty-one of her twenty-four years on the Committee, resigned due to advancing age and Elizabeth Greenshields returned to the Committee of Management rather than assume the position of First Directress as requested.[12] The same problem occurred in 1883–84. Margaret (Thomas) Coffin accepted the position of First Directress that year but resigned four years later, believing that "a younger and more active person could fulfill the duties more efficiently."[13] Circumstances such as these, as well as general insecurity or the challenges inherent in the work, could preclude other members from "undertaking any fresh duties"[14] or accepting office. Offered the position of Second Directress in 1884, long-time member Miss Blackwood, for example, declined "the honor, as she felt quite unable to fulfill the duties in a satisfactory manner." Not surprisingly, women elected to Directress positions were usually long-term and/or active members. Several were chosen in deference to their evident leadership and management skills.

Given their executive functions, Directresses had a substantial amount of power in the charities and did much of the actual work. Nonetheless, major policy decisions in both charities were made at the monthly meetings. The general POA Committee was also involved in most admission and placement decisions, since, except in urgent cases, these were done at the monthly meetings. In the LBS, as a much larger charity and one that dealt with several types of clientele as well as a high turnover, most admissions and departures were dealt with on an ongoing basis by the Directresses and the ladies acting as Visitors in any given month. The First Directress reported on these at the monthly meetings, and the Committee discussed individual cases only if there had been a gross irregularity, which was rare. This is perhaps one factor in explaining why the LBS often had problems securing quorum at meetings despite the Committee's large size.

Over the century, the process for making decisions in the LBS was centralized, and the position of First Directress became even more powerful. Under the 1874 By-Laws, the First and Second Directress were listed as ex-officio members of all subcommittees and given the power to act as a committee in their own right.[15] Much of this increased power was due to the personality of several Directresses combined with the general weakness in the Committee as a result of constant turnover. One woman who played a large role in this was Annie Wheeler, a doctor's wife (seen in figure 0.10), who from 1877 to 1882 brought her energy and organizing skills to the position of First Directress, making several administrative and organizational changes. In 1878 she established weekly meetings with the Monthly Visitors to review applications and make admission decisions and instituted a report on these at monthly meetings; in the 1880s she increased contacts with the Young Ladies' School Committee, a move that was facilitated by her daughter's presidency of that committee.[16]

It is unclear whether all of these innovations remained after her resignation due to poor health, but certainly the regular reports did. By the 1890s, some discontent had evolved with this highly centralized model, especially among the other Directresses. The situation came to a crisis in 1893–94 when a series of resignations occurred as a result of a conflict between the First Directress, Mary-Anne Cramp, and the Treasurer, Harriet (F.W.) Thomas, who accused her of a lack of consultation, although Annie Wheeler seems to have been implicated in this conflict as well.[17] A decisive shift of the balance of power back to the larger Committee and the Executive as a whole occurred in 1896 when the Committee forced the First Directress (a member since the 1860s) to resign, believing she had exceeded her powers when she fired the institution's doctor.[18] The following year when a teacher was needed, a hiring committee was named. In the past, hiring would have been left to the First Directress, but the Secretary indicated pointedly that the ladies now felt that "such an important duty should not be left to one person alone."[19] Clearly the LBS Committee was beginning to challenge the power First Directresses had assumed and to decentralize some decision-making. Not surprisingly, the stipulation that the First and Second Directress could act as an ad-hoc subcommittee was dropped in the 1897 revision of the By-Laws.

A similar pattern evolved in the POA. Despite the involvement of the larger Committee in most major decisions, the POA Directresses did most of the work between meetings and thus wielded a great deal of power. This centralization of real power in the hands of the Directresses was aggravated by the Ross-McCord family's hegemony over these positions for fifty years. By the late 1870s, the POA began to slowly shift to a model where more members were directly involved in running the institution between meetings. Long-term active members such as Louisa Frothingham (Molson), seen in figure 0.7, were instrumental in this change. Having already challenged the largely Anglican Directresses and the Anglican/Presbyterian Committee on the matter of discrimination against members of her Unitarian faith in relation to apprenticeship and adoption in 1851 (see discussion below), she would lead the charge for both the democratization and the feminization of decision-making and the improved quality of conditions inside the home for the children through the creation of a series of subcommittees.

The first of several ad-hoc subcommittees created for these purposes was formed in 1878 to look into necessary building repairs, another investigated possible improvements to the institutional diet, and a third would later be organized in connection with planning for the new building. Louisa sat on all of them. In the early 1890s a series of permanent subcommittees were formed, including a purchasing committee, a school committee, and a finance committee.[20] These subcommittees (both the ad-hoc and the permanent ones) broadened the ladies' participation in areas such as investments and also increased the number of POA members, especially non-Directresses, involved in ongoing work. Unfortunately this also increased the possibility of tensions or disagreements between members over decisions, and both Louisa and her sister-in-law, Anne Molson, resigned in 1892 over the choice of building plan for the new home.[21]

Although on the whole the two Montreal committees seem to have worked fairly harmoniously, there were several serious disagreements besides those mentioned above. Both charities were officially nondenominational, but the excessive influence of the Anglican Church, particularly in the early years when it was still an established church, caused some tension within the committees. In 1844, eight Presbyterian women left the LBS to protest the fact that Presbyterian inmates were forced to attend Anglican Church services with the matron. The First and Second Directresses, Sarah Ann Richardson and Ann Ogden, resigned, as did two managers, all of them Anglican, fearing the appearance of partiality. They were quickly re-elected and motions passed to allow attendance at the Presbyterian Church. The authority of the Anglican Church and its influence were maintained, nonetheless, by the distinction that religious instruction inside the home would be limited to Anglican scriptures. In the meantime, the "Episcopal Friends of the Society" donated £75 to support its work, a clear underwriting by the Anglican establishment.[22]

At the 1845 meeting, an entire new slate of Directresses was elected. The acuteness of this conflict was revealed the next year when a subcommittee visited ministers to propose that charity sermons be held in several churches on the same day. The Presbyterian ministers agreed as long as "some of the Ladies of their congregations be permitted to join the Society as members." The assumption, on the part of the clergy, that "permission" was necessary speaks volumes. The Presbyterian members returned that year following these discussions. Politely, and in an attempt to smooth over conflict, they explained their departure as "a misunderstanding."[23] Importantly, though, a proposal to enable

Presbyterian Church attendance was finalized.[24] At the 1846 annual meeting, ladies from all Protestant churches were solicited to join and the Committee grew to sixty-eight members, but this issue remained a sensitive one since matrons were always Anglican and led family worship.[25]

The above situation highlights the underlying difficulty of nondenominational committees. In a city such as Montreal it was paramount that Protestants work together in charitable undertakings. But the power and influence of the Anglican Church cast a large shadow. As a result, members of other denominations might find their religious views and their churches being slighted. If this was true for Presbyterians, it was even more so for non-conformist denominations. We see this in the POA in 1851, when two Unitarian members, Louisa Frothingham and Annabella (Eadie) Workman, both of whom would be long-term and dedicated members, threatened to resign over a proposed change to adoption policy that discriminated against members of their faith. That situation was diffused only by removing the offending restriction from the proposed by-laws before they were sent to print.[26]

Two key policy issues – the admission of board cases in the LBS and of non-orphans in the POA – also led to long discussions and some disagreement.[27] In both of these cases the institutional Charters established a policy orientation against such admissions, but some of the members felt that, rather than be constrained by an old Charter, they should adapt to changing circumstances and admit needy and deserving applicants whenever possible. The compromise in the LBS was to admit board cases as long as such admissions did not jeopardize space for the charity's specified work with destitute cases. In a similar way, the POA agreed to admit non-orphans in cases of extreme need or to "rescue" a child, although this stipulation was made even more flexible in the twentieth century.

The apprenticeship of children to city trades and the problems posed by the need for unusual apprenticeship arrangements not accommodated by the normal form also generated debate and disagreements in the POA that were only finally resolved in the 1890s. There were also disagreements about the institutional diet in both societies by late century and, in the early period, over the use of institutional funds to purchase goods such as pianos, which some ladies felt would be seen as luxuries. Many of these policy conflicts centred on changing client needs, but changes to membership were also a factor. As a new generation of women joined the Committees from the 1870s, we see the impact of changed perceptions of childhood, child protection, and appropriate conditions inside a child charity on policies, as well as the move to decentralize power and involve more members in making decisions, even those crossing gender lines, such as finance.

MANAGEMENT WORK

The work of charity management was multidimensional and time-consuming: attending meetings; visiting to ensure healthy living conditions inside the institution; hiring and supervising staff; purchasing supplies; admitting children into the institutions; overseeing their education and training; attending to the special needs of the elderly residents (in the LBS); making policies on admissions, apprenticeship, adoption, and the rights of relatives; arranging for the placement of children; finding ways to resolve problems in relation to that placement and to protect the children officially still under their responsibility; creating a budget; and raising the necessary funds through collections or fund-raisers. Since policy decisions were made at monthly meetings, attending meetings regularly was the best way to be involved. Some specific tasks such as purchasing, hiring, and supervising the school were done by subcommittees, and both Committees attempted to involve as many members as possible in the sometimes onerous and time-consuming tasks of visiting the institutional home and fund-raising. In this section we will consider the various aspects of management work and, in the process, also examine the participation of members in the work.

With regards to participation rates, it is important to remember that members brought their own personal likes/dislikes and individual needs to the work. A need for the companionship or emotional satisfaction gained from working with a group of other women or caring for children might lead some women to be more likely to attend meetings, organize social events such as bazaars, and act as Monthly Visitor. Others might be well-placed to take advantage of large networks of affluent and sympathetic friends and family and choose to act as fund-raisers. The amount of time involved and possibly the specific skill set required probably also influenced participation in any given activity. Serving as

Monthly Visitor, for example, demanded a lot of time and required supervising the staff and dealing with any and all problems as they arose. Thus it could be both time-consuming and challenging. Other activities involved varying levels of time commitment.

ATTENDANCE AT MONTHLY COMMITTEE MEETINGS

Members kept abreast of developments important to the charity's work and participated in policy discussions and decisions by attending Committee meetings, but this demanded much more effort than simply allowing oneself to be elected to a committee. Meetings didn't involve a lot of controversy and tension but they took several hours once a month. Since attendance was noted at each meeting, it is possible to establish attendance patterns. These records, as shown in table 3.1, reveal that a large number of members rarely attended meetings. Ladies who were members for only one year are listed as "missing" to avoid skewing the data; this included fifty-five women, or 25 per cent of POA members, and seventy-two women, or 19.5 per cent of LBS members. Forty per cent of POA members for whom we can establish an attendance record, and more than half of LBS ones, attended fewer than two meetings a year on average. Many never came at all. At the other extreme we find a small core of ladies who were very involved. Seven per cent of POA members and five per cent of those in the LBS attended seven or more meetings a year. Since normally meetings were suspended over the summer, this is an excellent attendance record. Another large group of members (53 per cent in the POA and 38 per cent in the LBS) attended on average between three and six meetings a year.

A clear correlation emerges between the length of membership and attendance at meetings. In both charities, long-term members (more than twenty years) attended meetings more regularly than the norm. One-third of them had almost perfect attendance. Conversely, the majority of short-term members (five years or less) left after a few years of public association, not of extensive involvement. Only 10 per cent of short-term members in the POA and 15 per cent in the LBS attended more than half the meetings in the years they were members. The majority (66 per cent in the LBS and 55 per cent in the POA) either didn't attend a single meeting or, at most, came to one or two meetings a year.

Table 3.1
Mean attendance at monthly meetings, per year, per member, for the Protestant Orphan Asylum and the Ladies' Benevolent Society, 1835–1900

Mean	No. POA	% known cases	% total cases	No. LBS	% known cases	% total cases
0	23	13.9	10.5	64	21.6	17.3
1, 2	43	26.1	19.5	105	35.4	28.5
3, 4	55	33.3	25	66	22.2	17.9
5, 6	32	19.4	14.5	48	16.2	13
7, 8	11	6.7	5	13	4.4	3.5
9–11	1	0.6	0.5	1	0.3	0.3
Known Cases	165	100	75	297	100	80.5
Missing Cases	55	–	25	72	–	19.5
Total Cases	220	–	100	369	–	100

Source: POA, *Minutes*, 1835–1900; LBS, *Minutes*, 1835–1900.

SUBCOMMITTEES

Subcommittees were organized for specific jobs such as purchasing, hiring staff, overseeing the school, and finance, or for special ad-hoc projects such as overseeing house repairs or building construction, investigating the diet, or revising the by-laws. The POA rarely used subcommittees before 1878, but the LBS used ad-hoc committees quite regularly and had several standing subcommittees. The LBS Purchasing Committee, created in 1857, consisted of one or two members; between 1857 and 1900, seventeen women acted in this capacity.[28] They purchased fabric, household items, and bulk food supplies and were in charge of maintaining the clothing cupboard and allocating clothing and fabric. Membership on this committee was a fairly time-consuming undertaking since the Purchasers also cut out the patterns for the clothing and bedding made inside the institution to minimize wastage and sometimes helped with the actual sewing. These latter duties could take entire days.

The methods used to hire staff varied over the century. Servants and household staff (cooks, laundresses, nurses to oversee the children) were generally hired by the Directresses or the Monthly Visitors. In the LBS many of these workers were recorded in the admission register as if they were inmates, and indeed some of them were women who had entered with their children. The main qualification seems to have been a willingness to live in the institution and abide by its rules. By late century and into the twentieth century the matron or lady superintendent hired many of these workers. The hiring of matrons and teachers, however, was much more structured and considered. Usually the charity placed an advertisement in the city papers or, in the case of a teacher, made inquiries at the Normal School. In the POA, from 1871 on, all applications for these positions were reviewed at the monthly meetings and a six-member hiring committee carried out the interviews and checked references.[29] In the LBS, the Directresses did much of the actual hiring for these positions, but on occasion a special hiring committee was struck.

Both charities ran schools inside the institutions, and this called for monitoring and supervision. In the POA where the hired (male) superintendent ran the school as part of his regular duties, the ladies attempted to avoid potential jurisdictional problems with him by minimizing what might be perceived as interference. A school committee was formed in 1849, but unlike a regular standing committee, it was not added to the by-laws. The annual report referred to it in the following way: "as many of the Ladies of the Board of managers as can make it" were invited to check on the students' progress on Fridays.[30] An actual functioning school committee was not established until 1890, but even then its jurisdiction was limited to specialized needs such as arranging training for children with infirmities. These limited committee duties were maintained once a female teacher assumed responsibility for the school in 1893, although School Committee members had asserted their position by the twentieth century.[31] At that point, forceful members such as Miss Van Horne inspected the school weekly and were responsible for at least one teacher being dismissed for failure to maintain discipline. They also implemented new teaching methods.

The LBS did not have to worry about the sensitivity of a male superintendent since they had a hired female teacher, and there was a clear power hierarchy between the teacher and the Committee. The LBS formed a School Committee to supervise the school in 1832, but it was disbanded and reconstituted several times.[32] As a result of this difficulty, the LBS assigned responsibility for the supervision of the school to a separate committee called the Young Ladies' School Committee in 1851. By 1900, this committee had had 160 members and 23 Directresses. The School Committee was virtually autonomous, with separate annual reports and budget statements, although they were supposed to submit quarterly reports to the larger LBS Committee.[33] Contact between the two committees was increased in the 1880s, when Annie Wheeler was First Directress and her daughter Isabella was School Committee President, but an official coordination was not created until the revised by-laws of 1897.[34] Thus, it was only at the end of the century that the LBS Committee regained some real input into the supervision of the school.

Two School Committee members visited the school weekly to ensure a general oversight of the children's education; they also organized the yearly exams and prizes as well as the Christmas celebrations. Some of the young women gave singing lessons and ran Sunday school classes for those too young to attend church.[35] By the 1890s members also gave classes in gymnastics and kitchen garden exercises. The School Committee received an annual budget grant from the LBS as of 1861, but by the late 1880s, because of the LBS's financial difficulties, it had donated money to the LBS General Fund several times and allocated $900 to the Permanent Fund debt from the profits of a bazaar in 1887.[36] It also raised money annually to buy schoolbooks, supplies, and fabric, and in 1888 purchased a piano for the classroom.[37]

Apart from the Young Ladies' School Committee and the Purchasers, membership on standing and ad-hoc subcommittees was not always indicated, and only twenty-six ladies can be identified as working on LBS subcommittees and a few in the POA. Almost all were long-term members who did other work such as visiting and collecting and who attended meetings regularly; a few served as Directress at some point. Here we find clear evidence of the small group of active members who largely ran the institutions.

VISITING THE INSTITUTION

It was imperative that the Committees maintain a direct supervision over household management, both to ensure that policy guidelines and rules on daily routine, health, exercise, diet, schooling, and medical procedures were implemented by the hired staff and to make certain that the children were being cared for adequately. To avoid these duties falling solely on the Directresses, both Committees instituted a system of "Monthly Visitors" whereby each month two members accepted responsibility for the institution's internal management. The LBS by-laws empowered them to make decisions on all issues that needed immediate action as long as there was no policy impact; the POA by-laws instructed them to "fulfill whatever duties may arise from existing circumstances."[38]

Specifically, Visitors supervised the matron and workers, gave out the weekly supplies (kept under lock and key), maintained the household inventory, approved any purchases, examined the accounts before they were paid, and made sure that everything ran smoothly. They checked the children's health, diet, conduct, and progress in school, and attended to any health problems or building repairs. The 1888 diphtheria epidemic in the POA, for example, was discovered when the Visitors sent two children with sore throats to the hospital. In that instance the Visitors attended daily to check on the other children to ensure no more cases developed and then arranged for a sanitary inspection and plumbing repairs.[39] Besides acting as the link between the Committee and the matron, Visitors also had the most direct contact with the children and their families. They received all admissions and arranged transportation for any child who was leaving. In the LBS, they also made decisions on admissions and apprenticeships jointly with the First Directress.

Visiting duty greatly increased a member's personal involvement with the institution and its residents, and it was common for ladies to bring special donations and treats during their month and even to arrange entertainment events for the children. But it was also a difficult, time-consuming, and onerous undertaking. The LBS by-laws specified that visitors should visit three times a week. According to the visits recorded in the LBS Matron's Journal, they tended to do this and more, visiting daily when sickness or problems required. Most made it a point to visit during meals, both to verify the quality of the food and to reinforce the personal links between the institution's residents and the Committee.[40]

Monthly Visitors reported on their work at the monthly meetings. Although these reports were usually short, they kept the general Committee informed about the state of the institution and the children. Occasionally they made recommendations in relation to the diet, the school curriculum, clothing needs, health problems, or necessary building repair. Most of the policy discussions on these matters were initiated by such comments. Visitor reports also served to transmit requests from the servants or the matron for extra pay or privileges.

Ideally every member would do this work once a year; thus, a committee of twenty-five was perfectly placed to supervise the institution in teams of two. But the ideal remained just that. Since members volunteered as Visitor at the monthly meetings, the brunt of the work tended to fall on those who regularly attended meetings. Both Committees attempted to distribute the work more evenly through alphabetical lists, but this was unsuccessful.[41] The early LBS minutes refer to fines in cases other than illness or absence from town, but there is no indication that this policy was enforced.[42]

The LBS Matron's Journal (1851–99) enables us to track visiting duty in that institution. Unfortunately a similar source is no longer extant for the entire period in the POA files. From 1851 to 1900, 150 ladies or 58 per cent of LBS members during those years acted as official Monthly Visitor. Therefore, although it involved a lot of responsibility and work, more than half of the members accepted Visitor duty at least once. But a full 42 per cent never carried out this crucial duty and would have only entered the institution for meetings. Furthermore, of those who did accept being Monthly Visitor, most did not do it very often. In fact, ninety-eight members served as Visitor only once (37 per cent) or from two to five times (28 per cent) over their membership. Only forty members (27 per cent) accepted Visitor duty once a year in the years they were members, the way it was designed. Twenty-one of these women filled the gap left by their companions and visited more than once if this was necessary. They were helped in this by twelve members who accepted Visitor duty from six to ten times over the period.

This visiting data reveals both the seriousness with which some of the ladies took charity work and the fact that the majority were involved only sporadically. Echoing the pattern we found with attendance at meetings, the likelihood of acting as monthly Visitor increased with the length of time a lady was a member. Short-term members were the least likely to visit. Only 35 per cent served as Monthly Visitor, and only 9 per cent (eleven ladies) accepted to do this annually. Conversely, 81 per cent of those who were members for more than ten years (or seventy-three ladies) served as Visitor. Twenty-two of them did it on an annual basis. This latter number includes twelve ladies who visited at least once a year for terms of office spanning more than twenty years.[43]

FUND-RAISING

Speaking at the annual meeting of the LBS in 1873, one male supporter reminded the audience of women's reputation for fund-raising: "One thing was quite certain, that if women had the faculty of speech, they also had the faculty of getting money."[44] The actual experience of these Montreal charities proves that popular assumptions such as these were not always based in fact. Fund-raising was a source of almost constant frustration and demanded a great deal of effort since both charities depended on some form of private support for a large part of their funds. Finding ways to encourage people to donate money – as subscriptions, donations, or legacies – or organizing special fund-raising events such as bazaars or concerts was a demanding job, and the Committees, especially the LBS, often had problems commandeering sufficient volunteers to raise more funds than the bare minimum.

The annual subscription fees paid by members were the backbone of the charities' finances until late century, but they never covered operating expenses. The early POA reports indicate that subscriptions (as well as donations) were collected at the annual meeting, an efficient method although one in which revenue would fluctuate with meeting attendance.[45] Subsequent reports do not specifically refer to this, but it might be taken for granted. Most importantly for our purposes, when subscribers neglected to pay, the money had to be collected, and in this way even subscription income could represent work. This was done by members collecting subscriptions from their friends, or by the matron collecting them when she delivered the annual report.[46] By the 1880s unpaid subscriptions had become such a problem in the LBS that the subscription list was regularly reviewed and unpaid accounts collected by the Treasurer and four ladies designated for that purpose.[47] Given the importance of a solid basis of subscription income, there was a constant pressure on members to interest "a generous public in their favour,"[48] and thus expand membership (and subscription income).

Both charities used their annual reports, the press, and specialized appeals to inform newly arrived families about the charities' work and financial needs.[49] Many of the LBS annual reports, for example, as published in the press, included specific sections on "The State of the Funds" or "The Needs of the Society." As the century progressed and many of the original supporters died or left town, appealing to newcomers became even more urgent. The POA began to refer to this problem in their annual reports by the late 1870s. In 1879, for example, the Secretary commented: "We record with regret that within the last few years we have lost, by death or removal from the city, many of those old and tried friends who were the early supporters of this Asylum," and assured supporters that "[i]f each member were to interest even one or two new friends in our behalf, we feel confident that the list of our benefactors would be restored to its former dimension."[50] Without this new influx of support, private funding from subscriptions decreased in the POA from 1877 on by almost 50 per cent. It was in this same period that the LBS began to depend on business donations for an increasing percentage of their funds.

At the same time as these two charities were attempting to interest new supporters, the claims on charitable donations in the city had increased, with the creation of a wide range of new institutions and services that directly competed with the older charities for donations. Furthermore, their Endowment Funds led some supporters to assume they no longer needed support. This combination of factors was of particular concern for the LBS due to their precarious budgets. The Secretary made a direct allusion to this problem in 1890: "The impression seems to have gone abroad, that the Ladies' Benevolent Society is never at a loss for funds, and some of the old helpers have stopped their subscriptions to it, and given their money to newer efforts. The Managers wish God-speed to every effort for good, but they *feel* the loss of their old friends, and they hope that those charitable citizens may see their way to help the new without cutting off this old and worthy Society."[51] The ladies mainly depended on their personal contacts and networks to attract supporters, but they remained convinced that "there was a mine of wealth unopened in Montreal."[52] Regular accounts of the charities' work and of their needs was one way to reach new supporters; the "collection" was another, albeit not a popular one.

THE COLLECTION

Certainly the least onerous way to collect donations was for members to appeal to their network of personal friends, and at several points special collecting cards were designed for this purpose, or members "promised to exert themselves to the utmost to procure subscriptions from their friends."[53] Attracting donations from businesses was another potentially lucrative source.

A few companies, including the Hudson Bay Company and the Montreal Savings Bank (in the early years) and the City and District Bank (annually from 1858), made regular contributions, but these donations were isolated. The POA never made a concerted effort to develop this source of income, but the LBS began to tap into it in earnest from about 1865 when two members of the charity's Gentlemen's Committee began collecting in the business district. From that point business donations to the LBS increased, and the combined subscription and donation income was usually the largest single revenue source.

The least popular collecting method was the general canvass. Although teams of LBS collectors were immediately named and assigned to designated streets in 1832, much of this general canvassing was really another form of calling on friends or known supporters.[54] It was only in 1863 that the LBS developed a plan for an actual collection, dividing the central Montreal area, where most of the members resided and the major businesses were located, into thirteen districts.[55] Fifteen ladies volunteered and between them covered eleven districts, but this was the most systematic that collecting ever got. The next year the collection was cancelled altogether due to a lack of interest.[56] Despite attempted reorganizations in both 1879 and 1884, collecting was very unpopular, and the LBS consistently "found it impossible to get a sufficient number of collectors to carry out the systematic plan they had arranged for that purpose."[57] In 1884, the Treasurer explained the LBS's deficit situation as "not for a want of kind friends, but from the great difficulty we experience in getting the Managers to collect."[58]

The major work of collecting was in fact done by a small number of members, and finding ways to divide the "burden of collecting so as to prevent too much duty from falling on only a few" was always problematic.[59] According to the annual reports, where this information is included from 1848, approximately one-third of LBS members in the period 1848 to 1899, or ninety-one ladies (including six School Committee members or Honorary Managers), collected for the society. However, almost two-thirds of them did so only once (twenty-nine) or two to three times (twenty-eight). In addition, many collected small sums that were probably nothing more than the subscriptions of friends. The bulk of the work was done by a group of twenty women who collected for periods longer than nine years, and another fourteen who collected for four to eight years. These ladies provided continuity and were responsible for the largest collections. Usually there were five or six of these regular collectors with large lists, supplemented by other members collecting smaller sums. Most of the ladies who collected were active in other areas as well, visiting, attending meetings, and doing subcommittee work; 40 per cent served as a Directress at some point and more than half were long-term members. But collecting was also the way in which a few ladies, such as Mary Ferrier, for example, made their major contribution. Marriage to James Ferrier, a successful capitalist, railway promoter, and politician, undoubtedly provided Mary with a network of wealthy friends that she could appeal to in her capacity as collector.

In 1889–90, having ended the financial year with a deficit several times, the LBS decided to make a concerted effort to solicit donations by hiring a collector for the major districts.[60] Thus, the general reluctance to do this work resulted in the awkward situation whereby scarce charity funds were used to pay someone to collect the money needed to run the charity. Originally, seven members helped the collector, but by 1896 she worked alone. Donations increased substantially and the number of donors more than doubled (to 1,400), but most, coming from the general public, were for small amounts, some as little as $0.10. The POA would hire a collector as well in 1900.[61]

Collecting appears to be the first area in which these bourgeois female charity directors reached the limit of volunteerism. In the face of rising costs and regular deficits they took a step towards professionalization by hiring a collector to take on the task most of the volunteers refused to assume. This general aversion to collecting was not limited to Montreal. Both Nancy Hewitt and Lori Ginzberg found that American committees also found collecting "too onerous," referring to it as "a thankless duty" and "never a pleasant task."[62] Furthermore, it was not limited to female-directed charities. In 1878, only fifteen years after its formation, the male-directed Protestant House of Industry also resorted to a paid collector to call on subscribers who had failed to deposit their subscriptions to the building fund as promised.[63] Interestingly, the Board originally agreed to pay the collector a 2.5 per cent commission, but this was later adjusted upwards to 4 per cent when he complained about the difficulty of the task. Luckily, there were more attractive options for raising money than the unpopular collection.

ENTERTAINMENT EVENTS

Just as charitable institutions, the LBS and the POA among them, shaped the physical landscape of Montreal, the Charity Bazaar, the Promenade Concert, and the "Fête" inserted themselves into the city's social calendar. Events such as these were regularly used by charities in England, France, and the US as sources of financing.[64] Although the Montreal charities used them, they were not used to their maximum potential. Curiously, they were rarely used by the POA, which held two such events to raise money towards its Building or Land Fund (a bazaar in 1850 and a concert in 1858)[65] but never for the General Fund, although in both 1854 and 1856 they helped with concerts organized for their benefit by a temperance organization, the Order of Rechabiltes, in exchange for some of the receipts. The LBS used entertainments more often, with some event annually from 1843 to 1852, and in most years from 1857 to 1869, but from 1870 to 1900 only five fund-raising events were held despite the charity's precarious financial situation.

Several factors were instrumental in this. First, the ladies were hesitant to appeal to the public too often, believing that supporters would respond more positively if appeals were made only when the need was pressing. On several occasions this was the reason given when they refused to lend their name to entertainment events in return for a portion of the proceeds. The POA Secretary's wording of the 1853 appeal, made after years of budget problems while they tried to pay both the building and land debt, reveals her sensitivity to these concerns: "with anxious hearts, therefore, but certainly not without hope, do the Ladies of this charity call upon the Protestant public to answer the present appeal, not made till the moment of real want is at hand."[66]

Questions of respectability and religious sensibilities were also instrumental. Commenting on the US, Mary Ryan notes that theatricals such as balls were never considered entirely respectable.[67] Certainly by the 1840s, many of the Montreal ladies questioned the use of Charity Balls and entertainment events for religious and moral reasons.[68] Thus, although they had accepted donations from several theatrical productions in the early years, the POA stopped this as of 1840.[69] Similarly, the LBS accepted the proceeds from a Charity Ball organized by a group of citizens in 1842 and organized their own Charity Ball in 1844 as "the most effectual way of securing the largest sums," but by 1849 they had promised the clergy not to accept funds from Balls or theatricals and voted eleven to seven against accepting money from the Oddfellows Ball.[70] Unfortunately, their discussions with clergymen did not include reciprocal promises of financial help. Charity sermons were an important source of funds in the 1820s and 1830s,[71] but from that point on this support was small, irregular, and involved very few churches. The LBS often referred to this with dismay and even sent delegations to request aid, but all to no avail.[72]

The Charity Bazaar and Promenade Concert posed fewer religious problems than the Charity Ball, although a minority of members questioned them for their commercialism. Accordingly they were used more often, but both involved substantial preparations. Finding enough members to do this work was a major problem and probably explains their irregular use by late century. In anticipation of the need for increased funds as a result of their larger building in 1856, for example, the LBS rejected suggestions for either a concert or a soiree as being "impracticable." Instead they made a special appeal in newspapers for donations during their open house.[73] They did, though, hold concerts in 1868 and 1878 and organized a bazaar almost on an annual basis from 1843 to 1852 and again in 1857, 1858, 1868, 1869, and 1881, but none after that.

These events appear to have been much less elaborate than the bazaars and fairs discussed by Beverly Gordon in her work on American fund-raising fairs, events that featured theatricality, amusements, and elaborate aesthetic settings.[74] Although some emphasis was placed on creating an attractive setting, the Montreal bazaars seem to have been simple sales of goods, possibly with a meal included, somewhat akin to a modern-day church bazaar; concert announcements carefully noted that dancing would not be included.[75] Still, the planning and preparation began months in advance. The events became the focus of much community support – tickets were sold by the Mechanics Institute and the national societies; the military and militia bands performed at the concerts, as did other city talent.[76] Countless other supporters and the husbands of Committee members helped by loaning halls, setting up, providing free advertising, selling tickets, bringing goods to be sold at bazaars, or donating material to be made into goods for sale; but the success of these events largely depended on the voluntary efforts of members.[77] They were responsible for making most of the fancy sewing and craft goods offered for sale as well as the baked goods and refreshments, for working at the various bazaar tables, for selling concert tickets and making decorations, and for overall organization and coordination.

Several of the entertainment events were planned by others, the ladies helping by selling tickets and providing the refreshments. By far the most interesting example of this is a series of very popular "Fêtes" arranged by the husbands of several LBS members from 1858 to 1865 that netted profits in excess of $1,000 annually. These events were much more elaborate than those organized by the ladies themselves. This direct involvement of men seems to have been unusual and was more than likely driven by the lack of enthusiasm on the part of the female managers. Certainly Prochaska never refers to men organizing entertainment fund-raisers for female-directed societies in Britain, and Gordon argues that fairs were one area where American women operated independently of men, although she notes that the elaborate events in the post–Civil War period were often organized in coordination with men.[78] The LBS Committee recognized that profits from the "Fêtes" were "nearly necessary to the existence of the Society,"[79] but they did not attempt to organize many events themselves when the men were no longer able to do so. Bazaars were held in 1868, 1869, and 1881, and other fund-raisers in 1875, 1878, 1879, and 1889. None occurred thereafter.

It tended to be the Directresses and a small group of ladies who took responsibility for the bazaar tables. Other members contributed goods for sale, but numerous appeals for all members to help in these events point to the fact that only a few ladies undertook this work. In the 1881 Annual Report, the LBS Secretary referred to the bazaar of that year as "the effort of a comparatively few of the managers," and hoped that all members would help in future efforts.[80] The ladies' reluctance to engage in this extra work almost certainly explains why the 1881 bazaar was the first to be held since 1869, and also the last. Only twenty-eight ladies are known to have worked in the bazaars. Several were active members in other areas as well or had been Directresses, but bazaar work was one area that appealed to a few ladies who were not active in other areas. This less-than-impressive commitment to fund-raising caused the charities, especially the LBS, a great deal of difficulty as it led to major financial problems, even deficits, in several years and left the weight on the shoulders of a few dedicated members.

"MANAGER" TYPES

Two patterns emerge from this examination of charity work. First, members can be divided into three groups. The majority contributed to the Societies financially by paying their annual subscription and helped to establish their respectability by being publicly associated with them. Otherwise, they formed a group of silent or token members, their membership possibly a question of social obligation or family pressure. They remained on the Committees for less than five years; rarely, if ever, attended meetings; and volunteered to do very little, if any, related work. At the other extreme we find a small group of dedicated, hard-working ladies with long terms of office. They consistently attended meetings, many of them for more than twenty years; supervised the institutions by doing visitor duty; canvassed for contributions when necessary; ran bazaars; and did subcommittee work. They were aided in this by a third, larger group who attended many meetings and thus participated in policy discussions and decisions, and helped with other work on occasion, some of them preferring one area of activity such as the collection or bazaars.

Second, there is a clear correlation between these "manager" types and length of membership. Most short associations of less than five years were characterized by little if any actual participation in the work of charity management. Long-term members – those who were members for periods of eleven years or more, and especially those with twenty-year-plus memberships – were all involved in some way, although here we find evidence of both the small core of very active members and the group of supportive ones.

Within the group of active members, two distinct sub-groups are identifiable. One was a small group of committed "worker-members." These women attended meetings regularly and did Visitor Duty, fund-raising, and committee work, but never held office. Some, such as Miss Emma Badgley, Miss Ray, and Isabella Dorwin, regularly ran the LBS institution over the summer months when the Directresses were out of town. All three were offered a position as Directress at some point, and refused, but very little pressure was brought to bear to persuade them. It seems that for some reason (perhaps their single status for two of them), they did not fit the image expected of a Directress. The same can be seen in the POA with the cases of Louisa Frothingham Molson and Eliza Ross.

The other group was the Directresses. These women did not necessarily attend every meeting (this was only expected of the First Directress and the Secretary) and were not, as a norm, expected to perform Visitor duties, although several visited regularly. However, they played a major role in all fund-raising and did most of the problem-solving between meetings. Many were long-term, active members. Several were clearly chosen in deference to their strong personalities and management skills. Interesting examples include Annie Wheeler and Harriet Thomas in the LBS, both of whom made major changes to the LBS's management structure, and Jane Davidson Ross and Anne Ross McCord in the POA, who actively managed that charity for several decades.

It is clear that women in both these groups of active members developed or perfected their administrative skills in their charity work. The amount of time and effort they invested in this is testimony to their level of dedication and to the important role charity played in the lives of some elite women. It is also clear, however, that many of the members were not actively involved and were not developing administrative skills as a result. Our study reveals that the majority of women whose names appeared on charity lists were indeed there in name alone, a situation that made the undertaking much more difficult for those ladies who were committed to the success of their benevolent project.

Examination of these charity Committees also reveals several trends over time in terms of participation rates. Looking at members by decade for both societies, we find the highest rates of participation in the 1850s to 1870s. Much of this was due to a group of very active ladies who joined between the 1830s and 1860s, some of them founding members, remaining active over long memberships. However, even in those years, most members were inactive, and it was in 1869 that the LBS attempted to reassert the expectation that members should contribute to the Society's work with the division of the Committee list between active members and Honorary Managers. This expectation triggered a trend to a smaller Committee size at that point and again in the 1880s. Only 56 ladies were members of the LBS over the 1890s compared to 128 in the 1850s. The new streamlined size, however, did not lead to more active involvement. In fact, a larger proportion of LBS members by the 1890s did not visit, the collection was done by a paid collector, and no major fund-raising event was organized. Nonetheless, alongside this trend, by the 1890s both the LBS and the POA began to use subcommittees more regularly and to limit the power they had accorded to the Directresses. In this way power was decentralized and more members were involved in the actual administrative and management work of the homes and in making important decisions.

Two other changes are visible over time. In the 1850s and 1860s a number of ladies as well as other supporters visited the LBS on Sundays to read scriptures with the elderly women. This habit decreased over the decades and special Sunday visits had almost entirely disappeared by the 1880s. Similarly, in the 1850s and 1860s, the LBS (and probably the POA, although the absence of Superintendent's Journals makes it difficult to verify) was considered one of the important city sites and many visitors to the city or patrons toured the institution.[81] This practice had virtually disappeared by the 1890s.

When visitors toured one of these charities, they were shown around by the matron or superintendent unless they were accompanied by a Committee member. Relations with the staff who worked for them were an integral part of the work of running a charity. They were also central to the ladies' attempts to make their institutions as home-like as possible. It is to this we now turn our attention.

RELATIONS WITH THE STAFF

Committee members were not actively involved in the day-to-day internal management of their institutional homes and the children's care, but their control was ever-present. Precise guidelines established the daily routine and activities, budgets and diet lists determined menus, and supplies were kept under lock and key to be distributed weekly by the Monthly Visitor. From the class perspective of these conservative ladies, there was little room for initiative or independence on the part of a hired matron and/or superintendent. In fact, these workers had less independence than some housekeepers in wealthy homes, who controlled the household stores, paid the bills, and hired and fired the junior staff,[82] and certainly less than that advocated by late-century professional charity superintendents such as Lyman Alden, who believed that superintendents, not management committees, should control all aspects of internal management.[83] This was the type of independence, for example, that the Boys' Home superintendent enjoyed. Again from this class perspective, the ladies expected obedience and subservience from their staff but, ironically, they depended on the matrons' organizational and budgetary acumen to run the institutions. This gave matrons a lot of power inside the institutions, especially over the other staff.

Gender entered into the equation in two ways. First, other than the POA superintendent and an occasional furnace man, the institutional staff were women. Both the POA and the LBS had hired a matron/superintendent couple in the early years. This parental model simulated home-life and had the advantage of providing a gendered division of labour. However, both societies had switched to an all-female staff model by the end of the century, the LBS within ten years in 1841, the POA in 1893. Second, the POA, which chose to retain the couple model for most of the century, mainly interacted with the matron and often had problems in their dealings with the male superintendent.

THE MATRON/SUPERINTENDENT

It was the matron's job to run the household in both institutions. Her work included supervision of the other workers, household maintenance and cleaning, the production of clothing, care of the sick, and attendance at the funerals of inmates.[84] In the LBS she was the first contact with parents in terms of applications, investigations, and board payment. The matron planned the weekly meals according to the institution's dietary list, and either she or the superintendent kept the books, including a daily journal and a register of all admissions and applications (subsequently copied by the Secretary into the official register). Most important, matrons served the role of mothers in the institutional home, overseeing the children's care. The ladies' belief that mothers had a central role in child nurture, and that such nurture was crucial to a child's growth, is discernable in rules that specifically required the matron to be present at all meals, to supervise morning and evening prayers, to accompany the children to church and Sunday school, and to teach them good habits and industry. Entries in the LBS matron's journal refer to her searching for runaways, disciplining the children in the home, and, since she knew the children better than the ladies did, reminding the Committee when children were old enough to be placed out, and defending apprentices who had absconded in the face of mistreatment or lack of remuneration. The emotional ties between the children and the matron were often very strong as a result, and it was mainly to her that children wrote letters and returned to visit from their apprenticeship homes or once their indentures were completed.

Shifting to an all-female staff in 1841, the LBS was run by a matron and a female teacher until 1860. This policy was jeopardized when several matrons left to be married. In 1860, the Committee proposed that the matron's husband, Mr Watson, live in as a paying boarder on the condition that he would give some attention to the house.[85] Moreover, although he lived in the institution, he was never hired as a superintendent and had no official dealings with the Committee. Following his death in 1879, the LBS reverted to the all-female model, hiring an assistant matron. This matron/assistant matron model was maintained until 1893 when the official management was given, "under the continued personal and vigilant oversight of the Ladies,"[86] to a lady superintendent, helped by a matron in charge of the household and the servants. The LBS also hired a man for furnace and other work, but he was never given a job title.

The POA opened in 1822 with a governess in charge but had adopted the matron-and-superintendent couple model by 1828. This appears to have been an economy measure. The salary went from $120 annually for the governess to $100 for the less qualified couple. The male superintendent ran the school as both organizer and teacher and the matron ran the house. This system was used until 1893, except for two short periods from 1862 to 1871 and 1880 to 1884, when the superintendent died and the widowed matron ran the institution with the help of a female teacher. In 1889 the POA voted to switch to a matron/ teacher model, but finally decided to try the former model one more time as they were already engaged in a hiring process.[87] In 1893, when this last couple proved unsatisfactory, the POA adopted an all-female model with a lady superintendent and a female teacher. Gender was definitely a factor in this decision. In the final twenty years of the century, the POA dismissed two matron-superintendent couples and had particularly negative dealings with the last superintendent, C. Thomas, who accused them of firing him for encouraging the children to aspire to upward social mobility. The letter he wrote to them in May 1893 in relation to the termination of his contract, which he claimed was illegal, showed his keen awareness of the class hierarchy in which he worked. Reminding the ladies that there was "no worse affliction than to be set adrift, destitute of means in a large city at our age," and requesting to be reinstated, he went on to conclude, "May God grant that it may end in no deeper trouble. If it should, it will not be the first time, that the tyranny of wealth and position has driven the less fortunate to despair."[88] Given the tenor of this letter, it is not surprising that the POA ladies decided to hire only female employees from then on, who they assumed would be less confrontational and more accommodating.

The matron's character, her ability to manage the institution economically, and her maternal influence on the children were important to a charity's reputation and respectability and the ladies regularly used their annual reports to reassure supporters of these facts. Carefully worded comments pay tribute to the matrons' "kind and worthy" nature, their "unwearied attention to their duties and patient kindness to the children," their "careful business habits and strict integrity," and their having "faithfully and untiringly performed their duties." Most matrons and superintendents appear to have been from the respectable working class, but the Committees used the new lady superintendent model in the 1890s to improve the quality of their employees. In both organizations, the position of lady superintendent was more respectable, received a higher salary, and required more qualifications than the position had previously.[89] Ideally they hoped to attract middle-class widows for the new position. The LBS was successful in this. Mrs Jarvis, the first lady superintendent, was personally known to several of the ladies; and the next two, Mrs Bone and J. Frances Evans, were both former Committee members.

A number of the matrons remained in their jobs for many years. This was particularly true of the POA, where Mrs Cribb was matron for thirty-three years, Mrs Campbell for thirteen, and three others for six years each. Miss McGivern, the lady superintendent hired in 1893, remained for twenty-five years. In the LBS, Mrs Watson was matron for twenty-four years and several others served for ten-year periods. The personal link between the ladies and the matrons based on years of service was reinforced by the fact that the Committee regularly gave gifts to long-term matrons, paid for vacations, and, in a few cases, paid for pensions and nursing care for elderly former matrons.[90]

Despite this paternalism, there was a clear power hierarchy between the Committee and the hired matron, and most of their interaction was very formal. Although the matron came into contact with the Directresses and the Monthly Visitors when the latter visited the institution, and the words of encouragement that were surely exchanged at these times would have been important to her relationship with the ladies individually, matrons or superintendents communicated with the Committee as a whole officially through their written journal. Even more important, it was the Secretary, not the matron, who read the journal entries at the monthly meetings. Despite the fact the meetings were held in the institution, neither Committee invited matrons to attend to make their own reports.

In the twentieth century the POA ladies showed very public appreciation for the lady superintendent over her twenty-five years of service. Every annual report indicated their gratitude and appreciation and often credited her with the work's success. They encouraged her to stay when she threatened to quit, paid for several vacations when she was ill, and added an elevator to the building to accommodate her age. When she finally left, they provided her with a life annuity of $25/month and a $500 present.[91] Nonetheless, the hierarchy held fast, and even she was never invited to attend a Committee meeting.

Another hierarchy existed inside the institution, where the matron was in charge of the household staff. Although they did not have hiring and firing powers, matrons supervised the work of the rest of the staff and could use their journal to influence the recording and thus the "retelling" of events. The position of teacher (other than the POA superintendent) was somewhat anomalous since the school was not under the matron's jurisdiction in either institution. However, to the extent that teachers lived in the institution and were required to supervise the children during the day and to help in the house when they could after school hours, they came under the matron's supervision. A matron could certainly influence the Committee in terms of a teacher's employment performance in these extra-curricular areas, and this gave her a lot of power.[92]

The contact between the ladies and the teachers and the other hired staff was even more circumspect than the relationship they had with the matrons. When one of the staff wanted to make a request of the Committee, she could either inform the matron (who would submit the request by way of her journal) or speak to one of the Monthly Visitors directly and ask her to present the request at the monthly meeting. Although many of the matrons remained for years, other staff members, including teachers, tended to leave after relatively short periods of time. An extremely heavy workload, low wages, and the restrictive institutional regulations explain this rapid turnover.[93]

THE TEACHER

The LBS had a teacher permanently on staff from 1850; before this, one was hired when finances allowed. In 1858, they instituted annual public examinations and hired an assistant teacher. By 1895, three teachers worked in the school and at least one of them needed to have a teaching diploma.[94] The POA school was run by the male superintendent. In 1858, the ladies hired another teacher for half-days to supplement his teaching. A teacher remained until a new superintendent was hired in 1871. A teacher was again on staff in 1880 when the superintendent died. A permanent teacher was added in the new 1893 staff model.

Charity schools were designed to instil good character and to train the children in useful work skills and industrious habits as much as to teach them basic literacy. Accordingly, alongside the normal school subjects, teachers were expected to teach practical skills such as needlework and knitting as well as singing, which was considered important to character development. They were also implicated in the children's moral education and were responsible for supervising them outside school hours until 8 p.m.[95] Teachers taught large classes consisting of children at different academic levels with a constant changeover in the group. In both the LBS and the POA, teachers lived in the institution. They were on call from 6 a.m. in the summer and 7 a.m. in the winter, until 8 p.m., with some time off on Saturday and Sunday and on Wednesday evenings. Institutional regulations were very restrictive, and staff, including teachers, were not allowed visitors. Although in the POA one teacher remained for seven years and another for four, and in the LBS one stayed for fourteen and another for five, most of the teachers remained for only one or two years.

OTHER STAFF

The children in both institutions and the elderly women in the LBS helped do much of the housework. Nonetheless, both institutions hired servants, cooks, and laundresses to do the heavy work, and women referred to as "nurses" to oversee the children and sleep in the dormitories. By 1900, to deal with one hundred children, about thirty elderly infirm women, and a number of convalescents, the LBS staff included three nurses, two maids, one cook, two laundresses, and five girls-in-training, besides the lady superintendent, the housekeeper/matron, and three teachers. In addition, a sewing woman was hired when the production of clothing was more than the matron and the children could handle.[96] The POA staff in the same year was proportionately larger. It included two nurses, three servants, one cook, one laundress, a teacher, and a lady superintendent for a home with thirty children.

Many of the workers in the LBS were themselves charity cases, and the ladies used this as a way to minimize labour costs. In the early days, the emigrant agent sent destitute female emigrants to work in the LBS for their board while they waited to secure passage elsewhere.[97] Later, workers were paid their wage in clothing,[98] or worked for free in lieu of paying board for their children in the institution.[99] After 1846, workers who were not inmates and had no children in the institution were paid cash wages, but the LBS tried to minimize their number. After 1858 even women with children in the institution received cash wages, but they were paid lower wages than the regular staff (in recognition of the board cost) and still represented a considerable saving. In a few years from the 1870s, the wage bill was further minimized by having some of the older girls help in the household before their apprenticeships, to train them as "capable and efficient servants," or by apprenticing a few girls directly to the Society for this purpose.[100]

The POA was a smaller institution, and, with no women residents who could double as workers, it had a small paid staff responsible for multiple duties. In 1881, for example, the cook also worked in the laundry.[101] In recognition of this general duty, the wages paid were higher than in the LBS.[102] Even in the POA, however, an effort was made to minimize wage bills by apprenticing girls to the Society to train as servants on several occasions from the 1850s or simply by postponing apprenticeships for several months.[103]

The LBS registers noted most admissions, including workers. They permit us to identify 303 working women. Most were between 25 and 40 years of age. Almost half entered the institution with their children, although this proportion is probably exaggerated by the data for the 1870s when few other workers were recorded. However, admitting women with their children was ideal for the LBS, since as well as reducing costs it enabled the maintenance of some parental discipline. Occasionally children were accepted for admission on the condition that their mother entered as well, but this was neither an official policy nor the norm.

Workers did not remain in the institution for long. A majority of those both with children in the LBS (85) and those without (101) left in less than one year, most within a few months. The 56 women for whom it is impossible to determine a precise length of employment probably also came and went in a very short period. Another fifty workers remained from one to five years. There was a small number, however, for whom the LBS served as an employer for several years. Eleven women remained more than five years, three of them between eight and nine years and one for fourteen. Several factors were at play in this rapid turnover. Some of the women seem to have used the LBS as a way to get short-term help, as a period of training, or to secure admission of their children. The heavy workload was almost surely an additional factor. So too were the strict rules of conduct. No tobacco or alcohol was allowed on the premises, and workers could be dismissed for rough language or disrespectful conduct. They could leave the institution only once a week, and then only for a few hours; they were never allowed visitors. Although these conditions were similar to those of regular resident servants, they posed difficulties for women accustomed to autonomy. There were constant references to drunkenness and to discipline problems, especially on the way home from church or on their weekly outings. The matron regularly used her journal to appeal to the Committee for compassion and leniency in the case of women who were faithful workers but had a weakness for alcohol. She also often requested bonuses for staff (such as a new dress) in recompense for extra work done during spring cleaning or during bouts of illness in the institution.

On several occasions, the LBS ladies demonstrated the same concern towards the institution's ill or elderly teachers and workers as they did for matrons. In 1847, they offered to care for a former teacher who was ill, and several ladies sent special bedding for her.[104] In 1889, a former laundress returned to the institution "to claim the shelter of its roof" when she was dying of consumption,[105] and in 1894 the ladies paid to send another laundress, who had worked for them for several years and was described as "worn out and ill," to the Murray Bay Convalescent Home.[106] In 1895, a woman who had worked as head nurse for six years was sent on a paid vacation to visit her family in England. She was also given a two-week bonus and money to buy presents for the other nurses.[107]

Although a large number of Montreal ladies were associated with these two Montreal child charities, for the majority this was a short and basically public association. The elaborate and careful record-keeping systems these incorporated Societies introduced to respect their Constitutions and maintain public support, enabled us to examine the work involved in managing a private charity and the extent to which individual members participated in this. An analysis of length of membership, attendance at monthly meetings, subcommittee work, visitor duty, and fund-raising has shown that a small number of dedicated, mostly long-term managers were responsible for much of the work; in this they were assisted by a larger group of managers who were involved in a lesser way or helped in a specific area such as fund-raising. Nonetheless, the majority of members were largely uninvolved in the hands-on work of charity management. The constant turnover as a result of short memberships as well as the minimal investment of time by many others often led to a scarcity of volunteers for crucial tasks such as visiting the institution and fund-raising, and made the management of these two institutions more difficult than it would otherwise have been. This caused funding problems and left the brunt of the work on those ladies who were dedicated to the cause. Many of these active members held the position of Directress at some point. The organizational structure centralized power in the hands of the Directresses and the duties of each position made many members hesitant to take on these roles. This centralized structure was in the process of changing by the 1890s as new subcommittees assumed ongoing duties and helped to democratize the Committees. A few policies led to debate and some conflict, including the admission of board cases and children with both parents in the LBS and of non-orphans in the POA, but the main tension resulted from the Committees being nondenominational and the Anglican Church holding an inordinate amount of influence. As with policy issues, the ladies found compromises to resolve this and placed a lot of emphasis on the inclusivity of their Committees by mid-century.

The ladies' conservatism led them to introduce structured rules for the internal management of the charity homes to be followed by the hired staff. The hierarchy between ladies and their staff was clear despite the fact that the matron was largely responsible for the children's care and creating a home-like atmosphere. At this point we will turn our attention to the internal management of the charity homes and the interface between the Committees and the poor families who appealed to them for help. The next chapter examines admission into these institutions and changes to services over time.

4

Admissions
The Children and Their Families

The Protestant Orphan Asylum and the Ladies' Benevolent Society were both formed early in the century to care for the growing number of children left orphaned or in need of help as a result of epidemics, immigration, or economic dislocation. Given that the Committees aimed to shelter these children and to create a wholesome environment for them, the institutions were basically protective asylums as described by Timothy Hacsi in his work on American orphanages.[1] Nonetheless, they served two other roles: that of religious salvation through Protestant instruction and example; and that of social regulation through the training and (re-)education of destitute children and the inculcation of Protestant middle-class values. It is important to note, however, that these traditional charities aimed to train and "socialize" working-class children according to middle-class values, not to create *bona fide* middle-class children. They were thus protective but minimalist and had no aspirations of providing social mobility for these children.

Examining the actual circumstances under which children were admitted, cared for, and discharged is the best way to understand the institutions, how they worked, and their interaction with families. The next three chapters do this using admission registers, supplemented by information in the minutes of Committee meetings, the matron's or superintendent's journals, and the annual reports. In the present chapter these sources are used to highlight the situations under which families placed their children in a charity, the children's general characteristics, and the admission criteria implemented by the Committees, as well as changes to these over time.[2]

Although it is difficult to ever know what life was really like for the children who found themselves inside the walls of an institution such as these ones, the same sources can help us gain some appreciation of their experience. This is the focus of chapter 5. The discussion in chapter 6 examines the tendency for children with parents to return to their families, and the placement of other children as apprentices or through adoption as well as modification to placement policies.

The discussion in these chapters also reveals the interaction of parents/relatives and the charity Committees. At the intersection of power, class, and gender, these charities serve as an excellent window on the existence and limits of working-class agency. Social institutions such as these child charities were an amalgam of power and agency, of conflict and accommodation. The main interaction between parents and the charity Committees occurred around the admission of children to the institutional "homes" and their subsequent departure, which could only occur with the Committees' approval. The application process was structured by the charity's power to determine admission criteria. This was one of the main ways in which social regulation took place, as private institutions defined eligibility and controlled access to services. As figure 4.1 shows, there was a wide gulf between "the parlour and the pavement," and access to help was largely controlled by those under the bright lights of the parlour.

Nonetheless, working-class applicants demonstrated agency by the very fact of applying for aid and, as we will see, often found ways to present their case in the best possible light, thereby managing to circumvent rules. Applying for aid could become a negotiating process and a "carefully orchestrated performance" that involved using the appropriate "language of desert," as Sandra Cavallo has called it.[3] An important part of this "language" was the demonstration of adequate deference and gratitude in recognition that charity was not a right, but rather existed within a "gift" relationship that was part of a complex ordering of social classes. A lack of gratitude was one of the only reasons these charities would refuse a request to re-admit a child, and the Committee Secretary occasionally made a specific note to that effect beside a child's admission record in the institution's register. This insistence on deference and gratitude was yet another component of the ladies' benevolent conservatism.

Figure 4.1 M.W. Ridley, *The Parlour and the Pavement*. Published in *L'Opinion publique* in 1876, this print shows an abandoned mother and child, now homeless, taking momentary refuge on the steps beside the home of a well-to-do family.

THE CHILD RECIPIENTS: GENERAL CHARACTERISTICS

Over the course of the nineteenth century, the POA admitted 939 children, and the LBS, 2,572.[4] From 1900 to 1921 a further 223 children entered the POA and 1,136 entered the LBS. Admissions policies were less restrictive than those of many Protestant child institutions across the country, but some restrictions did exist, mainly connected to parental status, age, religion, and residency.

The POA initially used the term "orphan" loosely to refer to any child in need of care. This changed in 1832 with the opening of the LBS to care for destitute widows and their children. After 1832, the POA used a very precise definition of "orphan," refusing children with any living parent. They would make an exception to this rule only in extraordinary circumstances. The LBS, on the other hand, was specifically designed for the children of destitute widows, and accordingly destitute single-parent children were always given preferential admission. But if space permitted – and increasingly over the century – the Committee admitted other children, including children with working parents (as boarders). After 1883, when the LBS was certified as an industrial school as well as a charity, children who had become wards of the state while their parents were in prison and others sent by the Recorder Court or the Provincial Secretary were admitted, and by the end of the century, so were illegitimate children.

From the 1850s, and unlike many private child charities elsewhere in Canada, the LBS, and to a smaller extent the POA, admitted some of what Rooke and Schnell have identified as "alarming or desperate cases." In other Canadian cities these "abandoned or neglected" children went into poorhouses or Catholic institutions.[5] Given Montreal's religious and ethnic particularities, the city's Protestant elite tried to avoid letting any Protestant child enter a Catholic institution; and since a real poorhouse did not exist until 1863, and even then admitted very few children, these children entered the mainstream child charities instead. Both charities also housed some children who had been abandoned or institutionalized as infants by parents unable to support them. These children in particular lived in the charity homes for long periods of time. Five per cent (121) of the LBS children and 12 per cent of POA children (108) had entered the institution from another child charity, usually the Protestant Infants' Home (which kept children until the age of four or five) after its founding in 1871, or, later in the century, the Foundling and Baby Hospital. Several children made the transition from the Infants' Home to the LBS, and then to the POA, as their parental situation changed.

Children with various disabilities were admitted to both institutions as long as they met other admission requirements, but neither institution was equipped to provide specialized care. The POA ladies taught one hearing-impaired girl, but normally they attempted to send these children to specialized institutions if acceptable payment arrangements could be made.[6] The

POA Secretary referred to the number of children who were constitutionally weak in the 1897 Annual Report, focusing mainly on three boys who were in constant pain and walked with crutches. The ladies had organized special manual training classes for them, both at the Mackay Institute and inside the POA, but feared that "infirmity will prevent them, in a measure, from earning a livelihood," indicating that "their future destination is a problem the ladies have yet to solve."[7] The Committee continued to worry about where they would be able to find situations for these boys once they were too old to remain in the Home. Looking back in 1904, they told supporters that the boys had been very delicate and helpless when admitted but that all three had been placed by 1903. Two of them were working as mechanics and the third worked on a farm.[8] It was a great relief for the Committee when positions were found, but these boys reappeared in the minutes for years needing additional help and support (which the Committee never failed to give them), since their work did not tend to put them in positions where they could advance financially.[9]

Through these cases the POA Committee showed its compassion for the children who had been in their care. We find no evidence of the imposition of cultural notions of "normalcy" as discussed by Veronica Strong-Boag,[10] although the Committee did begin to refer to the "limits" of inheritance in their twentieth-century reports, as the following comment from 1904 suggests: "we, who are parents, realize the difficulties [of child-rearing]; how immeasurably then are these difficulties increased in a large community of children whose antecedents and inherited characteristics are to us, in many cases, a closed book."[11] By 1916, a much clearer awareness of this type of eugenics-related fear is evident. In their industrial school contract that year, the LBS Committee negotiated a specific clause that would allow them to restrict the access of what they called "mentally-deficient and objectionable" children.[12] It is possible that this was more an attempt to secure some flexibility in terms of admissions than anything else, but the awareness of fears connected to eugenics is also evident, and the city accepted the terms.

The age profile of the children in the institutions was a result of a combination of two factors: admission policies that gave preference to children aged from two or three to twelve, and the stage at which families tended to need help. The most common age on entry was six or seven. There was a slight preponderance of boys over girls, a statistic that did not reflect sex ratios in the city, where the ratio of girls to boys was always greater than one. Boys made up 52.7 per cent of children for whom gender is known in the POA and 56.6 per cent in the LBS. In the LBS, the imbalance was particularly significant from 1880 to 1900, when the percentage of boys increased to 60 per cent.

Some of this imbalance, at least in the LBS, was because girls could also be admitted into the Hervey Institute, which, as a norm, did not take many boys. Gender roles also appear to have played a part in this, given that families tended to be more likely to keep a girl at home than a boy because young girls were more useful in domestic labour as well as a wide range of household tasks, including child-minding.[13] Added to this was the general perception that boys were "more difficult of management than girls because they are naturally less tractable."[14] This perception seems to have encouraged some families to give up boys more readily than girls. For their part, the ladies on the two Committees certainly believed that boys were more troublesome, and they made many more references to boys having discipline problems and running away.

Almost all of the children in these two charities were Protestant, and neither charity ever knowingly admitted a Catholic child. On the few occasions where Catholic children were admitted by mistake, they were discharged as soon as the error was discovered. In the LBS, even children with one Catholic parent were refused admission after 1888 on the advice of the institution's lawyer.[15] In one of the few discussions the LBS recorded about the admission of Catholics, the ladies decided that Catholics could not be admitted since even Protestants were sometimes refused due to a lack of space, and their first commitment was to their own community.[16] Above all else, the refusal to admit Catholics represented a refusal to use relief work for proselytizing, a reticence that was explained only by the fact that Protestants wanted to avoid Catholic retaliation.

The number of Anglicans among the children, especially in the LBS, is of particular interest. Although, according to the Census for 1851–91, the proportion of Anglicans in the city's Protestant population ranged from 40 to 43 per cent, 58 per cent of the children in the LBS or 69 per cent of those for whom we know religious affiliation were Anglican.[17] Other denominations are under-represented in relation to the city's religious profile, the next largest group of children being Presbyterian.

Despite the fact that both Societies were officially nondenominational and ministers from the two main Protestant churches presided at the annual meetings, the Anglican Church had a disproportionate influence in both charities as we saw in the last chapter. The leadership of staunch Anglican families, such as the Ross-McCord family in the POA, for example, was one factor in this. So too was the fact that the matrons, who led family prayer in both institutions, were always Anglican and the liturgy used was that of the Episcopal Church. Equally important, though, was the fact that the Rev. W.B. Bond, associated first with St George's and then Christ Church Cathedral, was very pro-active, visiting both institutions weekly for more than thirty years until his duties as Bishop made this difficult. Few other clergy undertook this task. Not being in a position to establish a network of charities like the Catholic Church, this was one way of integrating the child charities into his sphere of influence, both ensuring that children of his parish would be well-received and imprinting the stamp of Anglicanism on public space.[18]

The POA Committee did not appear to be concerned about this overtly Anglican influence, but the LBS Committee definitely saw it as a potential problem. Given their history of Presbyterian members leaving the Committee in protest from 1844 to 1846, they were conscious of any appearance of Anglican power. They discussed the situation in 1876 and resolved to speak to Rev. Bond. At the next meeting, however, they reversed this position, deciding to take a less confrontational approach – instead of asking Rev. Bond to visit less, they invited other clergy to attend as well.[19] Few did, other than city missionaries. On the other hand, the careful choosing of Anglican and Presbyterian ministers to preside at alternate annual meetings began at that point, giving at least the public impression of non-denominationalism.

It is possible that the Protestant poor were disproportionately Anglican, but the influence of the Anglican Church in these institutions is almost surely relevant to this religious profile. Possibly this visible Anglicanism might have discouraged the poor of other denominations from applying for aid. It is equally possible that it encouraged some families to identify themselves as Anglican in a deliberate bid to make their application more acceptable. Finally, a family in an Anglican congregation would have had access to the important web of information and contacts that were often crucial to securing help. Church visitors, ministers, and missionaries served as an unofficial information and referral network. They helped guide families to the service most likely to help them and often acted as spokespeople to recommend admission. Without these contacts, families had to rely on information from neighbours until the SPWC was formed in 1881.

Interestingly, the religious affiliation of a substantial number of children is unknown. In the POA this is largely a problem of data collection since denominational information was provided very irregularly. The recording of religion in the LBS records, however, was extremely precise. Membership in thirteen different denominations was noted, and many entries included references to specific churches and ministers, many of whom would have made the admission application on the family's behalf. With such precise information for more than 2,000 cases, it is unlikely that the 432 unknowns were mere omissions. It is more likely that a good number of these families had no connection to a specific church or denomination. This explains the concern Bishop Bond raised in the 1890s about the number of city poor without a church affiliation!

A large number of the families needing help were recent immigrants, who were not yet well-integrated into local community structures such as churches, and were without a well-developed kin network or family economy on which they could depend. The POA register does not systematically include information on origin since the orphanage did not use a residency rule, admitting children from across the province, from elsewhere in Canada, and even from the United States. Many recent British immigrants were admitted, including groups of children in both 1832 and 1847, although by 1885 the Committee told the Emigrant Agent that children should have been in Montreal "at least for a few months."[20] In years when there was room in the orphanage, the Committee advertised at both the Anglican and the Presbyterian Synods that they were "happy to receive orphans from rural areas."[21]

The LBS was much more restrictive, introducing a two-year residency rule in 1860 and using it to refuse several recent immigrants as well as children from elsewhere in Quebec.[22] This concern with residency explains why origin is specified in the register for 2,321 children or 90 per cent of cases. Despite the residency rule, a large majority of these children (1,591 children or 69 per cent) are listed as from the British Isles, almost half of them from England. Some of this is probably a result of the way data was recorded. Although by the end of the century the column "country" clearly indicated a child's place of birth, in earlier years it often referred to nationality rather than birthplace.

As a result, it is probable that some Canadian-born and even Montreal-born children are incorrectly represented as immigrants in the register. Over the century only 14 per cent of children are listed as Canadian and 12 per cent as from Montreal, but by the last twenty-year period from 1880 to 1899, 28 per cent of the LBS children were Montreal-born while another 24 per cent were Canadian-born. Still, during this last twenty-year period, 41 per cent of children were listed as from the British Isles, even though the proportion of British immigrants in the Montreal population had dropped to only 12 per cent in the 1891 census and only 9 per cent in 1901.[23] It appears that even at the turn of the century many recent immigrants, possibly with no kin to help them, were still facing problems adjusting to a new city and its ever-changing economy.[24]

PARENTS AND KIN

Children were brought to the attention of the Committees, or applications were made on their behalf, in a number of ways. A minister might send a recommendation for a child in his congregation or a Committee member might propose a case that she knew of. Most children, though, were brought to the charity by their parents (usually their mothers), other family members, or relatives. Research proves that kin served as the first line of defence against unemployment, death, illness, and poverty and as a support network during immigration or migration.[25] Kin could take in orphaned children, care for the children of parents hospitalized or jailed, find work for adolescents, share food, fuel, housing, and clothing, and provide daycare for working widows. Veronica Strong-Boag argues that maternal female kin (aunts and grandmothers in particular) were most likely to be at the forefront of this support network.[26] The Montreal charity files provide many examples of kin networks in action – a number of the children had already received help from relatives, others had siblings who were still with relatives; and, as Strong-Boag found, female kin predominate amongst these helping networks.

Ellen, Thomas, and James F., for example, were admitted into the LBS when their mother entered the lying-in hospital for the birth of another child. They came from a family of five children; their siblings were with an aunt who was also looking after their mother. A widow with children of her own, she was unable to take in the entire family.[27] Sophie and William T. were brought to the POA in 1860 by their grandmother when she was unable to care for them any longer. They remained only two days because the elderly woman found her home too lonely without them and came to retrieve them.[28] Arthur T.'s mother was dead, his father intemperate. He and his younger brother were placed in the LBS in 1865 by their grandfather, who could no longer support them. A sister removed the younger boy one year later, and Arthur, already eleven, was apprenticed.[29] Many examples of community support among the poor – families being helped by "kind neighbours," "friends," or even "strangers" – were also found in the charity records.[30]

The majority of the children in the POA did not have kin networks they might have depended on. Seventy per cent of those for whom we have parental information (or 64 per cent of all admissions) were orphans; across the entire century only four children in the orphanage had both parents still alive. Most of the non-orphans were admitted between 1822 and 1832 before the LBS opened. Afterwards the POA only deviated from its "orphans-only" policy in a few instances when the institution had empty beds, and for cases of particularly destitute one-parent families or children with parents the ladies considered immoral and therefore in need of "rescue." Charles K., described as "a great object of charity," is an example of one of these special cases; so is Fanny H., described as the daughter of a "depraved woman, still living and the ladies hope by removing the child from the haunts of vice, to reclaim and save her."[31] The POA did not have any preference for helping widows; the number of children from families headed by a father was slightly larger than those headed by a mother.

Although the LBS was designed for children from one-parent families and a policy against admitting children with both parents was established in 1839, the policy was not stringently enforced if circumstances were such that it was impossible for parents to care for their children.[32] Over the century, almost 500 children from two-parent families (19 per cent of children) were admitted. One such case, in which the father was hospitalized and the mother, being forced to work out as a wet nurse, was unable to supervise the children, illustrates the type of problems families might face.[33] Nonetheless, 72 per cent of the children in the LBS came from one-parent families, the majority of them from families headed by women who had been widowed or deserted. This over-representation of women is explained both by the LBS's specific mission to help widows, indicative of a clear gender-driven policy, and by the fact that a woman without the resources of a male wage-earner was likely to face poverty. Moreover, according to census data for Montreal from 1851 to 1901, the number of widows outnumbered widowers in all age groups.[34] With no daycare facilities available until the Day Nursery opened in 1888, a widow's dual roles as mother/wage earner competed for her time and energy, often making her situation untenable, especially if her children were too young to participate in income strategies or to be left alone without supervision. The LBS ladies often helped these women by taking in several children to "lighten her burden" and improve her chances of finding work.

Some widows or deserted mothers placed their children almost immediately; others were able to support their families until overcome by illness, unemployment, or other problems. Sarah J. was admitted with her brothers and sister; her twelve-year-old sister who was sick remained with their widowed mother. The LBS register indicates that they had been accepted for admission "at a former date but the Mother had struggled on and managed to keep them until now." Anna L.'s mother supported four children for five years following her husband's death, but when rheumatism forced her to enter the hospital she gave the children into the care of the LBS. She took them out five months later, one assumes as soon as she was out of hospital and up to the workload.[35]

Many widowers or fathers, left to raise children on their own, also turned to the LBS for help. Their children accounted for 22 per cent of cases. The B. family is a good illustration of this. The recently widowed father placed his four children in the institution in 1875. He removed them soon after but was forced to return them. They remained for nine more months before he was able to care for them on a permanent basis. Similarly, Mr M. put his four children in the LBS in 1886 when his wife died. In 1893 he took the two boys out, but allowed the girls to be apprenticed.[36]

For a number of children (16 per cent in the LBS and 11 per cent in the POA), a reference is made to only one parent but no information is provided on their situation.[37] Although it is impossible to know exact numbers, the category probably includes some widows/widowers and deserted husbands/wives. But there is a good possibility that it also includes some two-parent families who thought it more prudent not to mention a second parent, given the admission preference for one-parent families, as well as some unwed mothers who did not want to take the chance of their application being rejected on the basis of their status. Assuming this is so, it is an excellent example of the poor designing their admission applications to effectively circumvent the rules meant to control them.[38]

The charity files do not provide systematic information on the occupation of the children's parents. The POA Committee did not see this information as relevant to the admission process, and it is indicated for only 10 per cent of children. From this data we find the orphaned children of a number of skilled workers, professionals, farmers, and clerks as well as those of unskilled workers, seamen, soldiers, factory workers, and domestic servants in the orphanage at some point. Parent occupation was noted a bit more consistently for the LBS. We have data for about 22 per cent of parents, which, while not a very large sample, does give some idea of the occupational strata of families that used child charities. Although a few teachers, shopkeepers, small merchants, clerks, or government employees such as policemen were among them, most of the parents worked in unskilled jobs and almost all were working-class. Most of the mothers worked as domestic servants, laundresses, charwomen, seamstresses, or nurses, all service-related jobs where women could use domestic skills to earn a living.[39] The children's fathers were mostly unskilled workers, often labourers. A few worked in factories or on the railway away from the city. A number of skilled workers were listed, all of them widowers.[40] Several of these men worked in seasonal trades such as construction or as employees in city bakeries; others included a cutter, two hairdressers, and a furrier. Irrespective of their parents' occupation, the children found themselves in one of these charities because their families were facing some type of problem.

FAMILY SITUATION: POVERTY, ILLNESS, DEATH, AND LIFE CYCLE

Veronica Strong-Boag has reminded us that "[t]he fate of all youngsters is inextricably linked to families."[41] We can see this clearly in relation to child charities. For families faced with short-term challenges, placing children in a charity was one survival strategy among those available to them. It helped to decrease family costs and gave parents time to overcome temporary problems or to adjust to the death of a spouse. For those faced with more chronic problems, placing children in an institution was often the only choice they had to ensure survival. Although the institutionalized child carried the main burden of the family's decision – being separated from his/her family and treated as a charity child – the experience was not entirely negative. The institutions were heated, the diet was regular if monotonous, and the schooling and skills-training were potentially advantageous. Nonetheless, placing children in a charity meant applications and explanations, the emotional stress of separation, and probably some stigma; parents and even relatives did not make this choice lightly.

A number of parents applied to the LBS for the admission of their children because they were unable to care for them while they worked. Normally working parents such as these arranged to pay board towards the children's cost. Almost five hundred children were admitted under these circumstances. Their admission was often debated and is discussed in more detail later in the chapter. For the vast majority of LBS children and their families, however, the payment of board was not a possibility. Problems of unemployment, poverty, illness, and death all figured prominently in the explanations given to support admission requests, as we can see in table 4.1, which presents the family circumstances of children entering the LBS.

A large number of children (458) entered the LBS because their families were unable to support them due to unemployment or insufficient income as a result of chronic low wages. In light of the admission policy favouring destitute cases, this is probably also the case for most of the 608 children for whom parental situation is unknown. Another large group (351) were admitted while their parents were ill. Without savings, prolonged periods of illness that reduced income made children a financial burden that families were often unable to manage. Some of these children were in the LBS while their mother recuperated from the birth of another child; others had parents in the hospital.

More than three hundred children came from female-headed families that had been left homeless by the death or desertion of the male wage-earner, and their mothers entered the LBS with them. Some of these women worked in the institution as cooks, laundresses, or nurses; others simply needed a period of convalescence and rest. Most only stayed for a short while, leaving

Table 4.1
Family circumstances of child recipients on entry into the Ladies' Benevolent Society, 1832–99

Parent situation	Number	%
Works	499	19.4
Unable to support	458	17.8
Health problems	351	13.7
Mother in the LBS (homeless)	306	11.9
In jail	82	3.2
Family problems	98	3.8
Moral reasons[1]	170	6.6
Total known	1,964	76.4
Situation unknown	608	23.6
Total cases	2,572	100

[1] Refers to children for whom parental "immorality" was given as the major cause for admission.
Source: LBS, *Register*, *Minutes*, 1833–99.

once their health had improved or they found employment elsewhere. When they left, the LBS usually agreed to keep their children as boarders (despite the rule discouraging the admission of boarders). It is probable that this was a deliberate strategy for at least some of these women – entering the institution as a worker for a short time in order to circumvent the board rule restrictions and secure a cheap and safe boarding place for their children. If so, this is an excellent example of agency on the part of poor mothers. Still, all of these women and their children were homeless and are among some of the most tragic of the LBS cases.

James L. and his mother are a typical example of the difficulties such families faced. James entered the LBS with his widowed mother in January 1852. She left when she found a job in service three months later, but was again in the LBS from May to November 1853, at which point both mother and son left. Unable to support him, she returned James to the LBS a year later in November 1854. At age eleven, he finally went home in December 1855.[42] This was his last entry in the register, and we can assume that his mother succeeded in supporting the family, probably with his help.

Another small group of children (82) were cared for by the LBS while their parents were in jail, or were admitted with no information about their parents other than the fact that they were considered immoral, or that the children had been abandoned or were neglected (170). This was the case with close to 10 per cent of children in the LBS whose circumstances were known and 12 per cent of the non-orphans in the POA. Most of these children had been found and brought to the charities by ministers, bible women, missionaries, or Committee members. A few had been abandoned by parents unable to cope with the burden of child care under difficult circumstances, and the minutes and register include descriptions of children huddled under doorsteps, dressed in rags, famished, and in various states of disarray. However, some of these children were probably neither abandoned nor neglected; rather, they lived with parents who did not meet middle-class ideas of morality, or were found on the street, possibly scavenging for material that could help supplement family income. Despite the ladies' concern about parental "immorality," most of these children eventually returned to their parents.

Other diverse family problems, such as step-parents refusing to provide for children or mistreating them, were common. So too were cases of parents having left the city temporarily in search of employment. All of the circumstances pointed to situations in which families were unable to care for their children and turned to the charities for help with this, either temporarily or for a longer term.

Family life cycle was also a determinant factor in the placement of children in a child institution. Occasionally families would place one child, and then another when the first one left, a sort of revolving door; but, for the most part, siblings entered the charities together. More than half of the children in both institutions (52 per cent in the POA and 68 per cent in the LBS) had brothers and sisters in the institution with them. Available data does not allow us to determine exact family stage for all families, but indications point to a preponderance of relatively recent and small families with few, if any, children of working age. While families known to have more than four children represented only 13 per cent of admissions to the POA and 18 per cent in the LBS, a large number of children (44 per cent in the POA and 52 per cent in the LBS) had specific references to one or two siblings. For many children (43 per cent in the POA and 30 per cent in the LBS) there is no reference to any siblings, although only a few were clearly identified as an only child. This impression of families in their early stages is reinforced by the large number of children admitted while their mother recuperated from the birth of another child and by the fact that most of the mothers who entered the LBS with their children were in their late twenties or early thirties.

CHANGING ADMISSION POLICIES AND NEW SERVICES

Both of these charities were created early in the century. The founding Committees identified the services that were needed as they understood the situation in the 1820s and '30s, and based on their evaluation of what was best suited to solicit community support for their cause. As the city's economy industrialized, families with different problems began applying for aid. Although neither charity changed its overall orientation, over the course of the nineteenth century and into the twentieth both adjusted some of their admission policies in response to these new needs, and in this way poor families were moderately successful in influencing admission policies.

Four of these changing services or policies stand out as worthy of analysis. First, the child charities' response to major epidemics, such as the 1832 cholera epidemic and the 1847 fever epidemic, is important in measuring their overall social role in the city. Second, the admission by the LBS of children whose working parents were able to pay board was problematic for a charity specifically designed for destitute cases, but their need for shelter was undeniable and was not being adequately addressed. Another gaping hole in the Protestant charitable network was the lack of any reformatory institution. The LBS took the first step towards addressing this when it was certified as an industrial school for non-delinquent, "endangered" children in 1883. Finally, early in the twentieth century, the POA added an important service to the city network when it established a convalescent wing for both women and children (1910–21) following the closure of the Typhoid Emergency Hospital. These four special services are considered next.

EPIDEMICS AND SPECIAL ANNEXES

Crises such as recurring epidemics brought the charities to the fore. During the cholera epidemic in 1832, the POA admitted twenty-three children, coordinating the effort with the Friendless Emigrant Society through Peter McGill. A donation from the latter group enabled them to rent the upper floors in the building adjoining the orphanage to receive the children. Six children died, but the rest seem to have been subsequently shifted into the main institution or returned to families/relatives.[43] Three years later, four children were sent to Mr Scott in Lanark to be apprenticed to families in his neighbourhood.[44] This was an unusual procedure used again only in relation to the 1847 fever children; it is possible that the four had been cholera admissions, but this is unclear since these children were not clearly marked in the register. In the end, the POA was unable to cope with the massive need during the epidemic, especially among widows and their children. As a result, some of the women associated with the POA and/or the former Female Benevolent Society formed the LBS. The latter sheltered needy women and children and worked in coordination with the Citizens' Committee to run a soup kitchen during the crisis.[45]

During the 1847 typhus fever epidemic, the need was even greater. Although the state had assumed some responsibility for immigrants with the opening of the Quebec immigrant hospital, the Marine Emigrant Hospital, and the quarantine stations at Grosse Isle and other port facilities, the 1847 Irish famine immigration saw costs skyrocket as ship after ship arrived at Grosse Isle with fever on board. Some sick immigrants continued on to other entry points such as Montreal. The government now faced the problem of dealing with the large number of helpless orphans left alone when their parents died. In July 1847, the Grey Nuns and Bishop Bourget wrote to the Executive Council indicating their readiness to assume the care of the Irish Catholic orphans in Montreal on payment of a monthly stipend per child. In his letter, Bishop Bourget pointed out the main advantage of this model – that Church institutions would "relieve the Government from the expense of building or hiring a building for their [the orphans] reception."[46] The government readily agreed to the proposal.

The POA had admitted thirteen orphans over June and July but feared their presence endangered the health of the other children.[47] They wrote to the government requesting support, offering to take in Protestant orphans if paid actual costs, assuring Council that they would use the "utmost economy … in carrying out this arrangement."[48] Clearly unwilling to make an undefined financial commitment, Council recommended that Protestant orphans be placed with Protestant religious societies on the same terms as those agreed to by the Grey Nuns. This was done in Quebec City, but in Montreal where private charities, not the Protestant churches, had assumed responsibility for child welfare efforts, it was not a workable solution.

In the end, the POA reached an agreement with the Executive Council for per-diem payments on the same terms as the nuns with an authorization for additional funds to pay for medical assistance.[49] They used this separate funding to set up a special annex in rented premises on William Street near the docks (the main orphanage building was a few blocks away on St Antoine at the time).[50] A total of ninety-five orphans were admitted to the annex. The government had agreed to pay for the children until they went to rural apprenticeships, but directed that this should be done as quickly as possible.[51] Within one month they began to pressure the POA Committee to place the children. To ensure compliance, in October (after only five months) they ordered the POA to send the children to the Immigration Commissioner or to accept a reduction in the agreed-upon payment to one-third its original level.[52] The ladies refused to turn the children over to another group once they had been admitted to their care but proceeded to find placement homes for them as quickly as possible.[53]

As a result, most of the William Street children remained for only a few months or until they had recuperated sufficiently to be placed. To find situations for so many children so quickly, the POA used a method they would never use again – they sent the children in groups of five to seven, along with indenture forms, to contact persons in rural Quebec and Ontario. These people arranged to place the children with farmers in the area. The POA did not evaluate the final situations.[54] Thus the method circumvented the institution's normal apprenticeship rules, but the help provided for these children while they were stranded in Montreal was nonetheless crucial, and we can only hope that their indenture to families ensured some support until they were eighteen. The ladies convinced the government to provide funds for winter clothing, fuel, and a stove to maintain the William Street annex for the twenty-three children who were too young or too sick to be placed.[55] In May 1848, these children entered the main institution.[56]

The LBS had also written to the government offering to admit children of one-parent families and widows among the famine victims, but the government rejected the proposal.[57] A few children were admitted according to available space, but the lack of any additional funding made it impossible to set up a separate annex. As a result, many widows and non-orphaned children who needed help were left to fend for themselves with some help from the St Patrick's Society or the Protestant churches. In this way, when faced with the problem of large numbers of orphaned children in the immigrant sheds of Montreal, the Executive Council avoided creating government-run facilities. Instead, the state opted to use Montreal's confessional and private aid structure and pay Catholic and Protestant associations a small per-diem amount to care for the children and arrange apprenticeship situations. Furthermore, they carefully minimized government costs by limiting the payments, at least in the case of Protestants, to orphans (refusing to pay for single-parent children) and by restricting the payment period as much as possible. Through this process, though, private child charities such as the POA and the women who ran them asserted their important role and contribution in the public sphere, a role that was not limited to special circumstances such as epidemics.

THE LADIES' BENEVOLENT SOCIETY AS A BOARDING FACILITY

Over the century, the range of services provided by the LBS increased as the ladies became more sensitive to different needs among the city's poor. One of these was the need for an inexpensive boarding facility where working parents could leave their children in safety knowing they would be cared for and educated. Unlike many of the Protestant child charities in other Canadian cities, where some form of board payment or fee was common, both the POA and the LBS were designed for destitute children and neither charged board as a regular admission requirement. In the POA there is no instance of board payment after 1832. In the LBS, board was more common, but this situation led to much debate among the Committee.

Between 1832 and 1899, a little more than one-third of all LBS children paid some fees, never fewer than one-quarter at any point. This became much more common in the last twenty years of the century, when almost half of LBS children (including the seventy children in the industrial school) were boarders. This number and proportion was to grow substantially in the early twentieth century with the increase of both the number of children in the industrial school and the number of parents paying board. Nonetheless, board payment was never made a condition of admission and was mainly used as a way to justify the admission of children from two-parent or working families, both of which were questionable under the LBS Charter.

The LBS Committee discussed the admission of board-paying children on several occasions. Both the by-laws and the Charter specified destitute cases, but the society's precarious financial situation made the possibility of board receipts very attractive, and certainly many families needed this service. Financial considerations seem to have been influential mainly in the 1840s and '50s and again from 1880 to 1921. So many children were admitted as boarders in the first period that, in November 1854, the First Directress reminded the Committee that they were infringing on the policy that gave priority to destitute cases. In fact, some needy cases had been refused admission due to a lack of space. She proposed that boarders be discharged to free space for destitute children. The question was debated again in 1855; the majority refused to discharge children once admitted. The working compromise that was agreed to was to admit boarders as long as this did not jeopardize the admission of destitute cases. Once in the institution, however, board children would be allowed to remain even if the space situation worsened.[58] As they explained when the question was debated yet again in 1885, "the house is a 'Home,' [they] hope in the real sense of the word, and those who are in can not be put out."[59]

The records indicate the source of board payments for 98 per cent of the 919 children for whom board was paid. Government board for the 70 children in the industrial school accounted for almost 8 per cent of these receipts, while churches, national societies, or private individuals paid for 73 children. Importantly, parents or kin paid more than four-fifths (82.4 per cent) of the board the LBS received. Almost all of the working parents who applied to the LBS to admit children paid board for them. More mothers than fathers paid board in absolute numbers, but fathers were more likely to be asked to pay board. Fifty-seven per cent of the 574 fathers paid board, while this was true of only 32 per cent of the 1,271 mothers. In addition, in recognition of their low wages, many widows paid a reduced rate. Nonetheless, board payment was often a substantial part of a parent's wage. The case of Frank D. is fairly representative. His mother paid $3 a month, which was the standard payment for one child. Her monthly wages as a servant were $7.[60]

When a parent had agreed to pay board, the LBS attempted to enforce this payment, occasionally using pressure tactics such as removing visiting rights, writing to the parent's employer, or threatening to send children home.[61] In 1857 the First Directress was empowered to enquire about the Society's legal powers to refuse to release a child to parents for non-payment.[62] No follow-up is included in the minutes, but when one mother requested her daughter's release, she was told she must first pay the outstanding board for her son. We cannot be sure if the ladies meant to enforce this or not, since the mother stole the girl out of the institution instead.[63] No other incidents of children denied discharge are recorded, however, and occasionally we find references to parents not having paid board as arranged. Furthermore, no examples were found of a child actually being discharged or apprenticed as a result of the non-payment of board, despite threats to this effect. This is in stark contrast to many other Canadian child charities, where families often lost their right to retrieve children if they defaulted on board payments or were forced to surrender legal control over their children to the charity.[64]

In the twentieth century the number of children having board paid for them increased. This was a result of two factors, both connected to the LBS's dual role as a child charity and an industrial school.[65] First, the number of children admitted into the industrial school grew exponentially, most of them placed there by Montreal's mayor and the city courts.[66] From 1910, they normally represented about half the institution's children. As more beds went to court children, fewer were available for children placed by their parents. Thus space became a problem. This was complicated by the fact that, having converted some dormitories into an indoor playroom and increasingly conscious of the connection between overcrowding and health issues, the LBS

Committee was determined to ideally limit admission to less than one hundred children.

The second problem was financial. Although the society received board payment from the city for the court children, over time, this payment did not come close to covering actual costs. To address this situation, the Committee made the only decision open to them – they increased pressure on working parents applying to admit children to pay board if they were able, ideally at a rate close to the city fee.[67] As a result, the number of parents paying board and the income this represented both increased to the point of being roughly equal with city board. In 1922, for example, these amounts were $5,795 (city) and $5,610 (parents) respectively.[68] This created the unfortunate situation whereby many destitute families wanting to place children in the LBS were forced to apply to the municipal court to have their children admitted into the industrial school at city expense rather than applying directly to the LBS Committee, since they could not afford to pay board. This combination of state and private board led the ladies to fear that they would not be recognized as a charity under the Quebec *Public Charities Act* when it was implemented in 1921, which would have caused them even more financial problems. They were relieved when their status application was accepted.

THE LADIES' BENEVOLENT SOCIETY AS AN INDUSTRIAL SCHOOL

In its earliest legislation aimed at youth protection passed in 1869, Quebec created two separate types of institutions: reform schools (for young delinquents) and industrial schools for children who had not actually committed an infraction but were considered "endangered" because of their marginal circumstances. This included orphans and children (aged fourteen and under) who were homeless or vagrant without any visible means of support or proper guardianship, as well as children known to associate with thieves, or whose parents were in prison. Parents and charitable institutions could also apply for the admission of children they found uncontrollable or recalcitrant.[69] From 1884, amendments extended the scope of the law to include children with parents unable to care for them due to habitual illness, extreme poverty, or bad habits; infirm children; and child victims of violence or abuse; and also lowered the age to include children as young as six.[70] This increased the State's power to intervene in the social realm in the guise of protecting young people. Other amendments shifted much of the responsibility for the institutions from Quebec to municipalities, with mayors given the authorization to place children in the institutions (and pay for their board), a development that would come to have more and more importance for Montreal.

As Michelle Cale notes in relation to England, children were committed to an industrial school not for an actual criminal offence, but for what might be construed to become "unrestrained, unsuitable behaviour."[71] In a similar way, the categories of children subsumed under the Quebec *Industrial School Act* were intrinsically subjective and the distinction between "endangered" and "dangerous" was both blurred and ambiguous. In effect, industrial schools served as intermediate, non-penal institutions for what were feared might be pre-delinquent children. Not only could they provide the requisite protection for the children (away from unsavoury influences) but they could also provide protection for society through re-education, without being officially punitive, although much of the context of the law was very restrictive.

The 1869 Quebec legislation allocated this "child protection" work to the private sector with government financial support and enforced the respect of children's religion; that is, it opted for a private, confessional model. Choosing to apply this mixed public-private charitable model to reformatory institutions and closing the previous state-run ones was cost-efficient. It also reflected contemporary beliefs about the importance of private philanthropy as well as faith in the crucial role religion and morality played in character formation.[72] Private/church institutions with a certified teacher on staff could apply for state certification. If accepted, they received a per-diem payment (from the province and/or the city) and were subject to annual inspection.

Having lobbied for this private, faith-based model, Bishop Bourget had religious orders ready to take on the work, and three Catholic institutions were established in Montreal within a few years.[73] Some individuals in the Protestant community recognized the need to establish their own institutions, and the Protestant House of Industry considered doing this in 1872/73, only to falter over funding problems. Following a special appeal from the government in late 1882 for the community to open the requisite reformatory institutions, the Protestant House of Industry altered its Constitution to this end, but was again stymied by a lack of sufficient funds.[74] Both the POA and the Boys' Home rejected the idea.[75] For the LBS, however, the promise of board payments was a major consideration in the decision to apply for industrial school certification. With a diploma teacher already on staff, it met the only government requirement. Since it had occasionally admitted "endangered" children anyway (including those whose parents were in jail), the new status would ensure board payments for these children while incurring no additional costs. For an institution with severe budget problems by the 1880s, this was a winning proposition.

With its certification as an industrial school in March 1883, the LBS became Montreal's only Protestant industrial school and added an important service for Protestant families.[76] Before this, Protestant children who appeared before the Recorder Court had been placed in Catholic institutions by default. The LBS remained the only Protestant industrial school into the twentieth century, except for a brief period from 1916 to 1920 when the SPWC opened a school for Protestant boys in Sweetsburg. Reform schools were not opened in the Montreal area until the Boys' Home opened a reformatory in Shawbridge in 1908. The Girls' Cottage Industrial School (which really acted as a reformatory) opened in 1911 in St Lambert.[77]

It is important to note that the LBS believed their new status would be temporary, since they assumed that the Protestant House of Industry would open a reformatory in conjunction with their new country building.[78] However, the LBS quickly accepted their permanent status and, on occasion, checked to make sure that the Recorder was sending them all of the Protestant children who came before the court.[79] They also regularly applied to shift children already in the charity onto the industrial school list – that is, to have as many children as possible paid for by the state once they reached the legal minimum age of six.

The LBS therefore functioned as both a child charity and an industrial school from 1883. This situation was not totally unusual for Quebec. Religious orders were often certified to run both reform and industrial schools in the same building, and most admitted some free charity cases as well.[80] In this way their institutions served both a reform and a social welfare function. The difference was one of emphasis. In the Catholic reform institutions, charity cases represented a small proportion of the children. In the LBS, the opposite was true, and the institution's main function was as a child charity. Despite their special status, court children lived in the LBS home alongside the other children under the same regime. When additional manual training was added in the twentieth century to better respect industrial school legislation, for example, all the children benefited from it, not just the court children. The ladies did not consider these children as different from others in their care. From their perspective, all the children in the institution were "endangered" and needed training and protection.

Although the LBS Committee did not make a distinction between the court children and those normally admitted, some of their supporters did. As soon as the first industrial school case entered – a young Scottish girl sent by the police magistrate until her parents could be located – questions were raised. Several supporters opposed the new status and even reduced their subscriptions in protest. The outcry against the reception of these children was such that the LBS First Directress printed an explanation in defence of the decision in three of the city's newspapers.[81]

Undoubtedly there was some confusion among the city's Protestant Anglophones about what exactly an industrial school was. Since the government had not yet shaped a social assistance role, it was unusual for the state to intervene directly other than in cases of crime or deviance. The fact that a city court (or the Provincial Secretary) placed the children for a fixed term, and that the state paid for their board, reinforced the impression that these children were different from and somehow "less worthy" than those who normally entered the LBS. Moreover, although Quebec had passed two separate pieces of legislation that made a distinction between industrial schools (that would eventually be placed under the jurisdiction of social services) and reform schools (that were directly under the jurisdiction of the justice system), in practice, industrial schools in other places in Canada such as Ontario, as well as in the United States, England, and Ireland, tended to be single-purpose reform-oriented institutions run more like reformatories than protective institutions.[82] Thus there was an association between delinquency and government-assisted institutions that created a concern among some of the Protestant elite that the industrial school might admit "suspect" children.

The ladies' sensitivity to these concerns led them to downplay their certification as an industrial school. In their published annual reports they referred to the children as "city board children" and to government payments as board for "destitute children." (Certainly by the twentieth century both of these statements were true!) In fact, they rarely mentioned the industrial school at all except in relation to the inadequacy of board payments, despite the fact that after 1900 between a third and half of the children in the institution at any given time were actually in the industrial school, not the "charity."

It is of interest then to examine what children were admitted under the auspices of the industrial school. The LBS register identifies these children with a specific notation. However, in this they included children they hoped would be shifted onto "the city list" when they turned six and became eligible, even though they were already in the institution, as well as children placed by the SPWC under the same circumstances. These children have only been kept as court cases if a court file such as a renewal or an exit request was located. This type of search was possible since the files for the applications to place, remove, or re-admit children in the LBS Industrial School are still extant in the city archives for the period 1892–1915.[83] Cross-referencing these with the LBS files gives a fairly accurate indication of the number of court children. The estimate is probably low since some of the children placed by the Provincial Secretary might be missed, but indications in the Sessional Papers are that these numbers were small, never more than thirteen.[84] More relevant is the fact that the years 1916–21 cannot be cross-checked.

On the basis of this analysis we find that approximately 461 children were sent to the LBS Industrial School from 1884 to 1921. The number in the first few years was small. Between 1884 and 1899, court cases represented seventy of the 848 children who entered during that period, or 8 per cent of admissions. From 1900 to 1921, however, the number increased dramatically to 392 out of 1,113 admissions, or 35 per cent. The number of court children in the home at any one time was much larger than these numbers suggest since they tended to remain longer than the norm. As we will see in chapter 6, most of the other children remained less than one year, many of them for less than three months. In contrast, most of the industrial school children remained for at least the minimum one-year term. To leave earlier required special permission from the court or the mayor. In actuality, as seen in table 4.2, it was much more common for these children to remain even longer than the initial term. More than half of them had applications for re-admission made on their behalf and remained two years or more, with many upwards of four or five years, and remarkably almost 13 per cent for six years or more.

Table 4.2
Length of stay for children in the Montreal Ladies' Benevolent Society Industrial School, 1883–1921

Number of	1883–99		1900–21		Total	
years[1]	Number	%	Number	%	Number	%
> 1	10	14.3	45	11.5	55	12
1	19	27.1	99	25.3	118	25.6
2	8	11.4	53	13.6	61	13.2
3	7	10	54	13.8	61	13.2
4	6	8.6	43	11.0	49	10.6
5	3	4.3	27	6.9	30	6.5
6–11	15	21.4	44	11.3	59	12.8
Unknown	2	2.9	26	6.6	28	6
Total cases	70	100	391	100	461	99.9

[1] Parts of years have been rounded to the closest year.
Source: LBS, *Admission Book*, 1883–1921.

The profile of the court children mirrored that of children entered into the LBS by their parents. There were roughly equal numbers of boys and girls and the children were fairly young.[85] The average age is 7.8, with the most common ages being six, seven, eight, and nine. Although four of the children were orphans and thirty-eight had been abandoned, most had some reference to a parent. Sixty-nine per cent of the children came from single-parent families, their parents being either widowed or deserted by their spouse. About a quarter had both parents. Most of the parents were suffering from health problems, had inadequate income, were unable to supervise children while they worked, or were homeless. Other than the orphans who would have otherwise gone to the POA, these were exactly the type of children the LBS had always admitted except that the proportion of abandoned children and children with parents in jail was higher.

About a third of the court cases in the period 1892–1915 were brought by the SPWC or the Charity Organization Society intervening on their own initiative or at a family's request. During the same period, families applied for the admission/re-admission of 352 children or 43 per cent of cases. Gradually

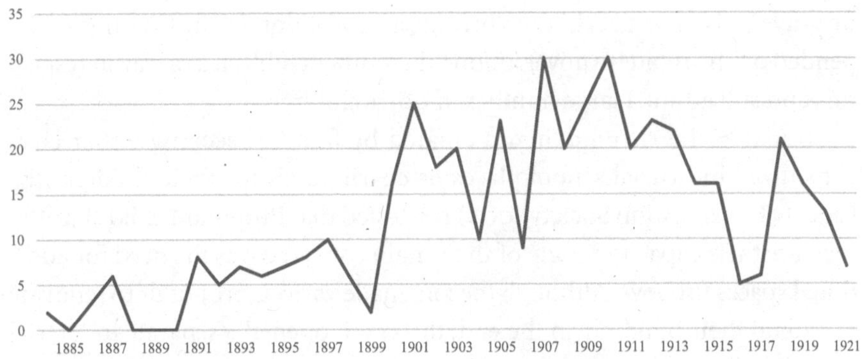

Figure 4.2 Number of children admitted to the Montreal Ladies' Benevolent Society Industrial School, 1884–1921. Source: LAC, Montreal Ladies' Benevolent Society, *Admission Book*, 1883–1921; AVM, 15, Bien-Être Social, série 3, *Enfants sans tutelle*, 1892–1915.

it became more common for mothers and other family members to appeal to the court directly to place their children at city expense; in many years from 1905 to 1915 they brought one-half or more of the applications.[86] As we noted earlier, families unable to pay board to the LBS often applied for admission to the industrial school instead. The city used the widened scope of the law that included illness and poverty to admit these children, especially once oversight for the schools' admissions and payments was placed under the Bureau of Municipal Assistance in 1907/08. Poor families were quick to take advantage. Looking at figure 4.2 we can see that the number of Protestant cases before the court had ranged from an annual low of zero to a high of ten in the 1890s, but increased after 1901 to as many as thirty a year in 1907 and 1909. All of these cases were paid for by the city; the majority were brought by parents.

As the number of court applications grew, the city became concerned about finding spots for these children in the appropriate institutions. This space issue became more urgent when institutions such as the LBS began to refuse court children due to a lack of space.[87] To address the problem, the mayor introduced contracts with the institutions to guarantee that beds would be available for industrial school children when he needed them.[88] In 1912 the LBS succeeded in putting an upper limit of fifty-five spaces into the contract, which was the number of court children they then had (and represented more than half their spaces), but in their 1916 contract, reserving fifty-five beds for court children became an obligation.[89] The Committee depended on the rapid turnover among their other children as a way to respect this and still admit a large number of other children.

To match the rising demand created by families seeking either city-subsidized industrial school places or charity beds for their children, the Charity Organization Society (COS) requested that Protestant child charities increase their capacity.[90] One of their main concerns was the need for additional spaces for boys. Although the LBS made various proposals to renovate or extend their building, in the end, the SPWC opened a separate industrial school for boys called Belmont Home that functioned from 1916 to 1920. From their protective perspective, the LBS ladies fought against this proposal, arguing that the distant country location in Sweetsburg would isolate boys from familiar urban surroundings and make parental visits virtually impossible. The male COS leaders, however, were determined to find a quick solution to the space problem and a new institution fit the bill. They were no doubt also influenced by the "wholesomeness" of the countryside and the appropriateness of having an institution to train boys managed by the male-directed SPWC (rather than a female charity). Although removing most of the boys from their industrial school during the 1916–20 period freed some space in the LBS, they were still somewhat constricted by their contract. While so many boys were going to the Belmont Home, the LBS considered reorganizing their institution as a training school for girls. This idea evaporated when Belmont closed and they had to admit its residents.[91]

The original government board payment was $5.50 per child monthly in 1884. By 1900 this was considered inadequate. In response to repeated requests to increase the amount, the city raised it to $7 for girls and $8 for boys in 1910. This gender differential was based on the assumption that industrial training cost more for boys than girls, and was the norm for all city-subsidized institutions in Montreal.[92] The LBS ran a deficit in 1913 as it tried to make do in the face of rising costs. By 1916, when the board payment was raised to $9 per child, the Committee estimated actual costs were $13.75; this had increased to $20.20 per child by 1919, or more than twice the subsidy.[93] The city raised the board payment to $12 in 1921, still much less than the actual cost, which had increased to $22.41 per child.[94] Again the charity found itself carrying much of the burden of the cost of the industrial school and, in effect, subsidizing state policy. Their wage bill made costs much greater than those of the Catholic institutions, but the city refused to take this into consideration and kept the payments similar to, or even less than, those negotiated with the Religious orders. This was a serious problem for the LBS since coping with the soaring war-related inflation was a major challenge.

One of the complications resulting from its dual role as charity and industrial school was that the LBS, as a private association with close to absolute control over its own space (admissions, policies, etc.), suddenly had to deal with inspectors and city officials much more than previously and was constricted by a legal contract that included directives in these areas. On occasion the managers found that these restrictions challenged their autonomy and a clash between public and private use of their space occurred.[95] Most of these negotiations were with Montreal as the city increasingly assumed responsibility for these institutions. Through this policy Montreal slowly took the first steps to mould a municipal social assistance role, an assistance that (not surprisingly) took the form that was typical of the Quebec system – the placement of children in an institution. Unfortunately, in the case of industrial schools, there was undoubtedly some stigma attached to this form of institutionalization.

THE PROTESTANT ORPHANS' HOME "WITH CONVALESCENT WARDS"

When the POA moved to its new home on Summerhill and Côte-des-Neiges in 1893, they found themselves in a building that was much bigger than they really needed. The Committee was reticent about changing their orphans-only policy, but they began to admit single-parent children after 1903. A new "field of usefulness" opened up when the Typhoid Emergency Hospital closed in 1910 despite the fact that many child patients were too ill to return home. The POA admitted them into their infirmary on the building's third floor. Fever cases were then received from the (Children's) Memorial Hospital, which had opened in 1903. Within a year eleven patients had entered and recovered.[96]

Designed as an infirmary in the building plans, the area had first been used in 1898 when ten children came down with scarlet fever within 48 hours and the hospital could not receive them. At the time the Secretary indicated that it "proved as near perfection as possible."[97] In 1902, the Committee hired a private nurse for four months to care for a former POA boy dying from consumption, during which time he rallied under the influence of the "pure air, good food and careful nursing," despite eventually succumbing to the disease.[98] Another former boy who the Committee learned was in the Grace Dart Hospital with TB was nursed for four months in the ward in 1910. The doctor had advised them that he would live if he went to the sanatorium but would need several months of complete bed rest before that. Once he had regained sufficient strength, they sent him to St Agathe as the doctor suggested.[99]

Convinced that this was an area of service for which their building was particularly well suited, and one that was sorely needed in the city, the ladies proceeded to take steps to alter their charter to take on the new function. To create space, they returned as many of the single-parent children in the institution as possible to their families, "feeling that greater good can be achieved by receiving convalescent children, than in keeping those who have a parent, who can support them."[100] The new charter, secured in 1912, added the care of convalescents as a legitimate function and changed the institution's name to "The Montreal Protestant Orphans' Home" to remove any negative associations surrounding the word "Asylum."[101] A reference to "with Convalescent Wards" was added to their stationery and reports but not the official name. This left the Committee free to alter this function if needed in the future without requiring a change to the charter.[102]

Renovations began immediately to convert one of the large front dormitories into a ward with ten cots, a sitting room, a diet kitchen, and a linen closet. There was also a wide veranda with cots and reclining chairs where "the little invalids can have the benefit of fresh air."[103] This was a more developed application of the Committee's long-term recognition that outdoor air was important for children's health. As Annemarie Adams and David Theodore explain in their work on children's hospitals, this concept was widespread; the Royal Victoria Hospital built outdoor corridors and even wards in tents for sick children, while others were brought out onto the lawn in their beds.[104] In 1913, with 171 patients having used the wards, and others on a waiting list, two new wards were converted.[105] Concern over the safety of the children – especially those in casts – should a fire break out led the

Committee to undertake the expensive construction of a special fire chute from the third floor near the children's convalescent ward, so that they could be wrapped in blankets on a cot to slide down.[106]

Although they originally referred to their new charter as giving them the power to "benefit a class of helpless and suffering children as well as orphans,"[107] many of those admitted were women. In 1912 the annual report indicates that fifty-five convalescents benefited during the year, "practically all of them women without homes to go to when they left hospital and very few of them able to pay."[108] In most years for which data is supplied, the ratio of women to children was three to one. On the day of the annual meeting in 1915, for example, there were seventeen adults and six children in the wards. In the last fourteen months from 1919 to 1920, ninety-two patients were admitted, twenty-three children and sixty-nine adults.[108] Probably this was as much an attempt to secure some self-financing as a function of demand. Orphans were admitted free of charge. Women were asked to pay something if possible; by 1915–16 the fee was $2.50 a week, although many paid nothing. When the wards were reopened in 1919 after being closed for a year due to financial problems, women were asked to pay $8 a week.[110]

Most of the children who were entered into the Convalescent Ward were put in a separate register that no longer exists, but fifteen convalescent cases, most of them early ones, are entered in the regular register. These cases reveal that the children were often older than the norm and many remained for short periods of time while they recuperated. On the other hand, one young girl was a resident for thirteen years, during which time she returned to the hospital for several operations. When she left she was seventeen and in good health. Several other children were cured of rickets and various bone problems or handicaps that made it difficult to walk. They left once they were "walking nicely."[111] In this way, the Ward admitted children who were "convalescents" leaving hospital, but also children with medical conditions that required long-term care, and children with mobility problems that families found difficult to deal with.

The description of the ward's aim given in the 1913–14 Annual Report indicated that working women and girls as well as boys to age ten were admitted "at little expense to themselves (orphans being free), patients may rest and recuperate and enjoy the benefits of fresh air, nourishing diet, and careful nursing."[112] The new service was expensive, as costs for special diets, treatment, dressings, and nurses' salaries were added to the normal cost of food, linens, laundry, fuel, and staff. These expenses forced the Committee to close the Convalescent Wards temporarily in 1917 for the summer despite the great need for such an institution in the city. They did not reopen in the fall as hoped due to the large expenses incurred the year before, one of them, ironically, the special fire chutes.

On 11 November 1919 the service was reopened. Despite having altered their charter, the Committee believed that their normal funds could not legitimately be used for the Convalescent Wards, and that hence the latter must be self-sufficient and not draw on regular operating funds or the Endowment Fund. Given the rising cost of food and wages post-war, this was even more difficult than previously. Their determination to continue the undertaking is shown by the fact that the ladies agreed that each of them would personally donate $100 into a fund as start-up capital. They hoped that this fund, along with an increase in fees for women and the opening of a private room at $15 per week, would be sufficient.[113] Meanwhile, they also talked of selling the building to some other philanthropic group to use as a Convalescent Home, so needed in the city, and then taking the profits and purchasing a smaller house for their work with orphans.[114]

This did not happen, and despite the personal effort they had made to ensure the undertaking's success, the Committee decided to close the Convalescent Ward for good in 1921. Several factors led to this decision. A lot of space had been committed to the Ward, nurses' salaries needed to be paid, and the superintendent dedicated a great deal of her time to overseeing its management. However, at points there were few patients, making the ward a serious drain on both funds and time, and impossible to run as a self-financing entity. Even more important were two additional factors: the demand for admission both from the families of soldiers and from orphans left in the wake of the influenza epidemic meant that the ladies needed to take back a ward in any case. A total of 757 patients had benefited from the service, and while it was open, it filled a pressing need in the city.

THE TWENTIETH CENTURY

We have noted some of the changes that the charities went through in the twentieth century in the above sections. The most important was the growing size of the industrial school inside the LBS and the corresponding impact that this had on the increase in the number of board-paying children in the institution. To some extent these changes balanced each other as many of the former destitute, dependent children were now entered into the industrial school at city expense, but with only half the number of places available and few of them actually free of charge, there were many families left with nowhere to place their children if they could not care for them. Where did these children go? Some went to the Hervey Institute. Although it also normally requested some board payment, its new building on Windsor/Claremont was quite large.

But many also went into the POA, and as a result, the orphanage changed almost beyond recognition in the twentieth century. Although the Committee refused applications from two widows in October 1902, in May 1903 they agreed to an application brought by the COS to admit non-orphans since they had "plenty of room."[115] By 1905 such admissions were increasingly common, and in most years orphans represented a minority of children. In 1908, for example, of sixty children who had been present at some point over the year, only eleven were orphans. A rather discouraged Committee noted in their December 1908 minutes that they were really doing the work of the LBS and the Hervey Institute, and that since both of the other societies charged board while they did not, it was clear why parents preferred to place their children in the POA. They proposed that a board policy should be implemented.[116] In 1912 they passed a motion that in the future only orphans and convalescents would be admitted; at that point only eight of the twenty-four children present were orphans.[117] In fact, the Committee was unable to implement such a policy. In the nineteenth century they would have stood adamantly behind their Charter and Constitution, but now the need to find places for these children was too great. When asked at the annual meeting in 1911 why so few orphans applied to the home, the ladies explained that relatives adopted them and/or that relatives did not like the POA rules about children remaining a minimum of one year and relatives being allowed to visit only once a month, and only if there was no threat of infectious disease in the city.[118] Their places were taken by children with parents, and over the years the total number of these children increased. Many of the 223 children who entered the POA from 1900 to 1921 still came in with their siblings, and the average age was about the same, but they had parents living in the city. This would impact substantially on departure patterns in the twentieth century, as we will see in chapter 6. During the war years the POA worked with the Patriotic League to admit motherless children with fathers overseas.[119] Some stayed for years even once their fathers returned. Alongside these children were, of course, those who had entered the Convalescent Ward.

Despite the elite's association of poverty with immorality, most of the families who applied to the LBS were experiencing problems connected to unemployment, illness, or the death of a wage-earner; a large majority of children admitted into the POA were orphans. As private societies, the Committees of elite women who managed the two child charities controlled access through admission rules; the clearest of these limited aid to Protestants. The LBS Constitution outlined the charity's role as helping destitute, single-parent children while the POA was identified as an actual orphanage; in both cases need drove admissions. In the interaction between charity Committees (especially the LBS) and parents around admission, we have seen that the poor could occasionally design their applications to circumvent restrictive rules. This might mean dissimulating information to present themselves as members of the predominant Anglican Church or as one-parent families, for example; or it might involve mothers entering institutions as workers to secure entry for their children. Thus working-class families demonstrated more agency than their position of relative powerlessness in this area suggests.

Over the century as new needs were identified, the ladies demonstrated a substantial amount of flexibility in adjusting their services or adding new ones, although this often resulted in debate and even dissent within the Committees. Thus the POA contracted with the government of United Canada to admit and care for orphaned children stranded in Montreal during the 1847 typhus fever epidemic, although the state refused to make a similar arrangement with the LBS for widows and destitute children. The LBS increasingly admitted children of working parents who were not in a position to care for their children but were able to pay board for their care, as well as children from two-parent families. The LBS also successfully applied for accreditation as an industrial school in 1883, and began to admit children sent by the

Provincial Secretary or the city Recorder Court. This particular policy shift caused some concern among supporters but the number of court children in the LBS home grew steadily. The twentieth century witnessed the charity Committees consciously asserting their place in the city's Protestant social services network. This was the case with the LBS Industrial School and the way it grew over the century; it was also the case with the POA Convalescent Ward, and subsequently, their cooperation with the Patriotic League.

The next chapter looks at the internal policies the Committees developed in their attempt to create an institutional "home" where children would be cared for, educated, and trained to become useful citizens, and what life was like for the children who lived there.

5

In the Institutional Home

Still the apparently hopeless plodding task goes on quietly but surely, day after day, and little by little the good finds a place, and the children begin to like the new life with all its great changes from their former one, they once thought so hard to bear; and obedience, cleanliness, and order, now become as much a part of their daily duty, as disobedience, dirt, and uncleanliness belonged to them before.

~ LBS, "School Report," 1863[1]

It was in this way that the LBS Young Ladies' School Committee Secretary juxtaposed institutional life's British Protestant bourgeois values with what she understood to be working-class life's "depravity," and explained the slow process whereby children apparently came to adapt to life in the LBS. The ladies believed that the children would benefit from a home-like environment designed to provide them with the education, moral training, and skills they would need in the future. Of equal importance was the ladies' belief in the possibility of religious salvation. The institutional regime was organized with these aims in mind and all aspects of the institution were brought to bear in this process. The building's design, the routine, the activities children carried out during the day, the school curriculum, attendance at church and Sunday school, the work skills they learned – everything reinforced bourgeois values and a religious upbringing.

It is difficult, if not impossible, to ever really know what children made of this experience. This chapter tries, nonetheless, to evaluate life inside these residential institutions and the extent to which the children saw them as homes and accepted the group of people who lived there as a family, if a contrived one. It is important to remember that, in the nineteenth century, many young people, including those from wealthy families, spent part of their childhood in an institutional setting. Even in a boarding school, children must have often felt lonely and isolated from their families, and certainly those institutions ran on a code of obedience and discipline. But a child charity was distinct from that type of institutional setting in that it was premised on class differences – the children in these institutions were poor children, treated as such by wealthy women with their own idea of what children needed to be taught as well as what conditions were "appropriate" for children of a lower class, and what was minimally necessary as "charity." The ladies developed internal policies aimed at creating a "safe" home, but with all the good intentions in the world, they often struggled with the contradiction between their protective instinct towards these children and their parsimonious management style, especially if it was coupled with budget restrictions.

Historians have written about the sense of abandonment, rejection, deprivation, and misery common among the British emigrant children surrendered by parents and sent to Canada where few accepted them; the testimony of many of these children confirms these conclusions.[2] The children in local charities must have experienced some of these same feelings on a lesser scale. The orphans in the POA had lost their parents and were alone in the world unless they had relatives who had then placed them in the charity; most of the children in the LBS had lost one parent and then had been surrendered or deserted by the remaining one – a double loss. A few of the children had lived for periods of time with relatives or neighbours and established new emotional ties – ties that were now also broken. Children with parents or relatives in the city might have been told that their stay in the institution was a temporary measure, but the emotional pain of separation must have been difficult even for them, and it is far from clear that young children could completely comprehend why they had been given by their families into the care of strangers. This must have been particularly perplexing and stressful for those who were placed to enable siblings to remain at home with the family. How did their young minds reconcile why they were the ones chosen for this treatment? The institutional environment, so different from the homes and districts to which the children were accustomed, was not likely to lessen any feelings of disorientation and loss. They came from overcrowded city districts with outdoor pit privies, often from wooden buildings with earth floors, where whole families lived in a room, or worse yet, in an attic or a cellar.[3] They played on back staircases or on dirty streets. They more than likely scoured the city for bits of coal or useable objects. They wore what they could and ate what little was available. Figure 5.1, showing houses in a poor district, provides some impression of what they might have been accustomed to. Finding themselves on the doorstep of one of the charities must have been somewhat intimidating, if only because of the scale of an imposing three-storey brick building.

Figure 5.1 Wm. Notman & Son, *Houses for Mr. Meredith, Montreal*, QC, 1903. Many of the houses in such older working-class districts as those from which the children came were in very poor condition.

Figure 5.2. Wm. Notman & Son, *Ladies' Benevolent Institution, Montreal*, QC, 1909. The home, situated on Ontario Street, dated from 1856. Three additions over the years meant that by 1909 the LBS was a large institution.

The reader will remember the illustration of the orphanage in figure 1.4: a large, somewhat ornate building with a massive oak door that had been the gift of Peter McGill. As was the case with many nineteenth-century charities, it had been built to impress – to assert the elite's role in accepting the social responsibility for charity while imposing their ideals of order and classical beauty. The original LBS building was more modest, but by 1900, three additional wings had been added. Figure 5.2 shows how massive this institution must have appeared to the children who entered it. Inside, the institutions were enormous compared to the homes from which children came.[4] Both of the buildings had a number of large dormitories on the upper floors (for younger children, older girls, older boys), as well as a classroom or two, a large dining room on the main floor where everyone ate meals together, a committee meeting room, a kitchen, a laundry, and rooms for the staff, as well as sundry additions such as a coal cellar and possibly a root cellar for supplies. The buildings had gardens or yards around them and were in the middle of the city's Anglophone upper-class district, in the case of the POA on St Catherine between Drummond and Stanley, and in the case of the LBS, on Berthelet (Ontario) between Bleury and City Councillors. The POA built a larger, more modern building in an even more remote area on the side of the mountain (Summerhill and Côte-des-Neiges) in 1893. There were a number of staff – matrons, nurses, servants, cooks, laundresses, and so on.

Children were immediately faced with the institutional reality when, on arrival, the visiting doctor gave them a physical examination to check for signs of communicable diseases and vaccinated them. They were then washed and dressed in institution clothes. Any child who needed delousing had his or her head shaved; others had their hair cut short to facilitate easy care and reduce the risk of head lice. The rules were explained to them and they joined the regular routine immediately. No transition period was built into the admission process, and nothing official was done to recognize the fact that many of these children had recently experienced a traumatic event such as the loss of a parent.[5] In short, children would need to adapt quickly to not feel too disoriented by the shock of these enormous differences. We know from the LBS School Secretary's comment that they often had trouble doing this and initially found the new environment "difficult to bear." For the children the experience almost certainly functioned as the kind of "emotional frontier" we spoke of in the Introduction where two different ways of "being, feeling, and knowing" collided.[6] New admits would begin their "new" education as soon as they joined the line of children marching to the next activity on their very first day.

The wearing of uniforms could create a feeling of shared identity among the children (or a feeing of being different from other children, as we will see later in the chapter), but for the ladies in charge it was probably driven more by questions of budget – to limit the purchase of clothing and its variety – and seen as a way to impose some uniformity and order on the institution. It is not entirely clear, though, to what extent the children in these two Montreal institutions actually wore uniforms. The first POA Committee meeting in 1823 decided on uniforms, and occasional references are made in the minutes and annual reports to these – the girls being dressed in blue frocks with blue checked pinafores and pink bonnets, the boys in grey with tweed trousers – but they might have been "good day" clothes and other clothing may have sufficed for regular wear.[7]

In the LBS, an attempt was made to have a uniform for times when the children appeared in public, but, due to budget constraints and the large number of children to clothe, children wore whatever clothes were available at other times. Annual reports regularly include requests for second-hand clothing as well as grateful thanks for any donations. This penury of clothing was rather problematic. In many years the LBS matron complained that the boys could not go out as they were "literally naked," that it was impossible to keep the children clean without a change of clothes, that the lack of extra clothes forced her to mend every night while the children slept, or that clothes were "no longer fit to be worn out of doors."[8] When coats and cloaks were made in 1882, children were given the first complete new outfit in a decade. The limited quantity of presentable clothing was particularly a problem on Sundays. In many years, children attended church and Sunday school in rotation since they needed to share clothes, especially in the winter when outdoor coats were necessary. In 1898, the Committee proudly noted that eighty children "dressed warmly" could now attend church at once; the other twenty children were still waiting for coats, caps, and dresses to be finished.[9]

Other than donations, all clothing was made inside the institutions. Regular references exist in the papers of both Societies to fabric being purchased, patterns being cut out by Committee members, and clothing then being made up by either sewing women or the matron and the girls. Ironically, the LBS purchased a sewing machine in 1859 to facilitate this but found that none of the women in the charity knew how to use it. They hired a sewing woman and the First Directress spent a morning teaching her, but this was not very successful. Another sewing woman was hired in 1869 to learn how to use the machine. As bourgeois women, the Committee members were accustomed to labour-saving machinery while the women in the charity or those they hired seemed less so this early in the century.[10] Boots and shoes were equally problematic. At various points the LBS matron suggested purchasing ready-made footwear, and donations were received from companies such as Childs and Scoles or Paton (whose wife was on the Committee),[11] but normally a shoemaker was hired to make them.

THE HOME

Like most Protestant philanthropists, the ladies running these charities modelled their institution on a home and designed the institutional routine and activities on what they understood to be a balance between nurture and an appropriate amount of discipline. In creating this "Protestant" home they emphasized the middle-class values they considered central to child-rearing, such as obedience, order, discipline, cleanliness, respect for authority, and industriousness – values that they believed were often lacking in the children's former upbringing. In effect, they aimed to recreate a Protestant family within their charity "homes" in which the matron and, by extension, the Committee members would assume the duties of mothers. As in any proper Protestant home, education, religion, and morals formed the bedrock of their project, what we could call their "benevolent design." It was in encountering this pattern of middle-class socialization, and the values that underlay it, that the children probably experienced an "emotional frontier," if the material differences between their former homes and the institution had not jolted them sufficiently. The lady managers and the matrons that worked for them had every intention of ensuring that these children learned more appropriate ways.

Religious instruction and moral education were central to this socialization. In fact, in most comments about their work inside their institutional homes, even those about education, the ladies always mentioned religion first. Although it is not surprising that religion was different in Montreal's Protestant child charities from the city's Catholic charities run by nuns, where the training regime and daily life were permeated by religion, it also seems to have been of a somewhat different nature from Chicago's Protestant child charities, where ministers led daily prayers and community churches were actively involved in the charities.[12] To decipher the reasons behind this difference, it helps to approach religion in the institutions from what Marguerite Van Die refers to as "lived experience."[13] We know by their continual invitations for clergy visits that these conservative ladies were more than willing to give the two mainstream churches an important role in their charity homes (like they had in Chicago), but that Montreal churches did not follow through on this. By default, then, the ladies applied the more domestic model that was becoming common among Victorian families, and, with it, the increased role for mothers this implied. As a result, in these two Montreal charities, daily religion was more of a family affair and one in which women (rather than male clergy) played a central role.[14] Family prayers were held twice a day, led by the female matron. This was supplemented by religious instruction as part of the school curriculum, taught by a male or female teacher, depending on the institution.

Children attended both church and Sunday school and ministers or missionaries visited regularly, but most of their religious training was domestic and largely led by women. Even more importantly, community churches, including the Anglican Church, were not directly involved in the charities' affairs, although early in the century some organized charity sermons to help fund-raising and, as we have seen, Rev. Bond visited weekly until he became Bishop. Dorcas associations made occasional donations of clothing but normally limited this to individual children or women for whom their church paid board. They did not take on the responsibility for making all the children's clothing like church groups did in Chicago, for instance. Although not as visibly religious as Catholic institutions, where religious symbols would have been on prominent display, these Protestant charities clearly focused on creating a domestic atmosphere where Christian nurture could flourish. Education and work were also central components of a proper Protestant upbringing; these activities took up most of the children's day.

Despite the ladies' desire to create a real "home," institutional life was highly regimented and routine. Part of this was necessary to maintain order in an institution with a large number of children (the POA usually had about 30 children but the LBS had as many as 110); part of it was driven by the determination to instil regular habits and values. Children followed a daily schedule of prayers, meals, school, and work, a routine that was rigorous and unchanging except on Sundays and holidays – and that began at 6 a.m. Days started with morning prayers, then breakfast, after which children made their beds and swept their rooms. School was scheduled from nine to noon followed by dinner at 1 p.m. After an hour of play, school resumed from 2 to 4 or 4:30 (LBS) or 2 to 5 (POA), followed by another play period until supper at 6. Evening prayers took place before bed at 8 p.m. Minor alterations in the winter had children rising later and retiring earlier. On Sundays they attended church and Sunday school. Bells rang out the time and signalled the different activities. It was the teacher's job to march the children to the appropriate room in orderly style and to keep them quiet. Silence was also the norm during meals, at least by the end of the century. The emphasis on rule, order, and quiet functioned as a form of moral regulation. This was not an environment in which the spontaneity and energy of childhood could find much place. There was certainly little room for freedom, individuality, or expression. Many of the dangers of the working-class street were absent, but so were the joys of laughter and the sounds of running feet, though some of the children probably developed close emotional ties with the other children in the institution. Outings and celebrations became more common by the last twenty years of the century, and throughout the period both charities made a concerted effort to create "family" events around holiday meals such as Christmas and Easter.

Determined to protect the children from what they saw as unsavoury and unhealthy influences, and especially to minimize their exposure to disease and infection, the ladies isolated the children in the institutional home.[15] After 1850 and into the twentieth century, the children attended school inside the institutions and for the most part had very little contact with other children, except at Sunday school and during occasional outings. Parents were allowed to visit, but these visits were limited to once a week on Saturday afternoon. Complaints about visitors bringing too many sweets and children being sick afterwards led both charities to limit parental visiting rights even further in the 1890s – in the POA, to once a month; in the LBS, to twice a month.[16]

The history of institutions, particularly child institutions, shows us that this isolation potentially represented one of the main threats to the children's well-being. How safe were children inside private institutions? The visiting patterns of the lady managers assured that they had some control over the conduct of the staff. Although discipline and obedience were core values in the institutional training mission and were considered necessary to maintain some modicum of order, determining an acceptable level of discipline, or the punishment associated with it, could be problematic. The sources for these two institutions indicate that punishment existed (and was defended by the Committees) but that excessive force was not tolerated. Although no POA staff lost their jobs for using excessive force, in 1848 a boy accused the superintendent of "undue severity and harsh treatment." The superintendent was exonerated after investigation.[17] The fact that in the LBS, however, both a teacher and a matron were dismissed for what was referred to as "cruel" treatment points in the direction of vigilance on the part of the Committee to protect the children.[18] The School Committee investigated the case of another teacher, but found that she was "assiduous in her endeavours" and had not used excessive discipline to maintain order.[19]

These early cases had been raised internally, but in the twentieth century outsiders made charges of excessive use of force against the LBS on two occasions. In 1907 a father brought a lawsuit against one of the LBS nurses for the ill-treatment of his son. The matter was dealt with by lawyers, and although the Committee and their advisors requested an investigation, they also expressed confidence that the nurse had "only done what was necessary to maintain discipline in the Institution."[20] Soon after, in 1910, a sewing woman complained to the SPWC that LBS children were being whipped. In response to this case, the Committee decided to get a regulation school strap (to replace the piece of rubber hose staff had been using) and told staff that no child was to receive "more than a few palmies."[21]

It is clear from these examples that physical punishment was used in the institutions, and that although the Committees initiated some form of investigation when cases were brought to their attention, they had a tendency to defend the use of what they considered "reasonable" force. In 1889, the POA Committee increased the scrutiny over their staff by adding a specific rule requiring the superintendent to record in his journal any time he used severe punishment. However, since they specified that judicious punishment was allowed, this was a matter of interpretation.[22] The next year the ladies highlighted the balanced treatment they aimed at when they applauded their matron and superintendent, the Campbells, who "by their judicious discipline, tempered with kindness and love, render the children under their care useful and happy."[23]

There are, of course, many ways to maintain order and to discipline children. As mothers, Committee ladies would have been aware of how effective psychological techniques such as praise or disapproval could be. It is probable that these methods as well as the removal of privileges were used inside the institutions to replace physical punishment on occasion.[24] Certainly the POA Committee members used these methods to encourage runaway apprentices to return to their placements. In the same way they used the encouragement of good behaviour prior to children leaving for their apprenticeships to try to ensure that problems did not occur.

This environment, with its isolation, its routine, and the emotional strain of separation, possibly even alienation, caused a number of children, especially boys, to run away.[25] Forty-five boys ran away from the LBS but only nine girls, while twenty boys and five girls ran away from the POA. In the case of the LBS, most runaways returned to their families and this appears to be directly linked to adjustment problems or simply missing their family. For the POA, however, where most children did not have family, the fact that boys might have felt more comfortable alone in the streets than girls did, or found it easier to secure employment, probably played a role in this gender imbalance. We will see later that boys, at least in the LBS, ran messages for the Committee and therefore were out on the streets alone occasionally, while girls never were. This gave boys both an opportunity and a knowledge base to run away that girls, tucked away inside the institutional home, lacked.[26]

Sometimes, though, children ran away for short periods of time simply looking for adventure. The ladies found this particular type of agency on the part of the children problematic, even unacceptable, if it occurred too often. In the LBS, they simply sent the children home. This was not an option for the POA, and there was a limit to how much of this behaviour the ladies would accept. In 1908, when several older boys ran away repeatedly and compounded the situation by taking younger ones with them, the POA Committee applied to the Recorder to send them to the Sherbrooke Reformatory. Recorder Weir refused, proposing he would meet with the boys weekly to influence them to improve their behaviour.[27] When two of the same boys enticed others to leave with them yet again and this time stole money, the committee took decisive action and the boys were sent to Sherbrooke. Within a few months the boys wrote to the Superintendent asking her to send them warm winter undergarments and stamps so they could write again.[28] Normally the Committee helped children with any request after their departure, but on this occasion, they refused. Agency in this form on the part of older boys, with the disruption it caused and the bad example it set, was not the type of behaviour the ladies were willing to accept or encourage.

CONDITIONS IN THE INSTITUTIONS

The ladies believed that charities called for healthy but simple conditions. Depending on private funds for most of their income, they were always conscious of possible criticisms of extravagance; and with budgets that were often barely at the break-even point, economy and thrift, even parsimonious management, were obvious in all aspects of the charity households. Certainly what one might call equipment or furnishing was minimal for a long time. Scattered references to this provide some idea of just how minimalist. In 1851 the house the LBS was renting at the time had no running water, a situation that the matron referred to as "utter folly" for a large institution facing a Canadian winter.[29] For most of the century, the LBS also had problems in their dining room; insufficient tin mugs and spoons meant that children took turns eating. Knives and forks were not purchased until 1866, and then only for the older children. It is not clear how much they were used, since as late as 1908 the Visiting ladies recommended that children be taught to eat with knives and forks rather than spoons.[30] Even the POA, which tended to be more financially secure, shared this type of problem, particularly in terms of basic furnishings. References exist in both institutions in several years to children being forced to stand either during meals or during school due to a lack of furnishings such as chairs.[31] Granted, it was probably difficult to maintain furniture in institutions with so many children using it over many years. The need for bedding and for clothes was ongoing in both charities, although some of these problems eased up by the 1880s.

Despite the difficulties the two Committees had furnishing their institutions, they took nineteenth-century notions of sanitation – the fear of dirt and contagion, the need for fresh air and ventilation, the importance of isolation during illness – as well as women's responsibility for ensuring healthy conditions in the home very seriously.[32] To this end, they developed clear policies on health, diet, outdoor exercise, and sanitation, including quarantine.[33] Reporting in 1909 on her visit to the POA, the city inspector, Dr Marion Hansford, was enthusiastic in her praise of "the entirely Sanitary Condition and the healthy looking well-cared for children."[34] But for much of the nineteenth century other factors could compromise their efforts. Budget constraints often made it difficult to implement policies, and occasionally the ladies' class bias, especially notions of "appropriate" conditions inside charitable institutions, proved a barrier to creating what we would today consider ideal conditions.

HEALTH

Health policies were generally designed to keep mortality rates down and limit disease as much as possible. Mortality rates among the children were relatively low at just under 3 per cent for the LBS and 8 per cent for the POA, but this latter statistic is distorted somewhat by the inclusion of 75 of the 1847 fever children, who had a mortality rate of 17.4 per cent and accounted for 22 per cent of all POA deaths.[35] In the "City of Wealth and Death," as Jean-Claude Robert has called Montreal, with an infant mortality rate of 24 per cent, this was remarkable.[36] Admission policies were designed to minimize health risks. Neither institution admitted infants or children who were visibly ill, and, from mid-century on, children were vaccinated against smallpox as soon as possible.[37] Nonetheless, Montreal was a city where epidemics and disease ran rampant.[38] Just as the POA had admitted children in 1832 and 1847 but housed them in separate annexes, the charities restricted admissions when there was an epidemic in the city and visits from family were severely curtailed, if not completely stopped. As a result of conflict with the city over the impact this strict policy had on court children, the LBS returned to a weekly "open day" for mothers in 1905 but required parents to bring a certificate of good health.[39]

Despite the effort the Committees and their hired staff put into maintaining healthy conditions and caring for the sick as well as the strict admission policies implemented during epidemics, both institutions were affected by epidemics such as smallpox and both had problems with the serial contamination common to child institutions with regard to communicable diseases. This was particularly a problem for the LBS, with its large population and high turnover of children. Scarlet fever, measles, whooping cough, and diphtheria were very serious threats for a child charity and often occurred concurrently or in tandem. Complications could include inflammation of the lungs or influenza, both very serious in their own right. Ringworm also proved to be a problem for the LBS by the twentieth century with the increase in the number of children in the industrial school. Very contagious, it spread quickly if children were exposed to it and was extremely difficult and expensive to cure. In 1905, for example, the LBS spent $1,100 on medicine and nurses' salaries to get an outbreak under control.[40] The determination to avoid further problems led to several confrontations with the City Recorder, as the Committee refused to admit court children if there was a chance they had or would imminently develop the disease.[41]

Doctors who served as house physicians visited the institutions regularly and during outbreaks of disease on a daily basis; by the 1880s and 1890s oculists and dentists also donated their services. The contribution these male professionals made to the health of the children cannot be overestimated. Equally important was the help of businessmen such as the Lymans, who provided free medicines for as long as they ran their business, to be replaced by other free suppliers thereafter. Although both of the buildings had been planned with an infirmary in mind, neither institution consistently had a dedicated and equipped infirmary until late in the century. In the LBS this was due to space problems; in the original POA building, an infirmary was only outfitted in the early 1880s,[42] but the new building after 1893 had a large, functioning infirmary.

Very conscious of the importance of quarantine in containing epidemics, the ladies sent children with communicable diseases to the Montreal General Hospital (MGH) as much as possible. This access to hospitals was essential in keeping down their mortality rates. In 1854, for example, when first typhus fever and then whooping cough hit the LBS, so many children were infected that the MGH devoted an entire ward for three months to their care.[43] In 1853 the LBS lost the services of one doctor when, in their haste to isolate measles cases, they sent children to the hospital without waiting for his instructions. Although the Committee argued expediency, the doctor believed they had "infringed on his prerogatives."[44] Gender was clearly a factor here. As Dorice Williams Elliott notes in her examination of gender questions in nineteenth-century England, male specialists were not always willing to have women take initiative in domains they believed to be their own.[45] This type of tension decreased over the century and, by the 1880s, Visiting Ladies or Directresses sent children with diphtheria to hospital without waiting for medical advice without any protest from their physician. When it was impossible to send children to hospital, the Committee implemented quarantine procedures themselves, setting aside an area such as the meeting room as a temporary infirmary.

When sick children remained in the charity, the matron followed treatments outlined by the doctor on his daily visits. Mustard plasters, fly blisters, linseed poultices, beef tea, wine drinks, arrowroot, and currant jam all figured prominently in these treatment programs and provide a glimpse of the ordeals that awaited sick children. During these periods of serious illness the institution's staff acted as nurses, but additional nurses were hired if needed. In 1862 when smallpox hit the LBS two months in a row and several unvaccinated children fell ill, one of their mothers came to help.[46] An outbreak of contagious disease was followed by a clean-up process: staff would thoroughly disinfect and whitewash the house, wash the children with castile soap, clean all the clothes, and change the straw in the beds.[47] But sometimes, when one outbreak followed another, it could take months between the beginning of an epidemic and this disinfecting process. In the LBS, budget considerations occasionally led to the postponement of whitewashing.

Besides the long list of communicable diseases, the most common health complaints were ear, eye, and skin infections, along with colds and respiratory disorders. The age of the main buildings (1849 for the POA and 1856 for the LBS) meant that dampness and heating problems were rampant. Certainly for the LBS, heating was a major expense in light of their tight budgets; it is a comment on the ladies' determination to ensure at least minimal conditions that they often ran deficits to purchase the large annual wood or coal supplies, and these supplies loom large in their budgets. Nonetheless, both Committees had trouble finding adequate heating apparatus and the buildings had consistent problems caused by drafts. Given this, the children must have suffered from the cold on a regular basis.

The situation was complicated by the buildings' designs. Neither building had adequate double windows and this aggravated earaches and ear infections. Furthermore, the floors were neither insulated nor doubled; standing on such cold wood floors, often in bare feet, the children suffered from chilblains.[48] When the POA added double windows on the upper front floor in the late 1860s, the move was described as a "great addition to the comfort of the family" as well as a savings on heat.[49] Double windows were later added to the back and the basement, and the floor in the schoolroom (where children spent many hours every day) was insulated and doubled.[50] Another health concern was the fact that both buildings had been built with external water closets; by the 1870s these had been condemned by the Sanitary Police several times.[51] Shifting to indoor bathrooms was a considerable financial undertaking. The POA took advantage of major building repairs in 1888 to make this transition; the LBS were still working on it in the 1890s.[52]

As the buildings aged, poor ventilation and faulty drains were linked to many cases of infectious diseases and even deaths. The city sanitary inspector, who began making regular visits in the 1880s, identified problems in both buildings and major drain repairs were made in several years.[53] Some of this was the result of the city growing up around them. As streets such as St Catherine and Bleury were expanded, the institutions' original drains were compromised and backed up into their basements.[54] By 1904 the situation was so serious for the LBS that many Committee members were afraid to enter the building.[55] These problems were not inconsequential; from 1912 to 1914, there were ninety cases of infectious disease in the LBS (twenty of them diphtheria). Following drain repairs in the latter year, things improved and only one case of disease occurred from 1914 to 1916.[56]

To some extent, then, the ladies were determined to avoid their institutions becoming what Annemarie Adams calls "a trap for the four deleterious D's – Darkness, Damp, Dirt, and Disease."[57] The insufficiency of budgets made this difficult, but the ladies did what they could with the resources they had. This often came down to policy directives rather than costly innovations or building repairs. They made sure that the staff and the children kept the buildings scrupulously clean as a normal course of events; additional cleansing and ventilating were carried out following any health problem. They avoided exposing their residents to disease as much as possible by isolating them from the outside community, especially when contact was considered too dangerous. They regularly "aired out" the buildings, and at least attempted to address questions connected to drains, sewage, and the like, even if they met with minimal success in this. They also attempted to ensure personal cleanliness and hygiene. In the summer of 1884 a small group of POA managers personally provided each child with their own brush, comb, toothbrush, and bag and equipped the dormitories with cupboards subdivided for every child's belongings.[58] This not only addressed sanitary issues but was also a way to recognize and establish some individuality for each child. From the same perspective, the LBS considered buying a washbasin for every child in 1897, but, finding the cost prohibitive, purchased more to facilitate so many children washing at the same time.[59]

Building problems would be resolved at least for a while for the POA when they sold their St Catherine Street building in 1893 and constructed a new one in a sparsely populated area on Côte-des-Neiges hill. They hoped the fresh air and spacious grounds would provide a healthier environment for the children and that a newly constructed building would eliminate the problems they had been having. To ensure this, they asked the city inspector to verify the sanitary specifications for their new building and implemented his recommendations, except for tile in the bathrooms, which they considered an unnecessary luxury.[60] This was the year before the government established minimum norms for public buildings, requiring that construction plans be submitted to a government inspector for approval, and fifteen years before the requirement was officially extended to orphanages (1908).[61] Requesting this input long before it was legally necessary is an indication of how seriously the ladies took these matters. Unfortunately, what the POA Committee had failed to consider in their choice of a building site halfway up the mountain was water runoff, and they continued to be plagued by drainage problems. The LBS, for their part, added a new wing to their building in 1898; this resolved their problems of overcrowding if not all of their health and sanitary issues.

Summer was a particularly dangerous time in city institutions due to the increased risk of disease in the city. After 1873, both charities sent a few frail or sickly children accompanied by a nurse to Eliza Hervey's Murray Bay Convalescent Home (in La Malbaie). The children and the occasional woman sent by the LBS remained there from several weeks to a month in the hope that they would regain their strength breathing the fresh air on the banks of the lower St Lawrence. By the late 1890s, Anglican children went to the Robert Jones Convalescent Hospital for Children in Lachine. In 1896 the LBS had the use of six beds in this institution, sending children for three-week stays.[62] Starting in 1873, the LBS also began to send home a few of the children who had parents living in the country, to get them out of the city for a summer holiday. By the 1890s, this summer vacation was a common practice, and almost all of the children visited relatives or friends for several weeks even if they lived in the city. In this way at least they were out of the institution with its increased summer risk of serial contamination. The policy had the added advantage of reinforcing family ties, and many of the children remained with their families in the fall.

Overcrowding was a problem; in both institutions children slept in gender-segregated dormitories, but up to three children shared a wooden bed and its straw mattress. This situation would raise concerns on several levels today, but the ladies were mainly worried about health issues and neatness; no reference to questions connected to morality is found in the sources.[63] The issue of shifting to single iron beds was raised in the LBS in 1855 and the POA in 1873, but budget constraints kept them from making massive purchases.[64] Furthermore, the original purchases had proved unsatisfactory due to their inferior quality – the LBS matron explained that the beds "bend nearly double when the children get into them."[65] The first iron beds were purchased for the LBS Convalescent Ward. The LBS gradually shifted to using them for children between 1878 and 1898; the POA made the shift in 1888.[66] The move to iron beds included the even more important step of securing an individual bed for each child.[67]

DIET

Institutional diets were simple, bland, and limited by budget considerations, the seasonal availability of food, and storage problems. The ladies believed in the advantages of "simple, hearty fare" – consistent with their understanding of children's health needs, but not more. Although at points early in the century the charities owned cows and rented grazing land, this was never found cost-efficient for long.[68] Both charities maintained vegetable gardens when they could and, thanks to a donation of twenty-three apple trees, the POA had a small orchard.[69] Without access to a farm, the Committees had to purchase most of their food, although they received donations of milk and vegetables from Committee members with estates on the mountain and from nearby farmers. Despite this, the LBS needed to buy at least four gallons of milk a day, since much of the donated milk was sour and neither the young children nor the elderly residents could digest it.[70] Other dairy products such as butter were seen as luxuries. In fact, the provision of milk and butter was one of the areas where class influenced policy discussions, although budget considerations were also decisive.

The original POA diet list, as drawn up in 1823 and revised in 1849, provides an example of diet in Montreal child charities.[71] (See table 5.1.) Carbohydrates predominated, providing the children with caloric energy, but the diet was low in fat, at least dairy fat, and the minimal quantities of fruits and vegetables probably resulted in some deficiency in minerals and vitamins. For breakfast and supper the main staples were bread, porridge, or "pudding."[72] At dinner, soup, meat, or fish with pudding, or vegetables, and beans and pork as well as milk, cocoa, rice, and molasses might be included.

The question of dairy products generated a lot of discussion in the POA meetings by the 1870s and 1880s. The contentious issue was whether whole milk and butter were necessary for good health and in what quantities. Butter was added to the Sunday menu in 1872,[73] but a motion to provide it daily was rejected in 1882. At the same time, the Committee decided that children should have roast meat once a week and milk twice a day, preferably whole milk.[74] To that point they had used a solution of milk mixed with water and treacle (a cheap sugar syrup), but several of the ladies believed whole milk was necessary for the children's health. For her part, the matron opposed the use of whole milk, arguing that it made some children sick and that the children preferred the treacle mixture. It was finally decided to permit children to request whole milk if they wanted it; otherwise, they would have the mixed solution more frequently to acquire the additional nutritional value.

This debate over butter and milk led to the establishment of a subcommittee of three ladies in 1888 to investigate the entire diet. They studied the dietary lists of institutions such as the MGH, and their suggestions were incorporated into a new diet that was more nutritious.[75] The MGH had informed them that a child needed half a pound of meat, one pint of milk, four ounces of bread, and two servings of potatoes daily. These recommendations were not followed completely, but children now had butter daily and milk twice a day; the amounts of beef, mutton, and fish, vegetables (carrots, cabbage, turnips, and onions), rice, and molasses were all increased – so that meat or a substitute was eaten daily; and potatoes and apples were added to the diet.

No detailed diet lists remain in the LBS papers. It is likely, however, that budget constraints kept their diet less varied than that of the POA. In 1848, for example, the LBS Committee drew up a reduced-cost diet list in which potatoes were added to supplement bread, the latter being more expensive at that point.[76] Special considerations were also necessary for the elderly women residents, the cost of which reduced the Committee's flexibility in terms of the children's diet. A resolution in 1853 added rice to the diet once a week and mutton for the elderly women; eggs had been added to their Sunday dinner the year before.[77] Butter was gradually added to the elderly women's diet between 1864 and 1869.[78] An 1878 discussion rejected butter for the children on the grounds of its prohibitive cost and the fact that it was not thought necessary for their health, but

Table 5.1

Diet list for the Protestant Orphan Asylum, 1823/49 and 1888

	1823 (revised 1849)	1888
Breakfast		
Sunday[1]	Cocoa and bread	Cocoa or tea, bread and butter
Others	Hasty pudding, boiled rice with molasses or milk, or milk porridge as the season admitted	Porridge and milk, bread and butter
Dinner		
Sunday	Roasted meat with pudding or vegetables	Joint of beef roasted, boiled potatoes, bread, pudding or apple dumplings
Monday	Soup	Boiled beef, carrots, turnips or cabbage and potatoes, bread
Tuesday	Boiled meat with pudding or vegetables	Soup with meat in it, thickened with rice or barley, bread, pudding
Wednesday	Soup	Quarter of mutton roasted, boiled potatoes, bread
Thursday	Beans or peas with pork	Soup with beans or peas and pork, bread, boiled rice with molasses
Friday	Broth made of mutton	Fish and potato pie, or fresh fish in white sauce
Saturday	Fish	Irish stew with mutton, potatoes, and onions, bread
Supper		
Sunday	Milk pudding thickened with flour, oatmeal, or cornmeal, bread and butter	Milk pudding thickened with flour, oatmeal, or cornmeal, bread and butter
Others	Hasty pudding, boiled rice with molasses or milk, and porridge as the season admitted	Monday: milk, bread, molasses Tuesday: milk, bread, stewed apples Wednesday: milk, bread, baked apples Thursday: milk, bread, butter Friday: milk, bread, molasses Saturday: milk, bread, butter

[1] In 1823, Monday was the distinct diet day, but in later references it was Sunday.

Source: POA, *Minutes*, 1823, 1888.

it was added twice a week in 1883.[79] In 1885 and 1894 investigations took place, responding to complaints from residents, but the Committee concluded that the diet was "suitable and plentiful and good."[80] In 1908 several ladies thought the children needed more substantial food. The final decision was to add some variety, the doctor having indicated that the diet was nourishing enough.[81] Still, the fact that twelve children were treated for malnutrition in 1920 raises some questions, although they might have been new admits.[82]

SCHOOL

Education was central to the mission of child charity, and both institutions operated schools inside the institution where children spent between five and six hours a day.[83] This is interesting if one considers that schooling was not yet compulsory in Quebec and the availability of schools was limited. Although the 1841 *Education Act* had opened the way to the formation of common schools, the Montreal Protestant School Commission really only began in 1846 and it had difficulty keeping up with the demand for schools in many working-class areas similar to those from which these children came, so it is possible the children would not previously have had access to a public school at all.[84] Furthermore, the children attended school for most of the year with only a few weeks off over the summer months. A child who spent some time in one of these institutions would have had as much schooling as at a public school (if not more), from which families often removed children for economic or health reasons.[85] Granted, some of these "school" hours were spent learning practical skills or working in the institution.

In the POA, the male superintendent ran the school for much of the century, a specialized teacher being considered "inconsistent with economy," but in 1858 a female teacher was added for half-days to cover the "many useful branches of education in which they [the children] were deficient."[86] A permanent teacher was added in the new administrative model adopted in 1893, but it was not until the twentieth century that the POA required the teacher be certified. At points they experimented with a day teacher, but a resident "governess" was the norm. Although the LBS internal management model included a hired teacher by 1846, the school was sporadic in the first years. As a result, occasionally from 1846 to 1850, boys attended the National School and girls either went to the School of Industry day school or were taught by the LBS School Committee.[87] Following problems with the boys' lack of progress at the National School, the LBS school was reintroduced in 1850 to ensure adequate education.[88] By 1858 the school had a teacher and an assistant teacher; another assistant was added in 1895 and from 1882 at least the main teacher had a teaching diploma.[89] All were women and two of the assistant teachers were former LBS girls who had been sent to the McGill Normal School for training.

Schools in both institutions used a version of the Lancastrian system, in which older, more advanced children served as monitors to help teach younger children. This system allowed the institutions to limit the number of teachers and keep costs down while still ensuring that children of different ages were taught appropriate material and skills.[90] At least in the LBS, where there was usually a ratio of forty to fifty children per teacher, the help these monitors provided was significant. While large, however, this class size was not much larger than that found in other city schools.[91]

Schooling inside the institutions was multi-faceted and included basic literacy, skills training, and moral and religious instruction. Both the religious and the "civilizing" roles of this education are clear in the POA description in 1873: "guiding and supporting those little ones entrusted to our care, so as to bring them up in the 'nurture and admonition of the Lord'; and fit them to occupy the positions in life they may be deemed to fill."[92] Their curriculum included "spelling, reading, writing, arithmetic, geography, and grammar"; boys and girls received the same education.[93] The LBS curriculum focused on a slightly more basic education: reading, writing, arithmetic, and geography. Still, this was not simply the 3 R's, as one might expect for children the ladies believed were destined for "lowly positions." The inclusion of geography was not accidental. The maps that Committee members donated to hang in the schoolroom would have had British "territory" across the world clearly marked in pink. These maps played a key role in teaching the children about the importance of the British Empire and their place in it. By 1903, the Protestant school commissioner who inspected the LBS school was said to be "very much pleased." The POA received a similar review in 1923, with the children being described as "well trained … bright and attentive."[94]

Skills training complemented the academic subjects and some of this training was done during school hours: both boys and girls were taught to make beds, to mend clothes, and to knit. Other training was gendered, with girls learning sewing, cooking, laundry, and general household cleaning while boys learned to clean boots, shovel snow, chop wood, garden, and do general work on the grounds. By the end of the century, this was supplemented in both institutions with specific and gendered "manual training," which, in effect, was an early version of vocational education: domestic service and cooking classes for girls and carpentry classes for boys. The LBS also introduced cobbling, basket-making, and weaving for boys while the POA taught boys chair caning and book-binding. Some of these skills helped children secure employment once they left the institution.[95]

Moral and religious education was assured through religious instruction, regular attendance at church and Sunday school, and structured prayers both morning and evening. Furthermore, the institutional routine, the discipline, and the household chores were designed to build character and instil those Protestant qualities of cleanliness, obedience, and respect for order and authority that the LBS School Secretary alluded to in her comment in 1863. Singing classes and school recitation exercises (in which children spoke all together with one voice) served as a moral framework within which to teach discipline and to build a sense of group cohesion.[96] School prizes presented at the annual meetings reflected these moral values and priorities. The POA awarded prizes for progress and proficiency in literacy, sewing, and knitting. Other prizes were given for "helpfulness and good example," "respectful obedience and industry," and "good conduct and faithfulness." The LBS offered a prize for "neatness in dress," "politeness of deportment," "application to study," and "good conduct."[97]

In light of budget constraints, some of the necessary school equipment including maps, blackboards, books, blinds, and even desks was donated, much of it by Committee members.[98] By the end of the century the school committees were actively involved in supervising, visiting, and helping with some of the teaching. Support from others in the community enabled them to implement new educational approaches, including callisthenics and gymnastics classes as well as "kitchen garden" exercises to help teach domestic service skills, by the 1890s.[99] A few of the older girls attended the YWCA cooking school. Temperance volunteers organized branches of the children's Band of Hope, and in the twentieth century, Boy Scout and Girl Guide troops were added.[100] These organizations served to informally reinforce lessons of socialization, proper values, and gender-appropriate activities, while providing the children with an “attractive and fun educational environment” outside of their normal routine.[101]

A public school opened on Berthelet Street near the LBS in 1886. The children began to attend this school in 1917, as soon as it was large enough to accommodate their numbers. The Committee kept one teacher on staff to supervise pre-school children and after-school homework. The POA maintained their in-house school until 1930 when the children began to attend Victoria School, located on Saint-Luke (de Maisonneuve) near Saint-Mark.[102] To reach this school they had to cross several major streets including Sherbrooke and walk about seven city blocks, many of them uphill on their way home.

WORK

There was a lot of work to be done in these large institutions with so many residents and few labour-saving devices to lessen the load. Like children in working-class homes and in other institutions, children in the LBS and the POA were expected to contribute to this work.[103] Not only did this train them in housework skills, discipline, and industrious habits, it also kept them busy and saved on wage bills. Both boys and girls helped with the housework, cleaning, and tidying, while gender-specific jobs were divided: girls answered the door, set the table, and helped with food preparation and clean-up; boys helped with the grounds and gardening, shovelled snow, carried water and coal, chopped wood, cleaned boots and shoes, and ran messages. As we noted, in both institutions children made most of the clothing, helped by the matron and Committee ladies; seamstresses were hired only when entire new outfits were needed. Children also knit stockings and other woollen items, and mended clothes. Comments in 1835 and 1836, for example, stated that the POA children were “all well and knitting warm stockings and making comfortable winter cloaks under the supervision of the Matron.”[104] In 1883, the LBS Committee, checking into the girls’ sewing practice, found that they sewed two hours a day making all of the institution’s underclothing.[105] Once manual training was begun, the children used their new skills to help reduce the institutions’ bills even further. The LBS 1899 Annual Report explains that the boys did all the carpentry repairs in the house and outdoors, and all the patching, soling, and heeling of the boots; while the girls grew vegetables in their gardens.[106] In that year a knitting machine had been purchased as a time-saver and the children had produced fifty pairs of socks in one month.[107]

A few of the boys, especially in the LBS, helped Committee members with their gardens or by running errands. The practice of using boys as messengers (for the institution or for ladies' private errands) was disputed by some members, who argued that it allowed the boys to circulate unescorted in the city where they might commit delinquencies or be reunited with questionable acquaintances. The LBS School Committee also protested, pointing out that boys missed school as a result. In 1874 the Committee attempted to address this issue with a by-law that limited the use of messenger boys to official LBS business and directed that boys should be sent out as messengers as infrequently as possible.[108] Twenty years later, though, boys still ran messages and teachers still complained of the resulting disruption to their schooling.

This child labour was important in both charities. The LBS matron frequently appealed to the Committee to postpone apprenticeships because she needed the older children's help in the house; this happened on occasion in the POA as well. In 1858, for example, the LBS matron explained that it was necessary to take the children from school several times a week to help with the cleaning, a situation she indicated could be avoided if she were allowed to hire more working women.[109] To address this need for additional labour, both charities occasionally apprenticed girls to the Society or simply kept them in the institution (but not in school) to train them as servants. Their work meant that the institution could often avoid hiring servants to do the light work of maintaining the house, leaving only demanding and specialized work such as cooking, laundry, and major cleaning to be done by hired workers. Working in the institution was also thought to reinforce the children's self-reliance. As one woman, remembering her experience in the Coombe Orphanage in Hespeler, Ontario, commented when summarizing her overall experience there, "Yes we learned to work, take responsibility, finish jobs, enabling us the children from the Coombe to go out and make successful lives for ourselves."[110] Children from the Montreal homes could have undoubtedly made a similar remark.[111]

Despite all the work they did, the Montreal children were better off than those in some child charities – the Halifax Home, for example, where children did all of the work without any hired help.[112] Furthermore, budget constraints never resulted in a situation where children were required to earn income, as was the norm in many child institutions.[113] This type of constant work was even more common in industrial schools. In both England and Ireland, many institutions had the children work or hired them out. Even closer to home in the industrial and reform schools run by religious orders, girls did laundry work or helped produce goods for sale, while the older boys at Montfort, a few miles from Montreal, worked in the bakery, in the workshops, and on the farm.[114] This was one important way in which the LBS Industrial School differed from the norm.

PLAY

In accordance with the nineteenth-century discourse on the health advantages of the country, both Committees considered fresh air, nature, and physical exercise as crucial to the children's health, despite the fact that their institutions were in the middle of the city. Hence it is not surprising that having some area available for a yard was high on their priority list when they searched for buildings to rent in the early years, and in the building plans of their permanent institutions. In 1856 the POA bought an additional lot beside the orphanage for this purpose. Importantly, both homes used at least some of this outdoor "natural" space for a garden. Gardening was thought to have educational and character-building qualities in addition to being a healthy form of exercise, a wholesome outdoor activity, and a cost-effective way to produce vegetables.[115]

Although most of the children's time was spent at school or doing household chores, set times were designated in the schedule of both institutions after lunch and before supper for "play," demonstrating the recognition that some recreation or relaxing was a normal part of a child's upbringing. Unfortunately, the ladies' exaggerated sense of responsibility to manage donated funds efficiently and their fear of charges of extravagance created the awkward situation whereby they did not feel warranted to use charity funds to purchase toys or sports equipment. References to such items are rare until the end of the century, when occasionally skipping ropes, footballs, swings, and sleds are mentioned. When they existed, they had been received as donations at Christmas, though most patrons preferred to send food treats such as oranges, or books.[116] Despite the advocacy of organized play popularized by the YMCA and the playground movement by the 1880s, donations that would have enabled the child charities to implement this type of training were not forthcoming.[117] When the LBS Young Ladies' School Committee helped the children organize a sale of their fancywork in 1899, the children opted to use the profits to purchase skipping ropes and footballs for themselves.[118]

Furthermore, any playing the children did was within the confines of the institution or on carefully supervised outings. Fear of exposing the children to communicable diseases led the ladies to refuse most invitations to attend public activities. Forced to remain in the institution or on its grounds with a minimum of toys or equipment, children did not always take advantage of the allotted play hour. In 1889, the POA Visitors reported with evident dismay that the children remained sitting on their school benches at their noon break rather than playing outdoors, and that if they did go outside, only the boys went, "the girls being seldom or never seen with them."[119] This was very different from the description the Visiting Ladies recounted of the children in the Hamilton Orphan Asylum in 1869, where they "generally found [the children] in happy groups engaged about their toys."[120] The POA had an indoor playroom but it is unlikely any more equipment would have been found there. The LBS did not have space for a playroom until the twentieth century.

Even walks were not a regular activity. In both the 1840s and the 1890s, the Committees passed resolutions requiring daily walks or fresh air exercise,[121] but the matron's and the superintendent's journals reveal that this did not happen. In fact, other than the trek to church and Sunday school, walks were limited to perhaps once a week, sometimes twice a month. In the winter this was largely due to the logistics of dressing large numbers of children, and, at least in the LBS, the lack of warm clothing. In the summer, concern was expressed about the health dangers of the summer heat.

Still, occasional day-long summer outings and picnics were common from the 1860s. These were easier by the late 1870s once both St Helen's Island and Mount Royal were opened as parks. A free ferry service linked St Helen's Island to the city, and the incline railway on Mount Royal was constructed in 1885. Most of these outings were paid for by Committee members and supporters, who sent wagons to pick up the children and provided refreshments during the outing or afterwards. In the latter part of the century, several times a year, the ladies also organized indoor entertainments for the children, including magic shows and picture slide shows.

In the twentieth century, the Committees' attitudes to recreation became much more positive. Pianos were purchased; children watched movies, learned folk dances, and did exercise classes. Both institutions had indoor playrooms equipped with toys and outdoor playgrounds with sports equipment. Some of the entertainments were designed to teach citizenship, such as visiting the art gallery or watching biographical films about such heroes as Admiral Nelson; others were strictly for pleasure. By the 1920s, besides outings, the children spent a large part of the summer in the country. The LBS rented a lodge across the river in St Lambert to serve as a camp and several POA Committee members invited the children to their summer homes in rotation.[122]

Conditions in terms of health, diet, and play slowly improved over the century and into the twentieth century. The new generation of managers after 1870 were more flexible than their mothers, aunts, and grandmothers had been. Notions of acceptable conditions and the needs of children were also evolving. From the 1880s, as the discourse on the importance of "the home" and the "innocence" of children increased and attacks on child institutions began, the Committees attempted to make their institutions more home-like and their policies became more child-centred than ever before. At the 1896 annual meeting, the POA Secretary referred to comments that had come to her attention about extravagance in relation to their children. She reminded those present that "the aim of those in charge of all these children is to improve them physically, as well as morally, by giving them a liberal and varied diet and plenty of fresh air and keeping them warmly and suitably clothed, and with an elementary education for all, and a thorough training for domestic service for the girls they are eventually sent out into the world with a fair prospect of earning their own living as respectable members of the community."[123] Evidently, she did not consider this as extravagant, simply as normal.

We also find earlier budget-conscious comments about strict economy and the prudent use of funds being replaced by comments emphasizing the importance of meeting the children's needs. Thus in 1897 the POA boldly informed supporters: "We make no attempt at reducing the individual cost of each child to such a low figure, as to ensure the commendation of the public for our careful and economical management. Our chief aim is to lay out the money entrusted to us to the best possible advantage for the benefit of the children."[124] Similarly, although with a bit less bravado, the LBS Secretary closed her Report in 1898 with the following remarks: "In conclusion, the Committee desire to state that, as long as there is room, no deserving person who comes within the scope of the Society is turned away … The funds of the Society are as carefully and economically administered as possible, the first consideration being the health and comfort of the inmates."[125] In these comments we see the convergence of several different factors, among them the increased recognition of children's innocence and their need for protection and care. But they also reflect a shift in orientation for the two Committees. For much of the century the ladies approached their work from a social and religious viewpoint and identified themselves as the stewards of their society (hence their concern with stringent budget control of donations). However, after years of experience in charity work and of interaction with poor families, the ladies gradually began to identify the individual children themselves, and to a lesser extent, their families, as their real "clients" and developed policies on the basis of this more personal client-identification and the children's needs.

A HOME?

The "home" was a central concept in middle-class domestic ideology, and the ladies often spoke of their intention to make their institutions home-like. They did their best to make this happen within the realm of possibility. Patrons at the annual meetings often spoke of the children's happy faces and neat appearance, comparing the atmosphere favourably with institutions they had visited in other cities. The description of the children given by the journalist covering the LBS open house following renovations to the building in 1898 is an excellent example: "plump little bodies, sparkling eyes and shining faces. Surely, the old stories of institution children are only nightmares to be forgotten."[126] We have already seen that when the POA changed their Act of Incorporation in 1912 to admit convalescents, they took advantage of this to alter their name to the Montreal Protestant Orphans' Home because they believed the word "asylum" no longer accurately portrayed their work.[127] An "asylum" gave the impression of a temporary refuge, while the word "home" indicated something much more permanent. This is indeed how the POA explained their mission by the end of the nineteenth century – a free home where children would remain and be taken care of until they were old enough to support themselves.

In many ways the ladies attempted to make institutional life as comfortable as possible for their young charges, and they gradually placed more emphasis on this. The POA Annual Report in 1903, for example, referred to how many of the children were "very weakly from neglect and lack of food when they arrived" and stated that their improved condition in a few months was "quite remarkable." It explained that the society's aim was to develop the children physically and morally: "could we better carry out the wishes of the donors than by infusing into the lives of these little ones fate has deprived of their natural protectors as much comfort and happiness as possible."[128]

Looking at these two child charities, we find some evidence that, alongside the inevitable discipline and strict character-building regimen, the ladies recognized the importance of the psychological and emotional aspects of a family home for children and made some effort to nurture these. This was easier in the POA, a smaller institution with about thirty children and where many of the matrons and superintendents acted as surrogate parents to children over long periods of time. This stability was reinforced by the lengthy stays of many of the children themselves and the fact that most had siblings with them in the institution. Entering with siblings did not always guarantee spending time with them, however, since children were separated on the basis of age and gender. Siblings of a similar age and certainly of the same gender would have been together most of the time, but this was not the case for children who had very young siblings, since young children tended to be separated from the older ones. If older children had been used to protecting their little brothers or sisters, being separated from them for much of the time in a strange environment must have been very difficult. In fact, on the basis of his interviews with former residents of twentieth-century child institutions, David Maunders finds that several of them remember this separation as traumatic and something that substantially increased their feelings of loss and isolation.[129]

Notwithstanding the separation that occurred between children of different ages inside the institution, the POA Committee made some effort to recognize the psychological well-being of the children and the importance of sibling ties. This was especially true of their concern about children following their apprenticeship. As much as possible, they tried to apprentice siblings to families in the same community; a few even went to the same family. Further, letter-writing was introduced by 1860 as a way to "cement early ties of affection or friendship, although they [the children] were widely separated from each other in the world."[130] On "letter-writing day" children wrote letters to siblings who had left the POA (usually as apprentices); those without siblings wrote to one of the POA apprentices, preferably a boy or girl they had known in the institution.

This pen-pal policy was probably even more important for the apprentices than for the children still in the institution and represents a real appreciation on the part of the Committee of the possible difficulties and sense of alienation experienced by apprenticed children alone in a new family, especially if they were also in an unfamiliar rural setting, as well as an attempt to nurture a connection between the children and the orphanage. The Christmas letter was another policy directed at maintaining contact with the child apprentices. All apprentices were encouraged to write letters at Christmas to either the ladies or the matron. As a further incentive, those who did were sent a book. In addition, as we will see in the next chapter, from 1876 the matron made a yearly visit to most apprentices. This trip served to ensure that masters were respecting their contractual obligations and that apprentices were well, but had the further advantage of reinforcing the emotional link between the children and the institution. By 1878 the ladies reported that the apprentices looked forward to these visits with pleasure, since the matron was really a mother figure for most of them. In 1885 they pointed to the importance of the visits for the children as one of the visiting system's most important features, "as it tends to keep unbroken the tie which binds them to their former home, and causes them to feel that their welfare is closely watched over by those who gave them their early training."[131] Another indication of the recognition of the children's personal needs and interests is the fact that, if possible, apprenticeship placements were chosen with a boy or girl's particular capacities or likes/dislikes in mind. This personalized approach to apprenticeship was reinforced by the fact that the Committee met each child for a special goodbye filled with advice before she or he left with their master and after their photograph had been taken, a photograph that remained in the institution.

The LBS Committee members also tried to emphasize their institution's home-like quality, but it was harder to create a family atmosphere in a large institution with sixty to one hundred children present at the same time and most of them remaining less than a year. A further complication was the fact that the children shared the home with elderly women, although many of the women spent most of their time in their rooms. On the other hand, most of the LBS children had siblings with them and parents who visited on Saturdays, so they were not really alone. Further, for some, the transition to institutional life had been eased by their mothers entering with them, at least temporarily, and many children knew that they would be returning home as soon as possible.

Celebrations at Christmas and Easter, daily family prayers, and family dinners reinforced the sense of belonging to a family that did things together and helped form a group cohesion. Both institutions enforced very strict attendance at meals in the dining room, unless a child was ill. In the LBS even the elderly women came down for meals if they were ambulatory. Christmas celebrations in particular were very elaborate. This was one of the main times when the community at large rallied to make the holiday enjoyable for the children. The lists of donations in December were so generous they often took an entire page in the annual reports, and both institutions organized elaborate Christmas dinners with turkeys, roast beef, ham, vegetables, plum puddings, oranges, and other delicacies. Several Committee members attended with their husbands and, on occasion, their children. By the end of the century donations also included books and occasionally toys and sleds, as well as things that were considered useful. Gifts were distributed to the children at the Christmas tree celebration, usually on Christmas Eve or Boxing Day. The LBS held the celebration inside the institution; in the case of the POA, it was held at "Piedmont," the home of Louisa Frothingham (Molson), situated at the top of Durocher Street, that can be seen in figure 5.3. Louisa also provided all the gifts.

How did the children in these two child charities experience institutional life? Did they adapt or did they suffer from a sense of alienation or even trauma? It is impossible to answer these questions with certainty, but there

Figure 5.3 Graham Beryl, *"Piedmont," the Frothingham House, Durocher St., Montreal, QC*, 1885. This is the home of Louisa Frothingham (Molson) where the POA children had their Christmas tree celebrations for much of the nineteenth century.

are several indications that point to the fact that these two Montreal charity Committees had at least some minimal success in their efforts to create a semblance of a real home.

Many of the children lived in the institutions alongside their siblings. They also almost surely formed emotional ties with the other children. These emotional ties would have made institutional life a little more liveable and a little more family-like. In her books recounting the reunions of the children in Montreal's two Jewish child charities, Judy Gordon refers to them as "400 brothers and sisters" and speaks of the strong ties that they all remember forming with their fellow residents.[132] For children in these two Protestant charities, emotional ties were also maintained with parents or relatives when they existed. We know that families did not give up their children lightly. Many mothers kept them as long as they could, struggling to support them; they placed them with relatives, or friends, or neighbours if possible and only as a last resort appealed to the Committees. In the last chapter we witnessed mothers and fathers leaving their children with heavy hearts, only to retrieve them as soon as possible, as well as grandparents who missed their orphaned grandchildren so much that they left them in the institution for only a day or two before they were back to retrieve them. Those who did finally entrust their little ones to the Committees visited when possible. They brought candy as a treat, which was probably the only gift they could afford and something designed to spoil the children a bit. Clearly emotional ties between parents or relatives and children remained strong. Some parents tried to make a home for their children unsuccessfully and were forced to request re-admission. Only the strong need to have the children with them could explain this attempt to remove children before they were in a position to care for them. These emotional contacts with siblings, other children, and families surely contributed to the children's experience of the institution as a home, even if a temporary one.

Probably one of the factors that had a great deal of influence on the children's experience was the staff. These were the people who dealt with the children on a daily basis. The difference between a caring, understanding person and one who was too strict or even abusive would obviously impact a child's ability to cope with institutional life.[133] We saw that the Committees investigated a few complaints of excessive punishment but they maintained the need for "judicious" discipline. What is surely relevant here is the fact that many of the matrons and superintendents remained for long periods of time with no complaints being lodged and would have truly been like parental figures to the children. This was especially important for orphans in the POA but must also have helped create a sense of stability for the LBS children, who were always unsure if, and when, they would be returning home. In both institutions, there were a number of other staff. Teachers lived in the institutions and spent most of their time with the children. Given that all of them were young, single women, many must have developed a fondness for the children that quite likely was reciprocated. Staff the ladies referred to as "nurses" helped care for the children and slept in the dormitories in case they were needed during the night. These women were from the same social class as the children and a few had children in the home. Other staff including cooks, laundresses, and handymen often had children working with them as helpers, and bonds could develop through this interaction. In her review of letters, interviews, and autobiographies of former residents in Baltimore orphanages, Nurith Zmora finds that many children remember connections of this kind. Richard McKenzie confirms this on the basis of his own experience and that of others.[134]

The "family" that had been formed inside the institutional homes was a contrived one, in that it was composed of many children who found themselves together, "mothered" by a matron (who tended to come from the working class) and irregularly by Committee ladies, all of whom were of another social class. But there is some reason to believe that it was a "family" nonetheless. There are clear indications, for example, that the emotional ties between the children and their institutional homes continued after they had left. Many returned to visit; others sent letters, or attended the Christmas dinner or the summer picnic. Still others wrote to the matron, lady superintendent, or Committee members to ask for advice on their future endeavours, to inform them of their situation, or to request help in finding post-apprenticeship positions, or with financing projects such as buying a farm, setting up a garage, etc. Certainly in the POA, where most children did not have parents, the Committee and the matron/lady superintendent became their surrogate parents. This was especially the case with the Cribbs and the Campbells, who remained for several decades. It was also true of Miss McGivern, the POA lady superintendent who took over in 1893 and remained for twenty-five years. Writing in 1907 about her connection with the children, the Secretary commented that "the children are devoted to her, their welcome, when she returns from a holiday is a sight worth seeing, they are so delighted."[135] Similarly in their 1903 report the Committee informed supporters that "[b]oth boys and girls who have left the Institution for some years continue to look upon it as their Home, visiting it when opportunity offers, and consulting with the Lady Superintendent as to their plans and future prospects."[136] Indeed the minutes in 1917 recount a letter from one boy, now in Calgary, "full of gratitude to the Home and Miss McGivern for past kindness, in the only place where he was ever at home or happy."[137]

A few of the children helped the Committees with substantial donations. In the best-publicized instance of this, a former POA child contributed a total of $1,370. He had entered the POA as an orphan during the cholera epidemic in 1832, been apprenticed to a cooper, and subsequently moved to California where he became quite prosperous. He made a number of donations to the Endowment Fund from 1851 until his death in 1892, and his widow furnished a dormitory in the new building named in his honour.[138] Another former

POA boy donated $2,200 over a number of years. He had been in the institution from 1849 to 1855 when he was apprenticed to Mr Hunter of Caldwell Mills (Noyan), one of the families that took several POA boys over the years. The experience had been a positive one, and, now seventy-two and living in Iowa, he wanted his old home to share in his success. In relation to this case, the POA Secretary wrote in 1906, "It is pleasant to hear of gratitude, which assumes a practical form after so many years."[139] Other former children used the vocational skills they had learned to help the ladies, as in the case of two former LBS boys who helped lay new floors and do plumbing repairs in 1893.[140]

The connection between the institutions and the children was not just visible in terms of the children; the ladies also demonstrated this emotional connection. As the POA Secretary explained in 1905, "Our interest in the children does not cease when they leave."[141] Both Committees arranged for boys returning from apprenticeships to board in the Boys' Home and often used their personal influence to find them positions. We have already seen how the POA provided medical care for two boys suffering from TB before they had opened a convalescent ward and were equipped to take on this type of commitment, and provided ongoing help for the disabled boys for whom they found positions but who had trouble at various points afterwards. During the war, when a number of former boys enlisted, the ladies were very proud; the Committee provided supplies for them before they left, and then sent more to the front. The minutes kept all informed of their progress, any injuries, and where they were stationed. When a few died in battle, the ladies created a Roll of Honour and posted it in the institution. These were women who knew the cost of war first-hand, several of them having lost sons in the war; now they honoured the boys who had been a part of their charity home.[142]

Several historians studying child institutions in the mid-twentieth century with access to testimonies have found that former residents have mixed memories of their time in institutions. Many remembered the tedium of the diet, the routine, and the work, and the fear of what might happen, but others indicated that the institution provided a continuity and stability in their lives that had not been there before.[143] Memories also included the friendships, the fun, the outings, the regular food, the sense of security, and an appreciation of the self-reliance, the values, and the work ethic they developed as well as the care and attention they were given.[144] Certainly the older man the author of the present book met in the McGill library had only positive memories of the POA and the care he and his brothers had received there early in the twentieth century. Similarly, D.K, a woman the author met who had been a resident of the LBS and then the POA in the late 1930s, also had excellent memories of the POA, her friends, and the activities, although she remembered the LBS staff as rigid and condescending.[145]

In his interviews with former child charity residents in Chicago, Kenneth Cmiel found that the strict health policies institutions used to protect and isolate children from the outside world, as well as the wearing of uniforms, were experienced by some children as a form of "differentness," things that separated them from other children in the community and set them apart.[146] Being marched down the street in an orderly manner two-by-two on their way to church and Sunday school was experienced in the same way. Probably many of the Montreal ladies' well-meaning policies had similar unintended effects, and the children probably experienced some of them, such as the use of silence, as a form of psychological control. In child charities such as these ones, the children lived, at one and the same time, a uniformity inside the institution, where there was little room for self-expression or individuality, and a "differentness" outside it, where they were visibly set off from other children and possibly discriminated against. Figure 5.4, a photograph taken of the LBS children in 1909, provides us with an inkling of this. In it, the more than ninety children pose in the Home's backyard, all dressed in their Sunday uniforms, all with their hair cut very short.

Different charities created different conditions and were successful to varying degrees in their attempt to create a home and to protect the children in it. Different children experienced their lives there in different ways. Some must have been homesick for their former lives, not finding enough emotional support in the institutions, and we saw a few run away to join their families; others found it difficult to leave their institutional homes, the matron, and the other children and maintained contact if possible.

These two charities had characteristics of both protective and isolating charities. Although the Committees isolated children in their institutions with little outside contact and limited contact with parents, they did this from a protective perspective and for the most part did not try to break children away from their parents, as more isolating child charities tended to do.

Figure 5.4 Wm. Notman & Son, *Ladies' Benevolent Institution, Montreal*, QC, 1909. The children pose in the institution's back yard.

Their overall aim was to create a refuge for the children, especially orphans – to make a home for them, and to teach them skills that would help them in the future. In this they were also helping families who were having temporary or longer-term difficulties caring for their children. There were contradictions within this, however, and clear class overtones. Rather than simply protect or provide for, the ladies also aimed to educate and socialize. They were determined that the right environment, education, and religious training could turn children into useful, God-fearing citizens.

Although children might have found the education and skills useful, some of them must have had difficulty adjusting to the values and routine that were so alien to their former lives. Others probably appreciated the stability and friendships they found, especially if they had come from difficult or even abusive home situations. If we ask the question "who did the ladies 'see' when they looked at the children?" this combination of class and maternalism is the best answer. To take the term coined by Mona Gleason, they saw "small bodies," not in a medical sense, but in a class sense.[147] These were children who showed the marks of poverty, who could benefit from education and training; but they were also children who suffered from malnutrition, who needed to be cared for and protected, and, as much as possible, whose emotional needs needed to be recognized.

Many of the children did not remain in the institutions long enough to worry about whether they were really home-like. In both charities, but especially in the LBS, a large number of children returned to their families after a brief stay. For a good number, however, residence in one of these charities represented a substantial part of their childhood. Thankfully, the Committee ladies had a child-centred approach and at least attempted to make the institutional homes as comfortable as budgets would allow. The policies that governed the conditions under which children left the charities and the placement methods used are discussed in the next chapter.

6

Returning Home and Other Placement Policies

In May 1858, a Catholic mother applied for her five children to be released from the LBS, where they had been since February, so that she could place them with the Grey Nuns. Under strict orders from the Committee that the children be kept from the mother, the matron refused. Determined that her children would be raised as Catholics, the mother returned later that day and stole them from the LBS by having them climb over the fence during playtime. According to the matron's description in her journal and the register, the nuns had two cabs waiting to whisk the family away to their orphanage. Certainly the nuns sent back all the LBS clothes when the children were returned by court order in July, and demanded the LBS return the nunnery's clothing in exchange. The children remained in the LBS until they were apprenticed as they came of age, one by one.[1]

The experience of this mother and her children reveals how complicated the interaction between families and charity Boards could become. It also tells the tragic story of a family facing an unusual amount of marital discord, violence, and alcohol abuse.[2] In effect, the children had been admitted when their father committed suicide, having first assaulted their mother (in hospital as a result) during a joint drinking binge. Tellingly, this was not the children's first sojourn in the LBS. They had been admitted on two previous occasions for short periods in both 1856 and 1857 when their mother was arrested for drinking, and the ladies referred to the parents in one register entry as "worthless characters." On both occasions the father had retrieved them once the mother was released and was able to resume their care.[3] It was following the second of these episodes that the father had Rev. Bond baptize the three youngest children.[4]

The case demonstrates agency on the mother's part in stealing her children and then later using the courts to challenge the tutorship process that had effectively removed her parental rights, but it also shows her powerlessness when this challenge ultimately failed and the children were returned to the LBS. The mother tried again unsuccessfully to remove them in November 1858, but tragically, when her youngest daughter died of scarlet fever in September 1859, the Committee could not locate her to attend the funeral.[5] The case points with some poignancy to the complications of the Montreal context, where the conflict between Protestant and Catholic was never far from the surface. Aware of the children's Protestant baptisms, the motive listed in the register for their admission is unmistakably direct: "to keep them Protestant." Finally, the case reveals some of the complications involved in decisions over discharging children, including the influence of religion, the Committee's evaluation of the mother's character, and her rights as the remaining parent (albeit a mother and not the tutor). This chapter will address some of these issues as we look at children leaving the institutions.

The ladies who ran the child charities brought their Protestant upper-middle-class culture to their work, and attempted to create a family atmosphere and to build at least some fictive family ties inside their institutions despite circumstances that often made this difficult. Nonetheless, their primary focus was on protecting the children, educating them, and training them to be good Christians and good citizens – making their work more child-centred than family-centred. This focus, merged with their class perspective and their suspicion of poor families, influenced their departure policies. The Committee recognized the important role families played in socializing children and in providing them with an identity, but they did not believe that the rights of families were absolute. The respective rights of parents and of charities temporarily assuming responsibility for their children were occasionally unclear; and this situation could result in conflict over the release of children from the institutions or their apprenticeship to others. Nonetheless, most children with a living parent returned to their families, and some of the POA orphans were eventually taken in by relatives. Other children were generally apprenticed, although a few were adopted. The departure patterns for the two charities are laid out in Table 6.1.

Table 6.1
Departures of children from the Ladies' Benevolent Society and the Protestant Orphan Asylum, 1832–99

	LBS		POA	
Departure	No.	%	No.	%
To relatives	1,802	70.1	308	34.1
Left/ran away	(84)[1]	–	30	3.3
Apprenticed	253	9.8	393	43.5
To service	23	0.9	45	5.0
Adopted	15	0.6	18	2.0
Died	65	2.5	68	7.5
To another institution	89	3.5	23	2.6
Known cases	2,247	87.4	885	98
Unknown	325	12.6	18	2
Total cases	2,572	100	903	100

[1] Includes thirty children removed by parents (usually stolen) and fifty-four who ran away. These cases are included in the category "to relatives."

Source: LBS, *Register, Minutes*, 1833–99; POA, *Register, Minutes*, 1823–99.

RETURNING HOME AND PARENTAL RIGHTS

For the most part, both Committees recognized the rights of families to reclaim their children, and the institutions played a major role in shoring up families that were undergoing crises. Consequently, returning to the care of parents or relatives was the norm for more than 70 per cent of LBS children (1,802 children). This category includes the fifty-four children who ran away to join their families and the thirty who were removed by parents without permission (see below). Since records were carefully kept of children who died or were apprenticed, the 13 per cent of children for whom we do not have specific departure data probably also returned to their families. This likelihood is reinforced by the fact that many of them left on the same day as their siblings. With its high percentage of orphans, only 34 per cent of POA children (308) went to family or relatives, but this represents 78 per cent of children with a known parent. Sometimes parents failed in their attempt to support retrieved children. In 111 such cases in the LBS and five in the POA, children were re-admitted two or even three times.

Designed to protect, educate, and train destitute children, both charities had official policies against admitting children for less than one year. Despite these policies, the charity Committees, perhaps forced by circumstance, did accept many children for short periods of time. In fact, a large number of children entered and left within a three-month period, and fully half of all LBS children and approximately 30 per cent of those in the POA returned to their families in under a year.[6] This was certainly one way by which poor families successfully used the charities for a purpose other than that for which they were designed.[7]

Almost 1,100 children in the LBS and 540 in the POA, however, remained more than a year. One or two years were the most frequent stays, but some children were resident for a good part of their childhood, if not all of it, as can be seen in table 6.2. In the POA, some of this was due to a policy implemented in 1880 by which children were not allowed to leave until they were fifteen for girls and thirteen for boys, even to go to family or kin.[8]

Although Carmen Nielson has argued that its Act of Incorporation in 1852 authorized the Hamilton Orphan Asylum to "assume guardianship rights over children with living parents," by granting it the power to apprentice any child admitted to the institution, specific clauses of this nature were not included in the Incorporations for these two Montreal societies.[9] The preamble of the POA Incorporation in 1843 recognized that they had apprenticed children in the past, but that for the LBS in 1841 does not even include such a statement. More importantly, neither the revised POA Incorporation in 1860–61 nor that of 1912 includes this type of clause.[10] The 1912 POA Act, for example, outlines the association's powers clearly as "to admit and care for orphans of the Protestant religion and, if they wish, convalescent children"; no reference is made to the disposition of said children.

Relevant to this difference from Hamilton is the fact that Quebec's civil law made paternal power to control children's "*garde et éducation*" very clear.[11] Certainly the ladies were not under the illusion that this was one of the powers they had gained through incorporation. They often lamented the rights parents had under the law to claim children, particularly in (what they perceived to be) cases of parents waiting until children were finally of some

Table 6.2
Children's length of stay in the Ladies' Benevolent Society and the Protestant Orphan Asylum, 1822/1838–99

Length of stay	LBS No.	LBS %	POA No.	POA %
Less than 3 months	892	34.7	178	19.7
3 months to 1 year	454	17.6	88	9.8
1–5 years	912	35.5	347	38.4
6–10 years	172	6.7	168	18.6
More than 10 years	14	0.5	25	2.8
Known cases	2,444	95	806	89.3
Unknown cases[1]	128	5	97	10.7
Total cases	2,572	100	903	100

[1] For these cases exit date is not indicated.
Source: LBS, *Register, Minutes*, 1833–99; POA, *Register, Minutes*, 1822–99.

economic use and just about to be apprenticed before they took them home, or when they subsequently interfered with apprenticeships.[12] In spite of these misgivings, as a general rule both Committees respected the rights of parents and relatives to retrieve children, and even occasionally wrote to find out if, and when, families wanted their children. A number of children, however, were released to parents "unwillingly," a characterization that betrays a certain reticence.[13]

The reluctance to return children was not unusual among nineteenth-century charity directors. In her study of the Boston Female Asylum, Susan Porter Benson finds that it was only in the 1840s, after years of difficulty using apprenticeship and adoption, that it became common to return children to families, and that even then, relatives or parents needed to be "financially secure and morally responsible" and sign a standard indenture agreement to receive their children.[14] Many self-styled "child savers," in fact, saw the mere act of surrendering a child to a charity as proof of parental negligence and justification for keeping children from such parents. Charities might force parents to legally bind children when they applied for admission, making them sign surrender agreements that came into effect immediately or after a specific lapse of time. Some, such as the English emigration societies, used a form of what Joy Parr has called "philanthropic abduction," making consent to emigration a precondition for admission. In a similar vein, several of the American Children's Aid Societies sent urban children to rural "foster" families in "orphan trains."[15] Some Canadian child charities were just as vigilant.[16]

Close examination of these two Montreal charities reveals that they did not fit this mould as a general rule. Neither institution forced parents to legally bind their children to the society on admission, although both considered such a policy. In the end, only 9 children or 4 per cent of non-orphans are identified as legally bound to the POA and 68 children or 3 per cent of children in the LBS, and in at least one instance, the LBS Committee released bound children at the mother's request.[17]

Despite their general acceptance of the rights of parents (and relatives) to retrieve children, both Committees were ready to challenge parental power when they believed the interests of the child warranted it. This was especially true of the POA, where the rights of relatives were less clear. There were two situations in which this happened: one, when Catholic relatives or parents tried to claim a Protestant child, and two, when the ladies considered the parent or relative applying for the child to be completely unsuitable to raise a child. It is essential to emphasize that these cases only involved about one per cent of children in the POA (twelve) and even less than one per cent in the LBS (thirteen) and thus do not reflect the overall character of these charities, but they do demonstrate the Committees' resistance to absolute parental power. While the ideals of the family and the home were central to the ladies' maternal and Protestant values, when they considered the home in question to be a moral or a religious threat to the child, their protective concern for the child overrode other considerations.

The role these two charities played in keeping Protestant children away from Catholics was taken very seriously. Although the ladies did not use their institutions to proselytize and in this way cohabited peacefully with the city's Catholics, some tension existed between the Protestant charities and the nuns. When one girl ran away and was later seen in the Grey Nunnery, for example (presumably they had rescued her from the street), the POA sought legal help to secure her release.[18] Both Committees consistently refused to release a child to Catholic relatives, even parents, when they were convinced the child had been baptised Protestant, especially if the relatives wanted to place them in a Catholic charity rather than integrating them into their family home. The case with which we began the chapter demonstrates this; so does the LBS's refusal to release the two K. boys to their aunt and brother, who wanted to move them to St Patrick's Orphanage. The ladies turned the boys over only after the aunt produced a court order and Catholic birth certificates. Even then they forced them to pay board for the children's entire stay.[19] From this perspective, protecting children from Catholicism was seen as more important than parental rights, especially those exercised by kin.

In a similar way, the POA resisted turning orphans over to Catholic relatives if their parents had been Protestant. Believing that the parents' intentions were paramount, they required that relatives produce Catholic birth certificates as proof that the parents had intended to raise the children as Catholics. Anna M., for example, for whom the POA finally found Protestant baptism papers, was never released to her Catholic uncle even though he was already sending her brother to a Protestant church and promised to do the same for her. Backed by their lawyer, who advised that since they had the baptismal papers, they stood a fifty-fifty chance that the courts would uphold their refusal to release a child to kin on the grounds of religion, and by the minister who feared for her being "exposed to the dangers of the east end and of Catholic relatives," the ladies persisted. Eventually the uncle gave up, dropping all claims.[20] Father Dowd, of St Patrick's Orphanage, intervened personally to see if some arrangement could be made in another case of two children whom their older brother and aunt wanted moved to St Patrick's. When no baptism certificates could be produced for the two boys, they remained in the POA.[21]

The case of Emma R., whose uncle wanted to send her to Catholic relatives in Ireland, did end up in the courts. When the uncle applied in 1887, the POA refused to release her because she was Protestant. This case was further complicated by the fact that Emma, who was already twelve, did not want to leave the orphanage, preferring to remain there to train as a servant. The uncle began legal proceedings to become her official tutor and then took the case to court on the grounds of *habeas corpus*. The POA lawyer argued on the basis of religion and challenged the legality of the tutorship process since the man was an Irish citizen, not Canadian. The judge ruled that the rights of the tutor to possession of the child, not the question of the child's religion, took precedence and ordered the POA to hand over the child.[22] It is not clear if the ladies would have resisted releasing the girl had the uncle been her tutor when he first applied, since as a norm they were extremely respectful of the rights of tutors. Nevertheless, the case exposed the legal invalidity of their position in relation to religion and the rights of kin. The ladies feared the press coverage of the case would encourage other Catholic relatives to claim children, but, with the exception of one case, these fears proved unfounded.[23]

The Committees also occasionally resisted releasing children to families on moral grounds to protect what they believed to be the interests of the children. This occurred when they judged a parent to be totally immoral, or "wicked" as they called it. In 1889, for example, the LBS refused to return one woman's children and wrote to the man who had applied for their admission, suggesting he become their legal tutor, and thereby protect them from their mother.[24] In August 1850 and again in 1851, the POA Committee referred to their decision to keep a child for moral reasons, in spite of the fact they knew they had "no legal right to retain the child," since it was a parent applying for the child's release.[25] However, the ladies firmly believed that, unlike parents, relatives did not have absolute rights to claim children, and in 1852, began to request that relatives produce a certificate of fitness similar to that used for apprenticeships.[26] The rule was applied irregularly, but its existence probably served to intimidate some relatives, and it was certainly used in at least three cases after 1852 for relatives judged to be "undesirable."[27]

Furthermore, on a few occasions both the LBS and the POA deliberately apprenticed children to keep them from "questionable" parents or relatives. In one case the LBS Committee did this to keep a girl from an intemperate mother, and in another they decided not to tell a mother where her son was placed, as "she is known to be such a character that she would do him more harm than good."[28] In 1868, the POA apprenticed one boy with the following explanation: "it was very desirable to remove W … from the influence of his relatives in Montreal."[29] Another boy was apprenticed, even though his father was in town, to ensure that the child would "be out of his interference."[30] In both these cases the ladies' actions were precautionary, since neither of the families had applied for the boys. In the case of two other orphans, however, their actions were more deliberate. They apprenticed one boy in 1843 against his relatives' wishes, arguing that the family's position was "detrimental to the child's welfare" and that the ladies "stood in relation to parents to the children" and thus must protect their interests.[31] In the other case they apprenticed a girl to avoid returning her to her aunt, described as "very undesirable and intemperate," and then successfully rebuked the aunt's attempt to claim her afterwards by arguing that the child was under the legal protection of the society until her majority.[32]

Faced with this challenge to their rights and the Committees' unilateral actions, some parents and/or relatives acquiesced, but others, as we have seen, fought back and are examples of clear agency on the part of families. Some, such as Emma R.'s uncle, whom we saw appealing to the courts in 1887, turned to legal means; similarly the S. boys were removed from the LBS by court order in December 1870, as was a little girl in September 1873.[33] The brother of Jane L. sent a lawyer's letter demanding her release.[34] The use of lawyers on the part of families was rare, but the Committees themselves often had their lawyer send letters to families or relatives who confronted them too often. Most families who were unhappy with the charities' actions simply removed their children rather than taking legal action. Thirty children "left" the LBS in this way, and two the POA. These children disappeared from the institution grounds while playing, from the street while walking home from church, or from the house during a visit.[35] Some of these parents, such as the Catholic mother who stole her children from the yard, had applied unsuccessfully for their discharge. Others were refused visiting privileges when they appeared on the wrong day.[36] Fear of a similar refusal is the best explanation for the other abductions. There were also a few instances of parents or relatives enticing children to leave their apprenticeship homes.

Parental power over children was clear under the Quebec Civil Code. The *Apprenticeship Law* passed in 1871 began to clarify the rights of charities but ambiguities remained. This act was one of a series connected to industrial and reform schools and the creation of a state policy on child protection, the thrust of which gradually shifted away from absolute paternal power over children.[37] The law clarified the power of charities to apprentice a child under their care and their continued responsibility over said children once apprenticed: "the rights, power and authority of the parents over and in respect of such child, shall cease and be vested in and exercised by the managers." It also introduced the notions of parental fitness and the child's best interests. A parent could apply to the superior court to have the child "restored to his or her custody and control," but had to prove that they were "fit and proper person[s] to take charge of the child, and that the child's condition will not thereby suffer."[38]

As such, it provided the charity Committees with some legal justification in cases such as those cited above where they decided parents were unfit, and certainly the POA had lobbied for its passage.[39] These notions are crucial in any discussion of the respect or non-respect of parental rights. One must remember, however, that evaluations of parental fitness were subject to class- and gender-based interpretations, as the charity Committees and the courts imposed their middle-class definitions of appropriate behaviour on working-class individuals with a different culture and economic possibilities. At least one POA case points to the need to interpret the respective rights of charities, parents, and children with some measure of nuance.

The case of Sarah, a twelve-year-old mixed-race girl from New Orleans who ended up in the POA, exposes some of the problems involved in determining parental fitness and in drawing the line between the rights of parents and the interests of the child. Assuming Sarah was an orphan, the ladies arranged an apprenticeship placement for her as a domestic servant. Some months later they received a letter from a woman in New Orleans introducing herself as Sarah's half-sister (Sarah was the child of this woman's father and his housekeeper). The woman requested that Sarah be placed in a boarding institution or be returned to her mother. The ladies refused to divulge the apprenticeship address or to send Sarah to New Orleans unaccompanied, but agreed to return her if the mother came to Montreal and could prove her identity.[40]

Concurrently they wrote to a minister in New Orleans to ascertain more information. Having gone to meet the relatives, he warned the ladies that "people of her colour have a very dubious position in New Orleans, and he feared much for her future fate," and strongly advised them to retain the child if at all possible.[41] Meanwhile, oblivious to these events, Sarah herself was writing letters to the ladies telling them how happy she was in her apprenticeship home.[42] The ladies continued to refuse to return her without having met the mother. The intervention of the American Vice Consul finally forced their hand; they sent the girl to New York, where she was met by relatives.[43] Two years later, however, they received a letter from Sarah (now fifteen). Indicating that her mother "had no use for her," she requested a reference to enable her to go into service. No mention was made of the half-sister. The ladies sent her the reference, commenting in the minutes on their sadness that she "is now neglected in a strange country."[44] This case is one of the few in the charity papers where we have a follow-up on a case where the ladies had resisted releasing a child to relatives but had been forced to do so, and it exposes the complicated nature of child protection and the potentially negative impact on children.

Parental rights and fitness were not an issue for orphans or for children whose parents could not resume their care. These children, however, posed another problem for the ladies, since it was not the norm for children to remain in child charities once they were in their early teens; instead they were sent to live in families. This freed up spaces for other children, but more important than this was the strongly held belief that families were necessary to socialize children. The Montreal charities used two common methods of home placement: adoption and apprenticeship. Both created some form of new relationship between the child and the receiving family. Apprenticeship was regulated by law; in Quebec, adoption was not, until 1924. However, as modern social workers and adoption agencies know from experience, sending a child into an unknown family can be fraught with potential danger in any historical period, even if a legal contract exists. Using something similar to an early casework approach, the Committees dealt with each child and problems that arose on a case-by-case basis and were often forced to grapple with complex questions in relation to these placements. Over time, in response to problematic situations, they adapted their methods to retain their protective perspective.

ADOPTION

The legal status of adoption was ambiguous in the nineteenth century. Although an informal version or *adoption de fait* was used regularly inside families and communities, it was not included in the 1866 Quebec Civil Code.[45] Similar versions of informal adoption also existed in the United States, but an 1851 Massachusetts law legalized adoption in that state and began a major change.[46] Studying this, Michael Grossberg has found that prior to this legislation, many American judges ruled that a father could not arbitrarily make someone a member of his family.[47] This situation, likely influenced by English common law, which protected consanguinity as a form of property rights, posed several practical problems, since it meant that adopted children were not legally family members and therefore had no inheritance rights. Authors including Jamil Zainaldin have argued that the new 1851 legislation changed this, effectively creating a basic framework for legal concepts connected to child custody issues, including the "best interests of the child" and parental "fitness," thereby allowing the American case to evolve differently from England's.[48] By the 1870s, several American states had followed Massachusetts' example and outlined adoption processes and inheritance rights in laws. In Canada, New Brunswick introduced legislation in 1873 to specifically allow for the adoption of illegitimate children, and Nova Scotia passed a more general adoption law in 1896, but adoption legislation was not passed in other provinces until the 1920s.[49] Although the 1871 *Apprenticeship Law* had granted charities the right to send a child out to be "placed," it did not include any legal clarifications or definitions as to the process or the rights, obligations, and responsibilities of the various parties.[50] It was not until 1924 that the process of adoption was legally outlined in Quebec in a specific adoption law and that adopted children gained a judicial status and clear legal claims on their new family.[51]

Despite the lack of legal guidelines, many nineteenth-century charities gave children to families in an arrangement they referred to as "adoption." It is of interest that the two Montreal charities rarely used the method. Only fifteen children in the LBS and eighteen in the POA were "adopted." The POA adoptions showed a clear preference for girls, with thirteen girls and five boys, but this gender imbalance was not repeated in the LBS. Adoptive parents were all from Quebec and tended to be artisans and farmers. Unlike the modern preference for young children, families tended to want children who were between six and thirteen, slightly younger than apprentices but at an age at which they would soon be useful. Some Ontario charities established adoption age at under eight, but the Montreal Committees never discussed this type of policy.[52]

Adoption did not generate much discussion in the LBS, given that most of the children had living parents, but the POA discussed the process several times. In Boston, where Susan Porter Benson argues that adoption evolved out of apprenticeship, the Boston Female Asylum simply legally bound adopted children using a version of the indenture form until the 1851 law clarified the situation, and, she suspects, possibly even after this.[53] But the Montreal charities made a clear distinction between apprenticeship (with a legal contract) and adoption (without one). They placed children in a family under the first format (apprenticeship) to be educated and learn a trade, and in consideration of the work this would require, they enforced the terms of a legal contract and expected payment in exchange. They placed children in a family under the second format (adoption) and expected them to be treated as regular children entering an affective bond.

Although the ladies appear to have sincerely believed that adoption made a child a member of a family, not a helper like an apprentice, and hence there was no contract or payment, they were aware of the practical problems posed by the legal ambiguity of inheritance rights and of the possibility that families might use children as free labour. In the absence of any legislation, the POA made an adopting family sign a waiver relieving the charity of all responsibility for the child, but an actual legal transfer of parental rights was not possible.[54] Nevertheless, the ladies believed that the waiver gave adoptive parents rights over the child, and removed the POA's right to interfere to protect an adopted child. In her study of the Toronto POH, Charlotte Neff argues that "under simple rules of contract, any written agreement between a children's home and an adoptive family should have been enforceable between them," and thus the home should have been able to take back a child if needed.[55] The Montreal ladies, however, were not convinced of this. It was considerations such as these that led the Committee to use adoption infrequently.

Under these circumstances, the POA tried to use their own by-laws to tighten the rules governing adoptions and make it a safer option for children. The original POA rules included a trial period for three months; the application was designed for childless families with the father promising to make the child his heir.[56] These rules were strengthened in 1851. The new rules clearly stipulated that only childless families could adopt POA children, and then only on signing a legal waiver that specifically included the child in any future inheritance.[57] By attempting to make adoption a process centred on completing a family through the addition of a child, and one that involved the acceptance of familial obligations such as inheritance – that is, a contract based on sentiment, not economics – the POA hoped to reduce the chances of a family adopting a child if what they really wanted was a free apprentice. The childless family rule was also designed to minimize potential future conflicts with other heirs.

No rules, however, could actually eliminate the possibility of sending a child into an unhappy home, and in 1853 a young girl adopted under the revised rules died from overwork and starvation. Five-year-old Anna D. was adopted by a Granby couple in April 1851. The adoptive mother attended the Committee meeting seventeen months later in September 1852 to ask that the child be accepted back into the POA, since they could not control her and felt no affection for her. Although it was against the policy, the ladies agreed, since they felt that otherwise "the poor child might soon be cast upon the wide world," but they insisted that the couple deposit a penalty fee in a savings account for the child, a requirement the woman refused. Informed soon afterwards by people in the area that the home was "a very uncomfortable one," the POA wrote in December to ask the couple to return the child. Six months later they finally sent Rev. Dr Henry Wilkes, the Anglican minister who had given the couple their character reference, to collect her. Although when the child arrived it was found she had been "insufficiently fed and cruelly overworked" and had "little hope of a recovery," the institution's physician told the Committee that there were insufficient grounds for a criminal prosecution. The ladies did what they could to save her, but Anna died on 1 August 1853, aged seven years old.[58]

The ladies were deeply saddened and shocked by this case. As a direct result of this death, they removed adoption from their by-laws in January 1855.[59] Thus, recognizing their inability to ensure the safety of adopted children and possibly feeling some sense of responsibility and remorse for having acted too slowly in Anna's case to save her life, the ladies eliminated the possibility of the problem recurring. Retold as a cautionary tale, this case served to reaffirm the no-adoption policy in 1867 and 1873 when new members inquired as to the reason behind it.[60] After 1855, the charity only agreed to adoption in two exceptional cases. One was an abandoned infant; the other was a deserted mixed-race child who they feared would be difficult to apprentice. Both were adopted by childless couples as specified in the 1851 rules.[61]

Anna's case highlights the risk inherent in sending a young child into an unknown family and the difficulties involved in protecting their interests. Other charities probably experienced similar problems. Certainly the Boston

Female Orphan Asylum found that about twenty per cent of children adopted from their home had negative experiences, although none of them serious enough to lead to death.[62] The POA Committee attempted to prevent abuse by using their by-laws to fill the void in the province's legal code, but, faced with a family who treated a child badly, they imposed a fine and waited for the family to return the child as requested. The legal ambiguity of adoption as a process in Lower Canada complicated the situation somewhat, as the ladies were unsure of their legal right to intervene. As women, and given the fact that Granby was about 100 kilometres from Montreal, they were restricted in their freedom to intervene directly themselves, but their decision to have someone act on their behalf could have been more timely. The failure to press legal charges against the adoptive parents was also linked to this reluctance to actively intervene in the public sphere, as was their deferring to the male doctor's advice.

The reluctance of the POA Committee to bring legal proceedings in abuse cases was not limited to this one instance. In 1863, when an adopted girl was banished from her adopted home, the POA lawyer intervened and resolved the problem. But in 1869 when the girl consulted the Committee about legal action against these adoptive parents, from whom she had "experienced much unkindness," the ladies were sympathetic, but dissuaded her from proceeding.[63] Similar difficulties in protecting children from abuse, as well as a tendency to avoid legal action, will be apparent with apprenticed children.

APPRENTICESHIP

Like most nineteenth-century child charities, both the POA and the LBS favoured apprenticeship as a method to place orphans and children whose parents were unable to resume their care. In the POA, 393 or 44 per cent of children were apprenticed;[64] in the LBS, 253 or 10 per cent. Although, historically, trades apprenticeship was a means of acquiring skills, the form used by charities was more akin to pauper apprenticeship and focused as much on providing a family home and supervision as it did on skills training per se.[65] Nonetheless, the process involved a detailed legal contract modelled on that of a standard apprenticeship form that ensured financial recompense at the end of its term ("end payment"), and made the master or mistress responsible for continued schooling (or at least reading and writing), regular church attendance, the teaching of the skills relevant to the trade in question, and the provision of adequate support. The standard POA form specified that the master "doth hereby promise and undertake to feed and clothe the said child in a fit and proper manner, according to the respective station of the parties."[66] According to the same contract, the apprenticed child was expected to work both as training and as payment for room and board and was bound to "faithfully serve" and to "demean him/herself as a good and faithful apprentice ought to do."[67]

The lower status of the apprentice in relation to the master was clear in the wording, and the ladies were aware of this unequal power under the law.[68] They were also aware that, despite the legal contract, the potential for exploitation was real. As the POA Secretary noted in 1868, "There is always an anxious responsibility involved in placing out the Orphans, especially the girls, which the Ladies never undertake without prayerful deliberation."[69] In recognition of this, the contract clearly outlined the charity's right to remove an apprentice from an abusive situation or in the event of the master's death.[70]

Just as they had attempted to anticipate where abuses might occur in adoption and head them off if possible, the ladies attempted to reduce the risk of exploitation or abuse associated with apprenticeship by gradually increasing the age at which children were apprenticed, the fees paid, and their control over the mechanism. In the early years POA children were apprenticed as young as eight (six in one case), but this was raised to twelve by 1847 and to fourteen for girls and thirteen for boys by 1854.[71] By the 1880s, girls were indentured at fifteen, and boys at thirteen or fourteen depending on their strength. In the LBS, apprenticeship age was set at ten in 1835.[72] A few years later it was raised to twelve for boys and fourteen for girls, but was decreased again to ten for boys in 1876.[73] The contract ended at age eighteen.[74]

Annual fees for POA apprentices were raised over the period from the yearly rate of $4 to $6, to $8, and then to $10. Apprentices also received a new set of clothes on completion of their term as an end payment.[75] Although masters complained that these fees were high, they were less than those charged by some of the British emigration societies such as Barnardo's, where, by the end of the century, a boy could earn more than $100 in his final placement from fourteen to eighteen.[76] Apprenticed boys from the POA, indentured at thirteen for five years, would only earn $50, plus a new set of clothes; girls apprenticed at fourteen or fifteen would earn less.[77] More importantly, these fees were much less than the wages received by hired farm hands, who were often the same age as apprentices, and it was common for apprentices to complain of this to the matron or in their Christmas letters. The ladies reminded them of the advantages of being in a family and of the new set of clothes they would acquire. Some of the apprentices who absconded did so because of this wage differential, remaining in the area as a hired worker.

This was a structural problem with the apprenticeship contracts used by the Montreal charities, which paid the young trainee the same amount throughout the contract despite the fact that his/her human capital worth was increasing over time. By the end of the term, the apprentice was earning less than he/she would have been able to make on the labour market. End payments were meant to compensate for this, but this was not always a strong enough incentive to quell frustrations and keep apprentices from absconding. From 1897, the POA attempted to forestall this by giving boys small amounts of their apprenticeship fee monthly so they would not feel quite so exploited.

Other than these cases late in the century, the apprenticeship fees were placed in trust with the POA or LBS Treasurer, to be awarded to apprentices if and when they completed their term. Otherwise, all fees were forfeited. This procedure was designed to discourage apprentices from absconding. In the POA, forfeited fees were placed in a Reward Fund, established in 1876, to defray the costs of apprentices returning to Montreal for medical treatment, and to reward good service. From that point, apprentices who successfully completed their term received a $12 reward.[78] This served as a further incentive to complete an apprenticeship. Similar rewards did not exist in the LBS, and references suggest that forfeited fees were simply added to the charity's General Fund.[79]

To prove their eligibility to take an apprentice, both charities required prospective masters to produce a reference letter from their clergyman testifying to their church membership and their fitness to receive and raise a child. In the LBS, apprenticeships were arranged by the First or Second Directresses or by the Monthly Visitors and were not regularly discussed at Committee meetings. Although the application and reference letter were supposed to be submitted before the process could be concluded, many apprenticeships were arranged in the presence of the applicant without this procedure being respected. In addition, the LBS files refer to some children as being "sent on the same terms as" or "as if apprenticed."[80] Some of these took place in the early years before the LBS was sure of its power to indenture children who were not bound to the society. Their lawyer, J.S. McCord, made an agreement to use in these cases and they sent the forms to clergymen for delivery to masters after the fact. However, the Committee remained uncertain about whether these agreements were official contracts.[81] In 1846 they tried to clarify this by adding a by-law specifying their power to apprentice children if parents had no interest in them or if they had been in the institution for years.[82]

Dealing mainly with orphans, the POA took a much more pro-active approach and had developed standardized forms and procedures by 1835.[83] All prospective masters were requested to submit an application accompanied by a reference letter. The Committee reviewed these documents and ruled on each application at their monthly meetings. If accepted, the master/mistress attended the following monthly meeting to sign the forms, pay the first year's fees, and escort the child home.[84] Only in rare instances, such as the imminent closing of river navigation, would the POA agree to an apprenticeship being arranged without these delays being respected.

In one of their first public statements about apprenticeship at their annual meeting in 1840, the POA Secretary assured supporters of both their vigilance and their success: "Their charges, thus provided for with good and careful persons, are not lost sight of by the Directresses of the Institution, who require from their masters annual accounts of their behaviour and progress, and it is with sincere pleasure they state, that during the lapse of many years, with one solitary exception, the reports have been most satisfactory."[85] Even in the POA, however, very little investigation actually took place, and neither Committee questioned the validity of a single character reference from a person unknown to them, even if that person was a clergyman. Although a yearly report on the child's health and progress was stipulated, these were not always sent and there was no way to verify the contents. Thus the charities had few ways to ensure that apprentices were not being exploited or abused, although the files of both charities include references to Secretaries writing for information on apprentices if the requisite letter was not received. For its part, the LBS named a visitor to check on city apprentices in 1846, but did not institute follow-up measures for rural apprentices, who represented about half of the total.[86] The POA, however, distinguished itself from many nineteenth-century child charities by developing an organized visiting system to provide some follow-up for apprentices.[87]

The POA began to consider a system for visiting and monitoring apprentices when they named a visitor to carry out inspections of city apprentices in 1846 and in 1849.[88] Establishing a visiting mechanism for apprentices outside the city was much more difficult and occurred gradually. Whenever anyone connected to the society, including Committee members, was travelling, they made sure to visit any apprentices in the area. In 1859, for example, their legal advisor, J.S. McCord, visited two apprentices while he was in Brome.[89] A more systematic method was developed in the end, but it occurred almost accidentally. In the summer of 1876, the matron requested a vacation and used it to visit the POA apprentices in the region of Lachute, a reflection of her emotional attachment to the children who had been in her care. Her account of this visit convinced the Committee of its value, and from that point on, the matron or superintendent made an annual inspection tour of most of the rural apprentices. There is no specific mention of continuing reports on city apprentices, but it is possible that the matron checked up on them in the course of her normal duties or that the Committee trusted neighbours and supporters to inform them of any problems.

After 1876, the POA apprenticed as many children as possible into areas visited by the matron in order to facilitate the inspection tour and ensure most apprentices would be monitored.[90] Information from these visits also helped the ladies identify and respond to problems. In 1879, for example, the sisters of an apprenticed girl complained about her placement and requested permission to remove her. In the past, the ladies would have refused on the basis of the legal contract, but, having determined from the inspection tour that the farm in question was very isolated and undeveloped, they were concerned about leaving her in "so wild a place where she could learn very little." They cancelled her indenture once the sisters paid a penalty to the master.[91] In 1881, after a master returned an apprentice to the POA claiming he was too weak for the work required, all other applications from the area were refused.[92]

These cases exposed the problems inherent in selecting apprenticeship families solely on the basis of a character reference without verifying the type of work required and the skills that could be acquired. This led the ladies to increase their scrutiny of the placement home and to use the inspection tour as a form of pre-inspection. From 1882, rural applicants were requested to include the exact acreage, age, and location of their farm, as well as the type of work expected. The matron then verified these details during her inspection tour. Several farms were subsequently vetoed as too large, too rough and rocky, too new, too remote, or too far from either church or school.[93] The matron also used the tour to scout out potential apprenticeship homes or applicants for apprentices, based on her knowledge of the children who would soon be of age.[94] The homes of those applying for apprentices in the city were also visited if unknown, and on at least one occasion an application was rejected because of the unsuitability of the home.[95]

The POA introduced other policy restrictions as a result of the problems apprentices experienced. This was the case, for example, with the decision not to send girls out as nursemaids, where they would have major child-care duties.[96] This policy change was directly linked to an unfortunate accident involving a POA apprentice in 1858. In his application for a girl in January, Rev. Morris of Buckingham indicated that she would "be permitted to attend Academy with his daughter" and "could acquire every useful and ornamental branch of education."[97] Considering this an excellent opportunity, the ladies gladly sent Sarah P., then aged fourteen, off to Buckingham. In May, Morris sent Sarah back to Montreal with a friend. The letter the Secretary had received from him in April explained that there had been a terrible accident that had resulted in the death of his only child, an eight-month-old baby. The child had died when Sarah, trying to hold the infant while pouring water from a kettle, had scalded her. In this way Sarah was directly to blame. The POA minutes indicate she was "much afflicted" by the experience.[98]

The case raises several issues. First, it is clear that Rev. Morris misrepresented his family situation and the work he expected in his application. His child was not attending the Academy but was eight months old. As a result, rather than going to school, Sarah was expected to carry out childcare duties. This exposes the problem of verifying information on an application. The ladies depended on the testimonial from a clergyman and, later, the annual visit to do this. In this case, since Morris himself was a clergyman, they had more than likely trusted his integrity. As the annual tour had not yet begun and Buckingham was outside of the region where any of the ladies tended to visit, they were unable to confirm any information in that way. Second, the master simply returned the girl with no mention of the legal contract by which he was bound, although it is unlikely that the Committee would have held him to it. Third, the case reveals that problems and abuse could take many forms. Was Sarah unhappy, overworked, discouraged by the unexpected circumstances she found herself in, or "inattentive"?[99]

The Committees also attempted to minimize potential abuse by introducing flexibility into the process. The LBS almost immediately introduced the possibility of waiving one year's fees if the apprentice proved to be sickly or unable to work.[100] By 1840, they had outlined a process for transferring an indenture, although the original master retained ultimate responsibility for the apprentice's well-being.[101] The POA had a stricter interpretation of the apprenticeship contract. The original by-law established that a contract could only be broken on the grounds of abuse or the master's death, but on several occasions in the 1840s and 1850s this was done for other reasons.[102] To increase flexibility, an 1856 by-law permitted masters to break a contract for "incompatibility of character," on the payment of a $20 fine that was waived if the master arranged a transfer.[103] There are many references to masters using this rule to transfer an apprentice to another farmer or a tradesman.[104] By 1871 the POA also allowed masters to cancel apprenticeships on the grounds of an apprentice's delicate health.[105]

This type of flexibility could be instrumental in avoiding abusive situations. On the other hand, since transfers were made infrequently, apprentices did not experience the same level of instability as found in organizations that used trial periods or moved young people regularly.[106] Ideally the POA used their inspection/visiting system, once it existed, to resolve problems before they became too serious and in this way minimize transfers. As the Secretary explained in 1885, "any little difficulty or misunderstanding … can be much more advantageously arranged than could be by means of writing."[107] If problems persisted, apprentices returned to Montreal and the ladies found new places for them.[108]

APPRENTICESHIP OCCUPATION AND LOCALITY

Generally, both charities apprenticed children to respectable lower-middle-class families such as farmers, skilled artisans, or shopkeepers, or even merchants and professionals including doctors, lawyers, and ministers. A large number of children were indentured to farmers to work on the farm (boys) or in the house (girls). Although some of the apprenticed children were learning the master's trade, many were also apprenticed to learn general domestic skills. The sixty-one apprentices who went to merchants or professionals, for instance, were probably in training as servants. This was also the case with boys apprenticed to dressmakers and girls apprenticed to tailors, chandlers, or watchmakers. The occupation of masters and mistresses to whom children were apprenticed is known for 74 per cent of POA apprentices, or 291 children. In the LBS, occupation is known for only 34 per cent of apprenticeship masters, but we find the same tendencies (although a reduced likelihood to apprentice children to farmers).

The clearest trend in the POA apprenticeships is the number of children apprenticed to farmers; at 143 children, they made up 36 per cent of all apprentices but 49 per cent if we consider only those for whom we know the master's occupation. This was the result of a combination of factors. First, most of the applications for apprentices came from farmers, who made up a majority of Quebec's English-speaking population and could almost always use the cheap labour an apprentice represented.[109] Equally important, though, was the fact that the ladies believed, as did most North American charity workers, that the country (and especially farm life) was more wholesome and held fewer temptations for young people than the city.[110] These factors were reinforced by the belief that the apprenticeship fee and subsequent wage work on a farm would enable boys to accumulate enough capital to buy a farm and provide for their future. For girls, domestic service on a farm was seen as excellent training for housewifery. On several occasions the POA Committee decided "that in every respect, a home in the country was preferable to town life,"[111] and passed resolutions to place children in country situations if possible in both 1872 and 1874.[112] The LBS Committee had the same idealized view of the country, but as they increased co-ordination with parents, the latter often vetoed apprenticeships in the country. This was the case, for example with sixteen LBS children sent to places in Montreal in 1877.[113]

The apprentices themselves could also have an influence on apprenticeship. The POA refused several applications on the grounds of a child's preference or aptitude, "deeming it their duty not to bind a child to a business for which he had no taste or for which he was unqualified,"[114] or skipped over boys to place another in recognition of their preference for a given trade or for the country.[115] The LBS matron occasionally would ask for volunteers for country placements.[116]

The POA Committee also preferred to apprentice children (especially boys) to trades (including farming) rather than as servants.[117] In line with this overall orientation, the final clause of the 1852 By-Laws instructed the superintendent to "make the boys acquainted with the various trades and manufactories in and about the City, in order that their knowledge may be increased, and their tastes and minds developed, with a view to their subsequent adoption of one or other useful trades or occupation."[118] They favoured apprenticeships with rural artisans, a situation that happily combined the advantages of trades-training and country living. An excellent example of this is John Adams, a La Tortue rope-maker, who trained nine POA boys and only stopped applying for boys when his rope-works burned down. Children also went to rural coopers, carpenters, saddle-makers, and so on.[119] Twenty-seven per cent of apprentices where the master's occupation is known, or seventy-nine children, went to artisans or shopkeepers; many of them, like Mr Adams, lived in the country. However, apprenticing young people to skilled trades in Montreal proved more difficult as the city industrialized and changes were made to the normal practices in trades apprenticeships (boarding arrangements, clothing provisions, age, etc.).

Apprenticeships in urban trades began to change in the early nineteenth century. Gillian Hamilton has found that most apprentices in the period 1791–1820 still received clothing and board, but that by 1840 only 20 per cent received clothing rather than a cash clothing allowance.[120] During the same period the average starting age had increased to fifteen, contract length had decreased to five years, fewer apprentices were living at their masters' homes, and the use of the entire system had decreased.[121] These findings are confirmed by studies done by Mary Anne Poutanen in relation to dressmaking and Joanne Burgess for shoemakers.[122] Given these changes, it is not surprising that when urban artisans applied for an apprentice, they often wanted a child on terms other than those specified in the standard charity apprenticeship contract, which was basically pre-industrial in its format. In particular, city tradesmen did not want to take responsibility for religious training or schooling. Even more importantly, they did not want to provide clothing, nor did they want an apprentice living in their family home. Finally, neither charity was in a position to pay any type of binding fee where this had become the norm.

By the 1850s, both charities experienced problems arranging apprenticeships to city artisans as a result of these changes. In 1857, for example, when a well-educated thirteen-year-old orphan was admitted to the POA and indicated a preference for printing, the Committee immediately approached their printer, John Lovell. Lovell was willing to accept the boy and even to pay him wages rather than the standard fee, but did not want him to live in his home. He proposed that the boy board in the POA instead. Before the end of the century, the ladies were reticent to let teens remain in or return to the institution for a substantial length of time for fear it might have an unsettling effect on the other children, therefore they refused. The boy was indentured instead to a tobacconist who accepted to board him in his house.[123] The LBS had had a similar experience when a cabinetmaker applied for a boy in 1851.[124]

The LBS case also highlighted the problem of age. Both charities apprenticed children, especially boys, before the age of fifteen, an age that was increasingly the standard age for urban apprenticeship.[125] This age differential is probably one of the reasons why so few city artisans applied for apprentices. The ladies tried to circumvent this problem by including the possibility of a future transfer in the indenture contract. The LBS boy in the 1851 case mentioned above, for example, was indentured the next year (at thirteen) as a servant, but the contract specified that in two years he would be transferred to a carpenter if he still wished.[126] Unfortunately it is unclear whether the LBS Committee had found an effective way to circumvent the age problem, since no follow-up exists. Based on a case in the POA later in the century, however, it appears the method was far from sure. In 1889 a boy's guardian applied to the POA for his release. The boy wanted to be a carpenter but a place could not be found. The guardian hoped to place him on a farm for two years to increase his strength and then to send him to a carpenter. The ladies vetoed this on the grounds that the same method had been used for his older brother, who had gone to four different places and still not learned a trade. They decided to keep the boy in the POA until they could arrange an apprenticeship with a carpenter.[127]

The subject of how to increase the number of apprenticeships to city trades was finally debated by the POA Committee in 1887. At that point, the Secretary noted poignantly that it had been "felt for some time past by several of the Committee that it would be desirable if possible to give the boys a trade, if they shewed any predilection for such."[128] The ladies identified boarding as the main problem and decided to organize carpentry classes inside the POA itself to provide boys with some skills training while they looked for a solution. The next year a city plumber applied for a boy. Although willing to pay the boy's board, he was unwilling to board him himself. The ladies arranged for him to board at the Boys' Home. The plumber paid his board as well as the standard indenture fee and gave the POA a clothing allowance of $0.50 a week.[129]

The new arrangement worked well, and the POA amended their by-laws in 1890 to allow indentures using an irregular form where the master was not responsible for lodging, schooling, clothing, or moral supervision.[130] The ladies were now free to secure situations "to the best possible interests" of the children.[131] In 1890, one boy was indentured to a plumber and another to a man working at the Grand Trunk Railway who promised to put him into a mechanical trade in two years.[132] By 1900, several POA and LBS boys lived in the Boys' Home while working as apprentices.[133] But, despite resolving the boarding problem, a lack of applications from artisans limited trades apprenticeships.

Thus, an analysis of the applications received for apprentices reveals that the ladies' preference for farmers as masters was not a deliberate plan by the Committees to limit the children's social mobility, nor the result of a class-based notion that charity children were more suited for menial occupations, as Rooke and Schnell suggest.[134] Many of the children were apprenticed to the occupation they chose and on several occasions both Committees indicated a preference for skilled trades, at least for boys. However, both the practical problems posed by the structural changes to urban apprenticeships and the Committees' hesitancy to modify the standard legal form to accommodate these changes, compromised apprenticeships to urban trades until the end of the century. Furthermore, even once the boarding problem was resolved, the age problem remained. As a result, very few applications were received from city artisans. It is also relevant that the ladies honestly, if somewhat naïvely, considered training on a farm as akin to a trade and as holding out the real possibility of future independence. This was the reason they preferred to apprentice boys to farmers, rather than as servants. Apprenticing girls as servants in the city or the country, on the other hand, was seen as relevant skills training.

Given the number of children apprenticed to farmers or to rural tradesmen, it is not surprising that almost three-quarters of POA apprentices went to situations in the country.[135] This trend was weakening by the end of the century, and in the final twenty-year period was true for only 58 per cent of apprentices. Over the century there was also a difference by gender, as more girls were apprenticed to city families and more boys went to rural areas. Most of the POA children (79 per cent, or 230) were apprenticed within a 100-kilometre radius of Montreal, with eighty-one remaining in the city itself.[136] Seventeen children went to the US (usually close to the border) and fifty-five to Ontario,[137] but only four children were sent outside Quebec after 1860. By mid-century the POA deliberately placed apprentices within easy reach of the city to facilitate the investigation of problems. Concentrations appear around Lachute (twenty-seven children) and towns nearby, spilling over the Ontario border into areas such as Hawkesbury (a total of fifty children). Around forty-four children went to places in the Eastern Townships, including Danville (twelve), Sherbrooke, and Cowansville. On a smaller scale, there were clusters with twenty-six children each on the south shore around Laprairie, St Phillipe, and La Tortue, and in the Richelieu Valley around Noyan, Lacolle, and Hemmingford.

All of these areas had large Protestant populations as well as churches and English-language schools. Geographic groupings of apprentices facilitated the inspection tour, but there were other reasons they occurred. Once the children were known in an area, applications from the region tended to increase; some families took a number of children in sequence. The Committees were "very glad to intrust [sic] the children into hands that have already proved themselves able and willing to train them up usefully,"[138] and preferred this type of application since they could evaluate them on the basis of previous experience and character references from ministers they knew. They also hoped to depend on these families to serve as protectors for apprentices in the area and believed these combined factors would reduce the chances of sending a child into an abusive situation.

Most LBS apprentices also went to families in Quebec, but apprenticeship did not follow the POA pattern. First, there was an almost equal number of urban (49.5 per cent) and rural (50.5 per cent) apprenticeships.[139] As a result, seventy-four apprentices remained in Montreal and others close by. At no point was there a clear rural preference. Some of this was due to a lack of rural applications; the fact that many parents vetoed apprenticeships to farmers was also instrumental in this. Second, we do not find a repetition of the POA pattern of large numbers of children being apprenticed into the same areas, or families taking more than one child. There were some smaller concentrations with four or five children each on the South Shore in Chateauguay, Hemmingford, Hemlock, and Lacolle, as well as Rawdon, Granby, and Farnham, and seven children went to the Lachute area.

PROBLEMS AND ABUSE CASES

The apprenticeship contract established a framework for basic conditions and outlined the responsibility of masters to provide adequate support; but placing a child, even a teenager, in the care of an unknown family carried the risk of exploitation or abuse. Documentation on particular LBS apprenticeships is sparse, but references are made to approximately sixteen problem cases, most of them from the early years. Six of these apprentices were returned to Montreal and found alternate situations.[140] In six other cases the Committee wrote for more information, but no follow-up is provided in the minutes.[141] Only two children were re-admitted after running away due to abuse. In one case the girl's fees were used to buy her clothes, indicating the ladies felt her charges were well-founded, but no action was taken against the master.[142] Several cases of ill treatment led to the apprentice taking shelter with neighbours.[143]

In the POA, slightly over ten per cent or thirty-nine of the 393 POA apprentices ran away or were sent back by their masters. Some of the runaways returned to the charity home, whereupon the Committee contacted the master to try to resolve the problem.[144] Failing that, they found another placement and transferred the indentures. Other runaways took refuge in a neighbour's home. Sometimes the indentures were transferred to these families, or the original indentures were cancelled, and the former apprentice remained with the new family as a wage-worker. The ladies were very concerned about an apprentice ending up alone without the protection and support of an adult. They criticized masters who did not immediately inform them about runaways, and if the child's whereabouts were unknown they sent the superintendent or even the police to find him, "so as to prevent, if possible, his becoming a vagrant and outcast in Society."[145] As the surrogate parent and signatory to the apprenticeship contract, the Committee had the ultimate responsibility for the children, especially in cases of contractual default or abuse.

About thirteen POA cases involved more serious problems than simply a misunderstanding, and the apprentice was removed by the ladies (or attempts were made to do this) or returned to the orphanage by his/her master. Terms such as "severely beaten and overworked," "dreadfully illused [*sic*]," "unhappily placed," and "cruel treatment in every way" describe their circumstances.[146] When the ladies used terms such as "ill-used" or "severely neglected," however, they could be referring to a range of situations from things that today would be considered minor, such as not attending church and Sunday school, to more serious circumstances such as a lack of schooling or insufficient clothing, up to and including overwork, physical abuse, or sexual assault. The POA files include much more detailed information on follow-up than those of the LBS. Analyzing these cases reveals the circumstances under which problems occurred and the difficulties the ladies encountered in their attempts to protect the young people indentured under their authority.

The first problem was information. The Committee usually learned of a problem through a letter from neighbours, the local minister, the apprentice's family, or either the master or apprentice themselves. They investigated all accusations by initially contacting the master and then writing to the local minister, or using their informal networks of friends in the area. Often this process involved lengthy delays. If the apprentice was in the city, a Directress or the matron went to investigate, which sped things up considerably, but most of the problem cases were in rural areas and the inspection tour did not cover all apprenticeship homes.

Denial of the accusations by either the master or the apprentice was also a problem. In several cases the Committee invited the master and apprentice to the monthly meeting but the children remained where placed.[147] In a few cases this was probably due to different understandings of abuse. One young girl, for example, was described as "deplorably neglected" but it appears the main problem was a lack of church attendance; not surprisingly the girl refused to leave and risk more serious neglect elsewhere.[148] In another case, a neighbour reported seeing a master strike a boy with a hoe. When the POA lawyer wrote asking that the boy be returned, the master sent his notary with affidavits from the boy denying all charges and requesting to stay. The master invited the matron to visit but she was unable to see the boy alone. Without proof of abuse, the ladies were only able to remove the boy three years later when the master died.[149]

In several cases where the ladies had determined the apprentice must be returned, the master took months to comply. In the case of one girl suffering from eye problems, for example, the total delay was two years, during which time many letters were exchanged and the Committee anguished over possible permanent eye damage.[150] When the girl was finally returned, they determined not to again place "a child where she could not be visited whenever necessity required."[151] In another case it took seven months after reports of ill-treatment reached the POA and the Committee had arranged for one boy's return, before the master finally sent him to Montreal. The ladies' exclamation that they were "glad to obtain possession of the boy" reflects their dependence on the goodwill of masters to comply with removal requests.[152] Distance was often a factor in these cases. The ladies tended to wait for a master to return a child and were hesitant to pro-actively send someone to remove them. The penalty fee could also add to delays. Although it was designed to protect apprentices, it often became a major stumbling block to having an apprentice returned quickly, since most masters attempted to avoid paying it by stalling for time. In a few cases the POA finally waived the fee, but the delay was lengthened by their initial attempt to impose it.

When a master refused to return an apprentice or to transfer the indentures, the range of possibilities was limited. Although the *Masters and Servants Act* gave masters many rights and extensive power over apprentices, they were legally liable in cases of undeniable violation of contract. The apprenticeship contract, the Society's by-laws, and the 1871 *Apprenticeship Law* established the Committees' right to intervene in cases of improper treatment or apprentices absconding.[153] However, proving abuse sufficient to unilaterally break an apprenticeship contract or proceed with legal action was not easy. When one master denied abuse charges, the ladies discussed their inability to prosecute without at least two witnesses willing to testify.[154] Finding no neighbours ready to do this, they were forced to abandon the idea. In another case they admitted they had not discovered anything serious enough "to admit of interference of the Corporation."[155]

A final relevant factor in explaining the Committees' response to problems is gender. As women, the ladies were limited in their ability to intervene personally to rescue young people miles away. They were also reluctant to intervene legally (and publicly) to challenge a master, and several times they dissuaded former apprentices from pressing charges themselves. In 1859, for example, they assured one master, who feared his apprentice intended to sue him for unpaid fees, that only the Committee, as signatory to the agreement, had the right to sue; that they did not do so if it could be avoided; and that they would not authorize an apprentice to sue for fees in their place.[156] In another case of a boy who had been apprenticed from the age of six to eighteen and had never learned to read or write (in clear violation of the contract stipulations on schooling), the POA voted him money from the reward fund to help pay for his schooling but withheld the money until he promised not to use it to prosecute his master, as the master feared.[157]

Nonetheless, legal action was initiated in two very serious cases: one for sexual assault and another for aggravated assault. In the first case, the girl's sister informed the POA of the situation. Confronted, the master confessed but disappeared once legal proceedings were begun. Once the girl was returned to the orphanage and the man was still not found, the charges were dropped. The Committee decided that sufficient punishment had resulted from him having been "disgraced and driven from his home."[158] The assault case involved a boy who had taken refuge with a nearby farmer. His feet were severely frozen and he had been inadequately clothed. The local magistrate's investigation found the master guilty of aggravated assault; he and his wife were fined $150 and the man served one month in jail. The boy was returned to Montreal and immediately hospitalized for an operation on his feet. The indentures were rescinded, but the POA did not force the master to pay the penalty fee, believing, in light of the boy's subsequent behaviour, that he probably shared some blame for the situation.[159]

Faced with the powers of masters over apprentices under the law; with masters who refused to comply with removal requests or did so tardily; with boys and girls who were attached to their masters, afraid what the unknown might hold, or simply afraid of the possible repercussions of complaining; and with long kilometres separating the charity and the apprentices formally under their care (and with restrictions on their ability to travel unescorted), the ladies attempted to protect the apprentices' interests and ensure they had a home to live in and some training. They also had to contend with differing notions of how much work a child should do and what level of discipline was acceptable, and with possible prejudice against charity children that masters might have, as well as the range of possible character problems children and teens might present. In addition to this, the ladies' own preference for the countryside influenced the fact that so many children were placed in rural regions in the first place. Occasionally they allowed untimely delays to occur while they tried to resolve a situation and hesitated about intervening in public space to rescue children or to prosecute masters, but overall they tried their best to get children out of bad situations and to deal with a range of problems.

Thus we see that the Committee's attempt to secure a positive family experience for the children under their care who did not have families or were unable to return to their own families was not always successful. They developed policies to attempt to avoid problems, and intervened when they could. It is some consolation, however, that the children were sent to adoptive homes or apprenticeships once they came of age (or according to specific requests and talents) and were not exposed to a monthly "visit" system like that used by some institutions.[160] It would be difficult to measure the emotional trauma of being put on show on a regular basis, always wondering if this time you would be chosen to join a family. The children of the LBS and the POA at least started their journey to a new home on a positive note. The ladies attempted to maintain some oversight of the quality of treatment and training the children received in these placements, but ultimately this mainly depended on the masters who signed the apprenticeship contracts or the families who adopted children.

POST-APPRENTICESHIP

One of the major problems with apprenticeship was that the term ended when children were still minors. After 1855, the POA arranged for a tutor (usually a male close to the society) to look after the interests of orphans until their majority.[161] This was rendered unnecessary by the 1871 *Apprenticeship*

Law, which made it legal for an apprentice over the age of fourteen to access his/her fees and legally discharge a charity from all future responsibility.[162] Nonetheless the Committees tried to find some adult supervision until the children's majority, encouraging masters to arrange positions for their former apprentices. On at least one occasion this led to a conflict with a boy's relatives, who accused the POA of separating families when they arranged this without informing the relatives in advance.[163] Many apprentices returned to Montreal at the end of their contract. They were admitted into the charities for a few days and isolated from the younger children while the Committee found them a position and arranged for board, or, for boys after 1870, secured their admission to the Boys' Home, which would find them a position and provide continued supervision.

We have very little data about what happened to the young people once they completed their apprenticeships, although some information can be gleaned from the POA minutes. The matron reported on former POA children still living in the Lachute area and others occasionally sent letters or visited the institution. As we saw, two former children (both artisans) sent substantial donations to the POA and several others inherited money. We also know that the ladies sent money from the Reward Fund to help several boys while they learned a trade or continued their schooling. They also sent money to help with land purchases, and three of these former children who now had farms took apprentices themselves. From data of this type on 101 former children, we find that most of the girls had married, many of them in the country; fifteen of the boys had bought small farms, and three had become ministers or teachers. A further thirty worked in trades, fifteen as servants, and three as farm labourers. Frail health had resulted in the deaths of twenty within a few years of their departure and at least five former residents spent some time in a Reform School or a prison. Unlike the results found by Carol Lasser in Salem, where a number of former charity children were later located in the poorhouse, only one reference exists to a POA child having entered the Protestant House of Industry, although without the institution's registers, we are unable to verify entry data. In the above case and that of the two former LBS girls who ended up in jail "for want of a home," the ladies removed them as soon as they found out where they were and found them situations.[164] One former POA girl returned to the POA to work as a servant, entering with her young child who was disabled, and, as we saw, two others returned to the POA when they were sick with TB. We have also already noted the support the Committee provided for former boys who enlisted as soldiers during the war.

TO SERVICE

Throughout the century, a number of children had occasionally left the charities to enter directly into domestic service for wages, instead of an apprenticeship. Most of the twenty-three cases in the LBS were teens admitted temporarily while the ladies found them a position or while they regained their health. In the 1890s a few boys were hired out to jobs in the city and boarded in the Boys' Home, and several of the girls remained in the institution under a new 1873 rule that girls could be trained for service in the LBS until eighteen.[165] Nonetheless, it was difficult for the LBS to implement such a rule on any large scale due to space restrictions and parents asking to remove their children. In the POA, however, forty-five children or 5 per cent left to go directly into wage work, and this represented a deliberate policy shift. After 1850 a few girls had been apprenticed to the POA and remained to train as servants rather than going into a family. In 1884, the Committee voted to keep girls to train them "when [it was] thought advisable."[166] The next year the ladies announced that they would retain girls in the asylum longer "to give them a more thorough training in household work."[167] From that point, girls began training in sewing and specialized domestic service at twelve or fourteen and did not leave the institution until they were between fifteen and seventeen and ready to work for regular wages. Almost no girls were apprenticed from the POA after 1890.

In part this policy shift was driven by the female charity directors' recognition of the limitations under which they worked and the potential risks associated with apprenticeship, particularly for girls. But it also had advantages. Since training was now done in the institution, the Committee avoided the problems apprentices had sometimes encountered. Furthermore, at $5 to $10 a month rather than $10 a year, the children earned a much higher level of remuneration as servants than as apprentices and the POA avoided collection problems. Finally, being placed at an older age, the young people were both stronger physically and in a better position to defend their own rights. Girls were found positions in Montreal as upper maids, usually with families known to the Committee. The method was used less regularly for boys, for whom it was more difficult to find positions, but a few boys, believed too weak to apprentice to trades or farmers, remained in the institutions and were then found positions in city offices as clerks.

Between the new training policy and the practice of not allowing any child to leave the POA younger than thirteen or fourteen even to return to relatives, children remained in the institution longer than in former years. Certainly they remained much longer than in the LBS. By the last twenty-year period from 1880 to 1899, for example, 54 per cent of new entrants to the POA remained more than six years, while this was true for only seven per cent of LBS children. Additionally, only five per cent of the children who entered the POA from 1880 to 1899 remained less than one year.

THE TWENTIETH CENTURY

Patterns for the LBS remained much the same in the early twentieth century, with most children returning home, although average length of stay increased slightly due to the number of industrial school children. The same could not be said of the POA, where major changes occurred with the suspension of the orphans-only admission policy. Although the average length of stay was three years, in many years there was a much larger turnover than the POA had known in the past. Furthermore, 123 of the 223 children who entered from 1900 to 1921 left to return to their family or relatives; ninety-three of them went to parents. As a result, the number leaving to go into service was reduced to only twenty-six cases. These were still very successful placements, with the children earning good wages. Many of the girls went to the homes of charity managers while boys went as office workers in the offices of doctors, lawyers, or people known to the Committee. Other boys went into wage work that Committee members found for them with supporters. Twenty-three boys were sent to the Boys' Home. The Committee used this as a way to organize board for boys who were working, but also as a way whereby boys who were more difficult to place or who had become difficult to manage would come under the supervision of a male Board of Directors and a male superintendent and be found positions as apprentices. Finally, one of the most interesting new trends was the revival of the use of adoption. Although adoption was not as yet legal in Quebec, twenty-two children were adopted to families. No discussion of this major policy shift is found, but it is probably connected to a number of factors, most important among them the gradual disuse of apprenticeship. By 1905 the practice of placing children in apprenticeship had decreased to such an extent that the POA Committee suspended the Reward Fund and absorbed the remaining money into the General Fund.[168] It might also be due to the normalization of adoption itself as it was increasingly legalized elsewhere. From early in the century the POA received a number of requests to adopt children, all of them for children over twelve (who would have been placed as apprentices in the past). Unfortunately one of these children needed to be rescued within a month of her placement, but this did not generate any major debate about continuing the practice of placing children without a legally binding contract.[169]

Over the century, the ladies running these two Montreal child charities grappled with issues such as the rights of parents or relatives to retrieve children, the rights of adoptive parents in relation to their new children, and those of masters in relation to apprentices, as well as with questions of child abuse and adequate education and training. For the most part, both Committees accepted to care for children temporarily and return them to families, often after a short period of time. However, they did not accept absolute parental rights in cases where they believed the interests of the child were morally or spiritually in jeopardy, a situation that led some parents to proactively resist these efforts. Their preference for rural placements for apprentices is clear, as is their preference to have boys learn a trade (even that of farmer) rather than be placed to train as domestic servants (though the latter was considered appropriate for girls); by late century they had finally resolved the practical difficulties in terms of urban trades apprenticeships. The ladies' attempts to protect the children who left their care to enter families other than their own, in either adoption or apprenticeship, and the problems they encountered provided them with the expertise needed to refine and modify their departure policies over the years. Class was a factor in terms of departure policy, as some of the ladies' assumptions about parental fitness and about ideal training were class-based. Gender was also an important factor as these upper-middle-class ladies intervened or hesitated to intervene in public space.

In her work on child charities in Toronto, Charlotte Neff argues that the nineteenth century saw a "heavy reliance on home care throughout the century," since even child institutions aimed to send children into placement homes as soon as possible.[170] This was never true for these two Montreal charities, which waited until children were in their early teens before they were placed. It became even less so over time. In fact, working on the basis of their experience and propelled by their protective child-centred approach, by the 1880s these two Montreal charities (and especially the POA) did the exact opposite and avoided sending children into families if at all possible unless it was to return them to their own family. Rather, the ladies were convinced of their ability to provide both a safer environment and superior training in their institutional homes. These policy issues and the logic behind them are discussed in more detail in the next chapter.

7

"Women's Social Sphere"

In the 1873 *Annual Report*, the Secretary, Fanny Evans, described the Ladies' Benevolent Society as a "Society, which is doing so much good in the quiet, unassuming manner characteristic of all institutions in which ladies are the working power."

~ LBS, *Annual Report*, 1873

This chapter treats the impact of the gendered discourse that presumed women would manage an institution differently from men because of their special "nature." Notions of special qualities and separate spheres of action could effectively limit women's power and authority outside of the home, assuming they allowed themselves to be influenced by such prescriptive ideas. The fact that the LBS Secretary chose to describe her organization's work in the above terms shows that the Montreal ladies had integrated at least some of this discourse, but, as noted in the Introduction, these definitions represented an ideal, not a reality. Charity management was closely associated with women's caregiving and domestic role as well as with the duty of Christian benevolence, and the exertion of moral and religious influence over the poor; and, as such, it was an accepted, even expected, undertaking for elite women. Effectively it took place in the social sphere, that intermediate space between the formal public sphere and the domestic private sphere, although managing institutions was a very public activity.

It is important to distinguish the Montreal ladies from reformist women who confidently and deliberately intervened in the public sphere to "reshape the city," as Sarah Deutsch has explained in the case of Boston, or to engage in municipal reform politics, as Maureen Flanagan found in Chicago.[1] As conservative women, they understood the legitimacy of their undertaking in terms of its religious, class, and domestic nature, not in terms of their own citizenship, and were constantly conscious of the limitations they believed gendered prescriptions placed on them. Thus the discourse of separate spheres was relevant to them to the extent it impacted their lives and their charity work in a very real way, despite the fact that their charities served a critical social function in the city and that the ladies themselves were regularly involved in public activities.

The women's social sphere, as represented by the gender-conscious and conservative Committees that ran the POA and the LBS, was characterized and inscribed in two ways: by the social/spatial restrictions imposed on women by prescriptions of polite society and by the empowerment these women gained from their own interpretation of women's special qualities and their authority within the women's sphere. This chapter looks at both of these aspects. The first part examines the limits placed on women's public appearances and on their public discourse by spatial restrictions and etiquette, as well as the ladies' tendency to depend on men to advise them in activities generally defined as male. The second part considers the empowering aspects by looking at policy development.

Both charities developed policies on the basis of their experience and the expertise they developed running the charities as well as their evaluation of need. In this, they challenged and resisted changing trends in charity work that were propagated by some members of the city's male elite and reformist women's groups. In the widespread re-evaluation of poor relief methods that took place in the second half of the nineteenth century, two major trends questioned institutionalization itself: the placing of children in foster families rather than in child institutions ("placing out") and the scientific charity movement that attacked traditional charity as sentimental, injudicious, and unscientific. The two Montreal charities rejected both of these movements, defending their policy choices and their institutional autonomy. These two movements and the ladies' response to them shape the third part of the chapter. The chapter ends with an examination of the interaction between the benevolent female societies and reformist groups such as the Young Women's Christian Association (YWCA) and the Montreal Local Council of Women (LCW), with whom the charities differed in basic orientation.

PUBLIC APPEARANCES

Given the nature of their work, it was imperative for these women to maintain the support of the male Protestant establishment. To some extent at least, they depended on this for their social legitimacy and their moral authority within the community, a moral authority that was class-based and that rested on their social status as elite women or ladies with the contingent connotations of female qualities. Public acceptance of the prevailing gender ideology on women's "proper" place was key to retaining this support.

The annual general meetings, open to the public and attended by a mixed audience, represented one of the most public activities these Committees performed. It was also here, in the context of the Secretary's and Treasurer's reports, that the political, economic, and administrative nature of their work was publicly exposed, although the official reports tended to underestimate these aspects of the actual work involved in charity management, and certainly its public nature. Recognizing how crucial these meetings were to their social acceptance and funding, the Committees were extremely careful to present an appearance of modesty and respect for the norms of polite society.

The clearest and most pervasive of these prescriptions regulated women's public appearances, or their incursions on geographic public space usually reserved for men. Under these norms, respectable women could attend public meetings, but social convention held that they could not address a mixed audience or speak in public.[2] Not speaking at public meetings was the norm for women throughout the nineteenth-century in Canada. When Lady Aberdeen addressed the mixed audience at the opening meeting of the National Council of Women in 1893, the *Toronto Empire* (which supported the organization) noted: "Hitherto it has not been the correct thing, from a Canadian society standpoint, for a woman to speak on a platform."[3] Similarly, when Julia Drummond addressed the public meeting held to organize the Montreal COS in 1899, it was said to be the first time a woman had given a public address in the city.[4] At their conference meetings, the YWCA could circumvent this rule by restricting much of the meeting to women only, thereby enabling women to address a same-sex audience and exchange ideas.[5] The private charities could not use this method at their annual meetings, given the legal obligations outlined in their charters as well as their need for public support.

In deference to this expectation against women speaking in public and the implicit restriction on women doing public work (or being seen to do public work), a public meeting of men often formally initiated nineteenth-century female charities. With the official framework (the legal structure, the Constitution, and the By-Laws) established, the men requested a Ladies' Committee to undertake the actual management, either alone or under the jurisdiction of a male Board or Advisory Committee.[6] A founding member of the Ottawa Protestant Orphan Home described this process in connection with that society as follows: "It was not customary for Ladies to occupy platforms in 1864 and they took over the business once the official arrangements were completed."[7]

The POA partially fits this pattern, having been formed at a public meeting called by Protestant ministers after the Female Benevolent Society was disbanded. In its *Historical Sketch* the POA credits Rev. John Bethune and Rev. Henry Esson with drafting the original Constitution.[8] However, the POA minutes reveal that the ladies themselves were actually very involved in this process, having written to the Boston Female Orphan Asylum to request copies of their Constitution and Rules. The Secretary notes that they selected their by-laws from those of the Boston association "where their wisdom and utility has been proved by more than twenty years of successful and beneficial experiment."[9] Hence, the ladies were actually responsible for much, if not all, of the working framework, having prepared it in advance through their contact with the Boston committee.[10] The account in the minutes also clarifies that the two ministers drew up a number of resolutions, read them, and then left. The women reread the resolutions, filled in the blanks, and voted on them one by one, in effect producing the actual working document.[11] This account gives the Montreal women a much more directive role than they had in the Ottawa example. Nonetheless, it is pertinent that in their official history the POA publicly associated their charity's foundation with the leaders of the Anglican and Presbyterian Churches, rather than with a committee of ladies who sought advice from Boston women and who finalized the details at a semi-private meeting of women.

It appears that this type of social expectation restricting public appearances and incursion into social space increased over the century. Thus the POA Committee in 1822 was less circumscribed in their actions than the Ottawa ladies would be in the 1860s. This is also clear in the case of the LBS (1815/32). The original Female Benevolent Society was set up in 1815 "by a number of Ladies" at a meeting convoked in city papers by three women, following a well-publicized subscription campaign.[12] The support of prominent men is clear by the Governor's patronage of the subscription campaign and the help of the Montreal Medical Institute in the ladies' work. Nonetheless, it was women who both convoked the meeting and organized the Society. Contemporaries such as Thomas Doige certainly credited women with directing the project, referring to the "bright example of superior benevolence evinced by the female sex."[13]

Similarly, the account of the founding of the LBS in 1832 makes no reference to men being present at the meeting, and specifically refers to a woman acting as chair: "At a meeting of Ladies called by Public announcement ... on Wednesday the 18th July, Mrs. Richardson having been called upon to preside and Mrs. Bancroft requested to act as Secretary, the following resolutions were proposed and unanimously adopted."[14] Since it was highly unusual for a woman to chair a public meeting, it is probably safe to assume that no men were present. The resolutions included the decision to form the LBS, to rent a house, and to hire staff. Those present drafted and adopted the Constitution and By-Laws and outlined the duties of office bearers.[15] In this case, then, women did all of the work associated with establishing the official framework of their organization.

Regardless of the events that marked their creation early in the century, the actions of these female Committees at the annual meetings in the years that followed, and certainly by the late 1830s, left no ambiguity concerning their respect for the rules of propriety that circumscribed public appearances by that point. These meetings served to provide subscribers and supporters with an account of the year's work and expenditures, as well as to officially elect the new officers and Committee of Management. They also provided the Committees with a platform to demonstrate both their own social usefulness and that of their organization. Committee members, subscribers, and supporters attended. Meetings were held in the institution, which gave patrons the opportunity to examine the home and the children and placed the meeting in the physical domain of the ladies' work – the home or a domestic sphere. Appropriately, this was a much less public place than a meeting hall elsewhere in the city; it was also a gendered space controlled by the ladies' Committees and one where only women and children resided. Nonetheless, the demonstration of female modesty and submissiveness was obvious at annual meetings by 1836.[16]

One place the increasing recognition of the rules of public etiquette is visible is in the reading of the reports. Accounts reveal that in the very early years, in 1824 and 1830, for example, "[T]he Secretary read the report," but by 1836, when Rev. Atkinson "at the request of the Ladies read aloud the Reports" as President of the meeting, this was no longer true.[17] From that point on, Committee members never again spoke at their public meetings, even though the meetings were held in the semi-public space of the institutional home and they had written all the reports. Rather, as was the norm in charities across America, women delegated men to speak on their behalf.[18] A minister always opened the meeting to set the religious tone and to establish the institution's moral authority. Male supporters, often the husbands of Committee members, read the annual report and the Treasurer's statement. Men moved, seconded, and spoke to all motions. Publicly, then, the male elite participated actively in these meetings, and, in this way, demonstrated their support for the charities, and provided credibility.

This prominent public role for men, however, masked the reality, which was that the ladies had completely orchestrated the meetings in advance and had agreed on the list of Directresses and Committee members at the monthly meeting preceding the annual meeting. The election of this slate at the larger meeting was strictly a legal formality. The Committee also chose and arranged for specific men to chair the meeting, to read the reports, and to move and second each motion. The motions were all prepared in advance; the men had only to read them and add some comment. Of course the ladies could not control what comments men added, and this occasionally posed problems for them; but the discussion in the next part of the chapter shows that they were very adept at avoiding unpopular suggestions or criticisms.

For most of the nineteenth century, men made the motions at the LBS meetings. The annual reports mention ladies seconding motions for a few years in the late 1840s, but these references ended by 1851. The POA meetings are much more intriguing and reveal an interesting example of female assertiveness within the bounds of the rules of public propriety. Early reports of these meetings indicate that "the members present" elected the Committee and officers, which suggests that possibly the women participated in the meeting by raising their hands to vote. Motions to name committees, accept reports, thank the chair, and so on were all made by men as was the norm. However, from 1860 on, although no lady spoke, their names were included as both movers and seconders in the text of each motion as it was read. The chair of the 1876 meeting explained this anomaly: "it was usual for the ladies to make the motions but as they did not speak he would call on the gentlemen present to support them."[19] In 1879, Rev. Bond, speaking to the acceptance of the Secretary's report, indicated that "[h]e wished he could get the ladies to speak themselves, as they were equally well qualified to do so as the gentlemen,"[20] but comments in the 1880s and 1890s such as "Canon Norman, speaking on behalf of Miss Blackwood" and "Mr J.C. Dunlop, on behalf of the secretary" confirm that the traditional method was still used at the end of the century.[21]

Changes in the nomenclature by which women presented themselves is another area where historians have detected a possible increase in public submissiveness. Suzanne Lebsock argues that clear changes occurred in Petersburg, Virginia over the century, from the use of first-name format to a married-name format – a change she interprets as indicating a loss of power.[22] In these Montreal charities, however, nomenclature is consistent. The Secretaries always signed the annual reports with their first names (for example, Anne McCord or Janey Evans), rather than the more formal and submissive Mrs or Miss. First names were also used publicly in newspaper appeals for donations or the official postponements of meetings. Even more important, they were used in official documents. The Acts of Incorporation refer to the founding members by their first names, and both Constitutions are signed with first names – the LBS in 1874 by C.K. Mackenzie and Fanny Evans; the POA in 1852 by Sophia Molson and Anne McCord. This is also the format used for official reports submitted to the government and letters directed to the Provincial Secretary in relation to requests for funding.[23]

The annual reports (other than the Secretary's signature) were the exception to first-name usage but this practice was consistent throughout the century. Here, Committee members and Directresses were always listed under their married names; so too were subscribers, Mrs and Miss being the norm. Furthermore, the married-name format used was often that which listed a woman under her husband's first and last name: that is, Mrs John Smith. As Leonore Davidoff and Catherine Hall have argued, this was a form of respect paid to middle-class women; in the Montreal case it was also often used to distinguish between multiple generations of the same family serving on the charity boards concurrently: for example Mrs John Greenshields and Mrs Greenshields.[24] The annual reports were the core of the societies' public discourse. It is important that in these key public documents ladies used their married names throughout the century, while in internal documents and correspondence with the government, which, while official, was not publicly seen, they quite naturally presented themselves using their given names.

Thus, a shift to increased "ritual submission" through a change in nomenclature is not evident in nineteenth-century Montreal, contrary to what Suzanne Lebsock found in Petersburg. Neither is there any evidence of the trend she found whereby the male elite moved to take control of female-directed charities or to set up competing male-directed ones in the areas already staked out by women's committees.[25] Jan Noel's contention – that Montreal merchant princes "overshadowed" female benevolent activities early in the century and turned "the women's wooden hospices and rented houses into the great pillared and iron-railed institutions of Victorian Montreal" – is borne out only by the early example of the Montreal General Hospital taking over the Female Benevolent Society's House of Recovery in 1822.[26] The formation of the MGH, though, did not point to the beginning of a trend for men to usurp women's role in charitable work with other women and children.

Male charity committees did not challenge the gender division of the Protestant network. Except for a few years in the 1860s, no children remained in the House of Industry any longer than it took to clarify their parental situation, at which point they were transferred to the appropriate female charity or sent out as apprentices. The Boys' Home and the Mackay Institute are the only examples of male boards directing organizations for youth, but neither was designed for young children, and due to their specialized services, they did not duplicate or infringe on the ladies' work. In fact, when the ladies' Committees appealed to the Boys' Home in 1896 to accept younger boys they refused. Thus, the main residential child charities were all managed by female committees and, as we established in chapter 1, these women played a major role in the city's Protestant charity network.

Furthermore, cooperation and collaboration between these elite women and their male supporters continued throughout the century. Donations from both businesses and men increased over the century, newspapers continued to provide favourable press coverage, lawyers represented their interests in many situations, medical professionals helped ensure the children's health, and politicians lobbied on their behalf for changes to incorporation charters, government grants, legislation, and so on. Rather than challenge the ladies' work, high-profile members of Montreal's establishment attended the annual meetings, praised the ladies for their "qualities" and their contribution to the city, and thanked them for their work. On at least one occasion, a speaker commented on the "great obligation they undertook, which actually ought to be fulfilled by the men,"[27] but the comment was meant as a compliment to their self-sacrifice, their management abilities, and the importance of their work, not as a threat of impending male incursion. The Montreal ladies' respect for social convention was surely one of the ways they maintained this enthusiastic public male endorsement. Their representation of their work as their "humble endeavours" emphasized this deference. And it was indeed in terms of these same adjectives that men also spoke of women's charitable work – descriptions that reflected the belief that women had special qualities which distinguished them from men.

GENDERED SPECIAL QUALITIES

It was especially a woman's work secretly and silently to gather the children in.
~ Rev. Burns, LBS, *Annual Report*, 1872

In this succinct description of the charity's work, Rev. Burns clarified the gendered nature of the endeavour and the qualities that made it so. The separate spheres discourse and the respectability associated with it were not limited to prescriptions on public appearances. At the core of the ideology was the concept of special qualities and separate activities. Women were thought to be natural nurturers and thus ideally fitted for home-making and child-rearing; among those activities normally defined as male were finance, business, and politics. On the whole, the Montreal ladies accepted these distinctions. Although the POA and LBS ladies were quite confident of their abilities to manage their institutions and to make decisions about admissions and departures, they looked for additional guidance when it came to constructing buildings and managing large investment portfolios, activities clearly within the "male sphere." In light of this, they depended on special male advisors or committees of men to help them with these specific matters. This had the added advantage of forging even stronger links to members of the male elite and providing an additional appearance of propriety and legitimacy.

Men's committees often existed in connection with female-directed charities. Several patterns existed. Where women's charities were originally set up by men, committees of women supervised domestic management but men maintained control over all legal and financial dealings.[28] Many other female-directed charities had official male Advisory Boards from their foundation, but the actual control of the charity rested firmly in the hands of the female management Committee. This was the case with the Hervey Institute, for example, which had a male Advisory Board and an official male Treasurer, but no one would have questioned that Eliza Hervey, the founding President, was really in charge. The POA and the LBS represent yet another pattern. Neither society formed men's committees at their inception, so had not depended on men's committees to legitimize the organization itself. Rather, they conceived of the men's committees once they were formed as task-specific – created when the task at hand fell clearly within the male sphere and/or required specialized knowledge and business contacts.

In the early years the ladies ran the charities in rented premises and relied on the husband of one of the Directresses to provide advice on business- and building-related questions. Once they began to contemplate constructing buildings, however, both Committees called on male supporters to aid them in a more formal way. The LBS decided in January 1852 that a Gentlemen's Committee "should be formed to act for them in cases of difficulty."[29] The Finance and Building Committee was formed the next year at a special meeting of men called to discuss the society's need for permanent facilities. It was specifically organized to carry out this construction project, and most of the twenty-one original members left the Committee once the new institution opened its doors in 1856. Only six of these men were connected to the LBS by family ties; other members included philanthropists such as Peter McGill, Alexander Simpson, John Frothingham, and William Workman. In this way, the Building Committee represented an effort on the part of the city's male charitable elite to put the LBS on a more stable footing.

The men's Committee was established on a more permanent basis in 1869 as the Finance and Advisory Committee, with eleven members. From that point the membership list was included in the annual reports. Membership was fairly consistent, with a few additions, but gradually members died or left due to other commitments and by 1887 only three remained. Beginning in 1889, new recruits were added, and the Committee had grown to thirteen members by 1897. A majority of the men, and certainly most of the active long-term members, had either a wife or a mother on the LBS Committee.

In 1853 the original Committee did most of the work involved with the new building on Berthelet (Ontario) Street: finding a site, overseeing the construction, and soliciting special funds to cover the debt.[30] The LBS Committee gave the final approval on all proposals, but left the initiatives to the men. They also left most of the subsequent decisions on renovations and additions "to the discretion of the Gentlemen's Committee,"[31] and one member of this Committee served as the regular special advisor on sundry matters such as repairs, landscaping, and fuel purchases.[32] Furthermore, the men managed the Permanent Fund and a few of them helped with fund-raising, organizing the "Fête," and collecting in the business district. On occasion the ladies requested help with other official tasks that they saw as out-of-the-ordinary or very important, believing that the men "would better understand the arrangements likely to ensure their success."[33] This was the case, for example, with the petition for government aid in 1856, when the LBS assumed a portion of the work of the defunct Protestant Industrial House of Refuge but hoped to receive the entire joint grant (see discussion below), as well as with the preparation of the address to the Governor General in 1873. Normally appeals for government aid were drafted and signed by the Secretary.

The POA also created a Gentlemen's Committee when it began to prepare for the construction of a permanent home on St Catherine Street in 1845. This Committee helped organize the financing and construction of the building, which was ready in 1849, and with special fund-raising campaigns in 1853 and 1856 to pay off the building debt and purchase the adjoining lot.[34] Members were again active from 1891 to 1893, when this building was sold and a new one constructed on Summerhill and Côte-des-Neiges. Although official membership lists were not published until 1887, the POA's minutes provide some information on who served on the committee before this. All of the men had wives or female relatives on the POA Committee.

Although the men did all the official work connected to the construction of the asylum buildings (1847–49, 1893) and often provided advice, the POA Committee discussed and approved all decisions. Even more importantly, in both instances a Ladies' Building Committee worked in coordination with the men and the professionals such as architects; similar subcommittees helped when renovations or major repairs were made.[35] In 1847, in fact, the Ladies' Committee was officially given the organizing work and the men requested to "aid and assist."[36] Thus, the POA ladies were more actively involved than was the LBS Committee, but their reluctance to act on their own in these areas is still evident. In 1878, for example, the POA Committee refused to act on the advice of their ladies' building subcommittee with regards to needed renovations, waiting until the Gentlemen's Committee had been consulted. In this instance the men gave the same advice as the subcommittee, a clear demonstration of the women's competence.[37]

Normally one of the men on the POA Gentlemen's Committee acted as a general advisor and another as the financial advisor. This system was informal and evolved naturally from family connections. J.S. McCord and D.R. McCord, respectively the husband and the son of long-time Secretary Anne Ross McCord, served as the special advisors for most of the century. The financial advisors were all related to the Treasurer and included R.S. Tylee, J. Greenshields, and E.B. Greenshields. These latter men invested monies, bought stock, or arranged for (investment) mortgages on behalf of the POA, and forwarded the weekly household funds if the Treasurer was out of town.

In 1874, in an effort to clarify these responsibilities and reduce the Treasurer's workload, the POA officially assigned the management of the Endowment Fund to the (men's) Finance Committee. The men submitted any suggestions in terms of changes to the stock portfolio or other investments to the monthly meeting for discussion and approval. The family advisor model (through the Greenshields family) was nonetheless effectively still in force until 1895.[38] From that point on, the entire Finance Committee, renamed the Advisory Board, worked in conjunction with the recently created Ladies' Finance Committee to make investment decisions, although with the resignation of D.R. McCord as their legal advisor in 1903, E.B. Greenshields became their special advisor on most matters and remained so until his death.[39] The new Ladies' Finance Committee reflected the shift we already noted toward involving more Committee members in active management by late century.

Willingly deferring to men's advice on matters of building and finance, which they identified as being in the men's sphere, the ladies kept their own counsel when it came to managing their charities and caring for their residents, areas they identified as within the women's domain. Furthermore, they did not hesitate to both develop and defend policies in opposition to the views of male advisors or supporters. In this, their beliefs about separate spheres and special qualities actually empowered them; so did the experience they had acquired through years of running their charities.

THE REJECTION OF PLACING OUT

An institution is not a home and never can be made such.
~ J.J. Kelso, *The Canadian Magazine*, 1894[40]

Formed in 1822 and 1832, the POA and the LBS were at the beginning of the trend to form specialized institutions for destitute children in Canada; the concerted push to create separate children's institutions took place in the second half of the century.[41] Not all who worked on behalf of children, however, believed that institutions were the best answer to the problem of child destitution. Although English Canadian historiography often associates foster care with J.J. Kelso and the Ontario Children's Aid Society from 1893, the original version of this method, known as "placing out," began as a trend in North American social work when the Children's Mission in Boston and, even more famously, Charles Loring Brace of the New York City Children's Aid Society sent the first "orphan trains" in the 1850s on their westward journey, taking children away from the city to distant rural homes.[42] Arguing the superiority of families over institutions to socialize children, supporters of this method believed that "neglected" children needed a home and a family, preferably far away from the influence of both the urban environment and their parents.

The debate between the two approaches was high-profile and public. Many of the new professional child-care workers favoured placing out, and used the American National Conference of Charities and Corrections (NCCC), and subsequently the Canadian Conference, formed in 1898, to lobby against institutional care.[43] From the late 1870s, speakers at these meetings attacked institutions, arguing that rule and routine stunted growth and development, eradicated individualism and initiative, and created an institutional child with "stunted mental and moral faculties" "who show[ed] a want of pluck, [and] dependence on others."[44] Advocates also insisted that institutions were expensive, increased health risks, and encouraged parents to forsake their duties by using charities as temporary boarding houses.

Defenders of institutions claimed that, without a judicious choice of placement homes and a strict follow-up inspection system, placing out could lead to exploitation and child abuse, as children were often considered workers and not family members, and since neither of these safeguards existed, the method was fraught with danger.[45] Nonetheless, touted as the "modern" method, placing out was adopted by several American states and its use spread through private institutions such as the Children's Aid Societies (CAS) as these were created across the continent.[46] By 1901 there were thirty CAS in Canada, some of them, such as those in Ontario and British Columbia, supported by state legislation giving them the power to intervene in families.[47] Alongside these newer groups, institutional child charities continued to exist and new ones opened, but a decisive shift away from seeing institutions as good places to raise children gained momentum.

The challenge to Montreal's institutional model began in the late nineteenth century and grew in force in the early decades of the twentieth. Veronica Strong-Boag has argued that the introduction of foster care in Canada was driven by the attempt to "affirm male leadership" and government oversight (through quasi-public structures including the CAS) in an area where working-class families and traditional methods such as female-managed orphanages had prevailed.[48] Certainly the early advocacy for family placement in Montreal had a gendered aspect, if not a governmental one. Beginning in the 1870s a number of high-profile Montreal men wrote to our two Committees and used the public platform of their annual meetings to request that they adopt placing out in one form or another, as the superior, modern method.

The most vocal Montreal advocate was Rev. Robert Lindsay. As chair of the Anglican Synod Committee on Works of Mercy (and later one of the founders of the Associated Charities) he was an influential leader among the Protestant benevolent elite. In 1875, he addressed the LBS annual meeting on the subject, as recounted by the Secretary: "He thought that there might be too rigid conservatism in their works of mercy; as the world advanced, people engaged in philanthropy prepared new plans and devised new modes of carrying out the work." Referring to the example of Ireland, where "for these several years, the children, no matter how young, were almost farmed out, being placed in families," he concluded that "this was the true principle."[49] Later that year he wrote to the POA about the foster placement system used by Annie Macpherson in her Knowlton home.[50] He argued that "everything should progress with the spirit of the age" and that children should be "placed out by adoption at all ages."[51] In the ensuing discussion at the POA Committee meeting, several members questioned the no-adoption policy. In response, the Secretary read the account of the death of the young child in 1855 that had led to the rejection of adoption as a placement method. The Committee reconfirmed their refusal to place children in a family without a legal arrangement such as apprenticeship, and filed Lindsay's letter away.

Lindsay made another pitch for the superiority of adoption or placing out at the POA annual meeting in January 1876 and was supported by several other men at the meeting. E.E. Shelton, for instance, informed the audience that "he had offered to take children out of this institution and bring them up as his own, but could not get them."[52] Since the ladies could not speak in a public meeting, it fell to their lawyer, D.R. McCord, to defend the Committee by explaining the circumstances behind the removal of adoption from their charter in 1855. Rev. Henry Wilkes concluded the meeting with the hope that the ladies would "exercise their judgement correctly" in their consideration of changes to the policy.[53] Rev. Green raised the subject again at the 1879 meeting. Using a Boston example, he recommended that as many children as possible be adopted into families.[54]

Despite these letters, speeches, and even public invitations to reconsider their institutional approach and to implement the use of adoption (or placing out), the POA and the LBS refused such a policy shift. Their deference to male authority kept them from openly debating or challenging the suggestions made by men. Appropriately, their rejection of all such proposals was at one and the same time demure and effective. They politely filed away letters without a response that we know of, and listened quietly to speeches at meetings, but they never raised the issue of a policy change at their monthly Committee meetings. As Amanda Vickery found for the women she studied, "[m]asculine authority was formally honoured but practically managed," and women "would brook little interference" in areas connected to childcare and housekeeping.[55] For the Montreal women under study, they considered these areas, as reflected through their internal policies, to be well within the female sphere of influence and competence.

The Montreal child charity managers did not see placing out as a new method, as men such as Lindsay claimed, but rather as a new name for old methods of adoption that they had used for years and that left children in an unknown family without contractual protection and potentially exposed to danger; therefore, they were not impressed by its growing popularity as the most "modern" method. Even more importantly, the combination of their personal protective approach and their acquired expertise as child charity managers led them to reject the assumptions underlying placing out – assumptions that advocated removing children from their natural families and that postulated the superiority of placement homes over institutions. First, other than in a few rare cases, neither charity deliberately separated families. Second, their experience with the dangers of placing children in the families of strangers convinced the Committees that the pro-family ideology was both idealized and impractical. Even the legal contract of apprenticeship had not always protected children from problems of overwork and abuse; the lack of such a contract was simply irresponsible and foolish.

Increasingly both Committees even questioned the use of apprenticeship. Since the children generally did their apprenticeships as helpers in lower-middle-class families, they worked hard but the training was not always well-directed and did not adequately prepare them for independent action. For girls, it limited their access to jobs other than domestic service and compromised their ability to move up inside the servant ranks from the position of general servant or kitchen helper. The same was true for the boys unless they were apprenticed to skilled trades. Most of the other boys were apprenticed to farmers and afterwards limited to work as agricultural labourers or unskilled workers, unless they could save enough money to purchase land. Both Committees saw placement as an opportunity to live in a family and have the supervision and protection of an adult, but also as a period of paid training. From this perspective, the respective advantages of training in the institution and in a lower-class family became a crucial consideration over time, one that further strengthened their opposition to placing out and led to policies directly in opposition to this movement.

The LBS first discussed the limitations of apprenticeship for girls in 1848 and decided that keeping girls in the institution longer was the best way to improve their training. Space and budget considerations, however, made it impossible to implement this policy. For the same reason, an 1873 resolution that allowed girls to remain as "servants-in-training" until eighteen was only implemented in the 1880s.[56] With it, a few girls were apprenticed to the LBS and received the usual fee, as we have seen. This sort of in-house training enabled the ladies to oversee the girls' training and had the added advantage of reducing the home's costs, given the differential between the apprenticeship fee and a servant's wage. In 1887, the ladies defended themselves against criticism that too few girls were sent out as apprentices, pointing to the right of parents to remove children, the difficulty of finding workers for the institution, and the advantages of training girls in the institution: "that the Managers might keep them under their care, at an age when it is so important that they should be carefully watched over."[57] This in-house training for girls, however, did not entail an overall re-evaluation of apprenticeship policy. Boys were still apprenticed to families and the LBS reduced apprenticeship age for them from thirteen to ten, based on their belief that boys would benefit more from their training if they started at a younger age, as well as on complaints from masters that adolescent boys were hard to discipline.[58]

The POA had also occasionally apprenticed girls to the Society from the 1850s to reduce wage bills. By 1881, the Committee began to address the problems they had identified with apprenticeship. The first of these was the lack of education. They decided better preparation in the asylum prior to children's departure might help.[59] However, their fears about schooling and the quality of training were not assuaged and, in 1884, they informed supporters that they were "convinced that, as soon as they leave our threshold, the children enter upon the duties of life, and have few opportunities for further instruction and training."[60] Believing that it was therefore up to them to ensure proper training and socialization, the ladies launched their new policy to keep girls in the institution longer in 1885.[61] Under the new policy, girls, and some boys, were kept in the POA until their late teens, when they were old enough to be placed directly as workers.

Under the new regime, from age twelve girls spent part of their day in school and part of it training as specialized servants (nursemaids, table maids, housemaids) in preparation for being sent out once they had "a fair prospect of earning their own wage."[62] Consistent with their overall conservatism, the ladies did not challenge the choice of domestic service as an occupation for girls, but they did aspire to some limited social mobility by training girls as specialized servants rather than general help, and at least one supporter called the decision "most apropos" given the paucity of well-trained servants.[63] The new policy was gendered. Some boys were trained as office boys, and the Committee placed more emphasis on manual training inside the institution. Other boys were still apprenticed, including a few to skilled trades now that the board problem was resolved. The result of this policy was that by the end of the century, most POA children were trained in the asylum, not in a family. Girls left between the ages of fifteen and seventeen, going directly into Montreal middle- or upper-class homes (some of them of Committee members) as upper maids. If not apprenticed, boys were sent to Montreal professionals or businesses as office boys or clerks. Evaluating the success of the new policy in 1900, the Secretary indicated that the young people were doing well and that several were "already receiving considerable increases in wages."[64]

With this policy shift, the Montreal Committees had decided that the quality of training the children received was more important than socialization in a family. Moreover, their experience with past abuse and their suspicion of potential abuse in placement situations led them to feel safer monitoring the children's care themselves. Institutions were not alien to them as places to raise children – many upper-class children spent time in a boarding school – and they were not fearful of creating an "institutional child," as professional child-care workers appeared to be. This increased emphasis on child protection was not limited to training; it paralleled a number of health and sanitary improvements in the last part of the century, as we have already noted.

Thus, rather than swelling the ranks of placing-out advocates, these two Montreal child charities deliberately rejected the method and even began to re-evaluate their use of apprenticeship. In direct contradiction to the arguments in favour of placing out, the POA, and to some extent the LBS, claimed that their experience using similar methods such as adoption and apprenticeship proved that, in fact, the only way to ensure proper care, education, and training in a protective environment was to keep children (certainly girls) in the institution under constant supervision, not to place them in unknown families. With this new approach, the ladies took the institutional model to its logical conclusion – their institutions became the substitute home most of the children would not leave until they were young wage-earners and could go out on their own, unless parents removed them before. What is interesting about this is not that the ladies rejected placing out, since many other child charities did that,[65] but that they did this against the publicly articulated wishes of many of their male supporters. At the very moment that placing out for children of all ages was gaining widespread acceptance, the POA developed a policy of in-house training and increased institutionalization. The LBS continued to offer temporary care and used in-house training for girls when possible.

As we will see in the Epilogue, the confrontation between foster care and institutional care became much more direct in the twentieth century and the terms of the debate shifted. In the nineteenth century, placing out was often linked to parental morality and child rescue – sending urban children to rural families far from the "dangerous" influence of both parents and the city. Foster care, as it was called in the twentieth century, was linked, at least as it evolved in Protestant Montreal, to scientific charity, professionalism, and cost efficiency just as much as to a pro-family and anti-institution ideology. This highlights the second way in which these Committees were out of step with new developments. Alongside the attack on institutions as proper homes for dependent children, there was a more general attack on traditional charity per se. The Montreal ladies tenaciously rejected the movement known as "scientific charity" and defended both their autonomy and their own beliefs about the accessibility of relief.

OPPOSITION TO "SCIENTIFIC CHARITY"

> An uncharitable, misjudging world is somewhat prejudiced against ladies' benevolent societies. It is believed that the kind-hearted women who compose them have no very definite aims; that their exertions in the cause of the distressed are spasmodic and that the money which they collect is not always as judiciously expended as it might be.
>
> ~ *Montreal Herald*, 1856[66]

The author of this *Montreal Herald* article went on to defend the Ladies' Benevolent Society from the above charges, assuring readers that "it is not an association of Lady Bountifuls who meet at irregular intervals to find congenial occupation for time that hangs heavily on their hands, who are regarded by impostors of many kinds, but earnest and self-sacrificing women with definite and practicable objects."[67] Nonetheless, the statement highlights the attack on traditional charity methods that was part of the re-evaluation of poor-relief policy over the century. The shift to find a more scientific approach to relief gained considerable influence with the formation of the London Charity Organization Society (COS) in 1869, although its ideological foundations dated from early in the century.[68] The movement spread to the United States in 1877 with the Buffalo, New York COS. By 1893, nearly one hundred COS-type societies existed in the United States. Toronto established an Associated Charities in 1880 and Montreal in 1883, although the latter was short-lived and reorganized as a COS in 1899. By 1900, similar organizations existed in Hamilton, Kingston, London, Ottawa, and Victoria.[69]

The advocates of scientific charity or "philanthropy" argued for an organized, systematic approach to poor relief aimed at reforming, even rehabilitating, the poor and ultimately eliminating "pauperism" in the process. They believed that traditional charity, based on personal service or individual giving (even when voluntary associations acted as an intermediary) and focused on relieving need, could aggravate the situation by providing indiscriminate aid and creating dependency.[70] As Mariana Valverde pointed out when differentiating between charity and philanthropy, philanthropists "sought to eliminate both the impulsive and the individual elements of giving" and believed that "the problem with charity was … that there was too much of it and the poor were becoming pauperized by dependence on abundant charity."[71] Proponents claimed that this situation could be resolved through the centralized coordination of relief in a city, the cooperation of agencies, and the investigation of all applicants to eliminate fraud. Reflecting liberal concepts of the poor's moral deficiencies, supporters advocated relief that forced the poor to become self-reliant rather than dependent on aid; in connection with this, the moral influence of volunteer visitors was key.[72]

Although a permanent COS was not founded in Montreal until the turn of the century, steps in the direction of organizing charity began much earlier. The assumption that poverty was mainly the result of immorality and bad habits led logically to the conviction that poor relief was counterproductive unless it addressed this underlying problem. By mid-century many also believed that the overall cost and the volume of aid were out of control, and feared the rise of pauperism as a result. As the *Montreal Herald* quotation indicated, they blamed this situation as much on "sentimental, indiscriminate" aid (that is, traditional charity and alms-giving) as on the "unworthy poor" who took advantage of the availability of relief. In Montreal, the attack on traditional charity took place on two levels: the move to reorient the purpose of aid and to limit it to the "deserving," and the move to rationalize relief services to reduce costs and avoid fraud.

From early in the century, ministers warned that aid must be inspired by moral principles and aimed at removing the cause of distress, not simply relieving suffering – that is, that it must "go to the root of the evil," as Montreal Methodist minister Rev. W. Taylor told the Masons in 1843.[73] Speaking twenty years later, J.W. Williams, Anglican Bishop of Quebec, called specifically for a more organized system of charity: "On all sides organization promotes efficiency. And more than that, it elevates benevolence from a casual impulse into a permanent principle."[74] Articles in the religious and secular press supported the careful distribution of aid to the deserving and advocated charity as a personal duty that needed to be mediated by discretion – that is, considered philanthropy rather than old-fashioned charity.[75] Writing in 1881, at a time when the scientific charity movement was well-established, the editor of the *Canadian Illustrated News* put the position succinctly: "careless, unreasoning, uninvestigating, indiscriminate giving ... is not charity – it is mere impulse."[76] The editor of the *Canadian Magazine* added that "indiscriminate charity is one of the most hurtful of Society's modern values."[77]

As Sarah Deutsch points out in her discussion of the resistance to scientific charity by Boston's female-directed Fragment Society, the "efficiency versus sympathy debate" "contrasted nineteenth-century woman's culture with the ascendant business values."[78] This was also a factor in Montreal. The ladies who ran the child charities conceived of their institutions in terms of sympathy and personal service rooted in Christianity; in other words, they practised traditional charity, not philanthropy. Like all nineteenth-century middle-class citizens, they were aware of concepts of the deserving poor and generally attempted to verify the accuracy of application information, assuring supporters that they gave aid only to the deserving, emphasizing that "nothing could be more foolish than to be engaged in giving rashly without any knowledge of the conditions of those who received gifts."[79] Yet the examination of their admission policies revealed that in actual fact these Committees worked more from a perspective of responding to families' needs than from one of reforming the poor. Neither charity used a restrictive admission policy (other than religion) – the POA admitted every orphan whose application was noted; the only real limit on admission to the LBS was available space and residency. Therefore these traditional female Committees rejected the restrictive and moralist concepts behind scientific charity, and defended the needs of families against arguments of efficiency.

Even more importantly, the two Committees rejected scientific charity's aim to centralize and coordinate services in the city to remove duplication and to systematize relief. Both defended their institutional autonomy against male-led initiatives from mid-century on to rationalize the city's charity services, and both refused to cooperate with any move to reorganize child welfare.

Attempts to rationalize the female charities occurred sporadically from the 1850s. The first such attempt was made in 1854 by the male Advisory Committee associated with the newly opened Protestant Industrial House of Refuge. This committee had the responsibility "to suggest what ought to be done to interest their friends and the public in the Institution, so that means may be obtained for its support, and to extend its usefulness."[80] Rather than focusing on this mandate and the institution's needs, the men understood the directive within a larger perspective and immediately addressed the issue of overall poor relief in the city. David Davidson wrote to both the POA and the LBS about the need to make the "measure of relief" in the city "more efficient and comprehensive," since "misery and want" would likely increase as Montreal's population grew.[81] His proposal entailed the entire restructuring of existing Protestant charities. First, the POA would become the only child charity. Second, the other three female charities – the LBS, the House of Refuge, and the School of Industry (Hervey Institute) – would be merged into one central institution that would provide institutional care for the blind, elderly, infirm, incurables, convalescents, and unemployed women as well as outdoor relief to needy widows.[82] In effect, the proposal would reduce the number of charities from four to two: one for children, the other for the elderly and women in need. Other services, including the industrial departments, were left in abeyance.

In her study of the 1871 Chicago fire, Maureen Flanagan found that women and men responded differently to the provision of aid to victims – while women pro-actively addressed actual need, men's approach was much more restrictive.[83] The situation in Montreal during the 1854 economic slowdown reveals similar gendered responses to singular events. Viewing the economic crisis Montreal was experiencing as a temporary situation, the ladies managing the House of Refuge attempted to provide direct aid and/or industrial relief for all the women and families who applied for it, and ran a small deficit in the process. The men's Advisory Committee, on the other hand, approached the question from an ideological and business perspective, addressing the long term; they were more concerned about efficiency and cost. To this they added a preoccupation with organizing and eliminating any duplication of services in the overall network. If they expected the female charities and their Managers (many of whom were their wives) to share their orientation and their proposals, they were sorely disappointed.

The LBS Committee refused the proposal and rejected Davidson's suggestion to hold a public meeting to discuss it, finding such a meeting unnecessary on the grounds that "twelve managers are sufficient to determine any question regarding the interests of the Institution."[84] The POA's answer was less defensive, but equally final. They refused to accept any children from the other institutions until their Endowment Fund was large enough to finance triple the number of children that were in the POA at that point. In effect, the ladies made two basic arguments: that it was irresponsible to reorganize poor-relief services without clear funding commitments, and that changes must respect a charity's existing Constitution and not compromise its legal obligations.[85]

The men launched their second rationalization attempt almost immediately. The next year, as chairman of the 1855 LBS annual meeting, Rev. Dr Donald Fraser suggested that the Industrial House of Refuge and the LBS be amalgamated since the latter had a spacious new building.[86] Pressures continued. The Protestant Poor Relief Committee was created in 1855 to centralize outdoor relief and distribute the special emergency aid grant from the city.[87] Funding support for the Industrial House of Refuge fell accordingly and the work departments were cut back in relation to 1854–55 levels. At their second annual meeting in 1856, the women running the institution bemoaned the lack of support and indicated that there was too much work for so few of them.[88] In response, the men from the Advisory Committee present at the meeting voted to abolish the institution and to rationalize services to widows by amalgamating it with the LBS. They formed a special all-male committee to meet with the LBS for that purpose.[89]

In their discussion of this proposal at their monthly meeting, the LBS Committee also discussed a brief prepared by their Secretary for the Children, Catherine Ogden, who was a founding member and had served as a Directress for many years. She argued "against admitting Strangers [the men's committee] into the consultation of the Managers as unconstitutional," and stated how "injurious the proposed connection would be in every way to the temporal and spiritual interests of [the] Institution." Her position "had a very strong effect upon the meeting against the proposed amalgamation," but in the end, fearing it would be "considered discourteous to refuse to hear the views of the [male] Committee," the LBS instructed the Secretary to request the proposal be sent to them in writing to buy time for reflection.[90] When they resumed discussion of the proposal several days later, they formed a subcommittee to draft a reply stating their objections.

The LBS Committee initially refused an amalgamation outright, citing the lack of space and funds to take on new work, the technical and staff requirements of an industrial department (which they assumed would remain), and the moral and religious complications of mixing the vagrant poor with their regular residents.[91] Instead, they finally offered a compromise they felt they could live with but assumed the men would refuse. They agreed to accept two of the House of Refuge's services – the sheltering of female immigrants and convalescents – in return for its entire $600 government grant. The men agreed and the amalgamation took place on the LBS's terms, which meant that the laundry, the sewing rooms, the soup kitchen, the night refuge, and all the outdoor relief services were discontinued. Thus the first successful rationalization effort resulted in the closing of an institution and a substantial decrease of services to widows and families. Even in this early version of scientific charity, the opposition between sympathy with the needs of families and the efficiency of services was clear. So too was the preference for institutional aid, as all the industrial and outdoor relief services disappeared.

Rationalizing charitable services was also linked to the move to establish a centralized structure to coordinate the private charities. Initiatives in this direction were made in Montreal from the 1870s. In 1874 Rev. Gavin Lang of St Andrew's Presbyterian Church spoke at the LBS meeting on the advantages of a single centralized "financial Board for the combined charities of the city."[92] In 1878 motions were passed at the annual and half-yearly meetings of the Protestant House of Industry "to unite the various charitable societies in one effort in the relief of the poor through the city."[93] In October 1881 discussions began about the possibility of organizing an Associated Charities.[94]

The real push to form a coordinating body came as a result of discussions with the government on the need for a Protestant reformatory. After meeting with the government about possible per-diem payments like those paid to Catholic institutions, Rev. Robert Lindsay reported that the government promised Protestants the same financial aid as long as they made "their demand as a united body, and not as separate Institutions."[95] An Associated Charities was formed that year (1883) to act as an umbrella organization to coordinate Protestant charitable efforts and to implement scientific charity principles. The *Montreal Witness* explained its aim as "[t]o secure the concurrent and harmonious action of the different charities of Montreal in order to raise the needy above the need of relief, prevent begging and imposition and diminish pauperism."[96] The POA sent two delegates to the preliminary meeting, but the LBS files do not refer to any representation. The Associated Charities immediately addressed the gaps in the Protestant relief network. The meetings in relation to reformatory institutions resulted in the LBS successfully applying for industrial school certification. The efforts in relation to the foundling problem, especially the attempt to force the Infants' Home to accept foundlings, however, were controversial and the Associated Charities was disbanded after a few years. Neither the LBS nor the POA had participated in its work, and during the discussions on foundlings they sent their lawyer to represent their inability to use their funds for purposes other than those outlined in their Incorporation.[97]

To that point, the thrust to rationalize and coordinate relief had come from the male elite, and part of the ladies' resistance was gendered as they defended the network of female charities (with its duplication of services and its emphasis on "sympathy" and "need") against male incursions and "efficiency" at all costs. The ideological aspects of their resistance became clearer, however, when a group of women led by Julia Drummond and the Montreal Local Council of Women (LCW) worked to help form the Montreal Charity Organization Society (COS) in the late 1890s. Gender was no longer a factor in their resistance.

The members of the National Council of Women of Canada (NCWC), and certainly leaders such as Julia Drummond, who headed the Montreal Local Council, were maternal feminists and "progressive" reformers.[98] They agreed with the COS perspective that poverty was a moral problem that called for well-directed charity with an emphasis on inducing self-help as well as some understanding of the material circumstances surrounding any given case.[99] As Julia Drummond explained in her address on Charity Organization at the 1894 NCWC meeting: "True charity needs for its fulfilment all the forces of wise minds and gentle hearts. For its ultimate aims are nothing less than these – not only to relieve poverty, but to cure it; not only to redeem the feeble and the vicious, but to do away with the conditions that create them."[100] Central to this, she argued, was an organization to centralize information on all applicants and coordinate relief referrals, a system that "prevents indiscriminate and duplicate giving ... provides for the investigation of the case of every applicant for relief ... and is a means of communication between the work and the worker."[101]

Under Drummond's leadership, the Local Council took the formation of a COS in hand, creating a committee to this end in 1895 and working jointly with a committee of influential men from 1898 towards "the success of the undertaking."[102] The public meeting held in December 1899 to establish the COS elected a Board headed by Julia's husband, the Hon. George Drummond. Several Council members including Julia and Helen Reid were also elected to the Board, the Executive Committee, and the Ladies Auxiliary Committee.[103] The Montreal COS was designed to be non-sectarian, with representatives of the Catholic, Jewish, and Protestant communities, although the last were prominent.[104]

The LCW subcommittee recognized that the success of the enterprise depended on the "willing cooperation of all charitable societies and institutions," but believed that the societies would soon realize the mutual benefit.[105] Many of the city charities, however, were not at all convinced of the potential benefits. This reluctance is not surprising, and a centralized model was difficult to impose in Montreal, due to the nature of the network divided along confessional lines and the fact that private corporations tended to be protective of their independence and that some of them, including the POA and the LBS, did not share the COS ideology. An organization potentially designed to coordinate efforts, decide eligibility, and distribute cases was not likely to be popular. Finally, the COS's well-publicized views on poverty and pauperism and its vehement criticisms of private charity understandably led many to be on guard against it. In this, Montreal serves as another example of the trend Robert Humphries found in England, where many of the provincial COS did not find ready local support outside London.[106]

Both the LBS and the POA refused to participate in the establishment of the COS despite their affiliation with the Women's Council.[107] Neither was willing to forgo any control over their institution and their autonomy. They believed such interference was a strong possibility, given the COS's advertised ideology and the various proposals that had already come their way from earlier versions of rationalization initiatives. They were not alone in this, and several private charities met centralizing proposals with either suspicion or disinterest until well into the twentieth century. Rooke and Schnell found the same resistance on the part of other Canadian female-directed child charities, and Lori Ginzberg notes that in terms of local women's societies in the United States there was not a "universal rush to embrace the new emphasis on efficiency."[108]

In 1900, the Secretary General of Montreal's newly formed COS, Francis H. McLean, demonstrated no ambiguity about the distribution of relief, stating that "moral disease ... must be met by the force of intelligence and sympathy – not with bread and fuel."[109] He clarified that "relief-giving" must be "accompanied by actual curative or preventative work," and specified the need for "recreational, intellectual, aesthetic and social opportunities" for the poor, but these were long-term projects.[110] In the short term, he was particularly concerned with wasting charitable resources and duplicating relief (that is, fraud), hence the importance of using existing charitable services intelligently. Describing them as a "higher kind of charity," he hoped that the application of "scientific charity" methods would make the poor self-reliant and prevent "pauperism."[111] Accordingly, in its first year, one-third of cases were found to be ineligible for aid. Of the cases they accepted, staff found some form of outdoor aid from relatives or charities for about half, found employment for others, and referred still others to professionals such as doctors.[112] Reflecting this approach, the Annual Report for 1903–04 explains the Society's aim as the cooperation between charitable societies and charity workers, as well as the organization of relief from various sources, including family, churches or relief societies, and individuals.[113]

In effect, the COS was designed to be a centralized referral agency, not a relief agency itself. Quite quickly, however, advocates recognized that a strict application of this approach was problematic in Montreal due to the lack of a public relief structure where the "undeserving" could secure aid, and the COS was forced to provide aid to families.[114] They worked in coordination with the city to investigate applications made to the Bureau of Municipal Assistance, and much of the city's relief budget was distributed through the COS for both Protestants and Catholics.[115] The cost of direct relief had risen to $10,560 by 1915, almost all of which was paid for by a special $10,000 grant from the city, which also gave the organization a $1,500 annual grant.[116]

In line with their overall orientation, the Society placed a lot of emphasis on the investigation of applications for aid and the referral of cases to the correct service as well as training social workers to do this effectively. A confidential exchange to centralize information on relief applications and provision (and prevent fraud) was created in 1915; by that point district committees existed and various social efforts such as the sewing group, a lecture series, and a social work library had been ongoing for several years.[117]

Notwithstanding the Committees' original suspicion of the COS, soon after its formation both child charities cooperated with the organization and its workers by accepting cases referred to them directly by the COS or indirectly through the Recorder Court to the LBS Industrial School, where a great number of the applications on behalf of families were made by COS workers. What is important here is the fact that in the end the COS basically coordinated relief applications, not relief agencies, so the Committees' fears about interference and an attack on their autonomy were unfounded.

Much of the LBS's and POA's resistance to rationalizing initiatives is explained by their defence of existing services for widows and destitute children. Yet, for both these Committees, the charity home itself (the institution) was the manifestation of their work, the physical proof and affirmation, so to speak, of their social usefulness; and in their resistance to centralizing tendencies they were also defending their continued existence as well as their policy independence. On the whole, the Committees displayed a suspicion of outsiders, even of other female-directed charities and groups such as the YWCA and the LCW, and rejected all proposals that threatened their autonomy. The interaction with these other groups of women was further complicated by the ideological differences between benevolent Committees and reform organizations whose members supported what they perceived to be "new" approaches such as placing out and charity organization.

COOPERATION AMONG THE FEMALE CHARITIES

The LBS and the POA were not against cooperation in principle. They often transferred children from one institution to another, and, as we have seen, several of the ladies worked on more than one Committee. Nonetheless, there was very little real coordination or cooperation between the various charities – few recorded meetings, no joint policy discussions, and no joint fund-raising efforts.[118] Although the LBS Secretary noted that "the Managers entertained the most kindly feelings towards their kindred charities" when they received a letter from the Home for Friendless Women expressing a wish for occasional joint meetings, there is no indication that such meetings took place.[119] They also rejected several rationalization overtures from the Hervey Institute, which served more as a training school than a charity. Also an LBS member, Eliza Hervey quickly proposed that the two Societies merge. The LBS Committee received this suggestion with open hostility. It also rejected proposals in 1853 and 1856 to transfer children, as well as the Hervey Institute's proposals in 1889 and 1896 to reorganize their work along gender lines to allow for more efficient training.[120]

The LBS and POA were equally reluctant about cooperating with the YWCA. In 1889 the YWCA invited the ladies to conference meetings to discuss methods of work among women charity workers. The LBS sent representatives only to the first meeting.[121] The POA refused to attend, noting that "[t]he Ladies present did not see how such a scheme could be made serviceable to them as their plan of work and rules was all laid down."[122] Just as they had done when faced with the House of Refuge proposal in 1855, the POA used their Constitution as a protection against incursions on their policy independence and refused to discuss methods with outsiders.

There are several reasons, both cultural and organizational, for this reaction. First, although meetings to discuss methods were normal in the YWCA, which held regular conferences, they were not the norm among the benevolent organizations. Charities occasionally discussed the transfer of residents and had even met to discuss which services were missing in the city, but never to discuss policy orientations. Each charity was a private corporation defensive of its autonomy, and little coordination existed among them. A charity's mandate and range of services as well as its orientation were outlined in the Act of Incorporation, Constitution, and Rules and By-Laws; most Committees saw these as prescriptive and declined discussing any modifications with non-members.

Furthermore, the YWCA meetings, which advocated shared "religious fellowship with like-minded women," tended to use public prayer and gospel hymns to create "emotional bonds among delegates and affirm their membership in a community of female believers."[123] This practice was not the norm at charity Committee meetings. Although they carried out their work in a context of religious benevolence, the LBS and the POA were much more circumspect in their religious demonstration, limiting it to an opening prayer. Finally, and most important, the members of the LBS/POA and the YWCA were not, for the most part, "like-minded women." YWCA members were more reformist than the benevolent Committees, basing their overall approach on an early version of maternal feminism and publicly supporting scientific charity principles.[124]

The LBS/POA ladies had a similar reaction to the reformist Local Council of Women. Organized in 1893, the LCW invited the LBS and the POA to join as affiliated associations. Both did, but with a marked lack of enthusiasm that persisted throughout the 1890s. The LBS Secretary noted rather ambiguously that "they could not well decline – that it could do no harm, and might do much good."[125] They named the Secretary as their delegate, but her attendance was irregular and no reports on the Council are recorded in their minutes. The POA was less ambiguous, naming the First Directress and another member as delegates and immediately taking advantage of their membership to invite Lady Aberdeen and her children to a Christmas tea in 1894. Announcements of Local Council events were made at meetings and attendance encouraged, but the level of participation is called into question by the fact that in 1899 the Council President attended the monthly meeting to report on their work and request that the POA attend the meetings.[126]

This less than enthusiastic response to the Women's Council is not surprising in view of the ladies' suspicion of coordinated efforts and their lack of interest in discussing methods and ideas with outsiders. Moreover, just as they had with the YWCA, the LBS and the POA had major ideological differences with the Council, in particular with its support of the COS and of placing out. Neither the YWCA nor the LCW organizers, which included Julia Drummond, ran a child charity, nor had they actually experimented with different child placement methods; their support for placing out appears to be based on their ideological pro-family perspective and their acceptance of it as the "modern" method. This must have been very frustrating for the charity managers, who worked from an experiential base, having tried versions of placing out for seventy years and found it fraught with serious problems.

Both the POA and the LBS, however, agreed to participate in a conference on work with children, organized in 1896, to discuss methods and improve "the knowledge of one another's work." To facilitate discussion, the Council prepared a questionnaire for each agency to complete. There was even a codicil designed to assuage the private societies' apprehensions about coordinating bodies: "It is hardly necessary to remind our Societies that the Women's Council expressly disclaims any right to interfere with them in respect to their methods of work."[127] Yet despite this codicil, the questionnaire was unabashedly in favour of new methods.

The questionnaire included rather pointed questions about the admission of illegitimate children and children from two-parent families to child charities (the LCW clearly disapproved of both), as well as questions about the age until which boys and girls could "safely" be kept in the same institution. Other questions, on how to avoid the "institutionalization" of children and the "overlapping" of institutions, revealed the Council's anti-institutional bias and their support of rationalizing efforts. Questions on the use of adoption and placing out were included, but there were no questions on the methods actually used by the POA and the LBS, such as temporary aid for families, apprenticeship, or training inside the institution. Overall, the entire questionnaire was openly incongruous with the policy orientation of the two charities and exposed the major ideological differences that existed between themselves and the Local Council. Unfortunately, no reports, even in the charity minutes, remain to evaluate the discussions.

Nonetheless, despite these divergences, the meeting did lead to more cooperation among charities. A joint meeting of the LBS, the Hervey Institute, the Boys' Home, and the SPWC was immediately organized to discuss the need for some charity to undertake the work of helping young adolescent boys too young to work and pay board (i.e. enter the Boys' Home) but too old to remain in the child charities, although no solution was found.[128] In 1899, another meeting of representatives of the main female charities was convened to discuss the problems inherent in work with dependent children. Both the LBS and the POA attended. The LCW had invited prominent placing-out advocate J.J. Kelso as the guest speaker. But the women present identified their most important problem as the right of parents to remove children from institutions at will, not the institutionalization of children itself: "The first step towards improving existing conditions should be to secure powers of legal control over children placed in charitable institutions, with which parents should not interfere, the trouble at present being how to keep children long enough to train them usefully for after life."[129]

Kelso's presentation on his work as Superintendent of the Children's Department in Ontario convinced his audience of the positive effects of the new Ontario laws and his own department's work, but they understood these within a Quebec framework based on child institutions, not placing out. Therefore, almost certainly to the dismay of the Council leadership, follow-up from the meeting focused on the needs of institutions, and no mention was made of adopting Ontario's method of placing out. An ad-hoc committee was formed to address the absence of clear rights and powers for child institutions under Quebec law and to use the Council's lobbying powers to correct the situation. The women wanted some restriction on the power of the Recorder to commit children to jail (instead of a child charity), the appointment of a superintendent for neglected and dependent children, and specific legislation to extend the 1871 *Apprenticeship Law* to increase the legal powers of child charities over children and to require parents to prove "fitness" before removing a child from a charity. Despite support from the mayor and the SPWC, the undertaking was unsuccessful and no changes were made to the law.[130]

As a result of their association with the Council and membership in its various committees, the ladies' defensive isolationism began to subside by the end of the century. In 1912 both the LBS and the POA took responsibility for some aspect of the Child Welfare Exhibition.[131] A number of the child charities joined forces in 1918–19 to form the Children's Bureau to coordinate applications and admissions. The LBS and the Hervey Institute were already sharing the cost of a social worker to investigate applications for them, a decision that removed much time-consuming work from the individual agencies. The Children's Bureau was a logical next step; the charities generally conceived of it as a joint board akin to one of their own management boards over which they would have control.[132] But the trained social workers who staffed the Bureau diverged sharply from the private agencies on their view of child welfare and best practices, and this proved very problematic for the child charities quite quickly, as did the structural reorganization of the Protestant network as of 1920. As we will see in the epilogue, which looks at this question in more detail, the ladies adjusted some of their services but steadfastly defended both their place in the community's social services network, the importance of the services they provided, and the validity of their policies.

Conclusion

Finding a means to address poverty is a problem society continues to struggle with today.

This was made even more difficult in nineteenth-century Quebec, where the absence of a public poor-relief system left the private sector responsible for any help that was available, even that for the homeless and the destitute. Montreal's dual ethnic and religious makeup resulted in a model that was somewhat unusual in the Western world. Without any public relief, two parallel social service networks developed along confessional and, for the most part, linguistic lines, with the Catholic Church building an extensive network of relief services for the French-speaking population and Irish Catholics while the Protestant elite provided for the remaining English-speaking population. As a component of the social regulation structure, poor relief was based on a dynamic whereby aid was recognized as a gift, not a right. The rise of liberalism, with its emphasis on individual freedom and responsibility as well as the association of poverty with moral weakness and even crime, resulted in a tendency to constrained benevolence on the part of the city's Protestant elite. Institutional aid, with its ability to both confine and reform/retrain recipients, formed the core of both the Protestant and the Catholic networks of support.

This book has examined female benevolence in nineteenth- and early-twentieth-century Protestant Montreal, and, in so doing, has shed light on little-known aspects of the community's response to social inequality. Montreal bourgeois women forged an essential role for themselves in the city's Protestant social services network, by establishing almost all of the organizations that provided relief services for women and children. In this they represented a crucial support for families faced with either temporary or long-term difficulties due to unemployment, insufficient income, or the death of a spouse.

Serving on a charity board was an accepted, even expected, activity for ladies of the elite; and, since charities were an integral part of the institutional structures that underpinned class relations, such service was a sign of a family's social importance and moral authority. Thus, a significant number of women, drawn mainly from the leading families in Montreal's Protestant elite – the wives and daughters of merchants, manufacturers, professionals, and clergymen – were associated with the charities as subscribers or as Committee members. As collective histories of the lady directors, but also as institutional histories, case studies such as this one enable us to understand the details and nuances of charity management work and the challenges the ladies faced, as well as their policy decisions and the circumstances behind them. Examination of these female-directed private charities reveals that managing a charity involved substantial administrative and organizational work, but that this work was not spread evenly among the many women who were publicly associated with the Committees. The majority were members for less than five years, rarely attended meetings, never supervised the institution as a Monthly Visitor, and did not participate in fund-raising. That left the bulk of the work and all of the decision-making to a small core of talented and dedicated members who invested a substantial amount of time and effort. They were assisted in this by another group, some of whom made a particular contribution in one area such as fund-raising or visiting. This lack of overall involvement made it more difficult to supervise the institutions and their schools and to organize fund-raising events than it would otherwise have been, and left real power in the hands of a few families for much of the century, although this highly centralized administrative model was in the process of changing by late in the century.

Run by women of the elite as private incorporated societies, these charities reflected the values of that elite – their Protestantism, their "Britishness," their class bias, their power, and their status – but more importantly, they reflected the values of Protestant elite women. As was typically the case in benevolent women's organizations such as these ones, these ladies tended to come from establishment families and to have a traditional conservative perspective, based on the centrality of religion, the Christian duty of charity, and the importance of family, as well as a class duty to help the less fortunate. Focused on responding to need and relieving poverty, rather than reforming the poor, they moderated some of the harshest moralist responses to vulnerable populations that constrained the benevolence of many in the elite and provided families with services they could not find elsewhere in the city. Nonetheless, the ladies understood child care from within their own class perspective and overall they aimed to "socialize," even "civilize," the children of the poor, making their charities an integral part of the city's social regulation system.

Class and gender intersected in the ladies' charitable work and their response to poverty, but gender was the determinant factor. Bringing their maternal and caring perspective to their work with children, the ladies structured their societies and their benevolent design around religious salvation, education, and providing a home for children who found themselves in need of one, and developed child-centred policies in the process. Their benevolent design was anchored by their evangelical faith in the possibility of religious salvation and structured by their determination to teach children "adequate" middle-class values.

In this, the ladies aimed to educate children deprived of parental protection to become good Christians and useful citizens, and their institutional regimes were designed with this in mind, with schooling, religious training, and work dominating the daily schedule. The Committees hoped to make their institutions into substitute homes, but their class perspective and their conservatism led them to focus on training poor children for their "proper" place in society, rather than aspiring to social mobility for them. Still, their respect for parental rights and their general willingness to provide temporary care for children, as well as their determined attempts to maintain conditions in the charity homes as healthy and comfortable as budgets permitted, made both societies protective in their approach. Nonetheless, the stark differences between the milieux from which the children came and the environment in which they found themselves once they crossed the threshold of one of these charities might have caused them a certain amount of emotional trauma and even been experienced on their part as an "emotional frontier" – that is, a collision of two different cultures or ways of being. From the perspective of one of these children everything must have seemed big, different, and intimidating. They would begin their new education, training, and socialization on the day of their arrival.

Placing children in a charity was one strategy families used to cope with familial difficulties or financial problems. The relationship between a charity director and a poor family was one in which the elite management Committee held significantly more power than the working-class applicants, but it was also an interactive dynamic, and working-class agency was an important factor in the process. Requesting aid was in itself a form of agency, and families needed to decide where their application was most likely to meet with success and then find the best way to present their situation to ensure acceptance. As was shown in the example of the LBS, this might mean presenting themselves as members of the predominant church or as one-parent families, or it might involve mothers entering institutions as workers for a short time to secure entry for their children. Many families were willing to do whatever it took to secure care for their children or to relieve the family of their cost. The main form of agency these families demonstrated, however, was requesting the discharge of their children as soon as possible despite rules on minimum periods of residence. In this context, on the rare occasion that the Committees refused to release children on the basis of religion or parental immorality, families demonstrated clear agency by stealing their children from the charity homes or challenging the societies in court. Thus working-class families were more assertive and more imaginative than their position of relative powerlessness suggests.

For the most part both Committees showed remarkable continuity and cohesion, yet conflicts arose at points over the dominant role of the Anglican Church and the centralization of power in the hands of Directresses. A few contentious policy debates occurred over the admission of non-orphans in the POA and of children with working parents able to pay board in the LBS. Most policy discussions, though, centred on policies used to place children leaving the institutional home: the difficulties associated with finding apprenticeship situations, especially in skilled trades; the inherent dangers in placement methods such as adoption, apprenticeship, and foster care; and the methods that could be introduced to make these placements safer and more advantageous for children. From the late 1870s, as new members joined or others were in a position to assert themselves, and as notions of childhood innocence became more common, the Committees began a modernization and decentralization process, adding new services and altering both internal policies and placement policies in an effort to improve conditions for the children and to increase both the quality of their training and their protection.

Although their efforts were often compromised by restricted budgets and class notions of minimal or appropriate conditions, both Committees attempted to make their institutions as home-like and safe as possible and in this way to create a "fictive" family. The regimen was strict, but family activities including prayer, meals, and holiday celebrations built family cohesion. In the last part of the century and into the twentieth, this was supplemented by entertainments and summer outings. Many children had siblings with them, and parents visited; some formed close ties with other children. Once they left, children apprenticed from the POA received letters from siblings or children they had known and were sent books at Christmas, as well as receiving a yearly visit from the matron. The children lived an experience of uniformity inside the institution, where individuality and spontaneity found little place, and of "differentness" outside it, as they were isolated from other children for the most part (to protect them from disease), except when they were marched to church and Sunday school in a group. Still, many of the children appear to have accepted the institutions as their homes and their fictive families. They wrote letters back, returned to visit after they left, donated their skills to help the Committees with building repairs, attended family celebrations when they were in town, and made financial donations if they became prosperous. For their part the Committee ladies helped children after their apprenticeships with funds, job placements, and medical care. In this way the Committees were successful in creating an institutional atmosphere that many of the child residents did not experience as alienating, despite having lost their parents or been placed in care. These findings confirm those from other cities, where the re-evaluation of child charities based on case studies and testimonies has found that many child residents found positive aspects in their experience.

Their place as women in a highly gendered society where women did not have the same legal, political, social, and economic rights as men impacted on the work of these female Committees. They worked in the social sphere where charity management was accepted, despite the public nature of much of the work involved, but they integrated certain aspects of the prevalent gendered "separate spheres" ideology that imposed norms of propriety and limited some of their actions in public. Created early in the century before such prescriptions were as common, these two charity Committees had more autonomy in terms of their foundation than those formed later in the century and neither had a male Advisory Board at its inception. Nonetheless, their respect for rules of public etiquette meant that by the late 1830s the ladies no longer spoke at their public annual meetings, and their acceptance of gender-defined special qualities led both Committees to request male supporters to form men's committees by mid-century when the task at hand (constructing buildings and investments) was clearly in the male sphere. However, unlike what historians have found in several other places, changes in nomenclature did not occur and the women's role in Montreal's Protestant network was neither challenged nor compromised.

Yet, these same gendered notions empowered the ladies when it came to policy decisions in terms of children and managing the institutional home, both seen as domestic by nature and based on women's moral and religious authority, hence within the women's sphere of competence. This gave them the confidence to base their policies on their years of experience, not on new trends, and to resist pressure from supporters to alter their policy orientations. Still, the ladies' gender did bring with it some limitations that had an impact on their work. They managed to side-step the legal restrictions placed on married women by incorporating their societies, but social restrictions remained. As women, they did not have the same freedom as men to intervene publicly to rescue children from abusive situations, and their reluctance to publicly prosecute apprenticeship masters in cases of abuse was influenced by gender considerations.

Gender is also an important factor in explaining the supportive women's culture that developed inside these charity Committees themselves and that influenced their protective, personal approach to charity work based on an ethic of care, as well as their pro-child and, at least to some extent, pro-family perspective. The ladies worked together on female committees made up of close networks of kinship and friendship. They brought with them a shared women's culture and value system, based in humanism and religious dedication. Their approach to charity was centred on their particular project or institution and the needs of the children or women in their charities – what I have referred to as a "person-centred approach." This kept them focused and pragmatic.

It has been shown that both Committees developed policies on the basis of their experience managing the charities. In this they demonstrated a remarkable level of professionalism for volunteer committees. Admission policies were based on their understanding of changing needs, and the Committees demonstrated flexibility in their readiness to accommodate new needs among poor families (working families, two-parent families, and abandoned children) as well as those in the city in general (the 1847 typhus fever outbreak, the LBS Industrial School, the POA convalescent wards). Their emphasis on protecting the children increased as their experience grew and as they struggled with the many complex problems inherent in child charity work: those related to the rights of parents, the ideal institutional regime, and the risks inherent in placing children in other families.

Their protective approach is especially evident in changes they made to the placement policies they used for children who could not return to their parents. Both Committees were conscious of the potential problems and challenges associated with sending children into virtually unknown families. They attempted to minimize dangers while creating as normal a life experience as possible for children under their care. Neither charity used adoption very often because of its legal ambiguity under Quebec law, and the POA discontinued its use entirely at mid-century, when an adopted child died from abuse. Both Committees also tried to reduce the risk of abuse and exploitation in apprenticeship placements by making upward adjustments in apprenticeship age and fees, by adding flexibility into the process, and by attempting to visit apprentices once placed. This considered approach resulted in fairly advanced policies on apprenticeship – a visiting system, trial periods, and apprenticeship to trades. Still, several cases of abuse occurred and the ladies encountered a number of problems trying to deal with these in the child's best interests. By the 1880s, the ladies' increased emphasis on protecting the children and their lack of faith in the ability of placement families to educate, train, and care for children adequately led both Committees to reduce the use of apprenticeship for girls and for a few of the boys. Instead they opted for a policy of prolonged institutionalization where the Committee ladies themselves (with the help of their staff) were able to ensure both superior training and care.

These policy orientations as well as their traditional approach to charity meant that the Committees found themselves at odds with two new movements by the late nineteenth century: placing out and scientific charity. Reformers and many professional child-care workers argued that family life was necessary for an ideal childhood and advocated placing dependent children in foster families ("placing out") as early as possible rather than in institutions. The Montreal Committees rejected both the qualification of placing out as a new, more modern method and its use to deliberately break up poor families. Moreover, although the ladies certainly saw their work in the context of saving children, their pragmatism led them to value the expertise they had acquired over years of placing children in families more than vague ideological concepts about the importance of the family and the home, even if these concepts were central to their own middle-class culture and were advocated by many of their supporters. It is important to recognize that while the Committees' defence of institutional care might have appeared backward from the standpoint of English Canada (or the United States), it was the standard model for Quebec, both Protestant and Catholic.

In a similar way both Committees also rejected the scientific charity movement, which called for the establishment of centralized and coordinated charity structures to investigate applications for aid to avoid fraud and ensure aid was given only to those considered deserving, and then to design aid to force self-reliance. Their traditional and humanitarian perspective meant the ladies did not agree with the ideological assumptions behind this approach. In fact, they accepted need as the main basis for their admission policies (if not always in their public discourse) and were not overly concerned with notions of the deserving poor or of relief dependency. Thus they focused more on helping the poor with child care than on forcing them to become self-reliant, although they often passed judgment on parents' morality. The ladies also resisted attempts by the male elite to rationalize the female charities (and thus reduce services to families by eliminating duplication) or to centralize and coordinate the city's charitable services. In this they were defending both their range of services and their institutional autonomy.

Buoyed by their confidence both in their traditional world-view and in the expertise they had acquired through their experience running child charities, the ladies refused requests made by male supporters to adopt foster care as a placement method and effectively resisted attempts by the male elite in the nineteenth century to rationalize the network and merge institutions or remove services. Their defence of institutional care rather than foster care also put them at odds with both reformist women's associations and professional child-care workers in the twentieth century.

As benevolent women's associations, the ladies on these management Committees did not advocate reforming the poor, nor were they interested in intervening in the political arena as citizens, instead limiting their public intervention to what was directly linked to their committee tasks. In these ways they differed from women's associations formed later in the century, such as the YWCA and the Local Council of Women, that approached social questions from a more reformist perspective. These latter groups supported placing out as the modern method, arguing for its superiority over institutions; they also actively lobbied for scientific charity as the best way to force the poor to be self-reliant and to address underlying problems rather than simply to relieve destitution. As a result, they disagreed with the policy choices of the two charities under study and on occasion criticized benevolent associations. These ideological differences kept the benevolent women's groups from actively embracing policy discussions and cooperation with the reformist groups, although this was beginning to change by the twentieth century.

By the latter part of the nineteenth century, a number of contemporaries criticized female-managed private child charities (and other traditional benevolent societies) for being amateurish and for resisting what were seen as more modern approaches to charity. This study has shown that this is not a fair evaluation of these two Montreal charities. In fact, these women did not deliberately resist change. They based their benevolent design on years of practical experience and on their personal approach to charity work, centred on the children and their well-being. Their policies were neither static nor were they developed haphazardly or in isolation from the reality of poverty or charity. They evolved in response to the needs of the city's poor families (to increase the admission to the LBS of boarding children and children from two-parent families, for example, and the admission of convalescents and soldiers' children to the POA), and in response to actual cases of abuse and other problems in placement methods, as well as the ladies' evaluation of the best way to protect and train children. In fact, their more personal approach made them more sensitive to the needs of the industrial city's poor families than many charity reformers, even as it made them somewhat disrespectful of so-called "superior" methods.

Any qualification of the ladies and their approach as "sentimental" or "naïve" only made sense from a liberal perspective to poverty and the poor based on morals testing, forced self-reliance, and notions of the deserving poor. In fact the ladies worked from a perspective we could characterize as realism – if families had no income, were sick, or were homeless, then they needed help with child care, at least temporarily. The experience of the charities shows that most families who turned to them for help did not abuse this aid, removing their children as soon as they were able to resume their care.

The charity directors developed policies from a caring perspective, but class was a constant factor. They provided help when needed, but the help they provided for families was as much a form of civilizing, socializing, and spiritual salvation as it was support and child protection – that is, a full range of moral rescue and middle-class character-building. In this way, their realistic evaluation of need was mixed with an optimistic faith that they would be able to influence and educate the children of the poor into God-fearing and well-trained young people. As we saw, many of the children did not remain in the institutions long enough for this training to be very effective, but the ladies could always console themselves with the hope that what little influence they had had would bear fruit in the future. Over the nineteenth and into the twentieth centuries their benevolent design evolved. Centred on protection, religion, education, and health care in the nineteenth century, it shifted to a clearer emphasis on citizenship training in the twentieth.

The two charities under study are excellent examples of benevolent women who carried out extensive and challenging charity work within the limits of their social perspective. They faced many of the same challenges still grappled with today: issues of parental rights and fitness, of child abuse and child exploitation, of finding ways to relieve poverty. Their responses were limited by their attitudes to poverty, their suspicion of working-class morality, their belief in a hierarchical society and the superiority of middle-class culture, and the constraints imposed by their gender, but they forged a central place for themselves in the city's network of social services and provided important support for Protestant families.

Over the course of the nineteenth century, the two Committees demonstrated a remarkable level of independence, professionalism, and ingenuity.

They developed clear policies on diet, health, hygiene, and exercise. They improved the quality of their staff and increasingly recognized education as important. They adapted their admission and placement policies on the basis of their experience and of their evaluation of changing needs in the city. Finally, their general policy orientation was designed to recognize the needs of families and children and to protect the children under their care.

By the 1920s the Committees began to hire social workers to help with admission inquiries and joined the new umbrella organizations including the Children's Bureau and the Montreal Council of Social Agencies. This was to prove somewhat problematic for them in the end, since both of these organizations advocated the use of foster care as a placement method rather than institutions. Nonetheless, despite this openness to co-operating with new social agencies to coordinate services for children in the city, both Committees stood steadfast in their belief that a structured, protected environment such as a well-run residential institution provided a good home and excellent training and could be beneficial for many, if not all, children. Having assumed an important place in the city's Protestant social services network, the women who ran these two child charities over several generations fought to keep their place and to maintain services to as many families as possible. As we will see in the epilogue, by the 1930s their benevolent design included a defence of their existence as much as of their methods.

Epilogue

The nature of Montreal's Protestant social services changed profoundly in the interwar years. Recognizing that it spent much of its time actually working with families, the COS reinvented itself as the Family Welfare Association in 1920 and yielded the mission to coordinate the network to the newly formed Montreal Council of Social Agencies (MCSA). The Financial Federation (hereafter "the Federation"), set up in 1922 to coordinate fund-raising, ended separate efforts and centralized the allocation of funds. Both the LBS and the POA joined the new organizations rather unenthusiastically on the assumption they "could at any time withdraw,"[1] and after verifying that donations could be earmarked to specific societies and that endowment funds were not in jeopardy.[2]

With funding rationalized, the MCSA was free to address the organization of the network into a coordinated, well-structured whole that reflected modern social work and scientific charity principles and was designed to "better" serve the community.[3] In the process, the child charities became the target of a new series of proposals that challenged both their policy approach and their very existence.

The Children's Bureau was restructured and assumed additional powers. When it was formed in 1919, it was responsible for investigating applications and admissions. To this end, it opened a temporary Receiving Home in 1920, where all those admitted would remain for medical testing and observation before placement.[4] In October 1920, one of the four Bureau social workers was put in charge of supervising the four child charities.[5] In April of 1921 (one month after the POA/H finally joined the Bureau), the LBS First Directress reported that all "placements" would now be done by the Bureau.[6] Slowly this came to include discharges as well as admissions.

As members of these three structures, the LBS and the POA/H became part of an external administrative framework, a situation that circumscribed their autonomy to some extent. Given that the three associations – the Bureau, the MCSA, and the Federation – advocated the use of foster homes and eventually challenged the place of residential institutions within the network, the extent to which the policies of the two child charities went against the grain of the rapidly changing face of Protestant social work in the city was often uncomfortably clear. Both Committees defended the essential contribution they made to the child-care network and to the needs of families, all the while adjusting their services to accommodate community needs and the demands of the coordinating bodies.

The MCSA organized the various agencies into four Divisions. As members of the Children's Division, the child charities found themselves merged with representatives from the Bureau, the Women's Directory (which worked with mothers and infants), and the SPWC, as well as five at-large voting members. This effectively marginalized their influence on policy, since they could easily be out-voted. In 1923, the Children's Division invited C.C. Carsten, Director of the Child Welfare League of America, to study the city's child-care system and make recommendations. This was the first of several appeals to American "experts" for advice on what were considered to be needed reforms.

We have already noted that Montreal's child-care model, with its preponderance of residential institutions, very few of which used foster care, was the system used throughout Quebec but not the one that was increasingly popular in the rest of North America, especially among social workers and professionals. Thus it was no surprise that in his final report Carsten recommended (among other things) reducing the number of child institutions and developing a system of foster home placement under the supervision of the trained staff at the Children's Bureau. Working on the premise that ideally children should remain in their own family, he believed that when this was not feasible, family placement was preferable as much as possible. Although he noted how "home like" both the POA/H and the LBS institutions managed to be and commended them on their "atmosphere of kindliness," he recommended merging them and moving the resulting institution, organized on a cottage system, to the suburbs. He also recommended developing a coordinated plan (under the Bureau) where home placement and institutional care would supplement each other to the best advantage of each child.[7]

According to the 1923 Children's Bureau Report, both foster care and cottage-system institutions were already part of the Bureau's draft plan as outlined in 1921.[8] Thus, both the LBS and the POA/H responded positively to the idea of a merger if this enabled them to establish modernized services on a cottage system, but this was contingent on the sale of their buildings at fair market value, which never happened.[9] Neither, however, accepted the superiority of foster care as a method for all children.

When the child charities formed the Children's Bureau in 1919, it was mandated to oversee applications and admissions. Although it seems certain that they believed foster homes would mainly be used to supplement institutions, and naïvely assumed that institutional care would remain at the centre of the Montreal model as it always had been, the social workers hired to coordinate client investigation and admissions were convinced of the superiority of families (foster homes) as an environment for normal children, as were some of the Board members who represented other agencies and the at-large members in the Children's Division. Thus, although an early Bureau report in 1922 indicated that it placed "certain of its wards in foster homes," the respective roles of foster homes and institutions changed rapidly after 1924 and Carstens's Report.[10]

The rise of professionalization was at the crux of another point of contention between the Bureau and the child charities. The professional staff believed that all decisions connected to investigations, admissions, and discharges should be left to trained workers such as themselves, and not to volunteers such as the bourgeois women who ran the institutions. Groups such as the LBS had originally conceived of the Bureau as a way to have the onerous task of investigating admission requests done by trained workers in a centralized fashion. But they also believed that the managers of private charities, including themselves, had a role to play and that the expertise they had acquired running child charities for a century should be recognized. Furthermore, this new structure involved implications they had never imagined and almost certainly would not have agreed to.

Under the structural reorganization, agencies were considered "constituent units" of the Bureau. When the charity Committees had formed the Bureau, they thought they were gaining social workers to help with some of the work, but rather than the Bureau staff working for them, in the end they had placed themselves under a system organized on different principles. Hence, the Bureau, as the agency's representative, now signed contracts with the city, and payments from the Quebec *Public Charities Act* came to agencies through the Bureau, not directly. In April–May 1921, for example, the LBS, "as a constituent unit of the Children's Bureau," empowered the Bureau to sign the Industrial School Contract with the city on their behalf. The Bureau originally refused to sign due to the clause requiring responsibility for hospital costs, which the LBS had always assumed. The LBS appears to have lost its industrial school status soon afterwards. In February 1922, Quebec asked for their accreditation papers and, although the LBS minutes indicate the Bureau received a telegram from Quebec confirming this status, government payments at the industrial school level stopped soon after.[11] One can only assume that the Bureau staff did not agree with the dual function of the LBS as both a charity and an industrial school, or did not consider the extra income necessary, given the funding they now received for institutionalized children under the 1921 *Public Charities Act* in any case. Unfortunately, no discussion of this is recorded by either the Bureau or the LBS.

Even more importantly, as a result of the charities being considered "constituent bodies," the Bureau, not the agency where a child was resident, held quasi-guardian status. In effect, the private incorporated societies had lost whatever "guardianship" powers they had held under the 1871 *Apprenticeship Law*. These legal implications were never explained to them, and to some extent the Committees continued to understand their work in the context of their private institutional constitutions and their former way of doing things. In particular, the LBS and the POA/H both wanted to retain some input into the placement and supervision of children leaving their institutions, since they continued to believe they still were responsible for them, but this now raised issues of guardianship, confidentiality, and jurisdiction. They protested their lack of control and attempted to assert it with varying levels of success.[12] Inevitably this led to conflicts.

Members of both the MCSA and the Bureau advocated the scientific charity principles of self-reliance, centralization, and investigation. Their determination to keep families together in the family home if possible and to force them to rely on their own resources (or those of their extended family) rather than on charity led to more restrictive admission criteria whereby the number of accepted applications dropped substantially.[13] A number of families still appealed directly to the child charities, but the new centralized admission policy meant that the Committees could not admit children directly, and many of the requests they forwarded to the Bureau were refused under the new, more restrictive guidelines.[14] The Bureau's preference for foster care meant that by 1927 most children who were accepted were placed in foster homes rather than institutions. Moreover, additional social workers were hired to undertake ongoing investigations aimed at implementing a policy of family reconstitution (based on the principle of self-reliance), by which families were expected to resume the care of their children as soon as it was determined they were in a position to do so (and much more quickly than they had done in the past). The combination of these policies led to reduced numbers of children being sent to child institutions (by 1936, this represented a differential of almost three times more children going into foster care than to institutions) and a reduction in the length of time children remained residents there. Although a special Placement Committee was designed to oversee admission decisions, the charities found they had very little input and were under the impression that most decisions were made in advance of the meetings and that cases that had been refused were never discussed.[15] The combined result of these policies left both the POH and the LBS under-populated by the late 1920s, a situation they unsuccessfully appealed to the Federation to correct many times.

Both the MCSA and the Federation had a mandate to organize a community network. In their view, the child charities that overlapped not only one another but, more importantly, a service they thought should be performed by foster homes (under the Children's Bureau) were a luxury the city could ill afford. Believing that every funded member agency should serve a specific function in the network, they strove to redefine a "new" role for the "old" charities. Several proposals to this effect that would have completely altered the charities' mandates, such as the POA/H taking only convalescent children and the LBS serving as a home for "mentally deficient" children, were rejected.[16]

Of course the deliberate strategy of emptying the institutions increased their per capita cost, and running an institution at half capacity was wasteful and expensive. While the Federation worried about cost, the Bureau was sending fewer and fewer children to the charities. When the LBS and the POA protested against this, the Bureau offered compromise rather than a change in policy: that the charities accept more children on a temporary basis, that they accept more boys, that they lower their age limit to take younger children. Despite attempts to accommodate these requests, which included costly renovations in the LBS to reorganize dorms to admit more boys,[17] and in the POA to improve their capacity to care for sickly children, and even offers to accept children free of charge, only a few of these children were sent.[18] Carsten had recommended that normal children be placed in foster care and "problem" children in institutions. Although the charities resisted limiting their work to problem cases, the LBS accepted more and more children with psychological or intellectual difficulties, and children with medical problems, such as whooping cough and ringworm, entered the POA/H. To be able to do this type of work effectively, both Societies undertook the additional specialized staff training, including courses in Mental Hygiene, and hired more Registered Nurses.

The Committees had permission to maintain in-house training for girls over fourteen who had completed their schooling.[19] Discussions of this occurred sporadically, mainly about placement; this was a constant concern for the Committees, who were no longer in a position to hand-pick placement situations. By 1931, they had secured permission to arrange the placement (and supervision) of these girls and the POA/H also served as a "wage-home" for several girls working in the city and boarding in the institution.[20] In one particularly problematic case, the Bureau approved the tentative adoption of one of the older girls by an elderly couple despite the ladies' protests. Although the girl had been instructed not to communicate with the ladies, she wrote to the teacher about her lack of schooling and her excessive workload. Unlike their hesitancy to act in the nineteenth century, the Directresses found the placement address through her relatives, got into Caroline Angus's "motorcar," and drove to Knowlton to verify the situation.[21] In light of their report, the Bureau agreed to return her to the POA/H. Much had changed since the nineteenth century, but although the ladies themselves were now more capable of independent action, their Societies had lost much of their autonomy.

One aspect of the twentieth-century Committees that had not changed was the use of personal "private" charity. When a young boy with a cleft lip was admitted to the POA/H in 1930 (in their convalescent capacity) and the MGH doctors urged extensive treatment, the Bureau refused to pay, arguing it was not needed due to the boy's "retarded mental condition." Just as they had done when trying to save their Convalescent Wing in 1920, seventeen of the POA/H members personally donated the funds needed for three years of treatment for the boy.[22] While not a characteristic of bureaucracies, this type of personal charity remained part of the ladies' committees' benevolent approach.

In her biography of Jane Wisdom, the social worker who served as Executive Director of the Women's Directory in Montreal from 1923 to 1938, Suzanne Morton speaks of Wisdom's social scientific methods as being "broadly conceived ... to mediate between naively sentimental and harshly punitive responses to poverty" and applauds "the unity of professional technical expertise and humanistic values."[23] It was for what they saw as a lack of these qualities – the lack of humanity and what they felt was an exaggerated emphasis on rigid bureaucracy and a harsh attitude towards needy families – that the ladies' Committees criticized the Bureau (and its workers) in terms of the way they dealt with families and with the children in their charities. It would be an understatement to say that the Bureau's Executive Director, Mildred Kensitt, was not well-liked and appears to have made little effort to accommodate the charity Committees.

Given Quebec's largely private relief model, when the Great Depression hit in the 1930s, the Federation was faced with trying to pay for the mounting costs associated with massive unemployment and social dislocation at a time of faltering private fund-raising efforts and the reluctance of governments to intervene. In light of their worsening financial situation, the Federation began another rationalization attempt in 1932, striking a series of Survey Committees to look for possible cost efficiencies without too great an impact on services.[24] These committees worked on the basis of the Charity Organization principles that had underpinned the formation of the Council in 1919/20 – the organization of services to reduce duplication and to produce a streamlined, efficient structure. The working proposal of the Child-care and Protection Committee, submitted in 1935, included the abolition of the Infants' Home and the amalgamation of the LBS and POH. The joint LBS–POH would move into the Infants' Home building, the Federation would move its offices into the LBS building, and the POH building would be sold with the profits going to the Federation. It was suggested that the organizations' Endowment Funds could become part of "community assets."[25]

If the charities had been muted in their response to earlier proposals, in 1935 they argued that the time had come, in the words of the POA/H First

Directress, Caroline Molson Angus, "for the Child-Caring Institutions to state *their* case."[26] As they defended institutional care and challenged foster care, some of their arguments foreshadowed problems with foster care that would be exposed later in the century, but what is even more interesting is the extent to which, although their institutions had changed a lot, many of their arguments echoed back to those of the nineteenth century – the same defense of institutions as ideal milieux in which to provide socialization and protective care either long-term for children without families or temporarily for children eventually returning to their families. In the forefront remained the needs of children as future citizens and the best way to ensure this. The training of citizens had always been a part of the child charities' benevolent design, but in the nineteenth century more emphasis was placed on protection, education, and health care. Given the advances in these areas, citizenship training had become the main focus of their benevolent design by the 1920s.

The Committees pointed to several weaknesses they identified in the Survey Committee's plan to minimize institutional care.[27] First, although they agreed that a family home was ideal for many children, they affirmed that this was not a question of "one-size fits all," as many children benefited from the socialization with other children and the structure that a well-run institution offered. They were particularly critical of the traumatic experience several children had had being shuffled from one foster home to another before they finally found some stability in one of their institutions. Second, they addressed the overall availability of care – that need in the city was likely to grow and that there would never be enough "suitable" foster homes to be found; therefore, reducing institutional care was foolhardy. The core of their arguments centred on the questionable quality of foster homes and their inability to provide adequate training and health care.

Their defence of institutional care came down to an argument for the quality of their care and its advantages. Both Committees were cognizant of the discourse on the negative effects of institutionalization and had developed policies to address this. Their annual reports throughout the 1920s and 1930s emphasized the home-like qualities of their charity "homes": how children were treated as individuals, each with their own clothes and possessions, pocket money, and bank accounts; how children returned regularly to visit after they had left and that the Committees ran clubs for former children to facilitate these visits. The Committees built the case for the superiority of institutional care in terms of their spacious facilities, their large playgrounds, the varied recreational and social activities (including two months at summer camp), and the special training courses that were regularly organized for the children, all aimed at preparing them for their future. Perhaps even more importantly, children could socialize with their friends, attend public school, and receive regular visits from their families. Underlying this was an emphasis on the institutions' trained personnel, including Registered Nurses, and high standards designed to give children all possible advantages. As Caroline Molson Angus explained to the Survey Committee, "we are bringing up future citizens of the city and we want to do the best we can for them."[28] Their class bias convinced them that they were in a better position to do this than untrained working-class foster mothers were, and that their "Homes" were therefore superior to foster homes. The Committees remained convinced that foster homes were inadequately supervised and investigated despite the number of Bureau staff allocated to these functions, and that families took in children solely for economic reasons, which in itself was proof of their inability to provide adequate care.

Class is also a factor in their twentieth-century critique of scientific charity from the perspective of conservative benevolence. The ladies, who, as the POA/H informed the Survey Committee, "care[d] about humanity and kindness to children and kindness to the poor," were willing to open their charities to help as many poor families as possible. They were particularly critical of the restrictions that had been arbitrarily placed on admissions to encourage self-reliance and the number of poor families who were being turned down as a result despite needing help. Further, they felt that many needy families hesitated to even ask for help since the attitude of the Bureau's Executive Director was "arbitrary and lacking in sympathy to such an extent that only in extreme cases are applications made."[29] Both Committees also believed that the Federation had to recognize the value of volunteer workers and their place in the system.

The crux came, though, with the attack on their existence as private corporations. For underlying the MCSA's "community" approach lay a direct assault on the "private" nature of associative charities holding mandates outlined in Acts of Incorporation and obligations to foundation donors. The assumption that the Federation could simply change their mandate and take their buildings, and possibly even their Endowment Funds, threatened them to their core. Both categorically refused the proposals and, supported by their lawyer, the POH threatened to leave the Federation if it came to that.[30]

In the end, the aim to find some economy in the area of children's services was secured when seven agencies, including the Bureau, Big Brothers, Big Sisters, and the SPWC, merged under the SPWC's charter to form the Children's Services Association (CSA) and there was no need to implement the proposals connected to the POA/H and the LBS. One child institution was abolished when the foster care system was placed under the Infants' Home instead of the Bureau and headquartered in its building on Queen Mary. Interestingly, now that a committee of volunteer women were in charge, they addressed many of the problems the LBS and POA/H Committees had raised about the lack of training for foster mothers and the lack of inspection of foster homes for health and safety. The naming of E. Corbett as Executive Director of the CSA helped to ensure a smooth transition, as he had the entire confidence of the child charities due to his former work in the SPWC. The new Placement Committee appears to have worked better under the more streamlined structure and the child charities must have felt less under attack as a result, although foster care remained the policy of choice.

The two twentieth-century Committees had successfully defended some of their services and their existence from a major rationalization attempt. Through the process, they had forged a new role for themselves in the network as a complement to foster care. Both charities still provided temporary care for families and trained adolescent girls as servants or provided them with a home while they continued their education. However, they had added new services – for the LBS, the care and supervision of "troubled" children; for the POA/H, the medical care of children and the provision of a safe and supervised board option for girls who had "aged out" of the child-care system and started work.

Coordination between the LBS and POA/H increased, and they amalgamated on their own terms and of their own volition in 1946–47, when the LBS sold its building and moved its children into the POA/H building at 1595 Summerhill Avenue.[31] This building was sold in the 1960s when the joint agency altered its policy approach, shifting from institutional to group home care. The new agency, Summerhill Homes, was, in effect, a modern version of the cottage system they had hoped to adopt in the 1920s but had been unable to put into place.

Appendix

Protestant Charities in Nineteenth-Century Montreal, by Date of Establishment

Year	Charity/society	Service
1815–22	Female Benevolent Society	Widows, children, I,* O**
1822	Montreal General Hospital	Hospital, outpatient
1822	Protestant Orphan Asylum	Orphans, I
1832	Montreal Ladies' Benevolent Society	Children, women, I
1834	St George's Society	O
1835	St Andrew's / St Patrick's / German Society	O
1842	Inspector Street Mission	O
1843	Montreal Maternity	I
1848	Magdalene Asylum (Sheltering Home)	Women, I ("moral rescue")
1847	Home and School of Industry	Children, I, sewing
1851	YMCA	Mission work, referrals (work, board)
1853	Montreal Dispensary	Outpatient
1854–56	Protestant Industrial House of Refuge	Women, children, I, O
1855	Anglican Church Home	Elderly women, I
1856	Irish Protestant Benevolent Society	O
1857	St Andrew's Home	Immigrants, I
1861	Industrial Rooms	Women, sewing work
1862	Montreal Sailors' Institute	Men, recreational

1863	Montreal Protestant House of Industry & Refuge	Elderly, homeless, I, O
1865	United Board of Outdoor Relief	O
1867	St George's Home	Immigrants, I
1869	Mackay Institute for Deaf-Mutes	Deaf and blind children, I
1870	Protestant Infants' Home	Infants, mothers, I
1871	Montreal Boys' Home	Adolescent boys, I
1871	Murray Bay Convalescent Home	Convalescence
1874	YWCA	Boarding, educational services
1874	Home for Friendless Women	Women, I ("moral rescue")
1875	Victoria Mission	O
1879	Montreal Diet Dispensary (YWCA)	Sick poor, O
1882	Women's Protective Society	Women immigrants, work referral
1882	Nazareth Street Mission	O
1883	St Margaret's Home for Incurables	Incurables, women, I
1883	Belmont Park	Immigrants, O
1887	Fresh Air Fund	Outings, convalescence
1888	Montreal Day Nursery (YWCA)	Children, day care and work referral (women)
1890	Old Brewery Mission	O, shelter
1891	Montreal Foundling and Baby Hospital	Foundlings, babies, I
1892	Welcome Hall Mission	O, shelter
1895	Moore Convalescent Home	Hospital, chronic
1895	Andrews' Home	Immigrants, I
1895	Robert Jones Convalescent	Children, convalescence
1896	Centre Street Mission	O
1899	Working Women's Home (Salvation Army)	Women, board

* I = Institutional

** O = Outdoor aid to people in their homes (food, fuel, clothing, medicine, etc.)

Note: Hospitals other than the Montreal General have not been included in the list.

Notes

INTRODUCTION

1 Pearce and Mitchell, *History of the Montreal Ladies' Benevolent Society*, 9.

2 Until 2015, the two organizations (merged in 1946 and subsequently involved in other mergers) were under Batshaw Youth and Family Centres, which is now integrated into the Centre intégré universitaire de santé et de services sociaux de l'Ouest-de-l'Île-de-Montréal (CIUSSS). I would like to thank Batshaw for giving me access to their papers and Frank Campanile, Archives, for his help. The papers are deposited in Library and Archives Canada (LAC): LAC Summerhill Homes Collection, MG 28, I 388. For simplicity's sake, I will refer to the two charities hereafter as POA and LBS.

3 Smith, *Ladies of the Leisure Class.* Also Prochaska, *Women and Philanthropy.*

4 Upper Canada / Ontario would move towards some state support with the *House of Industry Act* (1837) and the *Charity Aid Act* (1874). Muratto, "Charity and Public Welfare in History."

5 Fecteau, *Un nouvel ordre*, 35–69. See also Baillargeon, "Orphans in Quebec"; Fecteau, "Between the Old Order," 306, 320, n44; Fecteau and Vaillancourt, "Charity in the City"; Morel, "L'enfant sans famille."

6 The announcement was carried in the *Gazette* and the *Herald* daily until December. Pearce and Mitchell, *History of the Montreal Ladies' Benevolent Society*, 9.

7 On being "British," see Colley, *Britons*, and Hall, *Civilizing Subjects.*

8 See Young, *Patrician Families* and *Respectable Burial.*

9 Gordon and Nair, *Public Lives*; McKenna, "The Role of Women,"and *A Life of Propriety*; Smith, "Women, Class and Family."

10 For a more extensive discussion of the women on these two Committees see ch. 2.

11 See note on language usage, p. 24.

12 *Statutes of Canada East*, 1841, 4 and 5 Vict., c. 66; 1843, 7 Vict., c. 52.

13 See Scott, *Making the Invisible Woman Visible*, 263; also Williams Elliot, *The Angel out of the House*, 14.

14 Fecteau, *Un nouvel ordre*. The following discussion is based on his *La liberté du pauvre* (*The Pauper's Freedom*). Page references are to the translated edition. See also Fecteau, "L'Autre visage de la liberté," and "L'histoire comme expérience."

15 Fecteau, *The Pauper's Freedom*, 4, 24, 170–5, 260, 269–70. See also Dean, *The Constitution of Poverty*.

16 Fecteau, *The Pauper's Freedom*, 87–91, 179–81. For pauperism see ch. 1.

17 For the place of charity in these survival strategies see Mandler, "Poverty and Charity in the Nineteenth-Century Metropolis." For child charity in Montreal, see Bradbury, "The Fragmented Family," and *Working Families*. For other Canadian cities see the articles in Iacovetta and Mitchinson, *On the Case*. For London, the US, and various European cities see the articles in Mandler's *The Uses of Charity*; Crowther, *The Workhouse System*; and Morton, "The Transformation of Catholic Orphanages." For the use of insane asylums by families see Mitchinson, "Reasons for Committal," and Moran, *Committed to the State Asylum*.

18 On the interface of institution and working class agency, see the articles in Fecteau and Harvey, *La régulation sociale*.

19 See Fecteau and Harvey, "From Agents to Institutions," and Vallgårda, "Can the Subaltern Woman Run?" 481.

20 See Hewitt, *Women's Activism*, 40–50, 231–3; Boylan, "Women in Groups," and "Timid Girls, Venerable Widows"; Ginzberg, *Women and the Work*. Also Luddy, *Women and Philanthropy*.

21 Parr, "Introduction," 2. For an overview of this "reconstructed" childhood in Canada see McIntosh, *Boys in the Pits*, ch. 2. For the US, see Mintz, *Huck's Raft*.

22 For early changes in attitude see Greven, *The Protestant Temperament*; Lomax, *Science and Patterns of Child Care*; McLoughlin, "Evangelical Childrearing," 20–34; Semple, "The Nurture and Admonition of the Lord"; Wishy, *The Child and the Republic*. For the "economically useless child" see Zelizer, *Pricing the Priceless Child*. Discussions of this in Canada include Comacchio, *Nations Are Built of Babies*; Lafferty, *The Guardianship of Best Interests*; Peikoff and Brickey, "Creating Precious Children"; Rooke and Schnell, *Discarding the Asylum*; Sutherland, *Children in English-Canadian Society*.

23 Katz, *Poverty and Policy*, 72–3, and *In the Shadow of the Poorhouse*, 103–8, 193–4; Meckel, "Protecting the Innocents." Children were still found in some Canadian poorhouses in the twentieth century. See Rooke and Schnell, *Discarding the Asylum*, 74.

24 Bellingham, "The 'Unspeakable Blessing,'" 304. Steven Mintz agrees that class is the most determinant factor in the construct of the innocent child. Mintz, *Huck's Raft*, iii.

25 Chen, *Tending the Gardens of Citizenship*, 19–22, 54–9; Mintz, *Huck's Raft*, 92–3, 154–8.

26 Mintz, *Huck's Raft*, ch. 8.

27 Gilfoyle, "Street-Rats and Gutter-Snipes"; Stansell, *City of Women*.

28 Adamoski, "Charity Is One Thing"; Chen, *Tending the Gardens*; Hogeveen, "The Evils with Which"; Houston, "The 'Waifs and Strays.'"

29 Examples include "Duties of Society towards Our Young Waifs," *Daily Witness*, 3 January 1873; "Street Children," *Daily Witness*, 28 May 1873; *Philanthropy, Care of Our Destitute and Criminal Population*. See also "The Coming Generation of Criminals," *Canadian Illustrated News* 4, no. 10 (1871): 150. For an analysis of this see Harvey, "Le risque et la ville."

30 For this movement see Dekker, *The Will to Change the Child*; Dupont-Bouchat et al., *Enfance et justice*; Sutton, *Stubborn Children*.

31 *Statutes of United Canada*, 1857, 20 Vict., c. 28–9. A reformatory was opened at Île-aux-Noix in 1858; it moved to Saint-Vincent-de-Paul in 1862. See Ménard and Strimelle, "Enfant sujet, enfant objet?" and Trépanier, "Juvenile Delinquency and Youth Protection."

32 *Statutes of Quebec*, 1869, 32 Vict., c. 18.

33 *Statutes of Quebec*, 32 Vict., c. 17. For the discussion of this see ch. 1 and 4.

34 On the larger child-saving movement in the US see Ashby, *Saving the Waifs*; Gordon, "Single Mothers"; Stansell, *City of Women*. For Canada, see Bullen, "Children of the Industrial Age," 189–237; Chen, *Tending the Gardens*; Fingard, *The Dark Side of Life*, ch. 5; Reitsma-Street, "More Control than Care"; Sutherland, *Children in English-Canadian Society*; Ursel, *Private Lives, Public Policy*. See Gordon, "The Perils of Innocence," for the continuing negative impact of these concepts.

35 The early SPWC also lobbied for protective legislation for women and children. See Douglas, "A History of the SPWC," 7–23. For a more critical evaluation of the SPWC and its over-zealous tendency to "rescue" Catholic children in its early days, see Sitara, "Humanitarianism in the Age of Capital and Empire."

36 For a short overview of the residential schools see Fahrni, *Of Kith and Kin*, 115–18. For an excellent study of these institutions see, among others, Milloy, *A National Crime*.

37 In particular, Sutherland, *Children in English-Canadian Society*; Mintz, *Huck's Raft*; and Magda Fahrni's recent history of the family, *Of Kith and Kin*. Collections include those by Janovicek and Parr, *Histories of Canadian Children and Youth*; Parr, *Childhood and Family in Canadian History*; Rooke and Schnell, *Studies in Childhood History*; Smandych et al., *Dimensions of Childhood*.

38 For these concepts and examples of their application see the articles in Gleason et al., *Lost Kids*, and Gleason and Myers, *Bringing Children*.

39 See Gleason and Myers, *Bringing Children*, 1–16, for these distinctions.

40 Gleason, "Avoiding the Agency Trap," 448.
41 Alexander, "Can the Girl Guide Speak?" 149; Gleason, "Avoiding the Agency Trap."
42 Vallgårda, "Between Consent and Coercion," 92.
43 Ibid., 88–92; Vallgårda, "Adam's Escape," 300, 311.
44 Vallgårda, Alexander, and Olsen, "Emotions and the Global," 21; Vallgårda and Olsen, "Historicizing Emotional Development," 146.
45 Vallgårda, Alexander, and Olsen, "Emotions and the Global," 22.
46 Olsen and Vallgårda, "Emotional Frontiers," 437–44.
47 Poovey, *Uneven Developments*, 6. For a discussion of the origin of these ideas in the Enlightenment see Colley, *Britons*, ch. 6, and James, *Changing Ideas.*
48 Ryan, *Women in Public*, 6.
49 For the early-nineteenth-century Canadian press, see Errington, *Wives and Mothers*; Maas, *Helpmates of Man*; Morgan, *Public Men and Virtuous Women.*
50 See, for example, "Industry and Economy Essential Qualification in a Female," *Christian Guardian* 1, no. 1 (21 November 1829): 5; "Woman's Mission," *Christian Guardian* 19, no. 8 (8 December 1847): 29; "Advice to Young Women," *The Montreal Museum* 1, no. 2 (January 1833): 65.
51 Morgan, *Public Men and Virtuous Women*, 10. See also de la Cour et al., "Gender Regulation"; Fahrni, *Of Kith and Kin*; Langland, *Nobody's Angels*; McKenna, *A Life of Propriety*. In Quebec, women lost both the right to vote and their automatic dower rights in 1849. See Bradbury, "Women at the Hustings"; Bradbury et al., "Property and Marriage"; Garner, *The Franchise and Politics*, 159.
52 See Hewitt, "Beyond the Search," and Kerber, "Separate Spheres." For its impact in Canada, see Guildford and Morton, *Separate Spheres.*
53 Davidoff and Hall, *Family Fortunes*; Davidoff, "Regarding 'Some Old Husbands' Tales.'" Also Bradbury, *Wife to Widow*, 119.
54 Baillargeon, *Brève histoire*, 8 (my translation).
55 Ryan, *Cradle of the Middle Class*, 217.
56 Morgan, *Public Men and Virtuous Women*, 214–15; Riley, *"Am I That Name?"*, 47–55.
57 Fahrni, *Household Politics*, 21.
58 Vickery, *The Gentleman's Daughter*, 10.
59 In her study of nineteenth-century Montreal widows, Bettina Bradbury confirms that most of the women she looked at "both preached and practiced some version" of the ideology although they regularly crossed boundaries. Bradbury, *Wife to Widow*, 119.
60 Strong-Boag, *Fostering Nation?*, 38.
61 Hacsi, *Second Home*, 55–9. See also Cmeil, *A Home of Another Kind*, and Zmora, *Orphanages Reconsidered.*

62 See Curtis, *Building the Educational State*; Graff, "Remaking Growing Up"; Rodgers, "Socializing Middle Class Children"; Ryan, *Cradle of the Middle Class*; Sutherland, *Children in English-Canadian Society*; Zeliger, *Pricing the Priceless Child.*

63 Deutsch, *Women and the City*; Flanagan, *Seeing with Their Hearts*; Geddes Poole, *Philanthropy and the Construction of Victorian Women's Citizenship*; Gordon and Nair, *Public Lives*; King, *Women, Welfare and Local Politics*; Spain, *How Women Saved the City*; Cohen, *Femmes philanthropes*; Kirkland, "Mothering Citizens"; Nielson, *Private Women and the Public Good.*

64 Sutherland, *Children in English-Canadian Society*, 95.

65 Footnotes for Committee minutes refer to the volume number in the original source, not the microfilm volume and file numbers found in the LAC Finding Aid.

66 See Valverde, "On the Case," 268–9.

67 See Davidoff, "Class and Gender," 21, and Morgan, *Public Men and Virtuous Women*, 210.

68 Denyse Baillargeon makes this point in her *Brève histoire*, 52.

69 Flanagan, *Seeing with Their Hearts.*

CHAPTER ONE

1 The city population went from 18,767 in 1821 to 203,178 in 1900.

2 For family income strategies in Montreal see Bradbury, *Working Families*; Olson and Thornton, *Peopling the North American City*; Copp, *Anatomy of Poverty*, 30–42.

3 See Bradbury, "Canadian Children Who Lived with One Parent," "Surviving as a Widow," and *Wife to Widow*, especially ch. 11.

4 Valverde, "The Mixed Social Economy" and "Six Dimensions of Social Governance." For a similar model in Europe see Cunningham and Innes, *Charity, Philanthropy and Reform*, esp. Cunningham, 1–14; Innes, "State, Church and Voluntarism"; Roberts, "Head versus Heart?"

5 On this, see Fecteau, "La construction d'un espace social" and *The Pauper's Freedom*. For Quebec City, see Daigle and Gilbert, "Un modèle d'économie sociale mixte."

6 For the role of the state see Nielson, *Private Women and the Public Good*, and Valverde, "The Mixed Social Economy." For the Catholic Church in Toronto see Mauratto, *Governing Charities.*

7 Fecteau, *Un nouvel ordre*, 58, 65–71, 152–5; Joyal, *Les Enfants, la société et l'État*, 38, 43.

8 Its incorporation was not accepted until 1819. Fecteau, "État et associationnisme," 147.

9 It was open 1817/19–23, 1836–37, and then sporadically until 1846. See Chureau, "La Maison d'industrie de Montreal," and Fecteau, *Un nouvel ordre*, 189–94.

10 The Montreal Protestant House of Industry and Refuge was formed in 1863; St Bridget's Refuge, administered by the Grey Nuns, in 1866.

11 A "Ladies' Bazaar" to raise funds was held in 1829, for example. POA, *Minutes*, vol. 1, March 1829, 113.

12 POA, *Minutes*, vol. 1, June 1823, 28, 30.

13 Fecteau, *The Pauper's Freedom*, 37, 102, 220, 260, 269–70.

14 Chureau, "La Maison d'industrie de Montreal," 37–52; Fecteau, "Between the Old Order," 299–300, and *Un nouvel ordre*, 147–98.

15 In the case of insane asylums only the short-lived asylum at Saint-Jean d'Iberville (1861–73) was state-run. For the development of the insane asylum model see Keating, *La Science du Mal*, and Moran, *Committed to the State Asylum*.

16 Quebec consistently paid lower fees than those paid to similar institutions in Ontario or the United States. See Paradis, "Le sous-financement gouvernemental."

17 For a more developed discussion of industrial schools see ch. 4.

18 Pitsula, "The Treatment of Tramps."

19 This stands in stark contrast with Ontario, where local councils in Toronto and Hamilton subsidized charities and the provincial legislature provided more substantial help as well as a much more developed legislative framework. See Neff, "Government Approaches," and Nielson, *Private Women and the Public Good*.

20 AVM, *Report of the City Treasurer*, 1887–99; Fecteau, "Un cas de force majeur," 112.

21 Under the original 1869 legislation, funding was shared by Quebec, the municipality, and parents, if able. Amendments in 1884, 1892, and 1894 changed this; by 1894, municipalities were responsible for 100 per cent of board for children placed as a result of parental poverty or illness. *Statutes of Quebec*, 57 Vict., 1894, c. 32, s. 7.

22 Fecteau, "État et associationnisme"; Stevens, "Framing an Appropriate Corporate Law."

23 McCarthy, "Women and Political Culture," 182.

24 Fecteau, "État et associationnisme," 146–51.

25 *DLAUC*, 1850, vol. 9, 879, 1136–7, 1194, 1529–30, 1626; 1852–53, vol. XI, 629–30, 1925–38, 1947–2005. *Statutes of the Province of Canada*, 1850, 13 & 14 Vict., c. 32.

26 *DLAUC*, 1856, vol. 13, 1645–51. Robert Gross points to a similar concern by US state legislatures to limit "concentrations of wealth." Gross, "Giving in America," 42.

27 *Statutes of the Province of Canada*, 1857, 20 Vict., c. 28.

28 Ibid., section 35.

29 "Report of the Inspectors of Prisons, Asylums, etc. For the Years 1867 & 68," Quebec, *Sessional Papers*, 1869, no. 23.

30 "Report of the Inspector of Prisons, Asylums, etc. For the Year …," Quebec, *Sessional Papers*, 1869–1900.

31 AVM, *Minutes of Council Meetings*, vol. 46 (11, 12, 1851), 47 (01, 1852); 56 (01, 02, 1855); 66 (12, 58); *Report of the City Treasurer*, 1851–99; W. Nelson, "Mayor's Address," in *Annual Report of the Protestant Industrial House of Refuge*, 1855, 8; 1856, 5; AVM, M. Coursol, *Mayor's Inaugural Address*, 1871. For health emergencies such as smallpox see A. Bernard, *Mayor's Inaugural Address*, 1873, 1874; W. Workman, *Mayor's Inaugural Address*, 1878; Bliss, *Plague*.

32 Fecteau, "Un cas de force majeure," 110. A bequest from Gustave Meurling provided the funds for the Meurling Refuge. See Aranguiz, *Vagabonds et sans abris à Montréal*.

33 Fecteau, "Un cas de force majeure," 107–13. For the "sou du pauvre" see Charest-Bourdon and Petitclerc, "Le 'sou du pauvre,'" and Charest-Bourdon, "Qui va Payer pour les Maladies Indigents?"

34 *Quebec Statutes*, 1921, c. 79. For this law see Petitclerc, "À propos de 'ceux.'"

35 For a discussion of these aspects of the law and their long-term impact, see Ferretti, "Du 'devoir de charité.'"

36 For a more in-depth discussion of the city's charitable network see Fecteau and Harvey, "Montreal's Network of Social Regulation," and the online exhibition *Pushing Back at Fate: Poverty, Families, and Institutions*, https://dejouerfatalite.uqam.ca/en (in French as well). The accompanying interactive maps can be found on the website or directly at https://schemaserveur2.uqam.ca/lhpm/map/run/2453.

37 For this see Roberts, "Head versus Heart?," and McCants, "Christian Charity."

38 For the Sulpicians see Fecteau and Vaillancourt, "Charity in the City"; Young, *In Its Corporate Capacity*. For the St Vincent de Paul Society see Fecteau and Vaillancourt, "The Saint Vincent de Paul Society," and Gauvreau, "Forging a New Space," 35–67.

39 Centre d'histoire des régulations sociales, charitable institutions database. Over the century, seven religious orders (six of them female) worked in the field of social welfare. D'Allaire, *Les communautés religieuses*, 151–2; Lapointe-Roy, *Charité bien ordonnée*. See also Laperrière, *Histoire des communautés religieuses*.

40 Tronto, *Moral Boundaries*, 32–8.

41 On the many-faceted aspect of poverty see Sandwell, "The Limits of Liberalism," 447.

42 See Dru Stanley, "Beggars Can't Be Choosers," and Fraser and Gordon, "A Genealogy of Dependency." On pauperism, see Fecteau, *The Pauper's Freedom*; Gagan, *Punishment and Welfare*, 39–40, 52; Procacci, "Geneologies of Poverty," and "Social Economy," 158–9. For the general uncertainty in relation to the poor, see Harvey, "Le risque et la ville"; Lupton, *Risk*; Young Choi, "Writing the Victorian City."

43 Gordon, *The Great Arizona Orphan Abduction*, 156, 183.

44 Fecteau, *The Pauper's Freedom*, 176–93; Petitclerc, "À propos de 'ceux,'" 227–39.

45 Anglican Diocese of Montreal Archives (ADA), Christ Church, Church Wardens, *Report*, 1871, 3.

46 St Andrew's Society, *Annual Reports*, 1867, 4; 1872–73, 19.

47 For a more developed discussion of the role of Protestant churches in the relief network see Harvey, "Les Églises protestantes et l'assistance."

48 Reports for Christ Church Cathedral and St Georges are in the Anglican Diocese of Montreal Archives (ADA). The papers of most Presbyterian churches are in the Archives nationales du Québec (ANQ-M). Reports on Congregational Churches are in the *Congregational and Canadian Independent*.

49 ADA, Christ Church, Temporal and Pastoral Aid Society, *Report*, 1839, 1851; Christ Church, Church Wardens, *Reports*, 1851–1900; St George's, *Poor Fund Annual Reports*, 1851–1900; Crescent Street Presbyterian, *Reports*, 1878–1900; St Paul's Church, *Reports*, 1878–1900.

50 McNeill, *The Presbyterian Church in Canada*, 142.

51 Cooper, *The Blessed Communion*.

52 ADA, Bishop Bond, "Bishop's Address," in *Proceedings of the Anglican Synod*, 1892, 20.

53 ADA, Bishop Bond, "Bishop's Address," 1895, 18; 1896, 18.

54 By 1904, the home had provided board for 2,339 individuals and served 34,844 meals annually. ADA, Andrews Home papers; Virr, *Andrews Home*. See Harvey, "La religion, fer de lance de l'aide," 16–20. Andrew's Home worked in direct competition with the Women's Protective Immigration Society (see Roberts, "Sex, Politics and Religion") and the Boys' Home. See discussion below.

55 SJEAC, *St Margaret's Home for Aged Women (1883–1958)*; Reisner, *The Measure of Faith*, 183–9. The Order ran their Home for Aged Women from 1920–75.

56 The Vitre Street Mission opened in 1918, St Michael's in 1928. SJEAC, *Centenary Book of the Parish of St John the Evangelist*, 81–2.

57 ANQ-M, American Presbyterian Church, *Annual Reports*; St Gabriel's Street Presbyterian Church, *Annual Reports*; Erskine Presbyterian Church, *Annual Reports*; St Paul's Church, *Reports*; *Congregational and Canadian Independent* (reports on various churches).

58 For this phenomenon see Trigger, "Protestant Restructuring in the Canadian City."

59 For this type of intervention see Christie and Gauvreau, *A Full-Orbed Christianity*.

60 ANQ-M, *Manual of the American Presbyterian Church*, 26–7; Lighthall, *A Short History of the American Presbyterian*, 28; St Paul's Church, *Reports*, 1878, 16; 1896, 18.

61 For a discussion of this see Perry, "Manliness, Goodness and God."

62 Crescent Street Church, *Annual Reports*, 1886.

63 For these missions see Harvey, "La religion, fer de lance de l'aide," 22–9; WHM,

Welcome Hall Mission, *Annual Reports*; Swift, *The Least of These*; MM, Old Brewery Mission papers. For a recent history of the Old Brewery Mission see Hustak and Demchinsky, *Soup to Self-Sufficiency*.

64 Atherton, *Montreal, 1835–1914*, 473.

65 Leitch, "The Importance of Being 'English.'"

66 St George's Society, "Historical Sketch," 1904." It was incorporated in 1860. *Statutes of Canada*, 1860, 23 Vict., c. 41.

67 *Narrative of the Proceedings of the St Andrew's Society*, 3–8, 1855, and St Andrew's Society, *A Summary of the First Fifty Years*, 1886. It was incorporated in 1858. *Statutes of Canada*, 1858, 21 Vict., c. 138.

68 It was incorporated in 1865. *Statutes of Canada*, 1865, 28 Vict., c. 61. For its history, see Collard, *The Irish Way*.

69 St Andrew's Society, *Annual Reports*, 1867–1900.

70 St George's Society, "Historical Sketch," 1904, 27. Since these figures count each family every time they received aid, the number of separate families was much lower.

71 Irish Protestant Benevolent Society, *Annual Report*, 1883, 7; 1889, 12; Cross, "The Irish in Montreal," 163–4.

72 A permanent home was constructed on Dorchester in 1866. In 1888 they moved to a bigger house on Mountain Street and in 1891 to one on Aqueduct Street.

73 St Andrew's Society, *Annual Reports*, 1894, 6; 1895, 6.

74 St George's Society, "Historical Sketch," 1904, 28.

75 Irish Protestant Benevolent Society, *Annual Report*, 1883, 6.

76 Council discussed the possibility in February 1855, January 1856, September 1859. See AVM, *Minutes of the Council Meetings*, Vol. 56, 58, 68; *Annual Report of the Treasurer of the City of Montreal*, 1856, 3.

77 Fecteau, *The Pauper's Freedom*; Poutanen, "Regulating Public Space." See also Sitara, "Humanitarianism in the Age of Capital and Empire."

78 The POA ladies wrote to the Boston Female Asylum (1800) for copies of its Constitution to use as a model.

79 Few specialized child and female charities were formed in Canada before the 1850s. Rooke and Schnell, "The Rise and Decline," 23.

80 Committees from Kingston, Ottawa, London, and Halifax wrote to the POA requesting information and copies of the Rules and By-Laws.

81 For example, the Ladies' Benevolent Society of Hamilton. See Bamman, "The Ladies' Benevolent Society of Hamilton," and Nielson, *Private Women and the Public Good*.

82 The School of Industry provided some relief services. See below.

83 Irwin, "Going About and Doing Good," 374.

84 POA, *Annual Report*, 1863.

85 LBS, *Annual Report*, 1858.

86 For Boston, see Holloran, *Boston's Wayward Children*; for Toronto, see Muratto, *Governing Charities*. Fear of Protestant proselytism also existed in Ireland; see Luddy, "Women and Philanthropy," and Raftery and O'Sullivan, *Suffer the Little Children*.

87 For a more in-depth discussion of each charity see Harvey, "The Protestant Orphan's Asylum and the Montreal Ladies' Benevolent Society," ch. 2.

88 POA, 10th Annual Meeting, in *Minutes*, vol.1, January 1832, 141.

89 Information on this early society is found in Pearce and Mitchell, *History of the Montreal Ladies' Benevolent Society*, 9–25. The reports they used are no longer extant.

90 They used a special £1,200 public subscription to cover expenses.

91 The register for 1822–1900 includes 951 children. The number used in most of our analysis is 903 – see ch. 4. By 1945, 1,551 children are listed.

92 "Statement Furnished to Hew Ramsey, Esq. by the Secretary, POA," *Minutes*, in Appendix, November 1848.

93 For a discussion of its founding see Pearce and Mitchell, *History of the Montreal Ladies' Benevolent Society*, 28–31.

94 LBS, *Minutes*, vol. 1, 30 April 1833, 42; LBS, "Rules and Regulations."

95 By 1946, the register records admissions of 4,624.

96 They applied to the government for special funding to rent larger premises but were refused. LBS, *Annual Report*, 1847; 1851–54.

97 Despite its name, this institution was never an official industrial school. For Eliza Hervey's contribution to the city's social services network see Harvey, "Eliza Hervey."

98 *Statutes of Canada*, 1875, 38 Vict., c. 59.

99 School of Industry, *Annual Report*, 1859, 3.

100 LAC, Weredale Homes, MG 28 I 405, The Boys' Home, "Annual Report, 1879," in *Weredale House General Minute Book*, February 1879.

101 Atherton, *Montreal*, 469.

102 School of Industry, *Annual Report*, 1859, 5; 1863, 6; 1864, 7.

103 In 1889, 40 per cent of the children were non-paying.

104 In 1859, they refer to twelve families receiving aid; in 1864, to eighty. School of Industry, *Annual Reports*, 1859, 4–5; 1864, 4–6.

105 Sherry Olson found that up to two-thirds of the infants born in the University Lying-In Hospital (45 per cent were Protestant) were abandoned to the nuns in 1859–60. Olson et al., *A Geography of Little Children*, 9. The nuns sent the infants to wet nurses until 1888. Peter Gossage calculates their mortality rates as more than 90 per cent during most of this period. Gossage, "Les enfants abandonnés." See also "Startling Figures. The Grey Nuns' Balance Sheet with the Public on the Foundling Question," *Daily Witness*, 11 August 1887.

106 School of Industry, *Annual Report*, 1855.

107 School of Industry, *Annual Report*, 1869, 5.

108 *Statutes of Canada*, 1870, 34 Vict., c. 56.

109 It was allied with the School of Industry for the first six months and Committee membership overlapped to a great extent. *General History of the Protestant Infants' Home*, 2; Atherton, *Montreal*, 469–70.

110 "The Poor of Montreal," *Montreal Daily Herald*, 7 November 1905, 10.

111 In effect the mothers were "employed" as nurses for a nine-month period until infants were weaned. Protestant Infants' Home, *Annual Report*, 1894, 5.

112 Only infants more than eight days old, with no signs of disease, were admitted. All infants were immediately vaccinated.

113 It existed after 1930 but added Weredale House to its name at that point. Charles Alexander was a Director of most male-led charities including the Boys' Home, the Mackay Institute, the Protestant House of Industry, the Verdun Insane Asylum, the SPWC, the SPCA, the Sailor's Institute, the MGH, and the Female Home. See *DCB*: Janice Harvey, "Charles Alexander."

114 *Statutes of Canada*, 1869, 32 Vict., c. 88.; 1876–77, 41 Vict., c. 42. The Home's papers are in the LAC, Weredale Homes Collection, MG 28, I 405 (hereafter Boys' Home). Boys' Home, *Minute Book*, vol. 1, 15 February 1868, 1; 12 January 1871, 37.

115 The Boys' Home Board refused Quebec's request to become an industrial school. Boys' Home, *Minutes*, vol. 2, 7 July 1896, 31; 3 September 1896, 34.

116 Boys' Home, *Annual Reports*, 1870–1900. For this institution, its approach, and its training program, see Harvey, "Former des citoyens protestants."

117 Boys' Home, *Annual Reports*, 1870–1900; *Register*, 1881–92; 1910–21.

118 It was located in the District of St Francis prison, Sherbrooke. Quebec Sessional Papers, *Reports of the Inspector of Prisons*, 1873–1913, "Sherbrooke Reformatory for Protestant Boys."

119 Boys' Home, *Minute Book*, 1906–08; *Annual Reports*, 1907–09. For the Sherbrooke Reform School, see Harvey, "L'école de réforme de Sherbrooke" and "The Sherbrooke Reformatory for Protestant Boys."

120 For Shawbridge, see Rains and Teram, *Normal Bad Boys*.

121 The organization retained the Boys' Home Act of Incorporation and effectively used both names for many years.

122 *Statutes of Canada*, 1869, 32 Vict., c. 89; Mackay Institution for Protestant Deaf-Mutes, *Annual Report*, 1883, 94. Annual reports exist for 1870–97.

123 Mackay Institute, *Annual Report*, 1883, 94.

124 *Quebec Sessional Papers*, no. 1, 1889–1900.

125 It was incorporated in 1900. Day Nursery, *Annual Report*, 1900, 11; *Statutes of Canada*, 1900, 63 Vict., c. 104.

126 Atherton, *Montreal*, 470.

127 Day Nursery, *Annual Report*, 1897, 4; 1902, 9.

128 See discussion in ch. 7.

129 LBS, *Minutes*, Vol. 10, February 1886, 154–5. The Associated Charities held a series of meetings over a two-year period from March 1886 to August 1888.

130 "Protestant Foundlings," *The Gazette*, 10 March 1886, 14 April 1886.

131 Numerous articles about this debate appear in city newspapers – *The Gazette*, *The Herald*, *The Witness*, and *The Star* – in April 1887, and in May, June, and August 1888.

132 Foundling and Baby Hospital, *Annual Report*, 1897, 3, 1905, 12. See Harvey, "Des femmes anglo-protestants," 46–7.

133 *Statutes of Canada*, 1914, 4 Geo., c. 151.

134 Foundling and Baby Hospital, *Annual Report*, 1897, 9.

135 Foundling and Baby Hospital, *Annual Report*, 1902, 5.

136 Baillargeon, "Fréquenter les Gouttes de lait," 29–66; Comacchio, *Nations Are Built of Babies*, 48–9.

137 See Gordon, *Heroes of Their Own Lives*, ch. 2–4, and her *Pitied but Not Entitled*. Also Clement, "Nineteenth-Century Welfare Policy."

138 For Canada see Christie, *Engendering the State*, and Little, *No Car, No Radio*.

139 ADA, Bishop Bond, "Bishop's Address, 1892," 20; *History of the Church Home*; *Outline of Church Home History*.

140 For this institution see Harvey, "Dealing with 'the Destitute and the Wretched,'" and Erickson, "Montreal's Great Experiment."

141 William Workman left a $20,000 legacy for construction costs. CHRS, Protestant House of Industry, *Minute Book*, February 1864, vol. 1, 48–9; June 1885, vol. 2, 589. The institution eventually became the Centre des Soins Prolongée Grace Dart Extended Care Centre, situated on St Catherine Street near Viau.

142 Protestant House of Industry, "Annual Report, 1887," in *Minute Book*, vol. 2, 684.

143 James Moore paid for the Convalescent Home. Protestant House of Industry, *Annual Reports*, 1885–1959; *Minutes of Meetings*, 1885–1959.

144 Protestant House of Industry, "Rules of the Night Refuge," *Minute Book*, vol. 1, 127.

145 Protestant House of Industry, *Annual Report*, 1866, 4, 6.

146 See Harvey, "Dealing with 'the Destitute and the Wretched.'"

147 Protestant House of Industry, *Minutes of Monthly Meetings*, 1920–54.

148 For the role of the city and access to medical charities see Charest-Bourdon and Petitclerc, "Le 'sou du pauvre.'" For a history of the MGH from a doctor's perspective, see Hanaway and Burgess, *The General*.

149 Montreal Sailor's Institute, *Annual Reports*, 1876–96. For work with sailors see Ingam, "Saving the Union Jack," and Fingard, "Evangelical Social Work," 25–33.

150 CHRS, "United Board of Outdoor Relief," in Protestant House of Industry, *Annual Reports*, 1863–1900.

151 CHRS, Industrial Rooms, *Annual Report*, 1883, 7. These reports are in the Protestant House of Industry, *Minute Book*, vol. 1–4.

152 School of Industry, *Annual Report*, 1869, 5; Industrial Rooms, *Annual Report*, 1883, 5–8.
153 Given their presence in the Protestant House of Industry building, the ladies also served as "visitors" to the elderly poor in the permanent ward.
154 Industrial Rooms, *Annual Report*, 1899, 6; 1900, 5–6.
155 Industrial Rooms, *Annual Report*, 1863, 15; 1883, 3; 1885, 5; "Constitution and By-Laws," in Industrial Rooms, *Annual Report*, 1885, 12.
156 There were always a few Catholics. Industrial Rooms, *Annual Reports*, 1865–1900.
157 Industrial Rooms, *Annual Report*, 1895, 3; 1899, 6.
158 Industrial Rooms, *Annual Report*, 1872, 4.
159 For a discussion of this see Porter, "Business Heads and Sympathizing Hearts," 303.
160 See Harvey, "Des femmes anglo-protestants," 50–2, and Rowan, *A Beacon of Hope*.
161 "Food for the Sick," *Montreal Daily Witness*, 7 June, 1882; "Diet Dispensary," *Montreal Daily Witness*, 8 March, 1901.
162 YWCA/Montreal Diet Dispensary, *Annual Reports*, 1884–99.
163 For the twentieth century, see Cohen, "De la nutrition des pauvres malades."
164 See Schmidt, "Domesticating Parks and Mastering Playgrounds."
165 Fresh-Air Fund Committee, *8th Annual Report*, 1894.

CHAPTER TWO

1 Lists of Committee members were included in the city Directory under "Benevolent or Religious Societies" sporadically from the 1840s and more regularly after 1867. *The Lovell's Directory*, 1842–1900.
2 Specific references to family connections in annual reports, minutes, and biographical sources were useful. See Atherton, *Montreal, 1835–1914, Biographical*; Brothwick, *History and Biographical Gazeteer*; Campbell, *A History of … St. Gabriel Street*, 1887; Lyman, *Genealogy of the Lyman Family*; Morgan, *The Canadian Men and Women of the Time*; Sandwell, *The Molson Family*; Woods, *The Molson Saga*. *The Dictionary of Canadian Biography* revealed many family interconnections but these are an underestimate as authors did not always consider family information relevant. Also extremely helpful was the database *Généalogie* on the BANQ website as well as the BANQ-numérique for newspaper references. A number of prominent families have recent biographies that were helpful.
3 See Cott, *Bonds of Womanhood*, 187–94, 201–3; Gordon and Nair, *Public Lives*; Lebsock, *Free Women of Petersburg*, 208; Porter Benson, "Business Heads and Sympathetic Hearts," 302–6; Smith-Rosenberg, "The Female World of Love and Ritual."
4 The following discussion is based on membership lists for the two associations

from 1822/32 to 1900, with membership being followed if necessary until 1932. The years in brackets indicate years of Committee membership.

5 Lyman, *Genealogy of the Lyman Family*: Susannah Lyman, #104, 64; Henry Lyman, #154, 45; F.S. Lyman, #214, 46.

6 Lyman, *Genealogy of the Lyman Family*: Elisha Lyman, #98, 30; Hannah Lyman, #101, 147; Hannah Jane Mills, #172, 147; Bradbury, *Wife to Widow*, 36, 188.

7 Abigail's father Theodore was Susannah's brother. Lyman, *Genealogy of the Lyman Family*: Theodore Lyman, #101, 52; Abigail Jones Lyman, #221, 53.

8 *DCB*: Alfred Dubuc and Robert Tremblay, "John Molson"; Alfred Dubuc, "Thomas Molson" and "William Molson"; Bettina Bradbury, "Anne Molson"; Sandwell, *The Molson Family*, tables 2–9; and Woods, "Molson Family," in *The Molson Saga*.

9 *DCB*: F.H. Armstrong, "John Torrance," "David Torrance," and "Duncan Fisher"; Margaret Gillett, "William Lunn"; Jean-Pierre Kesterman, "A.T. Galt"; Gerald J.J. Tulchinsky, "James Ferrier"; R.E. Rudin, "Edwin Henry King."

10 POA, *Minutes*, vol. 8, May 1870, 258–9.

11 Vickery, *The Gentleman's Daughter*, 13.

12 Other studies find the same predominance of the upper-middle-class, especially merchants' wives. See Boylan, "Women's Benevolent Organizations," 511, 520; Hewitt, *Women's Activism*, 153; Lebsock, *Free Women of Petersburg*, 207; Porter Benson, "Business Heads and Sympathetic Hearts," 303; Ryan, *Cradle of the Middle Class*, 215.

13 See Thompson, *The Making of the English Working-Class*, 9–12; Morris, *Class and Class Consciousness*, 27–31, and "Middle-Class Culture"; Noble, "'Class-ifying' the Poor," 109–11.

14 Beckert and Rosenbaum, *The American Bourgeoisie*, 2, 5. See also Beckert, "The Bourgeois Institution Builders," 104.

15 Hall, *Civilizing Subjects*, 9; Colley, *Britons*, xix, 6, 17. The main "other" is France.

16 For example, Anne McCord and Sophia Moffat were neighbours, as were Mary Lyman and Jane Savage. MacKay, *The Square Mile*; MacLeod, "Salubrious Settings"; Young, *Respectable Burial*.

17 Collard, *Montreal Yesterdays*, 204–20; Leitch, "The Importance of Being 'English.'"

18 Lamonde, "La sociabilité et l'histoire," 102; *Lovell Directory*. For the role of similar associations in building the ascendency of the bourgeoisie in the United States see the articles in Beckert and Baumgarten, *The American Bourgeoisie*.

19 See Davidoff, *The Best Circles*; Smith, *Ladies of the Leisure Class*; Vickery, *The Gentleman's Daughter*.

20 Rochester and Boston benevolent societies had the same predominance of married women. Boylan, "Timid Girls," 780–2; Hewitt, *Women's Activism*, 153.

21 These women have been included in the data as single; one of them died in childbirth a year after her marriage.

22 Kirkland, "Mothering Citizens," 60.

23 Anne Boylan finds the same general pattern in her study of New York and Boston. Boylan, "Timid Girls," 781–5.

24 Data was found for only fifty-two women in the POA and sixty-four in the LBS.

25 Young, *Patrician Families.*

26 LAC, MG 24 D 115, Senator Robert Mackay, Correspondence.

27 Her membership in the LBS was disjointed: 1832–35, 1847, 1855–69, Honorary Manager 1869–74. She was also on the POA Committee 1866–74.

28 Single women on the Providence Employment Society Committee tended to remain almost twice as long as the norm. Porter Benson, "Business Heads and Sympathetic Hearts," 304. See also Vicinus, *Independent Women.*

29 Lee Chambers-Schiller, "Single Women," found this was a crucial factor.

30 Louisa actively supported a number of the city's charities but her most extensive work was with the POA. See *DCB*: Janice Harvey, "Louisa Goddard Frothingham (Molson)."

31 See LBS, *Annual Reports*, 1861–87.

32 Anne Boylan also found that this was common. Boylan, "Timid Girls," 780–9.

33 Total contributions have been adjusted to remove contributors who could not be identified by gender. Those referred to as Mrs or Miss and married couples are counted as women. All first initial, last names are counted as men, as are companies. Due to the large number of contributors, the LBS lists were checked at five-year intervals.

34 POA, *Annual Report*, 1855.

35 The sale of the POA property in 1893 provided the funds for their new home; the surplus was added to the Endowment Fund. POA, *Annual Report*, 1893.

36 Investments included stocks, bonds, and mortgages. POA, "Statement of Investments and Revenue," *Annual Reports*, 1899.

37 The fund included mainly stocks and bonds. LBS, *Annual Reports*, 1899.

38 Lebsock, *Free Women of Petersburg*, 224; Prochaska, *Women and Philanthropy*, 33–5.

39 LBS, *Annual Report*, 1896, 1906.

40 POA, *Annual Report*, 1910; LBS, *Annual Report*, 1910.

41 Board payment was rare in the POA (only 4 cases). Any contributions received for children from relatives, etc. were invested for their future use.

42 LBS, *Minutes*, vol. 5, November 1853, 39.

43 Funding was a common problem for child charities. Rooke and Schnell, *Discarding the Asylum*, 109–11.

44 POA, "Address to the Governor General," in *Minute Book*, vol. 7, 1874.

45 McCord, *Historical Sketch*, 25.
46 POA, *Annual Report*, 1859.
47 POA, "Typewritten letter from Mr. Thomas to the POA Committee of Management," May 1893, 5, *Correspondence Files*, vol. 12, file 30.
48 For institutional visiting see Janet Miron, *Prisons, Asylums, and the Public*.
49 See the discussion in ch. 7 and the epilogue.
50 POA, "Insert," *Minutes*, June 1866, 66.
51 Hewitt, *Women's Activism*, 50–3.
52 LBS, *Minutes*, vol. 4, April 1852, 213.
53 LBS, *Annual Report*, 1852.
54 Compton Brouwer, "Transcending the 'Unacknowledged Quarantine'"; Christie and Gauvreau, *A Full-Orbed Christianity*; Davidoff and Hall, *Family Fortunes*; Prochaska, *Christianity and Social Service*; Van Die, *Religion, Family and Community*, and "A Woman's Awakening." See also Marks, *Revivals and Roller Rinks*, and Westfall, *Two Worlds*.
55 McCarthy, *Women, Philanthropy and Civil Society*, 5.
56 Prochaska, *The Voluntary Impulse*.
57 For similar "religious and philanthropic imperatives" among middle-class women in Glasgow, see Gordon and Nair, *Public Lives*, 222, 28–9.
58 Easton, *A Sermon*, 10.
59 Ibid., 18–20.
60 POA, *Annual Report*, 1864.
61 See, for example, "A Young Man's Duty to the Church," *Congregationalist and Canadian Independent* 43, no. 51 (December 1896): 3; "Benevolence," *The Christian Guardian* 18 (14 January 1847): 53; "The Christian Law of Giving," *Dominion Churchman* (August 1876): 372. These concepts were also current in the secular press. See for example "Charity and Its Motives," *Canadian Illustrated News* 2, no. 6 (August 1870): 82; Rev. W.R.G. Mellen, "Wealth and Its Uses," *Rose-Belford's Canadian Monthly* 2 (1879): 343.
62 "Religion True Benevolence," *Christian Mirror* 1, no. 16 (1842): 125. See also Julia B. Schauffler, "Concerning Women's Missionary Societies," *The Methodist Magazine* 35 (1892): 272, and "Why I Give," *Presbyterian Record* 7, no. 7 (1882): 199.
63 POA, *Annual Report*, 1852; LBS, *Annual Report*, 1852.
64 LBS, *Annual Report*, 1880.
65 POA, *Annual Report*, 1852.
66 POA, *Annual Report*, 1855.
67 LBS, *Annual Report*, 1867.
68 LBS, *Annual Report*, 1889.
69 POA, *Annual Report*, 1875.
70 POA, *Annual Report*, 1844.

71 See Parr, "Transplanting from Dens of Iniquity," for this important distinction.
72 The work of the LBS also included the care of elderly women and the chronically infirm, for whom the charity's religious mission took on a slightly different quality.
73 POA, *Annual Report*, 1878.
74 Prochaska, *Women and Philanthropy*, 225.
75 LBS, *Annual Report*, 1855.
76 Concern about this was common in the city's English press. See introduction, n29, as well as "Our Reformatory System," *Montreal Witness*, 23 December 1874, and "The Reformation of Our Youth," *Montreal Witness*, 5 December 1879.
77 LBS, *Annual Report*, 1861.
78 LBS, *Annual Report*, 1858.
79 LBS, *Annual Report*, 1871.
80 LBS, *Annual Report*, 1849.
81 LBS, *Annual Report*, 1854.
82 LBS, *Annual Report*, 1873.
83 POA, *Annual Report*, 1854.
84 LBS, *Annual Report*, 1857.
85 LBS, "The Eighth Annual Report of the Visiting School Committee," in *Annual Report*, 1859.
86 LBS, *Annual Report*, 1861, 1875.
87 LBS, *Annual Report*, 1875. For use of this technique by American charities see Bellingham, "The 'Unspeakable Blessing,'" and Schlossman, "The 'Culture of Poverty.'"
88 LBS, *Annual Report*, 1864.
89 LBS, *Annual Report*, 1872.
90 With the exception of 1875.
91 POA, *Minutes*, 28 December 1868, vol. 8, 193.
92 POA, "Insert," *Minutes*, 2 April 1866, vol. 8, 2.
93 Young, *Respectable Burial*, 86.
94 These are the only other portraits specifically mentioned in the minutes.
95 Pearce and Mitchell, *History of the Montreal Ladies' Benevolent Society*, 56.
96 For this ethic of caring in relation to twentieth-century women, see the essays in Baines, McEvans, and Neysmith, *Women's Caring*, esp. Baines, "Women's Professions." For a political analysis of the ethic of care see Tronto, *Moral Boundaries*; Held, *Justice and Care*; and Strong-Boag, *Fostering Nation?*
97 See Cott, *The Bonds of Womanhood*; Hewitt, "Beyond the Search for Sisterhood," 303–10; Lebsock, *Free Women of Petersburg*, 112–13; McCarthy, "Parallel Power Structure"; and Vicinus, *Independent Women*.
98 McCarthy, "Parallel Power Structure," 4.

99 Cmiel, *A Home of Another Kind*, 31, 118.

100 The ladies use their annual reports to thank the photographers for their help in this.

101 Jane Errington argues that eulogies had a code used to construct the qualities of the good woman but that they were also personal testimonials. Errington, *Wives, Mothers, Schoolmistresses*, xii–xiii.

102 John Cumbler, in his study of the Lynn, Massachusetts COS, and Sharon Cook, in her study of two homes for the indigent elderly in Ottawa, have also identified cultural and policy differences that they accredit to gender. See Cumbler, "The Politics of Charity," and Cook, "A Quiet Place … to Die"; also Cmiel, *A Home of Another Kind*, and Vicinus, *Independent Women*, 212–36.

103 LAC, Boys' Home, *Minute Book*, 1868–1909, vol. 1–2, files 9–10; *Annual Reports*, 1871–1909, vol. 1, files 3–24, and vol. 3, file 1.

104 Boys' Home, *Minute Book*, 15 May 1870, vol. 1, 29; *Annual Report*, 1882, in *Minute Book*, vol. 1, 79.

105 Boys' Home, *Minute Book*, 1906–08; *Annual Reports*, 1907–09. The government had consulted Alexander on the original reform school's design and "curriculum" in 1873.

106 CHRS, Protestant House of Industry, *Minute Books*, 1863–1900.

CHAPTER THREE

1 Hewitt, *Women's Activism*; Boylan, "Women in Groups"; Ginzberg, *Women and the Work*.

2 POA, *Annual Report*, 1863.

3 LBS, *Annual Report*, 1896.

4 Fifty-nine women served as Honorary Managers at some point between the 1860s and 1900. All but eight had been former Committee members.

5 Nancy Hewitt finds that 25 per cent of women associated with Rochester charities were members for more than fifteen years. Hewitt, *Women's Activism*, 229. This number is 22 per cent for the POA and 13.5 per cent for the LBS.

6 *The Lovell's Directory*, 1865–1900.

7 LBS, *By-Laws*, 1874, #II, III; 1897, #VIII, IX; POA, *By-Laws*, 1852, #III.

8 The LBS *Matron's Journal* records these visits.

9 LBS, *By-Laws*, 1874, #VII; 1897, #XII; POA, *By-Laws*, 1852, #IV.

10 LBS, *Minutes*, vol. 3, October 1843, 49; vol. 5, May 1855, 100–11; LBS, *By-Laws*, 1874, #VIII; 1897, #XIII.

11 LBS, *By-Laws*, 1874, #VII; 1897, #XII; POA, *By-Laws*, 1852, #IV.

12 Agnes (Hew) Ramsay, another long-term member, refused both positions. POA, *Annual Report*, 1871; POA, *Minutes*, vol. 8, 4 December 1871, 45; 22 December 1871,

51; 28 December 1871, 55. They had lost their long-serving matron in the same year.

13 POA, *Minutes*, vol. 11, January 1884, 13–14; September 1888, 309.

14 POA, *Minutes*, vol. 11, December 1883, 10.

15 This included investigating the diet and arranging for building repairs or purchases.

16 Annie Wheeler joined the Committee in 1875 and immediately began collecting large sums of money towards improvement projects such as the furnace. She was named First Directress in September 1877; the presiding Directress became Second Directress. She retained the position until 1882, when she left for health reasons. She would become a prominent member again in the 1890s. LBS, *Minutes*, vol. 8, April 1875, 133; vol. 9, September 1877, 52–3; January 1877, 79; February 1879, 115; vol. 10, May 1882, 22; LBS, *Matron's Journal*, vol. 5, file 3, January 1878, 270.

17 LBS, *Minutes*, vol. 11, March 1893, 61; September 1894, 110; November 1894, 118–21.

18 The position was offered to Annie Wheeler, who declined. LBS, *Minutes*, vol. 11, February 1896, 168; March 1896, 179–80; April 1896, 182; vol. 12, September 1896, 29.

19 LBS, *Minutes*, vol. 12, February 1897, 27.

20 Both the building and finance committees worked alongside the men's Advisory Committee and deflected at least some power from this male committee. POA, *Minutes*, vol. 12, November 1891, 144–5; December 1891, 147–8.

21 POA, *Minutes*, vol. 12, July 1892, 179. It was a few years later that Louisa F. Molson made a $10,000 living bequest to the LBS rather than the POA.

22 LBS, *Minutes*, vol. 3, December 1844, 62; January 1845, 64–6; March 1845, 68.

23 LBS, *Minutes*, vol. 3, August 1846, 93–5.

24 LBS, *Minutes*, vol. 3, September 1846, 95–7.

25 Ibid., 103; October 1846, 111. From then on they kept a list of members from each church and approached ministers for names when any Presbyterian Church was underrepresented, as in 1877, for example. LBS, *Minutes*, vol. 9, October 1877, 57.

26 With the conflict resolved, Louisa Frothingham paid to have the by-laws printed. POA, *Minutes*, vol. 4, September 1851, 172; December 1851, 192; February 1852, 202; POA, *Correspondence files*, vol. 12, file 32.

27 See discussion in ch. 4.

28 LBS, *Minutes*, vol. 5, October 1857, 194.

29 POA, *Minutes*, vol. 6, October 1858, 58; November 1860, 163, 167; vol. 8, October 1867, 130–1; November 1867, 132–3; November 1870, 275; vol. 9, December 1871, 47–50; vol. 13, April 1895, 20–2; LBS, *Minutes*, vol. 7, March 1871, 139; vol. 9, December 1876, 29; vol. 10, March 1882, 6; May 1887, 193.

30 POA, *Minutes*, vol. 3, March 1848, 184; May 1848, 198–9; POA, *Annual Report*, 1849, 1853; POA, *By-Laws*, 1852.

31 In 1891 training was organized for several boys at the Mackay Institute. POA, *Minutes*, vol. 12, May 1890, 75; November 1891, 145; vol. 13, April 1895, 24; March 1898, 203; April 1898, 206.

32 LBS, *Minutes*, vol. 1, August 1832, 24; March 1835, 69; vol. 2, June 1837, 48; vol. 4, February 1849, 89; August 1851, 187; LBS, *Annual Report*, 1847, 6.

33 None of these reports remain in the LBS archives.

34 LBS, *By-Laws*, 1897, #XVII, section 1.

35 LBS, *Annual Report*, 1860, 10; LBS, *Minutes*, vol. 6, December 1861, 140–1. Originally done on a volunteer basis, by 1897 this teaching was included in the by-laws as one of the Committee's duties. LBS, *By-Laws*, 1897, #XVII, section 8.

36 LBS, *Annual Report*, 1887, 9.

37 LBS, *Minutes*, vol. 6, December 1861, 140–1; vol. 8, November 1873, 78; vol. 10, December 27, 1887, 204.

38 POA, *By-Laws*, 1852, #VII, #VIII; LBS, *By-Laws*, 1874, #XI; 1897, #XIX.

39 POA, *Minutes*, vol. 11, April 1888, 255–6.

40 POA, *Minutes*, vol. 11, September 1884, 54–6; October 1884, 59.

41 POA, *Minutes*, vol. 3, March 1843, 23; LBS, *Minutes*, vol. 1, March–April 1833, 40, 42; vol. 5, March 1855, 105; May 1855, 109–11; LBS, *By-Laws*, 1874, #XI; 1897, #XIX.

42 LBS, *Minutes*, vol. 1, June 1835, 76; vol. 2, October 1836, 30. A system of fines also existed in the charities studied by Bonnie Smith. Smith, *Ladies of the Leisure Class*, 140.

43 However, long-term membership was not a guarantee of active participation, since almost half of long-term members accepted Visitor duty fewer than six times over their membership.

44 LBS, *Annual Report*, 1873.

45 POA, *Minutes*, vol. 1, "Annual Report," 1824, 56; "Annual Report," 1825, 81.

46 POA, *Minutes*, vol. 3, May 1848, 205; vol. 4, March 1849, 16–17; LBS, *Minutes*, vol. 3, November 1846, 117; July 1846, 92; vol. 4, October 1848, 73–4.

47 LBS, *Minutes*, vol. 10, October 1884, 101; October 1886, 171; September 1888, 233.

48 POA, *Annual Report*, 1851.

49 The POA carried out this type of targeted appeal in 1837, 1842, 1849, and 1897.

50 POA, *Annual Report*, 1879.

51 LBS, *Annual Report*, 1890.

52 LBS, *Annual Report*, 1887.

53 POA, *Minutes*, vol. 4, November 1853, 304; LBS, *Minutes*, vol. 3, November 1846, 117; vol. 4, October 1848, 73–4.

54 LBS, *Minutes*, vol. 1, July 1832, 17; vol. 3, September 1843, 39.

55 Discussions on this began in 1856. The main area was from St Denis west to Peel

(and later Guy) and from Sherbrooke south to St Antoine. LBS, *Minutes*, vol. 5, October 1856, 162; January 1858, 203; vol. 6, January 1859, 59; October 1863, 197, 211–14.

56 LBS, *Minutes*, vol. 6, October 1864, 259.

57 LBS, *Annual Report*, 1881, 5. In 1879, nine districts were covered; in 1884, only five. LBS, *Minutes*, vol. 9, October 1879, 148; October 1881, 213–14; vol. 10, March 1882, 10; October 1884, 101.

58 LBS, *Treasurer's Report*, 1884, 10.

59 Ibid.; LBS, *Minutes*, vol. 10, August 1886, 66.

60 LBS, *Minutes*, vol. 10, September 1889, 274; May 1890, 311–13; vol. 11, November 1890, 2.

61 POA, *Annual Report*, 1900, 5.

62 Hewitt, *Women's Activism*, 146; Ginzberg, *Women and the Work*, 44.

63 CHRS, Protestant House of Industry, *Minute Book*, vol. 2, January 1878, 128.

64 Prochaska, *Women and Philanthropy*, ch. 2; Smith, *Ladies of the Leisure Class*, 146; Ryan, *Cradle of the Middle Class*, 216.

65 Credited to the Building Fund (1850) and the Land Fund (1858), the receipts for these two events ($600 each) do not appear in the General Account Fund.

66 POA, *Annual Report*, 1853.

67 Ryan, *Women in Public*, 81.

68 Articles in the religious press late in the century were still raising objections to entertainment fund-raisers. See "The Masquerade Ball," *Canadian Methodist Magazine* 15 (January–June 1882): 179; Rev. W.A. Fyles, "The Method of Almsgiving," *Montreal Diocesan Theological College Magazine* 3, no. 2 (1894): 26.

69 Donations were received from the Gentlemen Amateurs in 1830 and between 1837–40. McCord, *Historical Sketch*, 7–12; POA, *Minutes*, vol. 2, February 1838, 76–7; February 1840, 116.

70 LBS, *Minutes*, vol. 3, August 1842, 20; December 1844, 62; vol. 4, January 1849, 82–4.

71 McCord, *Historical Sketch*, 7–12.

72 A subcommittee was set up in 1850 to visit the clergy on an annual basis. The LBS made a public complaint against the churches in its 1868 annual report. LBS, *Minutes*, vol. 3, August 1846, 93–6; vol. 4, May 1850, 139; LBS, *Annual Report*, 1868, 5.

73 LBS, *Minutes of Special Meeting*, vol. 5, April 1856, 148. The newspaper announcement appeared 17 May 1856: insert in *Minute Book*, May 1856, 156.

74 Gordon, *Bazaars and Fair Ladies*, esp. ch. 1–2. See also Prochaska, *Women and Philanthropy*, ch. 2.

75 The lack of dancing was probably driven by religious concerns, not work aspects.

76 Both societies had close contacts with the militia through J.S. McCord.

77 Notices requesting contributions were placed in city newspapers. LBS, *Minutes*, vol. 4, November 1850, 159–60; vol. 5, September 1855, 118; vol. 7, May 1868, 109.

78 Prochaska, *Women and Philanthropy*, 57; Gordon, *Bazaars and Fair Ladies*, 9–14.

79 LBS, *Minutes*, vol. 6, March 1864, 238.

80 LBS, *Annual Report*, 1881.

81 For this practice see Miron, *Prisons, Asylums, and the Public.*

82 See Horn, *The Rise and Fall of the Victorian Servant*, 62–4; Lasser, "The Domestic Balance of Power"; Leskyi, "A 'Servant Problem' or a 'Servant-Mistress Problem?'"

83 Alden, "Institutions for Children," *NCCC*, 1896, 319.

84 LBS, *Minutes*, vol. 1, February 1833, 39; May 1833, 43; April 1834, 56; vol. 2, September 1836, 22; April 1838, 66; vol. 3, August 1842, 20; POA, *Minutes*, vol. 8, March 1868, 157; May 1869, 215; December 1869, 191; vol. 9, May 1877, 283; LBS, *By-Laws*, 1874, #18, #25, #23, #24; 1897, #27, #29, #30, #34; POA, *By-Laws*, 1852, #20, #21, #22, #23, #24, #25, #26, #28.

85 LBS, *Minutes*, vol. 6, December 1860, 93.

86 LBS, *Annual Report*, 1893.

87 POA, *Minutes*, vol. 12, October 1889, 25; November 1889, 29; December 1889, 38.

88 POA, *Correspondence files*, vol. 12, file 30.

89 In the LBS the salary was almost doubled from $20 to $35 a month. In the POA, the salary had reached $1,000 annually by 1919.

90 POA, *Minutes*, vol. 9, October 1871, 39; February 1876, 230; July 1876, 248; vol. 10, November 1880, 117; March 1881, 144; February 1883, 274; LBS, *Minutes*, vol. 10, February 1882, 5; March 1882, 6.

91 POA, *Minutes*, November 1911, 55; February 1912, 83–4; February 1914, 127; May 1918, 227; January 1919, 241; February 1919, 252–3.

92 Three teachers were fired following a complaint by a matron or lady superintendent for disrespect, insufficient help, or incompatibility. LBS, *Minutes*, vol. 3, September 1846, 100–1; POA, *Minutes*, vol. 12, October 1894, 395; vol. 13, April 1895, 18–19.

93 Staff turnover was normal in child charities. See Rooke and Schnell, "The Rise and Decline," 27.

94 LBS, *Minutes*, vol. 10, March 1882, 6; vol. 11, October 1895, 153.

95 LBS, *Minutes*, vol. 3, December 1845, 87; vol. 5, February 1855, 144; vol. 9, December 1876, 29; January 1877, 32.

96 LBS, *Minutes*, vol.6, June 1859, 59; September 1861, 122; vol. 8, May 1875, 137; vol. 10, March 1882, 7; August 1882, 26.

97 LBS, *Minutes*, vol. 2, May 1841, 119.

98 Payment in clothing remained the method used for rewarding extra work.

99 LBS, *Minutes*, vol. 2, June 1841, 121; vol. 3, March 1842, 14; vol. 5, June 1858, 214; vol. 8, May 1875, 137.

100 LBS, *Minutes*, vol. 8, June 1873, 52. See also March 1873, 41; April 1873, 45; March 1875, 127. LBS, *Annual Report*, 1893; LBS, *Minutes*, vol. 12, September 1896, 102.

101 POA, *Minutes*, vol. 10, December 1881, 190.

102 For example, the monthly wage in 1873 for the POA cook was $8; the LBS cook made $4, although it is possible that she was also paying board for her children.

103 POA, *Minutes*, vol. 4, June 1851, 157; November 1851, 184; vol. 5, September 1854, 45; vol. 6, April 1858, 28; vol. 7, May 1863, 130; vol. 9, May 1875, 202.

104 LBS, *Minutes*, vol. 2, January 1841, 124.

105 LBS, *Annual Report*, 1889.

106 LBS, *Minutes*, vol. 11, May 1894, 94.

107 Ibid., May 1895, 144–5.

CHAPTER FOUR

1 Hacsi, *Second Home*.

2 In accordance with access rules, the real names of children and their families have not been used and surnames are represented as initials.

3 Cavallo, "The Motivations of Benefactors," 56. For the "logic of charity" see McCants, "Christian Charity." See also Lees, "The Survival of the Unfit"; Ross, "Hungry Children"; Katz, "The History of an Impudent."

4 Only 903 children have been included in the POA database for analysis, which is the number once re-admissions and a number of the 1847 epidemic children, who were very unlike the norm (older and remained only a few days), are removed. The register includes 951 children.

5 Rooke and Schnell, *Discarding the Asylum*, 81, 111–12; "The Rise and Decline," 165.

6 The annual cost for one visually impaired boy sent to the Blind Asylum in Brantford was $80. The LBS paid $36; the balance was paid by one of the Committee members. LBS, *Minutes*, vol. 8, May 1872, 271. In a similar case a girl's fees were paid for jointly by the POA, the LBS, and the Anglican Church. POA, *Register*, 18, #343; LBS, *Minutes*, vol. 4, September 1852, 226.

7 POA, *Annual Report*, 1897, 4.

8 POA, *Annual Report*, 1904, 4.

9 One worked as an elevator operator for years and often wrote to the Committee about his financial problems. They helped him on several occasions.

10 Strong-Boag, "Children of Adversity," 413–32. Also see Clarke, "Sacred Daemons."

11 POA, *Annual Report*, 1904, 4

12 Harvey, "The Montreal Ladies' Benevolent," 326. See discussion below on the industrial school.

13 Bettina Bradbury refers to the help of daughters as "invaluable." Bradbury, "Gender at Work," 192.

14 Rev. Newcomb, "The Management of Boys," *Mother's Assistant*, February 1847, quoted in McLoughlin, "Evangelical Childrearing," 23. In her study of the applications for the Halifax orphans in 1917, Suzanne Morton finds similar conceptions of girls being more obedient, affectionate, and adaptable. Morton, "To Take an Orphan." See also Mintz, *Huck's Raft*.

15 Discussion of this occurred throughout the century. LBS, *Minutes*, vol. 2, April 1837, 42; vol. 9, November 1876, 26; vol. 10, April 1888, 203; vol. 12, January 1899, 95.

16 LBS, *Minutes*, vol. 9, November 1876, 26.

17 *Census of Canada*, 1851–91.

18 For Bishop Bond see DCB: Richard Virr, "William Bennett Bond."

19 LBS, *Minutes*, vol. 7, April 1872, 174; vol. 8, May 1872, 3.

20 POA, *Minutes*, vol. 11, May 1885, 99.

21 POA, *Minutes*, vol. 8, February 1870, 250.

22 LBS, *Minutes*, vol. 6, March 1860, 63; vol. 10, June 1883, 64; January 1884, 87. This policy was changed in 1917. LBS, *Annual Report*, 1917–18, 8.

23 *Census of Canada*, 1851–1901.

24 See also Gauvreau et al., "The Harsh Welcome of an Industrial City."

25 For the role of kin as a support network see Bradbury, *Working Families*; Fahrni, *Of Kith and Kin*; Gossage, *Families in Transition*; Ross, "Labour and Love,"and *Love and Toil*; also Anderson, *Family Structure*; Davidoff and Hall, *Family Fortunes*, ch. 7; Dyhouse, "Mothers and Daughters"; Katz, *Poverty and Policy*, 17–54, and "The History of an Impudent"; Roberts, *A Woman's Place*, ch. 5.

26 Strong-Boag, *Fostering Nation?* 21. For grandmothers in this role see Dillon, *The Shady Side of Fifty*.

27 LBS, *Register*, vol. 1, 112, #1737, #1738, #1739.

28 POA, *Register*, 22, #631, #632.

29 LBS, *Register*, vol. 1, 79, #1106, #1107.

30 POA, *Register*, 39, #820, #821, #822, #823; 29, #715; 35, #783; 15, #548; LBS, *Register*, vol. 1, 12, #256; 93, #1335; vol. 2, 212, #2887. For a discussion of neighbourhood support elsewhere see Ross, "Survival Networks," 4–27, and Winter, "Widowed Mothers and Mutual Aid," 115–25.

31 POA, *Minutes*, vol. 2, October 1840, 121; vol. 5, October 1854, 51–2; vol. 9, May 1873, 108; vol. 13, October 1896, 138. A discussion of this policy occurred in 1842 when it was decided to admit "objects of charity" if well-recommended; ten such cases were admitted, but this was unusual. POA, *Minutes*, vol. 3, March–April 1842, 17–18.

32 LBS, *Minutes*, vol. 2, August 1839, 94, 100.

33 LBS, *Register*, vol. 1, 29, #447, #448.

34 *Census of Canada*, 1851–1901.

35 LBS, *Register*, vol. 1, 117, #1838, #1839, #1840; vol. 1, 97, #1395, #1396, #1397, #1398.

36 LBS, *Register*, vol. 1, 104, #1548, #1549, #1550, #1551; vol. 2, 48, #2128, #2129, #2130, #2131.

37 These children have been included in the above statistic for one-parent families.

38 Cross-checks with the parent removing these children only revealed a few cases where the unknown parent retrieved the children, and it is possible these were recent marriages.

39 Before nursing was established as a skilled profession, most "nurses" were untrained and their work was closer to that of a servant. The MGH opened English Montreal's first nursing school in 1890. See Kenneally, "The Montreal Maternity," 86–93.

40 In her study of the (Catholic) Saint Alexis Orphanage, Bettina Bradbury found the same tendency towards working-class occupations (90 per cent). However, in her sample based on 10 per cent of children, the number of skilled workers was larger than in the LBS at almost 30 per cent. Bradbury, "The Fragmented Family," 117, 206.

41 Strong-Boag, "Forgotten People," 36.

42 LBS, *Register*, vol. 1, 27, #439; 39, #571. His mother is #438 and #538. LBS, *Matron's Journal*, vol. 2, 13 December 1855, 60.

43 POA, *Minutes*, vol. 1, July 1832, 147–9; August 1832, 154.

44 POA, *Minutes*, vol. 2, July 1835, 26.

45 Pearce and Mitchell, *History of the Montreal Ladies' Benevolent Society*, 31.

46 LAC, *Canada State Books*, vol. G, Reel C–113 (hereafter *Canada State Books*), "Executive Council report on letter from the Bishop of Montreal," 12 July 1847, 111.

47 POA, *Minutes*, vol. 3, June–July 1847, 158–63.

48 *Canada State Books*, "Report by W. Morris on letter from the POA and the committee's recommendation," 12 July 1847, 113.

49 In the end, Council considered the doctor's bill too high and paid only one-quarter of it. *Canada State Books*, 26 July 1847, 214; 10 September 1847, 379.

50 POA, *Minutes*, vol. 3, August 1847, 164–7; *Canada State Books*, 26 July 1847, 214.

51 *Canada State Books*, 4 August 1847, 219. Compare this haste to the treatment of fever children in Saint John, NB where the Emigrant Orphan Asylum was kept open for two years while the 296 children were found positions. See Murphy, *Poor Ignorant Children*.

52 *Canada State Books*, 25 October 1847, 499; 3 November 1847, 560–2.

53 POA, *Minutes*, vol. 3, October 1847, 175–6.

54 The government paid for the travelling expenses. Some of these children went to the same Mr Scott of Lanark (now Perth, Ontario) who had taken children in 1832. POA, *Minutes*, vol. 3, November 1847, 179.

55 POA, *Minutes*, vol. 3, November 1847, 176–7; December 1847, 184, 187.

56 POA, *Minutes*, vol. 3, May 1848, 205; McCord, *Historical Sketch*, 16.

57 LBS, *Minutes*, vol. 3, July 1847, 140–2; vol. 4, August 1847, 1; *Canada State Books*, "Report on response to Ladies' Benevolent Society," 4 August 1847, 218.

58 LBS, *Minutes*, vol. 5, November 1854, 73; January 1855, 95; February 1855, 98–9; May 1855, 110.

59 LBS, *Annual Report*, 1885.

60 LBS, *Register*, vol. 1, 112, #1753.

61 LBS, *Minutes*, vol. 3, July 1846, 92; vol. 4, February 1852, 208; vol. 5, March 1858, 208; vol. 6, July 1859, 34; vol. 7, May 1867, 69; vol. 10, November 1887, 203; vol. 11, March 1891, 18.

62 LBS, *Minutes*, vol. 5, March 1857, 172.

63 LBS, *Minutes*, vol. 5, March 1858, 208.

64 For this, see Purvey, "Alexandra Orphanage and Families," 124, and Rooke and Schnell, "Childhood and Charity," 168–9, 175–8. For the US, see Hacsi, *Second Home*, 126.

65 See discussion in the next section.

66 The last year the LBS received board payments from the Provincial Secretary was 1905 when they received $59.90 for two girls. In the same year the city paid $2,195.59. LBS, *Annual Report*, 1905; Quebec, *Sessional Papers*, vol. 39, 2.

67 In March 1909 they decided to ask parents to pay $5 board. This amount was slowly increased. LBS, *Minutes*, vol. 13, March 2, 1909, 18–19; vol. 15, March 2, 1920, 73.

68 LBS, *Annual Report*, 1922.

69 *Statutes of Quebec*, 1869, 32 Vict., c. 17, s. 12, 14, 15.

70 *Statutes of Quebec*, 1884, 47 Vict., c. 23, s. 15; 1888, 51–2 Vict., s. 12; 1894, 57 Vict., s. 1; 1912, 3 Geo., c. 39, s. 4031.

71 Cale, "Girls and the Perception of Sexual Danger," 201. See also Joyal, "L'acte concernant les écoles d'industrie," 239, for Quebec.

72 For this, see Fecteau, *The Pauper's Freedom*, 146–58, and Dekker, *The Will to Change the Child.* The model was based on that of Britain, and specifically that of Ireland where religious communities ran the institutions. For England, see Hurt, "Reformatory and Industrial Schools"; Cale, "Girls and the Perception of Sexual Danger"; Moore, "Social Control or Protection?"; for Ireland, see Raftery and O'Sullivan, *Suffer the Little Children.*

73 Joyal, "L'acte concernant les écoles d'industrie."

74 CHRS, Protestant House of Industry, *Annual Report*, 1873, 1884; *Minute Book*, vol. 1, October 1872, 435; May 1873, 474; *Minute Book*, vol. 2, October 1882, 411; December 1882, 421; January 1884, 484.

75 POA, *Minutes*, vol. 10, January 1883, 264–6; February 1883, 273; The Boys' Home, *Minutes*, vol. 2, July 7 1896, 31; September 3, 1896, 34.

76 For a more in-depth study of the LBS Industrial School see Harvey, "Endangered Children."

77 Myers, *Caught.*

78 This understanding is clear in their discussions at the meeting following the public protest to their new status. LBS, *Minutes*, vol. 10, April 1884, 93.

79 See for example, LBS, *Minutes*, vol. 11, October 1891, 28.

80 See Gilbert, "Assister les familles de Québec," 493. Ten per cent of the children admitted to the Hospice Saint Charles in Quebec City (both a reform and an industrial school) were charity cases. For Montreal, see Strimelle, "La gestion de la déviance."

81 LBS, *Minutes*, vol. 10, March 1884, 90; April 1884, 93; "The Ladies' Benevolent," *Montreal Witness*, 30 April 1884.

82 For Canada, see Neff, "The Ontario Industrial Schools Act," 171–208, and "Government Approaches," 41, 81; Bennett, "Taming 'Bad Boys,'" 71–96; Hogeveen, "The Evils with Which," 37–68, and "Accounting for Violence," 147–74; Lafferty, *The Guardianship of Best Interests*, 3–6, 9–10; Matters, "The Boys' Industrial School," 53–70.

83 AVM, 15, Bien-Être Social, série 3, *Enfants sans tutelle*, 1892–1915. The series includes 891 applications to the LBS Industrial School. 106 of these were discontinued, 89 were refused, and 274 were to request a child remain in the institution for an additional 1-year term (re-admissions).

84 *Quebec Sessional Papers*, 1888–1904.

85 This gender balance is somewhat misrepresentative since it is influenced by the fact that from 1916 to 1920 boys went to the SPWC Industrial School instead of the LBS. From 1884 to 1916 more boys than girls were admitted as a norm.

86 AVM, 15, Bien-Être Social, série 3, *Enfants sans tutelle*, 1892–1915. See Myers, "The Voluntary Delinquent," for a similar tendency for parents to apply to the courts for help with "unwieldy" children.

87 For a more extensive discussion of the contract negotiations with the city, see Harvey, "The Montreal Ladies' Benevolent."

88 Contracts had been signed with some institutions from 1892 but they became more widespread and standardized in 1910. Burban, "Les origines institutionelles," 84–6.

89 It is unclear if this clause was enforced, and it was not included in the 1921 contract. LBS, *Minutes*, vol. 13, 2 January 1912, 106; vol. 14, 1 February 1916, 138; 9 February 1916, 141.

90 LBS, *Minutes*, vol. 14, 1 February 1916, 125–30, 137–9.

91 LBS, *Annual Report*, 1919. Their 1921 industrial school contract included an upper limit of 25 boys. Therefore some of the Belmont discharges went to the POA. LBS, *Minutes*, vol. 15, September 1920, 83–85; POA, *Minutes*, vol. 15, October 1920, 304.

92 LBS, *Annual Report*, 1909; *Minutes*, vol. 13, 4 February 1910, 47. In 1913, the Soeurs de Bon Pasteur received $10 for girls in their industrial and reform schools while Mont Saint Antoine received $13–15 for boys. Strimelle, "La gestion de la déviance," 169. For the Catholic boys' reformatory in Montreal see Ménard, *Des enfants sous surveillance.*

93 LBS, *Annual Report*, 1919, 8. The rates for Hospice Saint-Charles in Quebec City were even lower that this: $5.50 (1870); $6.50 (1915); $10.83 (1921). Gilbert, "Assister les familles de Québec," 476.

94 "Better Care for Indigent Child. City Enters into Agreement to Help Juvenile Protestants," *The Gazette*, 2 September 1921. The new fee appears to have been applied to all children sent in connection with the Bureau of Municipal Assistance.

95 See the discussion of admissions and health policies in ch. 5, for example.

96 POA, *Annual Report*, 1910, 3

97 POA, *Annual Report*, 1898, 4.

98 POA, *Annual Report*, 1902, 4–5.

99 POA, *Annual Report*, 1910, 3–4.

100 Ibid., 5.

101 *Statutes of Quebec*, 1912, 2 George V, c. 116, s. 7, 4.

102 POA, *Annual Report*, 1912, 3.

103 POA, *Annual Report*, 1911, 3.

104 Adams and Theodore, "Designing for the 'Little Convalescents.'"

105 POA, *Annual Report*, 1913–14, 4. By that point 223 had used the facilities.

106 POA, *Annual Report*, 1917, 3.

107 POA, *Annual Report*, 1911, 3.

108 POA, *Annual Report*, 1912, 4. In the nineteenth century these women would have gone to the Convalescent Ward in the LBS but it had been converted to provide additional space for children.

109 POA, *Annual Report*, 1915, 4; 1920–21, 4.

110 POA, *Annual Report*, 1915–16, 3; 1919, 6.

111 This referred to a young orphan adopted after a year of care. POA, *Register*, #1064.

112 POA, *Annual Report*, 1913–14, 4.

113 POA, *Annual Report*, 1920, 6.

114 Ibid., 4.

115 POA, *Minutes of Meetings*, vol. 14, October 1902, 77; May 1903, 105.

116 POA, *Minutes of Meetings*, vol. 14, December 1908, 269; January 1909, 271.

117 POA, *Annual Report*, 1912, 3.

118 POA, *Annual Report*, 1911, 3.

119 POA, *Minutes*, vol. 13, May 1918, 226.

CHAPTER FIVE

1 LBS, "School Report," in *Annual Report*, 1863, 13.

2 See Rooke and Schnell, "The 'King's Children,'" 387–99, and the accounts by some of these children included in Bagnell, *The Little Immigrants*; Corbett, *Nation Builders*; Corbett, *Barnardo Children in Canada*; Harrison, *The Home Children*; R.A. Parker, *Uprooted*.

3 See Olson and Thornton, *Peopling the North American City*; Copp, *Anatomy of Poverty*; and Ames, *The City Below the Hill*.

4 One former resident of the Montreal Hebrew Orphan Home remembered how "huge" the building was on his arrival at the age of five. Gordon, *Four Hundred Brothers and Sisters*, 137.

5 David Maunders makes this point in "Awakening from the Dream," 397. Of course, it might have been left up to the matron or teacher to address this. R.B. McKenzie, for example, who entered an orphanage in 1953 after his mother's death, remembers having "a complete feeling of emptiness … a total emotional vacuum" on his arrival. McKenzie, *The Home*, 29.

6 Olsen and Vallgårda, "Emotional Frontiers," 437–44; Vallgårda, Alexander, and Olsen, "Emotions and the Global Politics."

7 POA, *Minutes*, vol. 1, January 1823, 15; June 1823, 27.

8 LBS, *Matron's Journal*, December 1851, 60; February 1852, 74; April 1852, 92; July 1855, 115.

9 LBS, *Minutes*, vol. 12, January 1898, 66; LBS, *Matron's Journal*, February 1898, 110.

10 LBS, *Minutes*, vol. 6, May–June 1859, 30–2; vol. 7, May 1869, 8; LBS, *Matron's Journal*, October 1859, 131, 134.

11 LBS, *Matron's Journal*, April 1851, 10; June 1862, 17; November 1869, 110, 112; February 1883, 56; January 1885, 2.

12 Cmeil, *A Home of Another Kind*. For an example of a Catholic child charity see Giroux, "Accueillir, Vêtir, Nourrir," 80–5.

13 Van Die, *Religion, Family and Community*, 8–9.

14 On the importance of family prayer in the middle-class home and the increasing role of women's responsibility for this see McDannell, *The Christian Home*, 77–85, 112–16.

15 This type of isolation was common in children's charities. See Hacsi, *Second Home*, 128.

16 POA, *Minutes*, vol. 13, May 1895, 26; LBS, *Minutes*, vol. 12, February 1899, 98. The LBS had first tried to limit sweets. LBS, *Minutes*, vol. 9, May 1877, 43; vol. 11, April 1895, 144.

17 POA, *Minutes*, vol. 3, July 1848, 209–11.

18 The matron had also stolen property. LBS, *Minutes*, vol. 3, September 1846, 100; vol. 5, April 1853, 2, 19.

19 LBS, *Minutes*, vol. 3, April 1847, 133; May 1847, 135.

20 LBS, *Minutes*, vol. 12, 25 November 1907, 261.

21 LBS, *Minutes*, vol. 13, 1 February 1910, 45; 1 March 1910, 49.

22 POA, *Minutes*, vol. 11, May 1889, 362–3.

23 POA, *Annual Report*, 1889.

24 For the use of these methods in the Hamilton orphanage see Nielson, *Private Women and the Public Good*, 92–3. See also Mintz and Kellogg, *Domestic Revolutions*, 58–9.

25 For the tendency of boys to run away more than girls, see Murray, "Fates of Orphans," 148, and Zorma, *Orphanages Reconsidered*, 144, 152.

26 For this type of agency on the part of children or "efforts to negotiate alternative realities for themselves," see Gleason et al., *Lost Kids*, 7.

27 POA, *Minutes*, vol. 12, 4 May 1908, 257–8.

28 The boys had run away twelve times. POA, *Minutes*, 4 May 1908, 258; 5 September 1908, 263–4. The Sherbrooke Reformatory (inside the prison) was notoriously damp, cold, and dark.

29 LBS, *Matron's Journal*, August 1851, 35.

30 LBS, *Matron's Journal*, January 1852, 68; LBS, *Minutes*, vol. 7, March 1866, 27; vol. 13, 28 January 1908, 266.

31 POA, *Minutes*, vol. 3, July 1858, 44; vol. 11, August 1884, 57; LBS, *Matron's Journal*, June 1875, 80; *Minutes*, vol. 9, April 1879, 129.

32 For a discussion of domestic sanitation conceptualized as "within the physical boundaries of the home" and thus the women's sphere, see Adams, *Architecture in the Family Way*.

33 For similar policies elsewhere see Zmora, "Baltimore's Nineteenth-Century Orphanages," 201.

34 POA, *Minutes*, vol. 14, June 1909, 288.

35 Both the POA and the LBS had free burial plots in the Protestant Mount Royal Cemetery as of 1853. Young, *Patrician Families*, 201, and *Respectable Burial*, 57.

36 Robert, "City of Wealth and Death," 24–8.

37 POA, *Minutes*, vol. 3, February 1841, 5.

38 Tétreault, "Les maladies de la misère."

39 The city demanded that parents of industrial school children be allowed to visit more regularly to maintain family cohesion. LBS, *Minutes*, vol. 12, 28 December 1905, 222.

40 LBS, *Minutes*, vol. 12, 26 September 1905, 213.

41 For the conflict with the city see Harvey, "The Montreal Ladies' Benevolent," 324.

42 POA, *Annual Report*, 1849; POA, *Minutes*, vol. 10, December 1878, 41–2.

43 LBS, *Annual Report*, 1854.

44 LBS, *Minutes*, vol. 5, March 1853, 17.

45 See Elliott, *The Angel out of the House*, esp. ch. 4.

46 LBS, *Matron's Journal*, April 1862, 6.

47 LBS, *Matron's Journal*, January 1869, 6–65; February 1869, 68, 70.

48 POA, *Minutes*, vol. 9, June 1875, 205. The LBS bought moccasins (against the cold) in 1899 and 1907. LBS, *Minutes*, vol. 12, October 1899, 116; 26 November 1907, 262.

49 POA, *Minutes*, vol. 8, December 1868, 190; October 1869, 232.

50 POA, *Minutes*, vol. 8, October 1869, 232; vol. 9, June 1875, 205; February 1877, 270.

51 LBS, *Matron's Journal*, May 1858, 28; August 1870, 156; August 1872, 91; August 1873, 154; February 1877, 210; POA, *Minutes*, vol. 11, April 1888, 262.

52 POA, *Minutes*, vol. 11, May 1888, 268; LBS, *Minutes*, vol. 11, March 1893, 61; vol. 12, January 1897, 24; February 1897, 27.

53 LBS, *Annual Reports*, 1890, 6; 1893, 5.

54 POA, *Minutes*, vol. 11, April–May 1888, 258–9, 263.

55 LBS, *Minutes*, vol. 12, 29 November 1904, 197–8.

56 LBS, *Minutes*, vol. 14, 17 March 1914, 26.

57 Adams, *Architecture in the Family Way*, 82.

58 POA, *Minutes*, vol. 11, August 1884, 54–6.

59 LBS, *Minutes*, vol. 12, August 1897, 45.

60 POA, *Minutes*, vol. 12, March 1893, 223; September 1893, 319.

61 Joyal, *Les enfants, la société et l'État*, 106.

62 LBS, *Matron's Journal*, June 1896, 17–18.

63 LBS, *Minutes*, vol. 11, December 1890, 9.

64 LBS, *Minutes*, vol. 5, October 1855, 134; POA, *Minutes*, vol. 9, February 1873, 97.

65 LBS, *Matron's Journal*, June 1872, 82.

66 LBS, *Minutes*, vol. 7, June 1871, 229; vol. 9, March 1878, 85; *Matron's Journal*, January 1898, 107; POA, *Minutes*, vol. 11, May 1888, 272.

67 The POA shifted from straw to springs and mattress in the early twentieth century. POA, *Minutes*, vol. 14, November 1902, 81; May 1904, 137; June 1904, 139.

68 LBS, *Minutes*, vol. 2, July 1840, 108; vol. 3, October 1845, 81; October 1846, 113; vol. 4, March 1848, 34; March 1849, 97; vol. 5, February 1854, 57; POA, *Minutes*, vol. 1, December 1823, 48; vol. 2, February 1830, 24; vol. 9, August 1872, 90.

69 POA, *Minutes*, vol. 4, June 1849, 93.

70 LBS, *Matron's Journal*, July 1862, 23.

71 They used the diet list for the Boston Female Asylum as a model.

72 The hasty pudding was a simple boiled pudding made of powdered maize with milk, to which beans, butter, bacon, or currants could be added. "The Hasty Pudding," *Harper's New Monthly Magazine* 13, no. 74 (July 1856): 145–60; Higginbotham, *The Workhouse Cookbook*, 28–9, 32.

73 POA, *Minutes*, vol. 9, April 1872, 77.

74 POA, *Minutes*, vol. 10, February 1882, 211–12.

75 POA, *Minutes*, vol. 11, November 1888, 329–30.
76 In 1854 mutton replaced beef as well. LBS, *Minutes*, vol. 4, December 1848, 78; vol. 5, July 1853, 28; December 1853, 51; February 1854, 58.
77 LBS, *Minutes*, vol. 5, December 1853, 51; vol. 4, April 1852, 215.
78 LBS, *Minutes*, vol. 6, March 1864, 236; vol. 7, June 1869, 145.
79 LBS, *Minutes*, vol. 9, December 1878, 110; vol. 10, March 1883, 58.
80 LBS, *Minutes*, vol. 10, September 1885, 122; vol. 11, February 1894, 70; April 1894, 98.
81 LBS, *Minutes*, vol. 12, 28 January 1908, 265–6; 25 February 1908, 267.
82 LBS, *Annual Report*, 1920, 13.
83 LBS, *Annual Report*, 1917–18, 8.
84 Point St Charles, for example, only received a school in 1876 following a petition on behalf of five hundred children without access to schooling. MacLeod and Poutanen, *A Meeting of the People*, 102.
85 For Quebec see ibid., 131. For Ontario see Neff, "The Education of Destitute," 28.
86 POA, *Minutes*, vol. 6, July 1858, 45.
87 LBS, *Minutes*, vol. 3, October 1846, 121; May 1847, 135; June 1847, 157; vol. 4, November 1848, 77; October 1850, 158.
88 This might have been the result of discrimination. Certainly this was the experience of the Coomb Orphanage children at their local school. Langan, *Hespeler's Hidden Secret*, 29.
89 LBS, *Minutes*, vol. 5, April 1858, 211; vol. 10, March 1882, 6; vol. 11, October 1895, 153.
90 Information from http://constitution.org/lanc/monitorial.htm (accessed 16 August 2012).
91 See MacLeod and Poutanen, *A Meeting of the People*, 129.
92 POA, *Annual Report*, 1873.
93 POA, *By-Laws*, 1852.
94 LBS, *Annual Reports*, 1903; POA, *Minutes*, vol. 16, insert dated 23 April 1923.
95 While studying at McGill, the author met a former POA boy who had learned book-binding in the POA and worked binding old books in the McGill library. Conversation with J.
96 For the use of singing to teach discipline and working together toward a common goal in orphanages since the Renaissance, see Miller, "The Early History of Orphanages," 41.
97 These are the prizes for 1893 (POA) and 1881 (LBS). POA, *Annual Report*, 1893; LBS, *Annual Report*, 1881.
98 Books were also provided by a travelling library. POA, *Minutes*, vol. 6, July 1858; December 1858; vol. 4, February 1851; LBS, *Matron's Journal*, June 1869, 90; November 1869, 110.
99 LBS, *Minutes*, vol. 10, January 1888, 207; February 1888, 210.

100 For these organizations see Olsen "Happy Home"; Spurr, "Lower-Middle Class Masculinity"; Alexander, *Guiding Modern Girls.*

101 Olsen, "Happy Home," 218.

102 POA, *Minutes*, vol. 16, May 1924; *Annual Report*, 1930, "Superintendent's Report," 1. For Victoria School, see MacLeod and Poutanen, *A Meeting of the People*, 126–7.

103 Sutherland, "We Always Had Things to Do." For Ontario institutions, see Neff, "The Education of Destitute," 19.

104 POA, *Minutes*, vol. 2, November 1835, 29; October 1836, 39.

105 LBS, *Minutes*, vol. 10, May 1883, 62.

106 LBS, *Annual Report*, 1899.

107 Ibid.

108 LBS, *Minutes*, vol. 6, October 1863, 216; vol. 8, June 1875, 141; LBS, *By-Laws*, 1874.

109 LBS, *Matron's Journal*, August 1858, 49.

110 Langan, *Hespeler's Hidden Secret*, 29.

111 This was confirmed by D.K., who had lived in the POA during the late 1930s and had a very successful life as a businesswoman. Conversation with D.K. See also McKenzie, *The Home*, 4.

112 Rooke and Schnell, *Discarding the Asylum*, 94, and "Childhood and Charity," 178.

113 See the Coombe Orphanage (1905 to 1947), for example, where children worked a large market garden and a chicken coop. Langan, *Hespeler's Hidden Secret.*

114 See Hurt, "Reformatory and Industrial Schools"; Raftery and O'Sullivan, *Suffer the Little Children*; Strimelle, "Le soin des âmes," 29–31; Burban, "Les origins institutionelles," 146.

115 Davidoff and Hall, *Family Fortunes*, 373; Young, *Respectable Burial.*

116 All of these were common presents for children. See Holmes, "Toys and Games," 187–202.

117 For the playground movement in Montreal, see Schmidt, "Domesticating Parks"; for Ontario, see Curtis, "The Playground"; for the US, see Cavallo, *Muscles and Morals.*

118 LBS, *Minutes*, vol. 12, March 1899, 102.

119 POA, *Minutes*, vol. 11, March 1889, 354–5.

120 Nielson, *Private Women and the Public Good*, 91. They also refer to toys as Christmas gifts that year.

121 LBS, *Minutes*, vol. 3, February 1842, 12; vol. 4, March 1848, 35; vol. 11, January 1894, 87; POA, *Minutes*, vol. 2, May 1839, 100; vol. 11, March 1889, 354–5. LBS, *By-Laws*, 1897.

122 Pearce and Mitchell, *History of the Ladies' Benevolent Society*, 64; LBS, *Annual Reports*, 1917–21; POA, *Minutes*, vol. 15, June 1920, 299.

123 POA, *Annual Report*, 1896.

124 Ibid., 1897.

125 LBS, *Annual Report*, 1898.

126 Quoted in LBS, *Minutes*, vol. 12, April 1898, 73.

127 *Statutes of Quebec*, 1912, 2 George V, c. 116, s. 4.

128 POA, *Annual Report*, 1903, 4.

129 Maunders, "Awakening from the Dream," 398, 400, 404. Maunders interviewed former residents in Canada, the US, and Australia. The article is based on nine of these interviews.

130 POA, *Minutes*, vol. 6, March 1860, 131.

131 POA, *Annual Reports*, 1878; 1885.

132 Gordon, *Four Hundred Brothers and Sisters*, and *Four Hundred Brothers and Sisters: Their Story Continues.* See also McKenzie, *Home Away from Home*, xiii.

133 Individuals with bad memories of institutional life in places such as the Coombe Orphanage, for example, focus mainly on the abuse they suffered at the hands of some of the attendants or in the homes to which they were sent. Langan, *Hespeler's Hidden Secret*, 12, 16, 18, 22, 29.

134 Zmora, *Orphanages Reconsidered*, ch. 5; McKenzie, *The Home*, 119.

135 POA, *Annual Report*, 1907, 4.

136 Ibid., 1903, 4.

137 POA, *Minutes*, vol. 15, February 1917, 200.

138 POA, *Annual Reports*, 1852; 1853; 1854; 1866; 1873; 1878; 1882; 1887; 1892; 1895; "A Home for the Orphans," newspaper clipping in POA, *Scrapbook*, 12 May 1892.

139 POA, *Annual Report*, 1906, 5.

140 Pearce and Mitchell, *History of the Ladies' Benevolent Society*, 57.

141 POA, *Annual Report*, 1905, 4.

142 See also Westley, *Remembrance of Grandeur*.

143 Carp, "Two Cheers for Orphanages"; Cmiel, *A Home of Another Kind*, 104; Langan, *Hespeler's Hidden Secret*, 29; Maunders, "Awakening from the Dream"; McKenzie, *The Home*; Zmora, *Orphanages Reconsidered*.

144 McKenzie, "Orphanage Alumni," 119. McKenzie's results are based on 1,589 respondents to a survey he did in 1995.

145 Conversation with J.; conversation with D.K.

146 Cmiel, *A Home of Another Kind*, 26.

147 See Gleason, "Lost Voices. Lost Bodies."

CHAPTER SIX

1 LBS, *Matron's Journal*, vol. 4, file 11, 28 February 1858, 13; 24 May 1858, 29; 3 July 1858, 36; LBS, *Register*, vol. 1, 54, #771–5; #780–6.

2 This couple is one of those included in the 1840 cohort in Bettina Bradbury's *Wife to Widow*, where she outlines the history of family problems as well as the

mother's struggle with the courts. See Bradbury, *Wife to Widow*, 14, 39, 102–3, 237–9.

3 LBS, *Matron's Journal*, vol. 4, file 10, March 1857, 135; 5 September 1857, 168; LBS, *Register*, vol. 1, 44–5, #640–5; 51, #719–22.

4 The older children were already baptized at Trinity Anglican Church. Bradbury, *Wife to Widow*, 103.

5 LBS, *Matron's Journal*, vol. 4, file 11, 6 November 1858, 60; 6–7 September 1859, 122. The funeral was paid for by the tutor; the matron and two of the sisters attended.

6 If the 1847 fever children, most of whom remained less than three months, are removed from the data, we find that only 26 per cent of other children remained less than a year, a more realistic representation of the normal POA trend.

7 For other examples of this see Bradbury, "Fragmented Families," 117; Neff, "The Role of Protestant Children's Homes," 60; Purvey, "Alexandra Orphanage," 115.

8 In July 1887, for example, they refused to release one boy to his brothers even though he was already twelve. POA, *Minutes*, vol. 11, July 1887, 206–7.

9 Nielson, *Private Women and the Public Good*, 80, 71–2.

10 *Statutes of Canada East*, 1860–61, 23 Vict., c. 143; *Statutes of Quebec*, 1912, 2 George V, c. 7.

11 For a general discussion of paternal power under the law, see Joyal, "L'évolution des modes de contrôle."

12 LBS, *Minutes*, vol. 11, February 1891, 16.

13 LBS, *Register*, vol. 1, 43, #621, 622.

14 Porter Benson, "A Good Home," 34, 48.

15 Parr, *Labouring Children*. For orphan trains see the discussion in ch. 7.

16 Rooke and Schnell, "Childhood and Charity," 175–8. These organizations did not succeed in permanently separating families. See Parr, *Labouring Children*, ch. 4. For the US, see Bellingham, "Institution and Family," and "Waifs and Strays."

17 POA, *Minutes*, vol. 1, January 1824, 53; vol. 3, August 1844, 53; vol. 4, December 1852, 249; LBS, *Minutes*, vol. 3, May 1844, 55; February 1847, 127; LBS, *Matron's Journal*, vol. 5, file 1, May 1869, 82.

18 POA, *Minutes*, vol. 9, July 1871, 29; August 1871, 30–1.

19 LBS, *Minutes*, vol. 7, September 1870, 190.

20 POA, *Minutes*, vol. 10, September 1880, 112; November 1880, 119, 123–4; December 1880, 126; March 1881, 142–3; February 1882, 205–7.

21 POA, *Minutes*, vol. 10, February 1882, 205–7; March 1882, 214–15.

22 POA, *Minutes*, vol. 11, September–October 1887, 214–15, 218–19.

23 The brother of two boys applied for them in October 1887. He had applied before and been refused since he was Catholic. It was probably the court case that encouraged him to reapply, but he did not pursue the matter. POA, *Minutes*, vol. 11, October 1887, 225–6.

24 LBS, *Minutes*, vol. 10, March 1889, 104.

25 POA, *Minutes*, vol. 4, August 1850, 154; November 1851, 181–2.

26 POA, *Minutes*, vol. 4, March 1852, 206.

27 POA, *Minutes*, vol. 5, December 1855, 116; vol. 8, October 1870, 272; vol. 10, June 1880, 109.

28 LBS, *Minutes*, vol. 5, April 1855, 104; vol. 10, August 1886, 166.

29 POA, *Minutes*, vol. 8, June 1868, 166.

30 POA, *Minutes*, vol. 9, November 1875, 213.

31 POA, *Minutes*, vol. 3, July 1843, 28.

32 The Secretary noted, "it would never do to let her have the child." POA, *Minutes*, vol. 10, April 1881, 147; vol. 11, March 1887, 180–1, 184.

33 LBS, *Matron's Journal*, vol. 5, file 1, December 1870, 186; vol. 5, file 2, September 1873.

34 He wanted her discharged so that he could place her in a situation, but she was already placed. POA, *Minutes*, vol. 11, May 1889, 364.

35 For accounts of some of these removals see LBS, *Matron's Journal*, vol. 4, file 11, April 1858, 21; vol. 4, file 13, July 1864, 26; April 1865, 72; June 1865, 84; October 1865, 98; vol. 5, file 1, October 1870, 173; March 1871, 209; vol. 5, file 2, September 1873, 73; LBS, *Minutes*, vol. 7, October 1870, 272; vol. 12, March 1890, 295.

36 LBS, *Matron's Journal*, vol. 4, file 10, November 1857, 180; October 1859, vol. 4, file 11, October 1859, 131.

37 For this shift and the *Apprenticeship Law*, see Joyal, *Les Enfants, la société et l'État*, 76–7.

38 *Statutes of Quebec*, 1871, 35 Vict., c. 13. It appears that the law was not enforced since charities were still fighting for these conditions in 1899 (see ch. 7).

39 The ladies had originally asked their lawyer, George Macrae, to prepare a request to amend their Act of Incorporation "in order to have more power over the children." They were even happier with the law and thanked both Macrae and the Hon. Luther Holton, MLA, for advice, preparation of documents, and lobbying. POA, *Minutes*, vol. 9, September 1871, 35; December 1871, 54; POA, *Annual Report*, 1872.

40 POA, *Minutes*, vol. 10, February 1878, 7; March 1878, 11.

41 POA, *Minutes*, vol. 10, April 1878, 16.

42 POA, *Minutes*, vol. 10, March 1878, 13.

43 POA, *Minutes*, vol. 10, May 1878, 20–1; June 1878, 27; September 1878, 31.

44 POA, *Minutes*, vol. 10, December 1880, 132.

45 See Goubau and O'Neill, "L'adoption, l'Église et l'État," 100–3.

46 For an overview of these early versions of adoption see Askeland, "Informal Adoption"; Cahn, "Perfect Substitutes?"; Carp, "Introduction," 3–8.

47 Grossberg, *Governing the Hearth*, 268–80.

48 Zainaldin, "The Emergence." See also Carp, "Introduction," 5–6, and Porter Benson, "A Good Home," 28.

49 British Columbia in 1920, Ontario in 1921, Manitoba and Saskatchewan in 1922, Quebec in 1924, Alberta in 1927, and Prince Edward Island in 1930.

50 Adoption was also referred to with the same lack of clarification in pre-Confederation legislation. *Statutes* of *Canada*, 1863–64, 27–8 Vict., c. 63; 1864, 28 Vict., c. 145.

51 *Revised Statutes of Quebec*, 1923–24, c. 75; 1925, c. 196. See Baillargeon, "Orphans in Quebec"; Goubau and O'Neill, "L'adoption, l'Église et l'État," 97–130; Joyal, *Les enfants, la société et l'État*, 140–4; Quesney, "De la charité au Bonheur familial," and "Un Foyer pour chaque enfant!" 266–7. The Quebec law made children who had been abandoned in a charity for two years eligible for adoption. After much negative reaction, the law was modified in 1925 to limit adoption to illegitimate children and orphans.

52 See Neff, "Apprenticeship and Adoption," 367, and "Pauper Apprenticeship," 157. Also Rooke and Schnell, "Childhood and Charity," 174–5.

53 Porter Benson, "A Good Home," 37.

54 One adoption was done by the family's lawyer. POA, *Minutes*, vol. 4, November 1849, 111.

55 The Toronto institution established an adoption form sometime between 1866 and 1879 that might have helped to clarify this. Neff, "Apprenticeship and Adoption," 362.

56 POA, *Minutes*, vol. 1, November 1824, 77.

57 POA, *Minutes*, vol. 4, February 1851, 137; September 1851, 171–2.

58 POA, *Minutes*, vol. 4, April 1851, 148; September 1852, 235–7; December 1852, 250; June 1853, 282–3; August 1853, 293; POA, *Register*, vol. 1, 16, #557.

59 POA, *Minutes*, vol. 5, December 1855.

60 POA, *Minutes*, vol. 8, July 1867, 120; vol. 9, February 1873, 232.

61 Coincidently they were both in March 1866. POA, *Minutes*, vol. 8, March 1866, 54–5.

62 Porter Benson, "A Good Home," 39.

63 POA, *Minutes*, vol. 7, February–March 1863, 117, 121; vol. 8, September 1869, 228.

64 This included one-half of orphans and 20 per cent of children with parents.

65 For this distinction and the use of pauper apprenticeship by charities, see Neff, "Pauper Apprenticeship," and Murray and Herndon, "Markets for Children."

66 POA, *By-Laws*, 1852, XV.

67 Ibid.

68 For this law see Craven, "The Law of Master and Servant"; Hogg, "Legal Rights of Masters"; Young, *The Politics of Codification*, 138.

69 POA, *Minutes*, vol. 8, March 1868, 156.

70 POA, *By-Laws*, 1852, XV.

71 POA, *Minutes*, vol. 3, April 1847, 150; vol. 5, August 1854, 42; December 1854, 63.

72 LBS, *Minutes*, vol. 2, October 1835, 9.

73 LBS, *Minutes*, vol. 9, May 1876, 2.

74 Until 1847 the LBS contract ended at 21. LBS, *Minutes*, vol. 4, November 1847, 19.

75 POA, *Minutes*, vol. 8, December 1869, 239.

76 Barnardo's as well as some Ontario charities, such as the Toronto POH, used a sliding scale with fees increasing according to age. See Neff, "The Use of Apprenticeship," and Parr, *Labouring Children*, 85–8.

77 This was more, though, than the fees charged by some other institutions. See Neff, "The Use of Apprenticeship," 364.

78 This fund also paid for the books sent to apprentices who wrote their Christmas letter.

79 LBS, *Minutes*, vol. 4, January 1848, 27.

80 These children are counted as apprenticed for the purposes of this study.

81 LBS, *Minutes*, vol. 3, April 1843, 34. When one of these children was badly treated, the ladies believed they had no recourse. LBS, *Minutes*, vol. 4, June 1848, 54.

82 LBS, *Minutes*, vol. 3, March 1846, 76.

83 POA, *Minutes*, vol. 2, February 1835, 20; April 1835, 23.

84 The only cases of children sent to indentures on their own were in 1832 and 1847.

85 POA, *Minutes*, vol. 2, January 1840, 109.

86 LBS, *Minutes*, vol. 3, March 1846, 78; vol. 4, October 1848, 75.

87 For other charities in Canada, see Rooke and Schnell, *Discarding the Asylum*, 93–4.

88 POA, *Minutes*, vol. 3, May 1846, 123; POA, "Account of the Annual Meeting, 1849," *Minutes*, vol. 4, 66.

89 POA, *Minutes*, vol. 6, March 1859, 84; November 1859, 118. See also vol. 4, September 1852, 238.

90 These included mainly Lachute, Pointe Fortune, Hemmingford, and Lacolle.

91 POA, *Minutes*, vol. 10, October 1879, 80–5.

92 POA, *Minutes*, vol. 10, June 1881, 154–5.

93 One application was described as "a very out of the way place not fit for any of our children to be sent to." POA, *Superintendent's Journal*, vol. 2, May 1882, 51.

94 POA, *Minutes*, vol. 10, September 1881, 169.

95 POA, *Minutes*, vol. 4, November 1853, 305; December 1853, 308.

96 Applications were rejected on these grounds in both 1861 and 1862. POA, *Minutes*, vol. 7, September 1861, 43; April 1862, 91.

97 POA, *Minutes*, vol. 6, January 1858, 12.

98 POA, *Minutes*, vol. 6, May 1858, 32; POA, *Correspondence*, "Letter from Mr. Morris," 7 April 1858.

99 This was the description used when she was returned a year later from her second placement. At that point her sister assumed her care. POA, *Minutes*, vol. 6, June 1859, 98.

100 LBS, *Minutes*, vol. 1, May 1834, 57; vol. 2, August 1840, 138; LBS, *Matron's Journal*, vol. 5, file 3, July 1875, 84.

101 LBS, *Minutes*, vol. 2, July 1840, 107–8.

102 POA, *Minutes*, vol. 3, May 1847, 154; November 1848, 218; vol. 5, February 1854, 9–10; April 1855, 86; May 1855, 90.

103 POA, *Minutes*, vol. 5, April 1856, 86. The LBS rarely attempted to impose fines for default of contract and did not have an official rule on this.

104 In 1869, for example, a boy with "no talent" for farming but an interest in mechanics was transferred to pursue that interest. POA, *Minutes*, vol. 7, October 1869, 231.

105 POA, *Minutes*, vol. 9, November 1871, 42.

106 This was the case with the British emigration societies, for example. See Parr, *Labouring Children*, 92; Sutherland, *Children in English-Canadian Society*.

107 POA, *Annual Report*, 1885.

108 In the case of one boy in 1854, the ladies transferred him to the shoemaker who had already trained his brother. POA, *Minutes*, vol. 5, February 1854, 9–10.

109 See Rudin, *Forgotten Quebecers*, 71, 77–90.

110 For a discussion of this see Valverde, *The Age of Light*, 130–3.

111 POA, *Minutes*, vol. 4, March 1851, 143.

112 POA, *Minutes*, vol. 9, October 1872, 90; September 1874, 168.

113 LBS, *Annual Report*, 1877; LBS, *Matron's Journal*, vol. 5, file 5, August–September 1897, 83.

114 POA, *Minutes*, vol. 4, July 1852, 227.

115 This was the case with a boy who wanted to be a carpenter. POA, *Minutes*, vol. 5, July 1855, 100.

116 LBS, *Matron's Journal*, vol. 4, file 9, January 1853, 135; LBS, *Matron's Journal*, vol. 5, file 5, August–September 1897, 86.

117 POA, *Minutes*, vol. 5, August 1855, 100. See also vol. 3, November 1846, 135.

118 POA, *By-Laws*, 1852, XXVIII.

119 A number of these boys remained in the area or went to the US, always earning good wages and keeping in touch with the Orphanage.

120 Hamilton, "Market for Montreal," and "Decline of Apprenticeship."

121 Hamilton, "Decline of Apprenticeship," 629, 632, 637, 641–4, 653, 657.

122 Poutanen, "For the Benefit of the Master," 106–57; Burgess, "Work, Family and Community," 64–102.

123 POA, *Minutes*, vol. 5, May 1857, 203; September 1857, 219.

124 LBS, *Minutes*, vol. 4, April 1851, 177; *Register*, vol. 1, #347.

125 Burgess, "Work, Family and Community," 63, 82–3; Hamilton, "Decline of Apprenticeship," 629; Poutanen, "For the Benefit of the Master," 130.

126 LBS, *Minutes*, vol. 5, November 1852, 9; *Register*, vol. 1, #347.

127 POA, *Minutes*, vol. 12, September 1889, 15.

128 POA, *Minutes*, vol. 11, November 1887, 231.

129 POA, *Minutes*, vol. 11, November 1888, 323–4.

130 POA, *Minutes*, vol. 11, December 1888, 342. The plumber suggested the changes.

131 POA, *Annual Report*, 1889; 1890.

132 POA, *Minutes*, vol. 12, April 1890, 74; May 1890, 76.

133 The Boys' Home supplied education (at night) and moral supervision for these boys.

134 Rooke and Schnell, *Discarding the Asylum*, 94.

135 Some of these were rural towns. Only Montreal has been kept as urban.

136 The *Répetoire Toponymique du Québec 1978* and the *Canadian Book of the Road* were used to find locations that have changed names.

137 This included the 13 children in 1832 and 1847 who went to Lanark (Perth) and 8 across the border from Lachute.

138 POA, *Annual Report*, 1888.

139 Data on apprenticeship location is recorded for 78 per cent of cases.

140 LBS, *Minutes*, vol. 1, May 1834, 34; vol. 2, February 1840, 104; vol. 3, March 1846, 78; vol. 4, December 1847, 27; June 1848, 27; vol. 5, August 1857, 181.

141 LBS, *Minutes*, vol. 1, July 1835, 78; vol. 2, December 1835, 13; March 1840, 105; June 1840, 106; vol. 4, September 1848, 64; vol. 6, June 1861, 112.

142 LBS, *Minutes*, vol. 2, February 1840, 104; vol. 3, September 1845, 73–4.

143 In one of these cases the girl later married into the family that took her in. LBS, *Minutes*, vol. 5, February 1855, 98.

144 In one case the girl's uncle (who had made the complaint of abuse), the master, and the matron attended the Committee meeting to find a compromise. POA, *Minutes*, vol. 10, March 1882, 216–18.

145 POA, *Minutes*, vol. 4, March 1849, 79. See also vol. 9, February 1872, 65.

146 See cases discussed below and also POA, *Minutes*, vol. 6, October 1859, 114; vol. 8, December 1866, 84; vol. 12, June 1894, 370.

147 This happened several times in the LBS. LBS, *Minutes*, vol. 6, June 1861, 12; vol. 7, November 1866, 51; December 1866, 53; January 1867, 57–8.

148 POA, *Minutes*, vol. 4, July–August 1853, 291–2; vol. 5, May 1855, 92; June 1855, 96.

149 POA, *Minutes*, vol. 9, June 1874, 163; October 1874, 173; September 1875, 274; April 1877, 279. See also vol. 4, March 1849, 79; vol. 5, April 1854, 23.

150 POA, *Minutes*, vol. 10, December 1881, 196; February 1882, 208; February 1883, 276; March 1883, 282–3; April 1883, 290; vol. 11, December 1883, 12.

151 Originally the master had lived near Lachute. POA, *Minutes*, vol. 10, April 1883, 290.

152 POA, *Minutes*, vol. 3, May 1841, 176.

153 The POA added a by-law to this effect in 1850. POA, *Minutes*, vol. 4, May 1850, 87.

154 POA, *Minutes*, vol. 4, October 1852, 242.

155 POA, *Minutes*, vol. 5, April 1854, 23–4.

156 The master paid the fees. POA, *Minutes*, vol. 7, July 1859, 100; August 1859, 106.

157 POA, *Minutes*, vol. 6, February 1859, 78; March 1859, 85.

158 They held two special meetings to discuss legal proceedings and met with their lawyer about this as well as about possible financial compensation. But in the end nothing was done. POA, *Minutes*, vol. 10, October 1881, 174; November 1881, 176.

159 POA, *Minutes*, vol. 9, March 1871, 12–13; April 1871, 15–17; June 1871, 25.

160 The Catherine Booth Maternity Hospital used this method (interview with Muriel Doherty, former CBM nurse). See also Neff, "The Use of Apprenticeship," 154. For the impact of this method on the disabled, see Strong-Boag, "Children of Adversity."

161 POA, *Minutes*, vol. 5, May 1855, 90; vol. 6, November 1858, 61.

162 *Statutes of Quebec*, 1871, 35 Vict., c. 13, s. 6.

163 POA, *Minutes*, vol. 11, April 1887, 186–7.

164 Lasser, "Pleasingly Oppressive Burden," 171–4; POA, *Minutes*, vol. 8, February 1872, 66; LBS, *Matron's Journal*, vol. 5, file 1, January 1868, 4.

165 LBS, *Minutes*, vol. 8, March 1873, 41; May–June 1873, 52.

166 POA, *Minutes*, vol. 11, June 1884, 40–1.

167 POA, *Annual Report*, 1885.

168 POA, *Minutes*, vol. 14, February 1905, 161.

169 POA, *Minutes*, vol. 15, November 1901, 31; December 1910, 37.

170 Neff, "The Use of Apprenticeship," 374.

CHAPTER SEVEN

1 Deutsch, *Women and the City*; Flanagan, *Seeing with Their Hearts*. See also McCarthy, "Women and Political Culture," and Spain, *How Women Saved the City*.

2 For an excellent study of the restrictions on women's public appearances and how women managed to overcome some of these, see Mary Ryan, *Women in Public*.

3 *Toronto Empire*, 1893, quoted in MacDonald, *Adelaide Hoodless*, 36.

4 Collard, *Montreal's Yesterdays*, quoted in Wolfe and Strachan, "Practical Idealism," 72.

5 See Pedersen, "The Power of True Christian Women," 330–2.

6 See Prochaska, *Women and Philanthropy*, 142–4; Speisman, "Munificent Parsons"; Splane, *Social Welfare in Ontario*; Rooke and Schnell, "The Rise and Decline."

7 Rooke and Schnell, "The Rise and Decline."

8 McCord, *Historical Sketch.*

9 POA, *Minutes*, vol. 1, 7 January 1823, 8.

10 For the Boston charity, see Holloran, *Boston's Wayward Children.*

11 POA, *Minutes*, vol. 1, 16 December 1822, 2–4.

12 Pearce and Mitchell, *History of the Montreal Ladies' Benevolent Society*, 9. Also, Jan Noel, "Femmes Fortes," 75–6.

13 Doige, *Montreal Directory*, 1819, quoted in Pearce and Mitchell, *History of the Montreal Ladies' Benevolent Society* 16.

14 LBS, *Minutes*, vol. 1, July 1833, 1–10.

15 Ibid., "Rules and Regulations of the Montreal Ladies' Benevolent Society."

16 This was not unusual. Jane Lewis finds that even social activists such as Octavia Hill and Beatrice Webb respected propriety and the delineated separate spheres in public despite their active work in social service. Lewis, *Women and Social Action*, 8–9.

17 POA, "Annual Report," in *Minutes*, vol. 1, 1824, 56; 1830, 121; LBS, "Annual Report," in *Minutes*, 1836, vol. 1, 32. In 1835 Rev. Bethune had done the same.

18 See the Toronto Orphans' Home for example. Neff, "The Use of Apprenticeship," 340. Also Ginzberg, *Women and the Work*, 34–40, and Hewitt, *Women's Activism*, 246.

19 POA, *Annual Report*, 1876.

20 POA, *Annual Report*, 1879.

21 POA, *Annual Report*, 1881; 1895.

22 Lebsock, *Free Women of Petersburg*, 230–1.

23 LAC, *Canada State Books*, 1847, and ANQ-Q, *Registry of Letters of the Provincial Secretary.*

24 Davidoff and Hall, *Family Fortunes*, 273.

25 Lebsock, *Free Women of Petersburg*, xvi.

26 Noel, "Women and Social Welfare Work," 262, 278.

27 LBS, *Annual Report*, 1866.

28 Rooke and Schnell, *Discarding the Asylum*, 24–5.

29 LBS, *Minutes*, vol. 4, January 1852, 206; *Annual Report*, 1853, 4.

30 LBS, *Minutes*, vol. 5, December 1853, 50; January 1854, 52; April 1854, 61; December 1854, 91; January 1855, 95.

31 LBS, *Minutes*, vol. 7, October 1864, 73; October 1866, 166; August 1869, 148; March 1870, 178; vol. 8, April 1875, 133; vol. 12, May 1897, 39.

32 This included A. Simpson, C. Geddes, F. Mackenzie, T. Gordon, and F.W. Thomas.

33 LBS, *Minutes*, vol. 5, December 1856, 166; vol. 8, June 1873, 30.

34 POA, *Minutes*, vol. 3, April 1845, 86–7; May 1845, 89; July 1847, 163; vol. 4, September 1853, 244; vol. 12, February 1891, 109–10; July 1893, 306; September 1893, 316; October 1893, 321–2.

35 POA, *Minutes*, vol. 3, February 1847, 145; vol. 11, April 1888, 255–6, 258; vol. 13, December 1897, 188.

36 POA, *Minutes*, vol. 3, February 1847, 145.

37 POA, *Minutes*, vol. 10, December 1878, 41–2, 47; February 1879, 55–6; March 1879, 60, 63.

38 Miss Margaret Greenshields, whose uncle (John Greenshields) was on the Gentlemen's Finance Committee, became Treasurer when Mary-Jane Tylee resigned. Several other ladies had refused the position given its difficulty. POA, *Minutes*, vol. 9, November 1874, 175; December 1874, 183.

39 POA, *Minutes*, vol. 13, January 1896, 95–6, 104–5.

40 J.J. Kelso, "Neglected and Friendless Children," *The Canadian Magazine* 2 (1894): 214.

41 Rooke and Schnell, "The Rise and Decline," 23.

42 For Boston see Holloran, *Boston's Wayward Children*, 41–50. For the New York CAS, see Bellingham, "Institution and Family," and "Waifs and Strays"; Langsam, *Children West*; O'Connor, *Orphan Trains*. For other examples, see Gordon, *The Great Arizona Orphan Abduction*, and Patrick and Trickel, *Orphan Trains to Missouri*.

43 Ashby, *Saving the Waifs*; Tiffin, *In Whose Best Interest?* For Canada (and Britain) see Rooke and Schnell, "From Binding Out."

44 Minton, "Family Life versus Institution Life," *Proceedings of the National Conference of Charities and Corrections* (hereafter NCCC), 1893, 45–7; Richardson, "The Massachusetts System," NCCC, 1893, 65.

45 Alden, "The Shady Side of the 'Placing-out System,'" NCCC, 1892; Cummings, "Home-Placing," NCCC, 1900; Hubbard, "Dangers of Careless Methods," NCCC, 1899. For a re-evaluation of this movement see Holt, "Adoption Reform," 23–7, and "The Orphan Trains."

46 See Ashby, *Endangered Children*, and *Saving the Waifs*; Clement, "Families and Foster Care"; Tiffin, *In Whose Best Interest?*; Berebitsky, *Like Our Very Own*.

47 For Ontario, see Bullen, "J.J. Kelso," and Jones and Rutman, *In the Children's Aid*, 83; for BC, see Strong-Boag, *Fostering Families*; for Calgary, see Klassen, "In Search of Neglected."

48 Strong-Boag, *Fostering Families*, 65–75.

49 LBS, *Annual Report*, 1875, 9.

50 Rev. Lindsay had served as a missionary in the Eastern Townships near Knowlton before coming to Montreal. ADA, *Anglican Synod Report*, "Obituary Notice," 1891, 21.

51 POA, *Minutes*, vol. 9, December 1875, 221–2. Since adoption was not legal under Quebec law, it was really a form of placing out irrespective of the terminology.

52 POA, *Annual Report*, 1876.

53 Ibid. This was the same Rev. Wilkes who had given the character reference for the couple responsible for the little girl's death in 1855.
54 POA, *Annual Report*, 1879.
55 Vickery, *The Gentleman's Daughter*, 285.
56 LBS, "Report for the Children," *Annual Report*, 1848, 16; LBS, *Minutes*, vol. 8, March 1873, 41; June 1873, 52.
57 LBS, *Annual Report*, 1887.
58 LBS, *Minutes*, vol. 9, May 1876, 2.
59 POA, *Annual Report*, 1881.
60 POA, *Annual Report*, 1884.
61 POA, *Annual Report*, 1885.
62 POA, *Annual Report*, 1896; 1897.
63 POA, *Annual Report*, 1884.
64 POA, *Annual Report*, 1900.
65 Hasci, *Second Home*, 29–37.
66 "Christian Charity," *Montreal Herald*, 19 October 1856.
67 Ibid.
68 For early organizations directed at improving the poor, see Huggins, *Protestants Against Poverty*; Rooke and Schnell, *Discarding the Asylum*; Smith-Rosenberg, *Religion and the Rise*; Stansell, *City of Women*.
69 *Women of Canada*, 323–4. For Toronto see Noble, "Class-ifying the Poor," and Pitsula, "The Relief of Poverty." Only a few of the Montreal COS Annual Reports have survived – see discussion below.
70 For a discussion of charity and philanthropy see Gross, "Giving in America," 30–1. Bremner's article "Scientific Philanthropy" remains helpful.
71 Valverde, *The Age of Light, Soap and Water*, 19. See also Valverde, "Moral Capital."
72 For two excellent treatments of the British COS see Humphreys, *Sin, Organized Charity and the Poor Law*, and Lewis, "The Boundary between Voluntary and Statutory."
73 Taylor, *Discourse Delivered before the Loyal Montreal Lodge*, 1843, 18.
74 Williams, *A Sermon Preached before the St. George's Society*, 1868.
75 See, among others, "The Poor in Montreal," *Montreal Witness*, 18 March 1848, 300; "Opportunity for the Poor," *The Anglo-American Magazine* 2 (1853): 575–6; "Relief of the Poor," *The Bystander* 13 (1883): 27–8; Rev. G.M. Meacham, "Hard Times, Their Causes and Remedies," *The Methodist Magazine* 39 (1894): 252–60.
76 "Discriminating Charity," *Canadian Illustrated News* 23 (1881): 266.
77 "Charity Organization System," *The Canadian Magazine* 6 (1896): 284.
78 Deutsch, *Women and the City*, 142.
79 LBS, *Annual Report*, 1861; 1857.
80 Industrial House of Refuge, *Constitution*, #10; *Annual Report*, 1855, 13.

81 LBS, *Minutes*, vol. 5, October 1854, 83–8.
82 Ibid.
83 Flanagan, *Seeing with Their Hearts*, 18–25.
84 LBS, *Minutes*, vol. 5, November 1854, 90.
85 POA, *Minutes*, vol. 5, November 1854, 55–6.
86 LBS, *Annual Report*, 1855.
87 AVM, *Minutes of Council Meetings*, vol. 56, 10 January 1855, 28; 21 February 1855, 10; *Report of the Treasurer*, 1855, 38; 1856, 34; Industrial House of Refuge, *Annual Report*, 1855, 8; 1856, 5.
88 Industrial House of Refuge, *Annual Report*, 1856, 6–7.
89 Ibid., 9–12.
90 LBS, *Minutes of Special Meeting*, vol. 5, April 1856, 149.
91 Ibid., 153–4.
92 LBS, *Annual Report*, 1874.
93 CHRS, Protestant House of Industry, "Annual Report, 1878," *Minute Book*, vol. 2, 14; "Half-Yearly Report, 1889," *Minute Book*, vol. 3, 189.
94 Protestant House of Industry, "Half-Yearly Report, 1881," *Minute Book*, vol. 2, 352.
95 Protestant House of Industry, "Annual Report, 1883," *Minute Book*, vol. 2, 433.
96 "Concentrating Charity. A Meeting to Inaugurate the 'Protestant Associated Charities of Montreal,'" *Montreal Witness*, 15 June 1883.
97 POA, *Minutes*, vol. 11, February 1886, 134–6. The PIH sent a letter. *The Gazette*, 9 February 1886.
98 For Julia Drummond's reform work, see Kirkland, "Mothering Citizens." Also Wolfe and Strathan, "Practical Idealism."
99 Morton, *Wisdom, Justice and Charity*, 31–3.
100 Mrs (Julia) Drummond, "Co-operation as Shown in Associated Charities," *Women Workers of Canada*, 57.
101 Ibid.
102 LAC, LCW, "Subcommittee on Charity Organization," in *Projects 1893–1958*.
103 Ibid.; Carrie M. Derrick, "The Origins of the COS of Montreal," in LAC, LCW, *Projects* (1919), 1–5; LAC, LCW, *Annual Report*, 1900, 9–10; 1901, 9; MUA, COS, Montreal, *Annual Report*, 1900, 3–5.
104 Morton, *Wisdom, Justice and Charity*, 67.
105 LCW, "Subcommittee on Charity Organization."
106 See Humphreys, *Sin, Organized Charity and the Poor Law*.
107 LBS, *Minutes*, vol. 12, January 1898, 67. The POA *Minutes* never mention the COS.
108 Rooke and Schnell, "The Rise and Decline," 31; Ginzberg, *Women and the Work*, 172–3.
109 COS, Montreal, *Annual Report*, 1900, 7, 18.

110 "Developing Self-Reliance. The Work of the Charity Organization Society," *Daily Witness*, 24 November 1900.

111 Ibid.; COS, Montreal, *Annual Report*, 1900, 7, 36.

112 COS, Montreal, *Annual Report*, 1900, 6, 18.

113 COS, Montreal, *Annual Report*, 1903–4, 2.

114 McLean, "Effects upon Private Charity," *NCCC*, 1901, 143.

115 Shepherd, "Genesis," 37, 38–9. The Annual Reports refer to their coordination with the city, the courts, and the police. COS, *Annual Report*, 1904, 8–9.

116 COS, Montreal, *Annual Report*, 1915–16, 30–33.

117 COS, Montreal, *Annual Report*, 1915–16, 33–9; 44–5.

118 Other historians have also found that, although rivalry between charities was rare, inter-agency cooperation was a twentieth-century phenomenon. See Holloran, *Boston's Wayward Children*, 41, and Purvey, "Alexandra Orphanage," 57–78.

119 LBS, *Minutes of Meetings*, vol. 9, May 1877, 44.

120 In the latter proposals, the Hervey Institute offered to take the girls and the LBS the boys. LBS, *Minutes*, vol. 4, December 1848, 80; vol. 5, October 1853, 36; April 1856, 151; vol. 10, February 1889, 260; October 1889, 283; November 1889, 287; vol. 12, October–November 1896, 14–16.

121 LBS, *Minutes*, vol. 10, January 1889, 257.

122 POA, *Minutes*, vol. 11, December 1889, 334.

123 Pedersen, "The Power of True Christian Women," 332–3.

124 Pedersen, "Providing a Women's Conscience," 198.

125 LBS, *Minutes*, vol. 11, January 1894, 83.

126 POA, *Minutes*, vol. 13, March 1899, 243; October 1899, 259.

127 LAC, LCW, "Questionnaire Submitted by the LCW and Covering Letter," *Scrapbook 1895–1899*, 49–51.

128 LBS, *Minutes*, vol. 12, November 1896, 17; Boys' Home, *Minutes*, vol. 2, July 1896, 31; September 1896, 34. The Hervey Institute took on this work after its move to Windsor Avenue in 1908.

129 LAC, LCW, "A Society to Be Incorporated to Look to Their Welfare," *Scrapbook 1895–1899*, 28.

130 "Destitute Children, Women's Council's Scheme for Legislation for Their Protection," *The Gazette*, 9 March 1899, in MLWC *Scrapbook 1895–1899*, 27. A Children's Aid Society was organized in 1908 in coordination with the SPWC but was not incorporated until 1946. LAC, SPWC papers, *History of Seventy-Five Years*; vol. 1, *Minute Book*, 96; vol. 12, Subject Files, *Letters Patent Incorporating "The Children's Aid Society of Montreal"*, 1946. See also Copp, "The Child Welfare Movement," and Douglas, "History of the SPWC," 29–30.

131 LBS, *Annual Report*, 1912; POA, *Annual Report*, 1912.

132 LBS, *Annual Reports*, 1900–21. The POA did not join the Children's Bureau until 1921. POA, *Minutes*, vol. 16, March 1921, 8.

EPILOGUE

1 LBS, *Minutes*, vol. 15, January 1920, 68; October 1921, 134, December 1921, 145.

2 The POA/H verified the experience of the Toronto Orphan's Home within a centralized funding body before it made its decision in terms of the Financial Federation. POA, *Minutes*, vol. 15, February 1920, 284; vol. 16, February–March 1922, 22–8.

3 For the MCSA's early history see MUA, Montreal Council of Social Agencies, *Origins, 1919–1921*, and MacLennan, *Red Feather in Montreal*.

4 MUA, Montreal Council of Social Agencies, Children's Bureau, "Annual Report," in *Welfare Work in Montreal, Federation Reports* (hereafter *WWM*), 1922, 32. Before it found a building, the Receiving Home was in the Day Nursery. The LBS had refused to take on this role. LBS, *Minutes*, vol. 15, June 1920, 54.

5 LBS, *Minutes*, vol. 15, October 1920, 59; November 1920, 60.

6 LBS, Minutes, vol. 15, April 1921, 113; September 1922, 187.

7 MUA, Montreal Council of Social Agencies, *A Study of the Children's Division Made by the Child Welfare League of America, February and March – 1924*, 4, 7–8.

8 Children's Bureau, "Annual Report," *WWM*, 1923, 64.

9 POA, *Minutes*, vol. 16, May 1924; Montreal Protestant Orphan's Home, "Annual Report," in *WWM*, 1924, 77; LBS, *Minutes*, vol. 16, April 1924, 24; LBS, "Annual Report," in *WWM*, 1924, 56. Both Societies discussed the possible sale of their buildings for years.

10 Children's Bureau, "Annual Report," *WWM*, 1922, 32.

11 LBS, *Minutes*, vol. 15, April–May 1921, 116–17; September 1921, 125; February 1922, 159; January 1923, 213.

12 The Bureau grudgingly accepted the idea of post-placement visits as long as they were done in the company of a social worker, but there is no evidence of these actually taking place. LBS, *Minutes*, vol. 16, Sept. 1924, 48; POA, *Minutes*, vol. 16, October 1924.

13 Children's Bureau, "Annual Report," *WWM*, 1924, 36.

14 The Committees note that they would have gladly admitted these cases. POA, *Minutes*, vol. 16, October 1929.

15 They provide many examples of this in their discussions with the Survey Committee investigating in 1935. LAC, Summerhill Homes, "Montreal Council of Social Agencies, Report of the Survey Committee, 1935, Section Two: A Report on Child Care and Protection," General Subject Files 14, no. 19.

16 POA, *Minutes*, vol. 17, May 1930, 15; LBS, *Minutes*, vol. 15, April 1923, 226.

17 The LBS made modifications to admit 35 boys instead of 25, but the City Inspector found the bathroom facilities inadequate. LBS, *Minutes*, vol. 16, October–November 1926, 77, 81; March 1927, 125.

18 For references to these requests and renovations, see Children's Bureau, "Annual

Report," WWM, 1927–35; LBS, "Annual Report," WWM, 1922–35; POH, "Annual Report," WWM, 1922–35; LBS, *Minutes*, 1922–35; POA, *Minutes*, 1922–35.

19 LBS, *Minutes*, vol. 16, February–March 1924, 6, 13; vol. 17, June 1931; POA, *Minutes*, vol. 17, February 1931, 45.

20 POA, *Minutes*, vol. 17, April 1931, 53; April 1931, 54; May 1931, 56.

21 Ibid., September–October 1934, 214–29; December 1934, 251–5.

22 Ibid., November–December 1930, 28–30, 34.

23 Morton, *Wisdom, Justice, and Charity*, 134, 161.

24 For the MCSA's efforts during the Depression and the work of the Survey Committee, see McLennan, "Charity and Change."

25 MUA, Montreal Council of Social Agencies, "Report of the Survey Committee, 1935, Section Two"; LAC, Summerhill Homes, "MCSA, Survey Committee Report on Child Care and Protection."

26 LAC, Summerhill Homes, "Stenographic Report of the Meetings with the Functional Committee, (POH) 1935." Subject Files 14, no. 7.

27 Their response is outlined in their interviews with the Functional Committee mandated to discuss the Report with the various agencies and make follow-up recommendations. "Stenographic Report of the Meetings with the Functional Committee (POH)"; "Stenographic Report of the Proceedings of the Meeting (LBS)," 14, no. 19.

28 LAC, Summerhill Homes, "Stenographic Report of Proceedings of Adjourned Meeting, (POH) 1935," Subject Files 14, no. 7, 84.

29 Ibid.

30 They were able to do this because their Endowment Fund made them less dependent on Federation grants than was the LBS. They also considered remaining in the Federation but leaving the Bureau and hiring a social worker to do admissions but not discharges. POA, *Minutes*, vol. 18, January 1936, 56–7; June 1936, 107.

31 LAC, Summerhill Homes, "Amalgamation of the Montreal Ladies Benevolent and the Montreal Protestant Orphan Home," Subject Files 16, no. 12–13.

Bibliography

PRIMARY SOURCES

Archival Sources

Anglican Diocese of Montreal (ADA)

Andrews Home, papers (reports).

Christ Church Cathedral Montreal, papers (reports, budgets).

The Church Home, papers (constitution, history, minutes, reports).

Proceedings of the Annual Synod of the Diocese of Montreal, 1861–1900. Montreal: Lovell.

St George's (Anglican Church). *Poor Fund Annual Reports*. 1851–1900.

Virr, Richard. *Andrews Home. Ninety Years of Service*. Unpublished paper, 1985.

Archives municipales de la ville de Montréal (AVM)

Fonds service des finances et du contrôle budgétaire.

Annual Reports of the City Treasurer/Auditor of the City of Montreal for the Civic Year, 1851–1899, VM002–Z–1–5.

Fonds Centre de documentation: Publications internes et externes.

Laroque, A.B. *Report of the Medical Officers of Health of the City of Montreal for the Year Ending 31st December 1875*, CA M001 XCD00–P4822.

Fonds Conseil de ville de Montréal (1833–2001).

Série 12 – Bureau du Maire (1854–1994). *Mayor's Inaugural Addresses, Valedictory Addresses* (1871–1899), VM001–12.

Série 10 – Procès-verbaux du Conseil de ville de Montréal. *Minutes of the Council Meetings*, 1850–1865, VM001–10.

Série 17 – Commissions spéciales et comités spéciaux – Dossier 22 Maison de l'industrie. *Minutes of the Special Committees, House of Industry*, VM001–17–D022.

Fonds Comité de santé – Bureau de santé (1832–1949).

Enfants sans tutelle, 1892–1915, VM045–3.

Bibliothèque et Archives nationales du Québec (BANQ)

BANQ–numérique.

BANQ–Généologie.

Archives nationales du Québec, Montréal (ANQ–M)

Fonds Conférence de l'Église Unie du Canada (P603).

S2, SS14, Montreal American Presbyterian Church, Montreal.

S2, SS40, Montreal St Gabriel's Street Presbyterian Church.

S2, SS96, Montreal Erskine Presbyterian Church.

Archives nationales du Québec, Québec (ANQ–Q)

Fonds Sécrétariat de la province (E4).

Registry of letters of the Provincial Secretary (Quebec).

Centre d'histoire des régulations sociales (CHRS), UQAM

"Archives MPHIR / Grace Dart, Documents administratifs, no boîte 10226."

Digital copies of Montreal Protestant House of Industry and Refuge papers, 1863–1959, and the Industrial Rooms papers, 1869–1904.

(Original documents are held at the Centre de soins prolongée / Grace Dart Extended Care Centre's private collection.)

Library Archives Canada (Collections) (LAC)

Canada State Books. vol. G, Reel C–113, July–November 1847.

Joseph Mackay Family fonds – MG 24 D 115 (R3512–0–9–E).

Summerhill Homes – MG 28 I 388 (R4930–0–7–E).

Montreal Ladies' Benevolent Society. Vols. 1, 2, 4, 5, 6, 21, 22, 23, 24. 1832–1936.

Montreal Protestant Orphan Asylum. Vols. 6, 7, 8, 11, 12, 13, 14, 25. 1822–1936.

Weredale House – MG 28 I 405 (R5583–0–3–E).

The Boys' Home of Montreal. Vols. 1, 2, 4, 7. 1868–1910.

Montreal Local Council of Women. *Annual Reports*. 1894–1900. MG 28 I 311 (R2857–4–2–E).

National Council of Women of Canada. *Annual Reports*. 1893–1900. MG 28 I 125 (R7584–0–0–E).

Society for the Protection of Women and Children, Montreal, Quebec. Sundry. MG 28 I 129 (R2726–0–4–E).

Young Women's Christian Association of Montreal. *Annual Reports*. 1876–1900. MG 28 I 198 (R4957–0–4–E).

McCord Museum of Canadian History (MM)

Old Brewery Mission papers #P688.

McGill University Archives / Osler Library / Rare Books and Special Collections (MUA)

Charity Organization Society, Montreal. *Reports.* 1900–03.
Montreal Council of Social Agencies fonds, MG2076.
Montreal Day Nursery, *Reports*, 1897–99, 1903–05.
Montreal Foundling and Baby Hospital, *Reports*, 1897–1911.

St John the Evangelist Anglican Church, Montreal – private collection (SJEAC)

Centenary Book of the Parish of St. John the Evangelist. In-house publication.
St Margaret's Home for Aged Women. Seventy-Five Years, 1883–1958. In-house publication.

Welcome Hall Mission – private collection (WHM)

Welcome Hall Mission, *Annual Reports*, 1893–1911.

Newspapers and Periodicals

Anglo-American Magazine
The Bystander
Canadian Illustrated News
The Canadian Methodist Magazine / The Methodist Magazine / The Methodist Magazine and Review
The Christian Mirror
The Christian Guardian
The Congregationalist and Canadian Independent
The Diocesan Theological College Magazine
The Dominion Churchman
The Dominion Illustrated / Monthly
Harper's New Monthly Magazine
Montreal Gazette
Montreal Herald
Montreal Witness / Daily Witness
Mother Assistant
Presbyterian Record for the Dominion of Canada
Rose-Belford's Canadian Monthly and National Review

Institutional Annual Reports

Collection Canadiana (CIHM)
Crescent Street Presbyterian Church, 1878–1900.
Fresh Air Fund, 1888–89, 1894.

The Female Home, 1870–79.
Irish Protestant Benevolent Society of Montreal, 1883, 1889, 1895, 1898.
Mackay Institute for Deaf-Mutes and the Blind, 1870–97.
Montreal Auxiliary Bible Society, 1857–91.
Montreal Diet Dispensary, 1884–87, 1890, 1894, 1897–99.
Montreal Home and School of Industry / Hervey Institute, 1855, 1859, 1863–64, 1868–70, 1889.
Montreal Sailor's Institute, 1876–96.
Murray Bay Convalescent Home, 1874–76, 1877–85.
Protestant Home for Friendless Women, 1876–78, 1888.
Protestant Infant's Home, 1871–79, 1885–88, 1893–98.
Protestant Industrial House of Refuge, 1855, 1856.
St Andrew's Society of Montreal, 1857, 1867–1900.
St George's Society of Montreal, 1876–77, 1903.
St Paul's Church Montreal, 1879–1900.
Women's Protective Immigration Society, 1888–1900.

Other Primary Sources

Alden, Lyman. "Institutions for Children. The Practical Details of Their Management." *Proceedings of the National Council of Charities and Corrections*. Grand Rapids, MI: 1896.

Atherton, William Henry. *Montreal, 1835–1914*. 2 vols. Montreal: Clarke, 1914.

Brothwick, J. Douglas. *History and Biographical Gazeteer of Montreal to the Year 1892*. Montreal: Lovell, 1892.

Campbell, Reverend Robert. *A History of the Scotch Presbyterian Church St. Gabriel's Street Montreal*. Montreal: W. Drysdale, 1887. (*CIHM*)

Census of Canada / Lower Canada. 1825, 1831, 1844, 1851/52, 1860/61, 1871, 1881, 1891, 1901.

Drummond, Mrs (Julia). "Co-operation as Shown in Associated Charities," *Women Workers of Canada. Being a Report of the Proceedings of the First Annual Meeting and Conference of the National Council of Women of Canada*, 1894.

Easton, Reverend Robert. *A Sermon Delivered Before the Members of the Female Benevolent Society, in Montreal, September 8, 1816*. Montreal: Lovell, 1816.

General History of the Protestant Infants' Home (later the Protestant Foster Home Centre) 1869–1951, privately published.

Gibbs, Elizabeth, et al., eds. *Debates of the Legislative Assembly of United Canada 1841–1867*. Montreal: Centre de recherche en histoire économique du Canada Français, 1978, 1981, 1991.

Kelso, J.J. "Neglected and Friendless Children." *The Canadian Magazine* 2 (1894): 213–16.

Lighthall, George R. *A Short History of the American Presbyterian Church of Montreal 1823 to 1923*. Montreal: [s.n.], 1923.

The Lovell's Directory, Main Series. 1842–1900.

McCord, Mrs A. *Historical Sketch of the Montreal Protestant Orphan Asylum from Its Formation on the 16th of February 1822 to the Present Day.* Montreal: John Lovell, 1860. Reprinted in POA, *Annual Report,* 1860, 7–12.

McLean, Francis H. "Effects upon Private Charity of the Absence of All Public Relief." *Proceedings of the National Council of Charities and Corrections.* Washington, DC: 1901.

Morgan, Henry James. *The Canadian Men and Women of the Times. A Handbook of Canadian Biography of Living Characters.* Toronto: William Briggs, 1912.

Narrative of the Proceedings of the St. Andrew's Society of Montreal from Its Formation on the 9th March, 1835 until the 1st January, 1844. Montreal: J.C. Beckett, 1855. (CIHM)

Pearce, N.C., and Mrs Alister Mitchell. *A History of the Montreal Ladies' Benevolent Society 1815–1920.* Montreal: privately printed, c. 1920.

Philanthropy, Care of Our Destitute and Criminal Population. Series of Letters Published in the Montreal Gazette. Montreal: Salter & Ross, 1857. (CIHM)

Proceedings of the Canadian Conference of Charities and Corrections. 1898–1903.

Proceedings of the National Conference of Charities and Correction (NCCC). 1882–1901.

"Public Accounts for the Province of Canada and Indexes." In *Journals of the Legislative Assembly for the United Canadas.* 1840–67.

"Public Accounts …" *Sessional Papers of the Legislature of Quebec,* no. 1. 1867–1900.

"Reports of the Inspector of Prisons, Asylums …" *Canada, Sessional Papers.* 1861–67.

"Report of the Inspectors of Prisons, Asylums …" *Sessional Papers of the Legislature of Quebec.* 1869–1900.

Statutes of Canada / Province of Canada / Statutes de bas Canada. 1818–1849.

Statutes of the Province of Quebec. 1867–1912.

St Andrew's Society of Montreal. *A Summary of the First Fifty Years Transactions.* Montreal: McQueen & Corneil, 1886. (CIHM)

St George's Society of Montreal. "Historical Sketch 1834–1903." In *Sixty-Ninth Annual Report of the St. George's Society of Montreal.* Montreal: James H. Oxley, 1904.

A Story of the Old Brewery Mission. Montreal: 1903.

Taylor, W. *Discourse Delivered before the Loyal Montreal Lodge of the Manchester Unity of the I. O. of O. F. at Their First Anniversary, November 7, 1843.* (CIHM)

Williams, J.W. *A Sermon Preached before the St. George's Society in the Cathedral, Quebec, 23rd April 1868.* (CIHM)

Women Workers of Canada. Being a Report of the Proceedings of the First Annual Meeting and Conference of the National Council of Women of Canada. 1894.

Women of Canada. Their Life and Work. Montreal: National Council of Women of Canada, 1900.

Interviews

Conversation with D.K., Montreal, November 2003.
Conversation with J., Montreal, 1974.
Conversation with Muriel Doherty, Montreal, 2014.

SECONDARY SOURCES

Adamoski, Robert. "'Charity Is One Thing and the Administration of Justice Is Another': Law and Politics of Familial Regulation in Early-Twentieth-Century British Columbia." In *Regulating Lives: Historical Essays on the State, Society, the Individual and the Law*, edited by John McLaren, Robert Menzies, and Dorothy Chunn, 145–69. Vancouver: UBC Press, 2002.

Adams, Annemarie. *Architecture in the Family Way: Doctors, Houses, and Women, 1870–1900*. Montreal and Kingston: McGill-Queen's University Press, 1996.

Adams, Annmarie, and David Theodore. "Designing for 'the Little Convalescents': Children's Hospitals in Toronto and Montreal, 1875–2006." *Canadian Bulletin of Medical History* 19, no. 1 (2002): 201–43.

Alexander, Kristine. "Can the Girl Guide Speak? The Perils and Pleasures of Looking for Children's Voices in Archival Research." In *Bringing Children and Youth into Canadian History*, edited by Gleason and Myers, 143–50.

– *Guiding Modern Girls: Girlhood, Empire, and Internationalism in the 1920s and 1930s*. Toronto: UBC Press, 2017.

Ames, Herbert Brown. *The City below the Hill*. 1897. Reprinted in Toronto: University of Toronto Press, 1972.

Anderson, Michael. *Family Structure in Nineteenth Century Lancashire*. London: Cambridge University Press, 1971.

Aranguiz, Marcela. *Vagabonds et sans abris à Montréal: perception et prise en charge de l'errance 1840–1925*. Montreal: Collection "Études et documents" RCHTQ, 12, 2000.

Ashby, LeRoy. *Endangered Children: Dependency, Neglect and Abuse in American History*. New York: Twayne, 1997.

– *Saving the Waifs: Reformers and Dependent Children, 1890–1917*. Philadelphia: Temple, 1984.

Askeland, Lori. "Informal Adoption, Apprentices, and Indentured Children in the Colonial Era and the New Republic, 1605–1850." In *Children and Youth in Adoption, Orphanages, and Foster Care: A Historical Handbook and Guide*, edited by Lori Askeland, 3–17. Westport, CT: Greenwood Press, 2006.

Bagnell, Kenneth. *The Little Immigrants: The Orphans Who Came to Canada*. Toronto: Dundurn Press, 2001.

Baillargeon, Denyse. *Brève histoire des femmes au Québec*. Montreal: Boréal, 2012.
– "Fréquenter les Gouttes de lait. L'expérience des mères Montréalaises 1910–1965." *Revue d'histoire de l'Amérique française* 50, no. 1 (Summer 1996): 29–66.
– "Orphans in Quebec. On the Margins of Which Family?" In *Mapping the Margins. The Family and Social Discipline in Canada, 1700–1975*, edited by Nancy Christie and Michael Gauvreau, 305–26. Montreal and Kingston: McGill-Queen's University Press, 2004.
Baines, Carol T. "Women's Professions and a Ethic of Care." In *Women's Caring*, edited by Baines, McEvans, and Neysmith, 23–46.
Baines, Carol T., Patricia McEvans, and Shelia M. Neysmith, eds. *Women's Caring: Feminist Perspectives in Social Welfare*. Toronto: Oxford University Press, 1998.
Bamman, Haley P. "The Ladies Benevolent Society of Hamilton, Ontario: Form and Function in Mid-Nineteenth Century Urban Philanthropy." In *The Canadian Social History Project*, Interim Report, no. 4, edited by Michael B. Katz, 162–217. Toronto: Department of History and Philosophy of Education, Ontario Institute for Studies in Education, 1972.
Beckert, Sven. "The Bourgeois Institution Builders." In *American Bourgeoisie*, edited by Beckert and Rosenbaum, 103–17.
Beckert, Sven, and Julia B. Rosenbaum, eds. *American Bourgeoisie: Distinction and Identity in the Nineteenth Century*. New York: Palgrave MacMillan, 2010.
Bellingham, Bruce. "Institution and Family: An Alternative View of Nineteenth-Century Child Saving." *Social Problems* 33, no. 6 (October–December 1986): S33–S57.
– "The 'Unspeakable Blessing': Street Children, Reform Rhetoric, and Misery in Early Industrial Capitalism." *Politics & Society* 12, no. 3 (1983): 303–30.
– "Waifs and Strays: Child Abandonment, Foster Care, and Families in Mid-Nineteenth Century New York." In *The Uses of Charity*, edited by Peter Mandler, 124–60.
Bennett, Paul W. "Taming 'Bad Boys' of the 'Dangerous Class': Child Rescue and Restraint at the Victoria Industrial School 1887–1935." *Histoire sociale / Social History* 21, no. 31 (May 1988): 71–96.
Berebitsky, Julie. *Like Our Very Own: Adoption and the Changing Culture of Motherhood, 1851–1950*. Lawrence, KS: University Press of Kansas, 2000.
Bliss, Michael. *Plague: A Story of Smallpox in Montreal*. Toronto: Harper Collins, 1991.
Boylan, Anne M. "Timid Girls, Venerable Widows and Dignified Matrons: Life Cycle Patterns among Organized Women in New York and Boston, 1797–1840." *American Quarterly* 38 (Winter 1986): 779–97.
– "Women in Groups: An Analysis of Women's Benevolent Organizations in New York and Boston, 1797–1840." *Journal of American History* 71 (December 1984): 497–523.
Bradbury, Bettina. "Canadian Children Who Lived with One Parent in 1901." In *Bringing Children and Youth into Canadian History*, edited by Gleason and Myers, 35–64.
– "The Fragmented Family: Family Strategies in the Face of Death, Illness, and Poverty,

Montreal, 1860–1885." In *Childhood and Family in Canadian History*, edited by Parr, 109–28.

– "Gender at Work at Home: Family Decisions, the Labour Market, and Girls' Contributions to the Family Economy." In *Canadian Family History: Selected Readings*, edited by Bradbury, 177–98. Toronto: Copp Clark Pitman, 1992.

– "Surviving as a Widow in 19th-Century Montreal." *Urban History Review* 17, no. 3 (February 1989): 148–60.

– *Wife to Widow: Lives, Laws, and Politics in Nineteenth-Century Montreal*. Vancouver and Toronto: University of British Columbia Press, 2011.

– "Women at the Hustings: Gender, Citizenship and the Montreal By-Elections of 1832." In *Rethinking Canada: The Promise of Women's History*, 5th ed., edited by Mona Gleason and Adele Perry, 73–94. Toronto: Oxford University Press, 2006.

– *Working Families: Age, Gender, and Daily Survival in Industrializing Montreal*. Toronto: McClelland & Stewart Inc., 1993.

Bradbury, Bettina, Peter Gossage, Evelyne Kolish, and Alan Stewart. "Property and Marriage: The Law and the Practice in Early Nineteenth-Century Montreal." *Histoire sociale / Social History* 26, no. 51 (May 1993): 9–39.

Brenmer, Robert H. "Scientific Philanthropy, 1873–93." The *Social Service Review* 30, no. 2 (June 1956): 168–73.

Bullen, John. "Children of the Industrial Age: Children, Work, and Welfare in Late Nineteenth-Century Ontario." PhD diss. Ottawa: University of Ottawa, 1989.

– "J.J. Kelso and the 'New' Child Savers. The Genesis of the Children's Aid Movement in Ontario." *Ontario History* 82, no. 2 (June 1990): 107–28.

Burban, Christelle. "Les origines institutionnelles de la protection de l'enfance au Québec: L'école d'industrie de Notre-Dame de Montfort (1883–1913)." Master's thesis. Rennes, France: Université de Rennes, 1996.

Burgess, Joanne. "Work, Family and Community: Montreal Leather Craftsmen 1790–1831." PhD diss. Montreal: Université du Québec à Montréal, 1986.

Cahn, Naomi. "Perfect Substitutes or the Real Thing?" In *Families by Law: An Adoption Reader*, edited by Naomi R. Cahn and Joan Heifetz Hollinger, 19–24. New York: New York University Press, 2004.

Cale, Michelle. "Girls and the Perception of Sexual Danger in the Victorian Reformatory System." *History* 78, no. 253 (June 1993): 201–17.

Canadian Book of the Road. Montreal: Reader's Digest Association, 1979.

Carp, E. Wayne. "Introduction: A Historical Overview of American Adoption." In *Adoption in America: Historical Perspectives*, edited by E. Wayne Carp, 1–26. Ann Arbor, MI: University of Michigan Press, 2002.

– "Two Cheers for Orphanages." *Reviews in American History* 24, no. 2 (June 1996): 277–84.

Cavallo, Dominic. *Muscles and Morals. Organized Playgrounds and Urban Reform, 1888–1920*. Philadelphia: University of Pennsylvania Press, 1981.

Cavallo, Sandra. "The Motivations of Benefactors: An Overview of Approaches to the Study of Charity." In *Medicine and Charity before the Welfare State*, edited by Jonathan Barry and Colin James, 46–62. New York: Routledge, 1991.

Chambers-Schiller, Lee. "Single Women: Family and Vocation among Nineteenth-Century Reformers." In *Woman's Being, Woman's Place: Female Identity and Vocation in American History*, edited by Mary Kelly, 338–44. Boston: G.K. Hall, 1979.

Charest-Bourdon, Noémie. "Qui va Payer pour les Maladies Indigents? La 'Philanthropie d'État,' du sou de pauvre à l'assistance publique au Québec (1905–1930)." Master's thesis. Montreal: UQAM, 2018.

Charest-Bourdon, Noémie, and Martin Petitclerc. "Le 'sou du pauvre', les municipalités, l'indigence et l'accès aux soins hospitaliers au début du XXe siècle à Montréal." *Histoire sociale / Social History* 51, no. 103 (May 2018): 75–97.

Chen, Xiaoben. *Tending the Gardens of Citizenship: Child Saving in Toronto, 1880s–1920s.* Toronto: University of Toronto Press, 2005.

Christie, Nancy. *Engendering the State: Family, Work, and Welfare in Canada.* Toronto: University of Toronto Press, 2000.

Christie, Nancy, and Michael Gauvreau. *A Full-Orbed Christianity: The Protestant Churches and Social Welfare in Canada, 1900–1940.* Montreal and Kingston: McGill-Queen's University Press, 1996.

Chureau, Damien. "La Maison d'industrie de Montréal (1836–1870)." Master's thesis. Angers, France: Université d'Angers, 1996.

Clarke, Nic. "Sacred Daemons: Exploring British Columbian Society's Perception of 'Mentally Deficient' Children, 1870–1930." In *Bringing Children and Youth into Canadian History*, edited by Gleason and Myers, 288–306.

Clement, Priscilla Ferguson. "Families and Foster Care: Philadelphia in the Late Nineteenth Century." *Social Service Review* 53, no. 3 (September 1979): 406–20.

– "Nineteenth-Century Welfare Policy, Programs, and Poor Women: Philadelphia as a Case Study." *Feminist Studies* 18, no. 1 (Spring 1992): 35–58.

Cmeil, Kenneth. *A Home of Another Kind: One Chicago Orphanage and the Tangle of Child Welfare.* Chicago and London: The University of Chicago Press, 1995.

Cohen, Yolande. "De la nutrition des pauvres malades : L'histoire du *Montreal Diet Dispensary* de 1910 à 1940." *Histoire sociale / Social History* 41, no. 81 (May 2008): 133–63.

– *Femmes Philanthropes: Catholiques, protestantes et juives dans les organisations caritatives au Québec (1880–1945).* Montreal: Les Presses de l'Université de Montréal, 2010.

Collard, E.A. *The Irish Way: The History of the Irish Protestant Benevolent Society.* Montreal: Price-Patterson, 1992.

– *Montreal Yesterdays.* Toronto: Longmans, 1963.

Colley, Linda. *Britons: Forging the Nation 1707–1837.* Revised ed. New Haven, CT, and London: Yale University Press, 2012.

Comacchio, Cynthia R. *Nations Are Built of Babies: Saving Ontario's Mothers and Children 1900–1940.* Montreal and Kingston: McGill-Queen's University Press, 1993.

Compton Brouwer, Ruth. "Transcending the 'Unacknowledged Quarantine': Putting Religion into English Canadian Women's History." *Journal of Canadian Studies* 27, no. 3 (Fall 1992): 47–61.

Cook, Sharon Ann. "'A Quiet Place … to Die': Ottawa's First Protestant Old Age Homes for Women and Men." *Ontario History* 81, no. 1 (March 1989): 25–40.

Cooper, John. *The Blessed Communion: The Origins and Histories of the Diocese of Montreal, 1760–1960*. Montreal: The Archives Committee of the Diocese of Montreal, 1960.

Copp, Terry. *Anatomy of Poverty: The Condition of the Working Class in Montreal, 1897–1929*. Toronto: McClelland and Stewart, 1974.

– "The Child Welfare Movement in Montreal to 1920." In *Social Welfare, 1850–1950, Argentina, Australia and Canada Compared*, edited by D.C.M. Platt, 45–59. London: MacMillan Press, 1989.

Corbett, Gail. *Barnardo Children in Canada*. Peterborough, ON: Woodland, 1981.

– *Nation Builders: Barnardo children in Canada*. Toronto: Dundurn Press, 2002.

Cott, Nancy. *The Bonds of Womanhood: "Woman's Sphere" in New England, 1780–1835*. New Haven, CT: Yale University Press, 1977.

Craven, Paul. "The Law of Master and Servant in Mid-Nineteenth-Century Ontario." In *Essays in the History of Canadian Law*, vol. 1, edited by David H. Flaherty, 175–211. Toronto: The Osgoode Society, 1981.

Cross, Suzanne D. "The Irish in Montreal, 1867–1896." Master's thesis. Montreal: McGill University, 1969.

– "The Neglected Majority: The Changing Role of Women in 19th Century Montreal." In *The Neglected Majority: Essays in Canadian Women's History*, edited by Susan Trofimenkoff and Alison Prentice, 66–86. Toronto: McClelland and Stewart, 1977.

Crowther, M.A. *The Workhouse System 1834–1929: The History of an English Institution*. Athens, GA: The University of Georgia Press, 1981.

Cumbler, John. "The Politics of Charity: Gender and Class in Late 19th Century Charity Policy." *Journal of Social History* 14, no. 1 (Fall 1980): 99–110.

Cunningham, Hugh. "Introduction." In *Charity, Philanthropy and Reform*, edited by Cunningham and Innes, 1–14.

Cunningham, Hugh, and Joanna Innes, eds. *Charity, Philanthropy and Reform: From the 1690s to 1850*. New York: St. Martin's Press, 1998.

Curtis, Bruce. *Building the Educational State: Pedagogy, Punishment and Popular Resistance in Canada West, 1850–1871*. London, ON: Althouse Press, 1988.

– "The Playground in Nineteenth-Century Ontario: Theory and Practice." *Material History Bulletin* 22 (Fall 1985): 21–30.

Daigle, Johanne, and Dale Gilbert. "Un modèle d'économie sociale mixte: la dynamique des services sociaux à l'enfance dans la ville de Québec, 1850–1950." *Recherche sociographiques* 49, no. 1 (January–April 2008): 113–47.

D'Allaire, Micheline. *Les Communautés religieuses de Montréal, Tome I: Les communau-*

tés religieuses et l'assistance sociale à Montréal 1695–1900. Montreal: Éditions du Méridien, 1997.

Davidoff, Leonore. *The Best Circles: Society Etiquette and the Season*. London: Croom Helm, 1973.

– "Class and Gender in Victorian England." In *Sex and Class in Women's History*, edited by Judith Newton, Mary Ryan, and Judith Walkowitz, 17–71. London: Routledge and Kegan Paul, 1983.

– "Regarding 'Some Old Husbands' Tales': Public and Private in Feminist History." In *Feminism, the Public and the Private*, edited by Joan B. Landes, 164–94. Oxford, UK: Oxford University Press, 1998.

Davidoff, Leonore, and Catherine Hall. *Family Fortunes: Men and Women of the English Middle Class, 1780–1850*. London: Hutchinson, 1987.

De la Cour, Lykke, Cecilia Morgan, and Mariana Valverde. "Gender Regulation and State Formation in Nineteenth-Century Canada." In *Colonial Leviathan: State Formation in Mid-Nineteenth-Century Canada*, edited by Allan Greer and Ian Radforth, 163–91. Toronto: University of Toronto Press, 1992.

Dean, Mitchell. *The Constitution of Poverty: Toward a Genealogy of Liberal Governance*. London: Routledge, 1991.

Dekker, Jeroen. *The Will to Change the Child: Re-education Homes for Children at Risk in Nineteenth Century Western Europe*. New York: Peter Lang, 2001.

Deutsch, Sarah. *Women and the City: Gender, Space and Power in Boston, 1870–1940*. New York: Oxford University Press, 2000.

Dictionary of Canadian Biography. Toronto: University of Toronto Press/Université Laval. www.biographi.ca/en/index.php.

Dillon, Lisa. *The Shady Side of Fifty: Age and Old Age in Late Victorian Canada and the United States*. Montreal and Kingston: McGill-Queen's University Press, 2008.

Douglas, Muriel H. "History of the Society for the Protection of Women and Children from 1822 to 1966." Master's thesis. Montreal: McGill University, 1967.

Dru Stanley, Amy. "Beggars Can't Be Choosers: Compulsion and Contract in Postbellum America." *The Journal of American History* 78 (March 1992): 1265–93.

Dupont-Bouchat, Marie-Sylvie, Éric Pierre, Jean-Marie Fecteau, Jean Trépanier, Jean-Jacques Petit, Bernard Schnapper, and Jeroen Dekker, eds. *Enfance et justice au XIXe siècle: essais d'histoire comparée de la protection de l'enfance, 1820–1914 (France, Belgique, Pays-Bas, Canada)*. Paris: Presses universitaires de France, 2001.

Dyhouse, Carol. "Mothers and Daughters in the Middle-Class Home c. 1870–1914." In *Labour and Love: Women's Experience of Home and Family*, edited by Jane Lewis, 27–47. Oxford, UK: Basil Blackwell, 1986.

Elliott, Doris Williams. *The Angel Out of the House: Philanthropy and Gender in Nineteenth-Century England*. Charlottesville, VA: University of Virginia Press, 2002.

Erickson, Kristofer A. "Montreal's Great Experiment: Poverty and the Montreal

Protestant House of Industry and Refuge, 1863–1901." Master's thesis. Kingston, ON: Queen's University, 2003.

Errington, Elizabeth Jane. *Wives and Mothers, Schoolmistress and Scullery Maids: Working Women in Upper Canada, 1790–1840*. Montreal and Kingston: McGill-Queen's University Press, 1995.

Fahrni, Magda. *Household Politics: Montreal Families and Postwar Reconstruction*. Toronto: University of Toronto Press, 2005.

– *Of Kith and Kin: A History of Families in Canada*. Don Mills, ON: Oxford University Press, 2022.

Fecteau, Jean-Marie. "L'Autre visage de la liberté: Dimensions historiques de la vulnérabilité dans la logique libérale." In *Penser la vulnérabilité: Visages de la fragilisation du sociale*, edited by Vivianne Chatel and Shirley Roy, 37–49. Quebec: Presses de l'Université du Québec, 2008.

– "Between the Old Order and Modern Times: Poverty, Criminality, and Power in Quebec, 1791–1840." In *Essays in the History of Canadian Law*, vol. 5, *Crime and Criminal Justice*, edited by Jim Phillips, Tina Loo, and Susan Lewthwaite, 293–323. Toronto: University of Toronto Press, 1994.

– "Un cas de force majeure: Le développement des mesures d'assistance publique à Montréal au tournant du siècle." *Lien Social et Politiques – RIAC, Généalogies de l'État-providence* 33 (Spring 1995): 107–13.

– "La construction d'un espace social: les rapports de l'Église et de l'État et la question de l'assistance publique au Québec dans la seconde moitié du XIXe siècle." In *L'histoire de la culture et de l'imprimé: Hommages à Claude Galarneau*, edited by Yvan Lamonde and Gilles Gallichan, 61–90. Quebec: Les presses de l'Université Laval, 1996.

– "État et associationnisme au XIXe siècle québécois." In *Colonial Leviathan: State Formation in Mid-Nineteenth-Century Canada*, edited by Allan Greer and Ian Radforth, 134–62. Toronto: University of Toronto Press, 1992.

– "L'histoire comme expérience de la violence." *Revue d'histoire de l'enfance "irrégulière"* 14 (2012): 15–28.

– *Un nouvel ordre des choses: la pauvreté, le crime, l'État au Québec, de la fin du XVIIIe siècle à 1840*. Outremont, QC: VLB Éditeur, 1989.

– *The Pauper's Freedom: Crime and Poverty in Nineteenth-Century Quebec*. Translated by Peter Feldstein (originally *La liberté du pauvre*, 2004). Montreal and Kingston: McGill-Queen's University Press, 2017.

Fecteau, Jean-Marie, and Janice Harvey. "From Agents to Institutions: An Historical Dialectic of Interactionism and Power Relations." In Fecteau and Harvey, *La régulation sociale entre l'acteur et l'institution*, 16–28 [French version 3–15].

– "Montreal's Network of Social Regulation." In *Montreal: The History of a North American City*, vol. 1, edited by Dany Fougère and Rod MacLeod, 670–708. Montreal and Kingston: McGill-Queen's University Press, 2017.

– eds. *La régulation sociale entre l'acteur et l'institution: Pour une problématique historique de l'interaction / Agency and Institutions in Social Regulation: Toward an Historical Understanding of* their *Interaction*. Sainte-Foy, QC: Presse de l'Université du Québec, 2005.

Fecteau, Jean-Marie, Sylvie Ménard, Véronique Strimelle, and Jean Trépanier. "Une politique de l'enfance délinquante et en danger : La mise en place des écoles de réforme et d'industrie au Québec (1840–1873)." *Crime, Histoire et Sociétés* 1, no. 2 (1998): 75–110.

Fecteau, Jean-Marie, and Éric Vaillancourt. "Charity in the City." In *The Sulpicians of Montreal: A History of Power and Discretion, 1657–2007*, edited by Olivier Hubert, 255–78. Montreal: Wilson & Lafleur, 2013.

– "The Saint Vincent de Paul Society and the Catholic Charitable System in Quebec (1846–1921)." In *The Churches and Social Order in Nineteenth- and Twentieth-Century Canada*, edited by Michael Gauvreau and Ollivier Hubert, 195–224. Montreal and Kingston: McGill-Queen's University Press, 2006.

Ferretti, Lucia. "Du 'devoir de charité' au 'droit à l'aide publique': la naissance de l'État-providence au Québec." *Les Conférences Gérard-Parizeau*, 11th conference, Montreal, 5 October 2011, Université de Montréal.

Fingard, Judith. *The Dark Side of Life in Victorian Halifax*. Porters Lake, NS: Pottersfield Press, 1989.

– "Evangelical Social Work in Canada: Salvationists and Sailor Friends, 1890–1920." In *Social Welfare, 1850–1950, Argentina, Australia and Canada Compared*, edited by D.C.M. Platt, 25–44. London: MacMillan Press, 1989.

Flanagan, Maureen A. *Seeing with Their Hearts: Chicago Women and the Vision of* the *Good City, 1871–1933*. Princeton, NJ: Princeton University Press, 2002.

Fraser, Nancy, and Linda Gordon. "A Geneology of Dependency: Tracing a Keyword of the U.S. Welfare State." *Signs: Journal of Women in Culture and Society* 19, no. 21 (1994): 309–36.

Garland, David. *Punishment and Welfare: A History of Penal Strategies*. Aldershot, UK: Gower, 1985.

Garner, John. *The Franchise and Politics in British North America 1755–1867*. Toronto: University of Toronto Press, 1969.

Gauvreau, Danielle, Sherry Olson, and Patricia Thorton. "The Harsh Welcome of an Industrial City: Immigrant Women in Montreal, 1880–1900." *Histoire sociale / Social History* 40, no. 80 (November 2007): 345–80.

Gauvreau, Michael. "Forging a New Space for Lay Male Piety: St. Vincent de Paul Societies in Urban Quebec and Ontario, 1846–1890." *Histoire sociale / Social History* 42, no. 83 (May 2009): 35–67.

Geddes Poole, Andrea. *Philanthropy and the Construction of Victorian Women's Citizenship: Lady Frederick Cavendish and Miss Emma Cons*. Toronto: University of Toronto Press, 2014.

Gilbert, Dale. "Assister les familles de Québec. L'école de réforme et l'école d'industrie de l'Hospice Saint-Charles, 1870–1950." *Revue d'histoire de l'Amérique française* 61, nos. 3–4 (Winter–Spring 2008): 469–99.

Gilfolye, Timothy. "Street-Rats and Gutter-Snipes: Child Pickpockets and Street Culture in New York City, 1850–1900." *Journal of Social History* (Summer 2004): 853–67.

Ginzberg, Lori D. *Women and the Work of Benevolence: Morality, Politics, and Class in the Nineteenth-Century United States.* New Haven, CT: Yale University Press, 1990.

Giroux, Marie-Christine. "Accueillir, Vêtir, Nourrir, Instruire, Éduquer et Soigner: La protection de l'enfance à l'hospice Saint-Joseph des Sœurs Grises de Montréal (1854–1911)." Master's thesis. Montreal: Université de Québec à Montréal, 2011.

Gleason, Mona. "Avoiding the Agency Trap: Caveats for Historians of Children, Youth and Education." *History of Education* 45, no. 4 (2016): 446–59.

– "'Lost Voices, Lost Bodies'? Doctors and the Embodiment of Children and Youth in English Canada from 1900 to the 1940s." In *Bringing Children and Youth into Canadian History*, edited by Gleason and Myers, 250–62.

Gleason, Mona, and Tamara Myers, eds. *Bringing Children and Youth into Canadian History: The Difference Kids Make.* Don Mills, ON: Oxford University Press, 2017.

Gleason, Mona, Tamara Myers, Leslie Paris, and Veronica Strong-Boag, eds. *Lost Kids: Vulnerable Children and Youth in Twentieth-Century Canada and the United States.* Vancouver: UBC Press, 2010.

Gordon, Beverly. *Bazaars and Fair Ladies: The History of the American Fundraising Fair.* Knoxville, TN: The University of Tennessee Press, 1998.

Gordon, Eleanor, and Gwyneth Nair. *Public Lives: Women, Family and Society in Victorian Britain.* New Haven, CT: Yale University Press, 2003.

Gordon, Judy. *Four Hundred Brothers and Sisters: The Story of Two Jewish Orphanages in Montreal, Quebec, 1909–1942.* Toronto: Lugus, 2002.

– *Four Hundred Brothers and Sisters: Their Story Continues …* Toronto: MJ Publications, 2004.

Gordon, Linda. *The Great Arizona Orphan Abduction.* Cambridge, MA: Harvard University Press, 2001.

– *Heroes of Their Own Lives: The Politics and History of Family Violence, Boston 1880–1960.* New York: Penguin Books, 1988.

– "The Perils of Innocence, or What's Wrong with Putting Children First." *The Journal of the History of Childhood and Youth* 1, no. 3 (2008): 331–50.

– *Pitied but Not Entitled: Single Mothers and the History of Welfare, 1890–1935.* New York: The Free Press, 1994.

– "Single Mothers and Child Neglect, 1880–1920." *American Quarterly* 37, no. 2 (1985): 173–92.

Gossage, Peter. "Les enfants abandonnés à Montréal au 19e siècle: La Crèche d'Youville des Sœurs Grises, 1820–1871." *Revue d'histoire de l'Amérique française* 40, no. 4 (Spring 1987): 537–59.

– *Families in Transition: Industry and Population in Nineteenth-Century Saint-Hyacinthe.* Montreal and Kingston: McGill-Queen's University Press, 1999.

Goubau, Dominique, and Claire O'Neill. "L'adoption, l'Église et l'État: Les origines tumultueuses d'une institution légale." In *Entre surveillance et compassion: L'évolution de la protection de l'enfance au Québec: Des origines à nos jours*, edited by Renée Joyal, 97–130. Sainte-Foy, QC: Presses de l'Université du Québec, 2000.

Graff, Harvey J. "Remaking Growing Up: Nineteenth-Century America." *Histoire sociale / Social History* 24, no. 47 (May 1991): 35–59.

Greven, Philip. *The Protestant Temperament: Patterns of Child-Rearing, Religious Experience, and the Self in Early America.* New York: Alfred A. Knopf, 1977.

Gross, Robert. "Giving in America: From Charity to Philanthropy." In *Charity, Philanthropy, and Civility in American History*, edited by Lawrence J. Friedman and Mark J. McGarvie, 29–48. Cambridge: Cambridge University Press, 2003.

Grossberg, Michael. *Governing the Hearth: Law and the Family in Nineteenth-Century America.* Chapel Hill, NC, and London: The University of North Carolina Press, 1985.

Guildford, Janet. "Introduction." In *Separate Spheres: Women's Worlds in the 19th-Century Maritimes*, edited by Janet Guildford and Suzanne Morton, 9–21. Fredericton: Acadiensis Press, 1994.

Hacsi, Timothy A. "Orphanages as a National Institution: History and Its Lessons." In *Home Away from Home*, edited by Richard McKenzie, 227–48.

– *Second Home: Orphan Asylums and Poor Families in America.* Cambridge, MA: Harvard University Press, 1997.

Hall, Catherine. *Civilising Subjects: Metropole and Colony in the English Imagination 1830–1867.* Chicago and London: The University of Chicago Press, 2002.

Hamilton, Gillian. "The Decline of Apprenticeship in North America: Evidence from Montreal." *The Journal of Economic History* 60, no. 3 (September 2000): 627–64.

– "The Market for Montreal Apprentices: Contract Length and Information." *Explorations in Economic History* 33 (1996): 496–523.

Hanaway, Joseph, and John H. Burgess, eds. *The General: A History of the Montreal General Hospital.* Montreal and Kingston: McGill-Queen's University Press, 2016.

Harrison, Phyliss. *The Home Children: Their Personal Stories.* Winnipeg: Watson & Dwyer, 1979.

Harvey, Janice. "Agency and Power in Child Charity: A Study of Two Montreal Child Charities, 1822–1900." In *Agency and Institutions in Social Regulation*, edited by Fecteau and Harvey, 328–42.

– "Dealing with 'the Destitute and the Wretched': The Montreal Protestant House of Industry and Refuge in Nineteenth-Century Montreal." *Journal of the CHA* 12, New Series (2001): 73–94.

– "L'école de réforme de Sherbrooke : modalités de contrôle social et séparation public–privé." Paper presented to the Institute d'histoire d'Amérique française (IHAF), Montreal, October 2017.

– "Les Églises protestantes et l'assistance aux pauvres à Montréal au XIXe siècle." SCHEC, *Études d'histoire religieuse* 69 (2003): 51–68.

– "Eliza Hervey : Fondatrice de la Home and School of Industry." In *Ces femmes qui ont bati Montréal: La petite et la grande histoire des femmes qui ont marqué la vie de Montréal depuis 350 ans*, edited by Maryse Darsigny, Francine Descarries, Lyne Kurtzman, and Évelyne Tardy, 90–1. Montreal: Les Éditions du remue-ménage, 1994.

– "Endangered Children and the Montreal Ladies' Benevolent Society Industrial School, 1883–1921." In *Youth and Justice in Western States, 1815–1950: From Punishment to Welfare*, edited by Jean Trépanier and Xavier Rousseaux, 131–60. London: Palgrave Macmillan, 2018.

– "Des femmes anglo-protestantes s'attaquent aux questions sanitaires. Les multiples facettes des soins de santé à Montréal au XIXe siècle et au début du XXe." In *L'incontournable caste des femmes*, edited by Thifault, 35–57.

– "Former des citoyens protestants: l'approche originale de la *Boys' Home of Montreal* (1871–1908)." In *Problèmes sociaux et citoyenneté: les régulations sociales en question (Québec-France, XIXe–XXe siècles)*, edited by Martin Petitclerc, Louise Bienvenue, Martin Robert, and Cory Verbauwherde, 43–62. Quebec: Presses de l'Université du Québec, 2020.

– "Mademoiselle Barber: La relance du Sheltering Home." In *Ces femmes qui ont bati Montréal*, edited by Maryse Darsigny et al., 111–12.

– "The Montreal Ladies' Benevolent Society Industrial School: An Interface of Public and Private." In *Modernidad, Ciudadanía, Desviaciones y Desigualdades: Por un Análisis Comparativo de las Dificultades del Paso a la Modernidad Ciudadana*, edited by Fernando López Mora, 309–27. Cordova, Spain: University of Cordova Press, 2010.

– "The Protestant Orphan Asylum and the Montreal Ladies' Benevolent Society: A Case Study in Protestant Child Charity in Montreal, 1822–1900." PhD diss. Montreal: McGill University, 2001.

– "La religion, fer de lance de l'aide aux démunis dans la communauté protestante montréalaise au XIXe siècle et au début du XXe siècle." SCHEC, *Études d'histoire religieuse* 73 (2007): 7–30.

– "Le risque et la ville au XIXe siècle : discours et interventions en matière de pauvreté et de santé dans le Montréal anglo-protestant." In *Pour une Histoire du Risque: Québec, France, Belgique*, edited by David Niget and Martin Petitclerc, 113–37. Quebec: Presses de l'Université du Québec, 2012. [Also printed, 111–33. Rennes, France: Presses Universitaires de Rennes, 2012.]

– "The Sherbrooke Reformatory for Protestant Boys: Tensions in the Child Protection System in Nineteenth-Century Quebec." Paper presented to the Social Science History Conference (SSHA), Montreal, November 2017.

Held, Virginia, ed. *Justice and Care: Essential Readings in Feminist Ethics*. Boulder, CO: Westview Press, 1995.

Hewitt, Nancy A. "Beyond the Search for Sisterhood: American Women's History in the 1980s." *Social History* 10 (1985): 299–321.
– *Women's Activism and Social Change: Rochester, New York, 1822–1872*. Ithaca, NY: Cornell University Press, 1984.
Higginbotham, Peter. *The Workhouse Cookbook*. Brimscombe Port, UK: The History Press, 2008.
Hogeveen, Bryan. "Accounting for Violence at the Victoria Industrial School." *Histoire sociale / Social History* 42, no. 83 (May 2009): 147–74.
– "'The Evils with Which We Are Called to Grapple': Elite Reformers, Eugenicists, Environmental Psychologists, and the Construction of Toronto's Working-Class Boy Problem, 1860–1930." *Labour / Le Travail* 55 (Spring 2005): 37–68.
Hogg, Grace Laing. "The Legal Rights of Masters, Mistresses and Domestic Servants in Montreal, 1816–1829." Master's thesis. Montreal: McGill University, 1989.
Holloran, Peter C. *Boston's Wayward Children: Social Services for the Homeless Children, 1830–1930*. Boston: Northeastern University Press, 1994.
Holmes, Janet. "Toys and Games." In *The Book of Canadian Antiques*, edited by Donald Blake Webster, 187–202. New York: McGraw-Hill Ryerson, 1974.
Horn, Pamela. *The Rise and Fall of the Victorian Servant*. Revised ed. Phoenix Mill, UK: Alan Sutton, 1990. Originally published 1975.
Holt, Marilyn Irvin. "Adoption Reform, Orphan Trains, and Child-Saving, 1851–1929." In *Children and Youth in Adoption, Orphanages, and Foster Care: A Historical Handbook and Guide*, edited by Lori Askeland, 17–29. Westport, CT: Greenwood Press, 2006.
– "The Orphan Trains as an Alternative to Orphanages." In *Home Away from Home*, edited by Richard McKenzie, 205–26.
Houston, Susan. "The 'Waifs and Strays' of a Late Victorian City: Juvenile Delinquents in Toronto." In *Childhood and Family in Canadian History*, edited by Parr, 129–42.
Huggins, Nathan I.H. *Protestants against Poverty: Boston's Charities 1870–1900*. Westport, CT: Greenwood, 1971.
Humphreys, Robert. *Sin, Organized Charity and the Poor Law in Victorian England*. New York and London: St Martin's Press, 1995.
Hurt, John. "Reformatory and Industrial Schools before 1933." *History of Education* 13, no. 1 (1984): 45–58.
Hustak, Alan, and Bryan Demchinsky. *Soup to Self-Sufficiency: The Old Brewery Mission*. Montreal: In-house publication, 2014.
Iacovetta, Franca, and Wendy Mitchinson. "Introduction: Social History and Case File Research." In *On the Case: Explorations in Social History*, edited by Franca Iacovetta and Wendy Mitchinson, 3–24. Toronto: University of Toronto Press, 1998.
Ingam, Darcy. "Saving the Union Jack: The Montreal Sailors' Institute and the Homeless Sailor, 1862–98." In *Negotiating Identities in 19th- and 20th-Century Montreal*, edited by Bettina Bradbury and Tamara Myers, 49–76. Toronto and Vancouver: UBC Press, 2005.

Innes, Joanna. "State, Church and Voluntarism in European Welfare, 1690–1850." In *Charity, Philanthropy and Reform*, edited by Cunningham and Innes, 15–66.

Irwin, Mary Ann. "'Going About and Doing Good': The Politics of Benevolence, Maternalism, and Welfare in San Francisco, 1850–1880." *Pacific Historical Review* 68, no. 3 (1999): 365–96.

James, Janet Wilson. *Changing Ideas about Women in the United States, 1776–1825*. New York: Garland, 1981.

Janovicek, Nancy, and Joy Parr, eds. *Histories of Canadian Children and Youth*. Toronto: Oxford University Press, 2003.

Jones, Andrew, and Leonard Rutman. *In the Children's Aid. J.J. Kelso and Child Welfare in Ontario*. Toronto: University of Toronto Press, 1981.

Joyal, Renée. "L'acte concernant les écoles d'industrie (1869): Une mesure de prophylaxie sociale dans un Québec en voie d'urbanisation." *Revue d'histoire de l'Amérique française* 50, no. 2 (Fall 1996): 227–39.

– *Les Enfants, la société et l'État au Québec, 1608–1989: Jalons*. Montreal: Éditions Hurtubise, Cahiers du Québec, 1999.

– "L'évolution des modes de contrôle de l'autorité parentale et son impact sur les relations entre parents et enfants dans la société Québécoise." In *Actes du Colloque entre tradition et universalisme*, edited by Françoise-Romaine Ouellette and Claude Bariteau, 245–58. Rimouski, QC: Institut québécois de recherche sur la culture, 1994.

Katz, Michael B. "The History of an Impudent Poor Woman in New York City from 1918 to 1923." In *The Uses of Charity*, edited by Peter Mandler, 227–46.

– *In the Shadow of the Poorhouse: A Social History of Welfare in America*. New York: Basic Books, 1986.

– *Poverty and Policy in American History*. New York: Academic Press, 1983.

Keating, Peter. *La Science du Mal: L'Institution de la psychiatrie au Québec, 1800–1914*. Montreal: Les Éditions du Boréal, 1993.

Kenneally, Rhona Richman. "The Montreal Maternity, 1843–1926: Evolution of a Hospital." Master's thesis. Montreal: McGill University, 1983.

Kerber, Linda K. "Separate Spheres, Female Worlds, Woman's Place: The Rhetoric of Women's History." *The Journal of American History* 75, no. 1 (June 1988): 9–39.

King, Steven. *Women, Welfare and Local Politics, 1880–1920: "We Might Be Trusted."* Brighton, UK: University of Sussex Academic Press, 2006.

Kirkland, Elizabeth. "Mothering Citizens: Elite Women in Montreal 1890–1914." PhD diss. Montreal: McGill University, 2011.

Klassen, Henry C. "In Search of Neglected and Delinquent Children: The Calgary Children's Aid Society, 1909–1920." In *Town and City: Aspects of Western Canadian Urban Development*, edited by Alan F.J. Artibise, 375–91. Regina: University of Regina, 1981.

Lafferty, Renée N. *The Guardianship of Best Interests: Institutional Care for Children of the Poor in Halifax, 1850–1969*. Montreal and Kingston: McGill-Queen's University Press, 2013.

Lamonde, Yvan. "La sociabilité et l'histoire socio-culturelle: le cas de Montréal, 1760–1880." *Canadian Historical Association, Historical Papers* (1987): 86–111.

Langan, Paul. *Hespeler's Hidden Secret: The Coombe Orphanage 1905–1947*. Cambridge, ON: Paul Langan, 2000.

Langland, Elizabeth. *Nobody's Angels: Middle-Class Women and Domestic Ideology in Victorian Culture*. Ithaca, NY: Cornell University Press, 1995.

Langsam, Miriam. *Children West: A History of the Placing Out System in the New York Children's Aid Society*. Madison: State Historical Society of Wisconsin, 1964.

Laperrière, Guy. *Histoire des communautés religieuses au Québec*. Montreal: VLB, 2013.

Lapointe-Roy, Huguette. *Charité bien ordonnée: le premier réseau de lutte contre la pauvreté à Montréal au 19e siècle*. Montreal: Boréal, 1987.

Lasser, Carol S. "The Domestic Balance of Power: Relations Between Mistress and Maid in Nineteenth-Century New England." *Labour History* 28, no. 1 (Winter 1987): 5–22.

– "A 'Pleasingly Oppressive' Burden: The Transformation of Domestic Service and Female Charity in Salem, 1880–1840." *Essex Institute Historical Collections* 116 (1980): 156–75.

Lebsock, Suzanne. *The Free Women of Petersburg. Status and Culture in a Southern Town, 1784–1860*. New York: W.W. Norton, 1986.

Lees, Lynn Hollen. "The Survival of the Unfit: Welfare Policies and Family Maintenance in Nineteenth-Century London." In *The Uses of Charity*, edited by Peter Mandler, 68–91.

Leitch, Gillian I. "The Importance of Being *English*? Identity and Social Organization in Montreal, 1800–1850." PhD diss. Montreal: Université de Montréal, 2006.

Leskyi, Helen. "A 'Servant Problem' or a 'Servant-Mistress Problem'? Domestic Service in Canada, 1830–1930." *Atlantis* 7, no. 1 (Fall 1981): 3–11.

Lewis, Jane. "The Boundary between Voluntary and Statutory Social Service in the Late Nineteenth and Early Twentieth Centuries." *The Historical Journal* 39, no. 1 (1996): 155–77.

– *Women and Social Action in Victorian and Edwardian England*. Stanford, CA: Stanford University Press, 1991.

Little, Margaret Jane Hillyard. *"No Car, No Radio, No Liquor Permit." The Moral Regulation of Single Mothers in Ontario, 1920–1997*. Toronto: Oxford University Press, 1998.

Lomax, Elizabeth M.R. *Science and Patterns of Child Care*. San Francisco: W.H. Freeman and Company, 1978.

Luddy, Maria. "Women and Philanthropy in Nineteenth-Century Ireland." In *Women, Philanthropy, and Civil Society*, edited by McCarthy, 29–64.

– *Women and Philanthropy in Nineteenth-Century Ireland*. New York: Cambridge University Press, 1995.

Lupton, Deborah. *Risk*. London and New York: Routledge, 1999.

Lyman, Arthur, ed. *Genealogy of the Lyman Family in Canada: Ancestors and Descendants of Elisha Lyman*. Montreal: Beaver Hall Press, 1943.

Maas, Barbara. *Helpmates of Man: Middle-Class Women and Gender Ideology in Nineteenth-Century Ontario*. Bochum, Germany: Universitatsverlag Dr. N. Brockmeyer, 1990.

MacDonald, Cheryl. *Adelaide Hoodless: Domestic Crusader*. Toronto: Dundurn Press, 1986.

MacDougall, Heather A. "Public Health and the 'Sanitary Idea' in Toronto, 1866–1890." In *Essays in the History of Canadian Medicine*, edited by Wendy Mitchinson and Janice P. Dickin McGinnis, 62–87. Toronto: McClelland and Stewart, 1988.

MacKay, Donald. *The Square Mile: Merchant Princes of Montreal*. Vancouver and Toronto: Douglas & McIntyre, 1987.

MacLeod, Roderick. "Salubrious Settings and Fortunate Families: The Making of Montreal's Golden Square Mile. 1840–1895." PhD diss. Montreal: McGill University, 1997.

MacLeod, Roderick, and Mary-Anne Poutanen. *A Meeting of the People: School Boards and Protestant Communities in Quebec, 1801–1998*. Montreal and Kingston: McGill-Queen's University Press, 2004.

MacLennan, Anne. "Charity and Change: Montreal English Protestant Charity Faces the Crisis of Depression." *Urban History Review* 16, no. 1 (June 1987): 1–16.

– *Red Feather in Montreal, A History*. Montreal: Red Feather Foundation, 1996.

Mandler, Peter. "Poverty and Charity in the Nineteenth-Century Metropolis: An Introduction." In *The Uses of Charity*, edited by Peter Mandler, 1–37.

– ed. *The Uses of Charity: The Poor on Relief in the Nineteenth-Century Metropolis*. Philadelphia: University of Pennsylvania Press, 1990.

Marks, Lynne. *Revivals and Roller Rinks: Religion, Leisure, and Identity in Late-Nineteenth-Century Small-Town Ontario*. Toronto: University of Toronto Press, 1996.

Matters, Diane. "The Boys' Industrial School: Education for Juvenile Offenders." In *Schooling and Society in Twentieth Century British Columbia*, edited by J. Donald Wilson and David C. Jones, 53–70. Calgary: Detselig Enterprises, 1980.

Maunders, David. "Awakening from the Dream: The Experience of Childhood in Protestant Orphan Homes in Australia, Canada, and the United States." *Child & Youth Care Forum* 23, no. 6 (December 1994): 393–412.

Maurutto, Paula. "Charity and Public Welfare in History: A Look at Ontario, 1830–1950." *The Philanthropist Journal*, 1 October 2004. https://thephilanthropist.ca/2004/10/charity-and-public-welfare-in-history-a-look-at-ontario-1830-1950.

– *Governing Charities: Church and State in Toronto's Catholic Archdiocese, 1850–1950*. Montreal and Kingston: McGill-Queen's University Press, 2003.

McCants, Anne E.C. "Christian Charity and the Politics of Orphan Care in the Dutch Republic." In *Home Away from Home*, edited by Richard McKenzie, 55–66.

McCarthy, Kathleen D. "Parallel Structures: Women and the Voluntary Sphere." In *Lady Bountiful Revisited: Women, Philanthropy, and Power*, edited by Kathleen D. McCarthy, 1–31. New Brunswick, NJ, and London: Rutgers University Press, 1990.

– ed. *Women, Philanthropy, and Civil Society*. Bloomington: Indiana University Press, 2001.

– "Women and Political Culture." In *Charity, Philanthropy, and Civility in American History*, edited by Lawrence J. Friedman and Mark J. McGarvie, 179–97. Cambridge: Cambridge University Press, 2003.

McDannell, Colleen. *The Christian Home in Victorian America, 1840–1900*. Bloomington: Indiana University Press, 1986.

McIntosh, Robert. *Boys in the Pits: Child Labour in Coal Mines*. Montreal and Kingston: McGill-Queen's University Press, 2000.

McKenna, Katherine M.J. *A Life of Propriety: Anne Murray Powell and Her Family, 1755–1849*. Montreal and Kingston: McGill-Queen's University Press, 1994.

– "The Role of Women in the Establishment of Social Status in Early Upper Canada." *Ontario History* 83, no. 3 (September 1990): 179–206.

McKenzie, Richard B. *The Home: A Memoire of Growing Up in an Orphanage*. New York: New York: Basic Books, 1996.

– ed. *Home Away from Home: The Forgotten History of Orphanages*, New York: Encounter Books, 2009.

– "Orphanage Alumni: How They Have Done and How They Evaluate Their Experience." In *Rethinking Orphanages for the 21st Century*, edited by Richard B. McKenzie, 103–26. Thousand Oakes, CA: SAGE, 1999.

McLoughlin, William C. "Evangelical Childrearing in the Age of Jackson: Francis Wayland's Views on When and How to Subdue the Wilfulness of Children." *Journal of Social History* 9, no. 15 (1975): 20–34.

McNeill, John Thomas. *The Presbyterian Church in Canada 1875–1925*. Toronto: General Board Presbyterian Church in Canada, Contribution of 1925.

Meckel, Richard A. "Protecting the Innocents: Age Segregation and the Early Child Welfare Movement." *The Social Service Review* 59, no. 3 (September 1985): 455–75.

Ménard, Sylvie. *Des enfants sous surveillance, la rééducation des jeunes délinquants au Québec (1840–1950)*. Montreal: VLB éditeur, 2003.

Ménard, Sylvie, and Véronique Strimelle. "Enfant sujet, enfant objet? L'enfant comme enjeu des nouvelles politiques pénales au Québec, de la seconde moitié du XIXe siècle au début du XXe siècle." *Lien social et politique–RIAC*, no. 44 (Fall 2000): 89–99.

Miller, Timothy S. "The Early History of Orphanages." In *Home Away from Home*, edited by Richard McKenzie, 23–41.

Milloy, John S. *A National Crime: The Canadian Government and the Residential School System, 1879–1976*. Winnipeg: University of Manitoba Press, 1999.

Mintz, Steven. *Huck's Raft: A History of American Childhood*. Cambridge, MA: Belknap Press of Harvard University Press, 2004.

Mintz, Steven, and Susan Kellogg. *Domestic Revolutions: A Social History of American Family Life*. New York: Free Press, 1988.

Miron, Janet. *Prisons, Asylums and the Public: Institutional Visiting in the Nineteenth Century*. Toronto: University of Toronto Press, 2011.

Mitchinson, Wendy. "Reasons for Committal to a Mid-Nineteenth Ontario Insane Asylum: The Case of Toronto." In *Essays in the History of Canadian Medicine*, edited by Wendy Mitchinson and Janice P. Dickin McGinnis, 88–109. Toronto: McClelland and Stewart, 1988.

Moore, Marianne. "Social Control or Protection of the Child? The Debates on the Industrial Schools Acts 1857–1894." *Journal of Family History* 33, no. 4 (October 2008): 359–87.

Moran, James E. *Committed to the State Asylum: Insanity and Society in Nineteenth-Century Quebec and Ontario*. Montreal and Kingston: McGill-Queen's University Press, 2000.

Morel, André. "L'enfant sans famille: De l'ancien droit au nouveau Code civil." In *Entre surveillance et compassion: L'évolution de la protection de l'enfance au Québec: Des origines à nos jours*, edited by Renée Joyal, 7–34. Sainte-Foy, QC: Presses de l'Université du Québec, 2000.

Morgan, Cecilia. *Public Men and Virtuous Women: The Gendered Language of Religion and Politics in Upper Class, 1791–1850*. Toronto: University of Toronto Press, 1996.

Morris, R.J. *Class and Class Consciousness in the Industrial Revolution 1780–1850*. London: McMillan, 1979.

– "Middle-Class Culture, 1700–1914." In *A History of Modern Leeds*, edited by Derek Fraser, 200–22. Manchester, UK: Manchester University Press, 1980.

Morton, Marian J. "The Transformation of Catholic Orphanages: Cleveland, 1851–1996." In *Home Away from Home*, edited by Richard McKenzie, 153–78.

Morton, Suzanne. "'To Take an Orphan': Gender and Family Roles Following the 1917 Halifax Explosion." In *Gendered Pasts: Historical Essays in Femininity and Masculinity in Canada*, edited by Kathryn McPherson, Cecilia Morgan, and Nancy M. Forestell, 106–22. Don Mills, ON: Oxford University Press, 1999.

– *Wisdom, Justice & Charity: Canadian Social Welfare through the Life of Jane B. Wisdom, 1884–1975*. Toronto: University of Toronto Press, 2014.

Murphy, Peter D. *Poor Ignorant Children: Irish Famine Orphans in Saint John, New Brunswick*. Halifax: McCurdy Printing, 1999.

Murray, John E. "Fates of Orphans: Poor Children in Antebellum Charleston." In *Home Away from Home*, edited by Richard McKenzie, 127–52.

Murray, John E., and Ruth Wallis Herndon. "Markets for Children in Early America: A Political Economy of Pauper Apprenticeship." *The Journal of Economic History* 62, no. 2 (June 2002): 356–82.

Myers, Tamara. *Caught: Montreal's Modern Girls and the Law, 1869–1945*. Toronto: University of Toronto Press, 2006.

– "The Voluntary Delinquent: Parents, Daughters, and the Montreal Juvenile Delinquents' Court in 1918." *Canadian Historical Review* 80, no. 2 (June 1999): 242–68.

Neff, Charlotte. "The Education of Destitute Homeless Children in Nineteenth-Century Ontario." *Journal of Family History* 29, no. 1 (January 2004): 3–46.

– "Government Approaches to Child Neglect and Mistreatment in 19th Century Ontario." *Histoire sociale / Social History* 41, no. 81 (May 2008): 165–214.

– "The Ontario Industrial Schools Act." *Canadian Journal of Family Law* 12, no. 1 (March 1994): 171–208.

– "Pauper Apprenticeship in Early Nineteenth Century Ontario." *Journal of Family History* 21, no. 2 (April 1996): 144–71.

– "The Role of Protestant Children's Homes in Nineteenth-Century Ontario: Child Rescue or Family Support." *Journal of Family History* 34, no. 1 (January 2009): 48–88.

– "The Use of Apprenticeship and Adoption by the Toronto Protestant Orphans' Home, 1853–1869." *Histoire sociale / Social History* 30, no. 60 (1997): 334–85.

Neilson, Carmen J. *Private Women and the Public Good: Charity and State Formation in Hamilton, Ontario, 1846–93*. Vancouver: UBC Press, 2014.

Noble, Joey. "'Class-ifying' the Poor: Toronto Charities 1850–1880." *Studies in Political Economy* 2 (Autumn 1979): 109–30.

Noel, Jan. "'Femmes Fortes' and the Montreal Poor in the Early Nineteenth Century." In *Canadian Women: A Reader*, edited by Wendy Mitchinson, Paula Bourne, Alison Prentice, Gail Cuthbert Brandt, Beth Light, and Naomi Black, 68–85. Toronto: Harcourt Brace, 1996.

– "Women and Social Welfare in the Montreal Region, 1800–1833: Preliminary Findings." In *Changing Roles of Women within the Christian Church in Canada*, edited by Elizabeth Gillan Muir and Marilyn Fardig Whiteley, 261–83. Toronto: University of Toronto Press, 1995.

O'Connor, Stephen. *Orphan Trains: The Story of Charles Loring Brace and the Children He Saved and Failed*. Boston: Houghton Mifflin, 2001.

Olsen, Stephanie. "'Happy Home' and 'Happy Land': Informal Emotional Education in British Bands of Hope, 1880–1914." *Historia y Memoria de la Educacion*, no. 2 (2015): 195–218.

– "Introduction." In *Childhood, Youth and Emotions in Modern History: National, Colonial and Global Perspectives*, edited by Stephanie Olsen, 1–11. New York: Palgrave Macmillan, 2015.

Olsen, Stephanie, and Karen Vallgårda. "Emotional Frontiers." In *The Oxford Handbook of Emotional Development*, edited by Daniel Dukes, Eric Walle, and Andrea Samson, 437–44. Oxford, UK: Oxford University Press, 2022. https://doi.org/10.1093/oxfordhb/9780198855903.001.0001.

Olson, Sherry, and Patricia Thornton. *Peopling the North American City: Montreal, 1840–1900*. Montreal and Kingston: McGill-Queen's University Press, 2011.

Olson, Sherry, Patricia Thornton, and Quoc Thuy Thach. *A Geography of Little Children in Nineteenth-Century Montreal*. Montreal: McGill University, Geography Department, 1987.

– *Infant Mortality in Montreal in 1860: The Roles of Culture, Class and Habitat*. Montreal: McGill University, Geography Department, 1987.

Paradis, André. "Le sous-financement gouvernemental et son impact sur le développement des asiles francophones au Québec (1845–1918)." *Revue d'histoire de l'Amérique française* 50, no. 4 (Spring 1997): 571–98.

Parr, Joy, ed. *Childhood and Family in Canadian History*. Toronto: McClelland and Stewart, 1982.

– "Introduction." In *Histories of Canadian Children and Youth*, edited by Janovicek and Parr, 1–7.

– *Labouring Children: British Immigrant Apprentices to Canada 1869–1924*. Montreal and Kingston: McGill-Queen's University Press, 1980.

– "'Transplanting from Dens of Iniquity': Theology and Child Emigration." In "*A Not Unreasonable Claim*"*: Women and Reform in Canada, 1880s–1920s*, edited by Linda Kealey, 169–83. Toronto: Canadian Women's Educational Press, 1979.

Parker, R.A. *Uprooted: The Shipment of Poor Children to Canada, 1867–1917*. Vancouver: UBC Press, 2008.

Patrick, Michael D., and Evelyn Goodrich Trickel. *Orphan Trains to Missouri*. Columbia, MO: University of Missouri Press, 1997.

Pedersen, Diana. "'The Power of True Christian Women': The YWCA and Evangelical Womanhood in the Late Nineteenth Century." In *Changing Roles of Women within the Christian Church in Canada*, edited by Elizabeth Gillan Muir and Marilyn Fardig Whiteley, 321–38. Toronto: University of Toronto Press, 1995.

– "Providing a Women's Conscience: The YWCA, Female Evangelicalism, and the Girl in the City, 1870–1930." In *Canadian Women: A Reader*, edited by Wendy Mitchinson, Paula Bourne, Alison Prentice, Gail Cuthbert Brandt, Beth Light, and Naomi Black, 194–210. Toronto: Harcourt Brace, 1996.

Peikoff, Tannis, and Stephen Brickey. "Creating Precious Children and Glorified Mothers: A Theoretical Assessment of the Transformation of Childhood." In *Dimensions of Childhood: Essays on the History of Childhood and Youth in Canada*, edited by Russell Smandych, Gordon Dodds, and Alvin Esau, 29–61. Winnipeg: University of Manitoba, Legal Research Institute, 1991.

Perry, Ann. "Manliness, Goodness, and God: Poverty, Gender and Social Reform in English-Speaking Montreal, 1890s–1930s." Master's thesis. Kingston: Queen's University, 1999.

Petitclerc, Martin. "À propos de 'ceux qui sont en dehors de la société': L'indigent et l'assistance publique au Québec dans la première moitié du XIXe siècle." *Revue d'histoire de l'Amérique française* 65, nos. 2–3 (Fall 2011–Winter 2012): 227–56.

Pitsula, James M. "The Relief of Poverty in Toronto, 1880–1930." PhD diss. Toronto: York University, 1979.

– "The Treatment of Tramps in Late Nineteenth-Century Toronto." *Canadian Historical Association, Historical Papers* (1980): 116–32.

Poovey, Mary. *Uneven Developments: The Ideological Work of Gender in Mid-Victorian England.* Chicago: The University of Chicago Press, 1988.

Porter Benson, Susan. "Business Heads and Sympathizing Hearts: The Women of the Providence Employment Society, 1837–1858." *Journal of Social History* 12, no. 2 (Winter 1978): 302–12.

– "A Good Home: Indenture and Adoption in Nineteenth-Century Orphanages." In *Adoption in America: Historical Perspectives*, edited by E. Wayne Carp, 27–50. Ann Arbor, MI: University of Michigan Press, 2002.

Poutanen, Mary-Anne. "For the Benefit of the Master. The Montreal Needle Trades during the Transition 1820–1842." Master's thesis. Montreal: McGill University, 1985.

– "Regulating Public Space in Early Nineteenth-Century Montreal: Vagrancy Laws and Gender in a Colonial Context." *Histoire sociale / Social History* 35, no. 69 (2002): 35–58.

Procacci, Giovanna. "Genealogies of Poverty: From Inclusion towards Exclusion." *Development* 50, no. 2 (2007): 26–30.

– "Social Economy and the Government of Poverty." In *The Foucault Effect: Studies in Governmentality*, edited by Graham Burchell, Colin Gordon, and Peter Miller, 151–68. London: Harvester Wheatsheaf, 1991.

Prochaska, Frank K. *Christianity and Social Service in Modern Britain: The Disinherited Spirit.* Oxford, UK: Oxford University Press, 2008.

– *The Voluntary Impulse: Philanthropy in Modern Britain.* London: Faber, 1988.

– *Women and Philanthropy in Nineteenth-Century England.* Oxford, UK: Clarendon Press, 1980.

Purvey, Diane. "Alexandra Orphanage and Families in Crisis in Vancouver, 1892 to 1938." Master's thesis. Vancouver: University of British Columbia, 1981.

Quesney, Chantal. "De la charité au Bonheur familial: Une histoire de la Société d'Adoption et de Protection de l'Enfance à Montréal, 1937–1972." PhD diss. Montreal: UQAM, 2010.

– "'Un Foyer pour chaque enfant!' Le rôle de la Société d'adoption et de protection de l'enfance à Montréal dans la désinstitutionnalisation des enfants sans famille, 1937–1972." *Revue d'histoire de l'Amérique française* 65, nos. 2–3 (Fall 2011–Winter 2012): 266–87.

Raftery, Mary, and Eoin O'Sullivan. *Suffer the Little Children: The Inside Story of Ireland's Industrial Schools.* New York: Continuum, 2001.

Rains, Prue, and Eli Teram. *Normal Bad Boys: Public Policies, Institutions, and the Politics of Client Recruitment.* Montreal and Kingston: McGill-Queen's University Press, 1992.

Reisner, M.E. *The Measure of Faith: Annals of the Diocese of Montreal 1760–2000.* Toronto: ABC Publishing Book Centre, 2002.

Reitsma-Street, Marge. "More Control than Care: A Critique of Historical and Contemporary Laws for Delinquency and Neglect of Children in Ontario." *Canadian Journal of Women and the Law* 3, no. 2 (1989–90): 510–30.

Répétoire Toponymique du Québec 1978. Quebec: Gouvernement du Québec, Commission de Toponymie, Éditeur Officiel Québec, 1979.

Riley, Denise. *"Am I That Name?" Feminism and the Category of "Women" in History*. London: Macmillan Press, 1988.

Robert, Jean-Claude. "City of Wealth and Death: Urban Mortality in Montreal, 1821–1871." In *Essays in the History of Canadian Medicine*, edited by Wendy Mitchinson and Janice P. Dickin McGinnis, 22–8. Toronto: McClelland and Stewart, 1988.

Roberts, Barbara. "Sex, Politics and Religion: Controversies in Female Immigration Reform Work in Montreal, 1881–1919." *Atlantis* 6, no. 1 (Fall 1980): 25–38.

Roberts, Elizabeth. *A Woman's Place: An Oral History of Working-Class Women, 1890–1940*. Oxford, UK, and New York: B. Blackwell, 1984.

Roberts, Michael J.D. "Head versus Heart? Voluntary Associations and Charity Organization in England, c. 1700–1850." In *Charity, Philanthropy and Reform*, edited by Cunningham and Innes, 66–86.

Rodgers, Daniel. "Socializing Middle Class Children: Institutions, Fables, and Work Values in Nineteenth Century America." *Journal of Social History* 13, no. 3 (Spring 1980): 359–67.

Rooke, Patricia, and Rodolph Leslie Schnell. "Childhood and Charity in Nineteenth Century British North America." *Histoire sociale / Social History* 15, no. 29 (May 1982): 157–79.

– *Discarding the Asylum: From Child Rescue to the Welfare State in English-Canada 1800–1950*. Lanham, MD: University Press of America, 1983.

– "From Binding Out to Boarding Out in Britain and English-Canada: A Transformation in Childhood Sentiment and Practice." *Paedagogica Historica* 24, no. 2 (1988): 461–91.

– "The 'King's Children' in English Canada: A Psychohistorical Study of Abandonment, Rejection, and Colonial Response (1869–1930)." *Journal of Psychohistory* 8 (Spring 1981): 387–99.

– "The Rise and Decline of British North American Protestant Orphans' Homes as Woman's Domain, 1850–1930." *Atlantis* 7, no. 2 (Spring 1982): 21–35.

Ross, Ellen. "Hungry Children: Housewives and London Charity, 1870–1918." In *The Uses of Charity*, edited by Peter Mandler, 161–96.

– "Labour and Love: Rediscovering London's Working Class Mothers, 1870–1916." In *Labour and Love: Women's Experience of Home and Family*, edited by Jane Lewis, 73–96. Oxford, UK: Basil Blackwell, 1986.

– *Love and Toil: Motherhood in Outcast London, 1870–1918*. New York: Oxford University Press, 1993.

– "Survival Networks: Women's Neighbourhood Sharing in London before WWI." *History Workshop Journal* 15 (Spring 1983): 4–27.

Rowan, Renée. *A Beacon of Hope: The Montreal Diet Dispensary*. Translated by Fred A. Reed. Montreal: Éditions Ordine, 2000.

Rudin, Ronald. *Forgotten Quebecers: A History of English-Speaking Quebec, 1759–1980*. Quebec: Institut Québeçois de recherche sur la culture, 1985.

Rutman, Leonard. "J.J. Kelso and the Development of Child Welfare." In *The "Benevolent" State: The Growth of Welfare in Canada*, edited by Allan Moscovitch and Jim Albert, 68–76. Toronto: Garamond Press, 1987.

Ryan, Mary. *Cradle of the Middle Class: The Family in Oneida County, New York, 1790–1865*. Cambridge: Cambridge University Press, 1981.

– *Women in Public: Between Banners and Ballots*. Baltimore: John Hopkins University Press, 1990.

Sandwell, Bernard K. *The Molson Family*. Montreal: Ronalds, 1933.

Sandwell, R.W. "The Limits of Liberalism. The Liberal Renaissance and the History of the Family in Canada." *Canadian Historical Review* 84, no. 3 (September 2003): 423–50.

Schlossman, Stephen L. "The Culture of Poverty in Ante-Bellum Social Thought." *Science and Society* 38 (1974): 150–66.

Schmidt, Sarah. "Domesticating Parks and Mastering Playgrounds: Sexuality, Power and Place in Montreal, 1870–1930." Master's thesis. Montreal: McGill University, 1997.

Scott, Anne Firor. *Making the Invisible Woman Visible*. Urbana: University of Illinois Press, 1984.

Semple, Neil. "The Nurture and Admonition of the Lord: Nineteenth Century Canadian Methodism's Response to Childhood." *Histoire sociale / Social History* 14, no. 29 (May 1981): 157–76.

Shepherd, William. "Genesis of the Montreal Council of Social Agencies." Master's thesis. Montreal: McGill University, 1957.

Sitara, Georgia. "Humanitarianism in the Age of Capital and Empire: Canada, 1870–1890." PhD diss. Victoria: University of Victoria, 2007.

Smith, Bonnie. *Ladies of the Leisure Class: The Bourgeoises of Northern France in the Nineteenth Century*. Princeton, NJ: Princeton University Press, 1981.

Smith-Rosenberg, Carroll. "The Female World of Love and Ritual: Relations between Women in Nineteenth-Century America." *Signs: Journal of Women in Culture and Society* 1 (Autumn 1975): 1–29.

– *Religion and the Rise of the American City: The New York City Mission Movement 1812–1870*. London: Cornell University Press, 1972.

Spain, Daphne. *How Women Saved the City*. Minneapolis: University of Minnesota Press, 2001.

Speisman, Stephen A. "Munificent Parsons and Municipal Parsimony: Voluntary vs. Public Poor Relief in Nineteenth Century Toronto." *Ontario Historical Society* 65, no. 1 (March 1973): 33–49.

Splane, Richard. *Social Welfare in Ontario 1791–1893: A Study of Public Welfare Administration*. Toronto: University of Toronto Press, 1965.

Spurr, Geoff. "Lower-Middle Class Masculinity and the Young Men's Christian Association, 1844–1880." *Histoire sociale / Social History* 47, no. 95 (November 2014): 547–76.

Stansell, Christine. *City of Women: Sex and Class in New York, 1789–1860*. New York: Knopf, 1986.

Stevens, David. "Framing an Appropriate Corporate Law." In *Between State and Market: Essays on Charities Law and Policy in Canada*, edited by Jim Phillips, Bruce Chapman, and David Stevens, 547–94. Montreal and Kingston: McGill-Queen's University Press, 2001.

Strimelle, Véronique. "La gestion de la déviance des filles et les institutions du Bon-Pasteur à Montréal, 1869–1912." PhD diss. Montreal: Université de Montréal, 1999.

– "Le soin des âmes : discours et programmes d'intervention des Sœurs du Bon-Pasteur d'Angers auprès des filles délinquantes et en danger à Montréal au XIXe siècle, 1869–1912." In *L'incontournable caste des femmes*, edited by Thifault, 17–33.

Strong-Boag, Veronica. "'Children of Adversity': Disabilities and Child Welfare in Canada from the Nineteenth to the Twenty-First Century." *Journal of Family History* 32 (2007): 413–32.

– "'Forgotten People of All the Forgotten': Children with Disabilities in English Canada from the Nineteenth Century to the New Millennium." In *Lost Kids*, edited by Gleason et al., 33–50.

– *Fostering Nation? Canada Confronts Its History of Childhood Disadvantage*. Waterloo, ON: Wilfred Laurier University Press, 2011.

Sutherland, Neil. *Children in English-Canadian Society: Framing the Twentieth Century Consensus*. 1976. Reprint. Waterloo, ON: Wilfred Laurier University Press, 2000.

– "'We Always Had Things to Do': The Paid and Unpaid Work of Anglophone Children between the 1920s and the 1960s." *Labour / Le Travail* 25 (Spring 1990): 105–41.

Sutton, John R. *Stubborn Children: Controlling Delinquency in the United States, 1640–1981*. Berkeley, CA: University of California Press, 1988.

Swift, Allan. *The Least of These: The Story of the Welcome Hall Mission*. Montreal: Welcome Hall Mission, 1982.

Tétreault, Martin. "Les maladies de la misère. Aspects de la santé publique à Montréal 1880–1914." *Revue d'histoire de l'Amérique française* 36, no. 4 (March 1983): 507–26.

Thifault, Marie-Claude, ed. *L'incontournable caste des femmes: Histoire des services de santé au Québec et au Canada*. Ottawa: Presses de l'Université d'Ottawa, 2012.

Thompson, E.P. *The Making of the English Working-Class*. Harmondsworth, UK: Penguin Books, 1972.

Tiffin, Susan. *In Whose Best Interest? Child Welfare Reform in the Progressive Era*. Westport, CT: Greenwood Press, 1982.

Trépanier, Jean. "Juvenile Delinquency and Youth Protection: The Historical Foundations of the Canadian Juvenile Delinquents Act of 1908." *European Journal of Crime, Criminal Law and Criminal Justice* 71, no. 1 (1999): 41–62.

Trigger, Rosalyn. "Protestant Restructuring in the Canadian City: Church and Mission in the Industrial Working-Class District of Griffintown, Montreal." *Urban History Review / Revue d'histoire urbaine* 31, no. 1 (Fall 2002): 5–18.

Tronto, Joan C. *Moral Boundaries: A Political Argument for an Ethic of Care*. New York: Routledge, 2009.

Ursel, Jane. *Private Lives, Public Policy: 100 Years of State Intervention in the Family*. Toronto: Women's Press, 1992.

Vallgårda, Karen. "Adam's Escape: Children and the Discordant Nature of Colonial Conversions." *Childhood* 18, no. 3 (2011): 298–315. https://www.doi.org/10.1177/0907568211407529.

– "Between Consent and Coercion: Danish Missionaries and Tamil Parents in Late Nineteenth Century South India." *Review of Development and Change* XIV, nos. 1–2 (2009): 87–108.

– "Can the Subaltern Woman Run? Gender, Race and Agency in Colonial Missionary Texts." *Scandinavian Journal of History* 39, no. 4 (2014): 472–86. https://www.doi.org/10.1080/03468755.2014.938112.

Vallgårda, Karen, Kristine Alexander, and Stephanie Olsen. "Emotions and the Global Politics of Childhood." In *Childhood, Youth and Emotions in Modern History: National, Colonial and Global Perspectives*, edited by Stephanie Olsen, 12–34. New York: Palgrave Macmillan, 2015.

Vallgårda, Karen, and Stephanie Olsen. "Historicizing Emotional Development." In *The Oxford Handbook of Emotional Development*, edited by Daniel Dukes, Eric Walle, and Andrea Samson, 146–57. Oxford, UK: Oxford University Press, 2022.

Valverde, Mariana. *The Age of Light, Soap, and Water: Moral Reform in English Canada, 1885–1925*. Toronto: McClelland & Stewart, 1991.

– "The Mixed Social Economy as a Canadian Tradition." *Studies in Political Economy* 47 (Summer 1995): 33–60.

– "Moral Capital." *Canadian Journal of Law and Society* 9, no. 1 (Spring 1994): 213–32.

– "Six Dimensions of Social Governance: Research Questions beyond the Dichotomy of 'Public' and 'Private.'" *Cahiers d'histoire* 17, nos. 1–2 (Spring–Fall 1997): 40–54.

Valverde, Mariana, J.R. Miller, Doug Owran, Shirley Tillotson, Bryan D. Palmer, Franca Iacovetta, and Wendy Mitchinson. "*On the Case: Explorations in Social History*: A Roundtable Discussion." *The Canadian Historical Review* 81, no. 2 (June 2000): 266–92.

Van Die, Marguerite. *Religion, Family and Community in Victorian Canada: The Colbys of Carrollcroft*. Montreal and Kingston: McGill-Queen's University Press, 2005.

– "'A Woman's Awakening': Evangelical Belief and Female Spirituality in Mid-Nineteenth-Century Canada." In *Canadian Women: A Reader*, edited by Wendy Mitchinson, Paula Bourne, Alison Prentice, Gail Cuthbert Brandt, Beth Light, and Naomi Black, 49–67. Toronto: Harcourt Brace, 1996.

Vicinus, Martha. *Independent Women: Women and Community for Single Women, 1850–1920*. London: Virago Press, 1985.

Vickery, Amanda. *The Gentleman's Daughter: Women's Lives in Georgian England*. New Haven, CT: Yale University Press, 1999.

Westfall, William. *Two Worlds: The Protestant Culture of Nineteenth-Century Ontario.* Montreal and Kingston: McGill-Queen's University Press, 1989.

Westley, Margaret. *Remembrance of Grandeur: The Anglo-Protestant Elite of Montreal, 1900–1950.* Montreal: Edition Libre Expression, 1990.

Whitley, Marilyn Fardig. "'Doing Just About What They Please.' Ladies' Aids in Ontario Methodism." *Ontario History* 82, no. 4 (December 1990): 289–304.

Winter, James. "Widowed Mothers and Mutual Aid in Early Victorian Britain." *Journal of Social History* (Fall 1983): 115–25.

Wishy, Bernard. *The Child and the Republic: The Dawn of Modern American Child Nurture.* Philadelphia: University of Pennsylvania Press, 1968.

Wolfe, Jeanne M., and Grace Strathan. "Practical Idealism: Women in Urban Reform, Julia Drummond and the Montreal Parks and Playgrounds Association." In *Life Spaces: Gender, Household, Employment,* edited by Caroline Andrew and Beth Moore Milroy, 31–64. Vancouver: UBC Press, 1988.

Woods, S.E. *The Molson Saga, 1763–1983.* Scarborough, ON: Avon Books of Canada, 1983.

Young, Brian. *In Its Corporate Capacity: The Seminary of Montreal as a Business Institution, 1816–1876.* Montreal and Kingston: McGill-Queen's University Press, 1986.

– *Patrician Families and the Making of Quebec: The Taschereaus and McCords.* Montreal and Kingston: McGill-Queen's University Press, 2014.

– *The Politics of Codification: The Lower Canadian Civil Code of 1866.* Montreal and Kingston: McGill-Queen's University Press, 1994.

– "Positive Law, Positive State: Class Realignment and the Transformation of Lower Canada, 1815–1866." In *Colonial Leviathan: State Formation in Mid-Nineteenth-Century Canada,* edited by Allan Greer and Ian Radforth, 50–63. Toronto: University of Toronto Press, 1992.

– *Respectable Burial: Montreal's Mount Royal Cemetery.* Montreal and Kingston: McGill-Queen's University Press, 2003.

Young Choi, Tina. "Writing the Victorian City: Discourses of Risk, Connection, and Inevitability." *Victorian Studies* 43, no. 4 (Summer 2001): 561–89.

Zainaldin, Jamil S. "The Emergence of a Modern American Family Law: Child Custody, Adoption, and the Courts, 1796–1851." *Northwestern University Law Review* 73, no. 6 (1978–79): 1038–89.

Zeliger, Viviane. *Pricing the Priceless Child: The Changing Social Value of Children.* New York: Basic Books, 1985.

Zmora, Nurith. "Baltimore's Nineteenth-Century Orphanages." In *Home Away from Home,* edited by McKenzie, 179–204.

– *Orphanages Reconsidered: Child Care Institutions in Progressive Era Baltimore.* Philadelphia: Temple University Press, 1994.

Index